Expanding minds and Opportunities

Leveraging the Power of Afterschool and Summer Learning for Student Success

A compendium of studies, reports, and commentaries by 100+ professionals and policy leaders on the best practices, impact, and future of expanded learning opportunities

Terry K. Peterson, PhD, Executive Editor

February 2013

ISBN: 978-0-9888332-0-3

COLLABORATIVE
COMMUNICATIONS GROUP

Collaborative Communications Group, Inc.
1029 Vermont Avenue, NW
Ninth Floor
Washington, DC 20005
www.collaborativecommunications.com

Collaborative Communications Group is a strategic consulting firm that builds the capacity of individuals, organizations and networks to work collaboratively to create solutions that are better than any single entity could produce on its own. Through dialogue and convenings, online and print publications and tools, and community conversations, Collaborative helps organizations and networks to identify, share, and apply what they know in ways that increase productivity and effectiveness. The ultimate objective of Collaborative's work is the improvement of the quality of public education and community life.

The inspiration for this seminal compendium came from the executive editor, Terry K. Peterson, PhD, who provided exceptional leadership during the entire development and editing processes. His idea to create this volume was inspired by the need to comprehensively share and shine a national spotlight on the powerful collective knowledge, research, partnerships, and best practices created during the past 15 years in the often-undervalued and unseen effort of those working to expand and improve learning opportunities across America in afterschool, summers, and even before school and weekends.

This publication was made possible with the generous support of the Charles Stewart Mott Foundation.

The content of this publication reflects the views and opinions of the authors, who are responsible for the facts and accuracy of the data presented herein. These views and opinions do not necessarily represent those of the editor, publisher, or funder of the publication.

Additional copies of and content from this publication can be ordered and downloaded online from the Expanded Learning & Afterschool Project website at www.expandinglearning.org/expandingminds.

Suggested citation: Peterson, T. K. (Ed.). (2013). *Expanding minds and opportunities: Leveraging the power of afterschool and summer learning for student success.* Washington, DC: Collaborative Communications Group.

Contents

Section 3: Recent Evidence of Impact

Section 4: The Power of Community-School Partnerships in Expanding Learning

Section 5: Afterschool and Summer Programs as Catalysts for Engaging Families

Section 6: A Growing Nationwide Infrastructure for Quality, Expansion, and Partnerships

Conclusion

William S. White
President and CEO
Charles Stewart Mott Foundation

Foreword

Expanding Minds and Opportunities: Leveraging the Power of Afterschool and Summer Learning for Student Success couldn't be more timely. Debate abounds today on how we should reform education to provide the learning experiences and opportunities students need to prepare for jobs in our sophisticated, technological age.

We all know there is no silver bullet for what ails our education system. Improving educational achievement will require the knitting together of multiple approaches. And as we look for workable solutions, I believe we should focus some serious attention on the hours before and after school—not because they are the answer to the problems facing our education system but because they can be an important piece of the puzzle.

To build a stronger system, we need to create more opportunities for young people to learn, to experience a full range of enrichment activities (including music and the arts), to be exposed to the latest in STEM (science, technology, engineering, and math) education, and to become more connected with their communities.

This book provides a window into how educators, schools, and communities are working together in cities, states, and towns—from San Francisco, California, to Dallas, Texas, to Woonsocket, Rhode Island—to provide these opportunities, develop solutions, and break down barriers to student success.

With almost 70 entries by leading educators, practitioners, policy makers, and researchers, *Expanding Minds and Opportunities* demonstrates the powerful benefits of afterschool, summer, and expanded learning opportunities for students, their families, and communities across America.

Of course, with so many diverse articles, representing so many different viewpoints and perspectives, not everyone will agree with all of the material presented here. But differences of opinion can often catalyze dialogue and stimulate new ideas that in turn can increase the quality and capacity of the field.

At the Charles Stewart Mott Foundation, through our years of funding community education and afterschool initiatives, we've learned that the productive use of time before and after school and during the summer can provide an important foundation for learning. That is why we have focused over the years on taking afterschool to scale across the country, including growing statewide afterschool networks from 9 in 2002 to 41 today, and supporting the development and implementation of the federal afterschool grant program known as the 21st Century Community Learning Centers initiative. Today, that program serves 1.6 million students across the country in rural communities, small cities, and suburban and urban neighborhoods.

Many of the articles in *Expanding Minds and Opportunities* illustrate how the 21st Century Community Learning Centers program, the networks, and many other afterschool efforts can be an important part of the solution to improving our education system. Moreover, they describe how these initiatives are successfully bringing multiple stakeholders to the table to support the education of children and their families, resulting in more cost-effective and efficient solutions.

There is no question that much remains to be done to ensure that all our young people have the opportunity to participate in high quality afterschool programming that expands their learning experiences and helps them succeed in school and life. Continuing to build strong programs and policies are fundamental to that effort. This publication—which contains a wealth of wisdom gleaned from experts—should help advance this important agenda.

Acknowledgments

Terry K. Peterson, PhD
Executive Editor

In a long-term project such as the development and production of this landmark compendium, with almost 70 articles and 100 authors, many individuals and organizations were involved, and their contributions deserve to be recognized and appreciated.

So THANK YOU to the following:

Our authors are very busy people making a difference in their own regular work, but they graciously took the extra time to write their article for this seminal publication. Some of our authors rarely have a chance to share their own good works and positive results because they are trying daily to make their own programs work well; others have written many articles, but were able to reflect on the overall development of this field of expanded learning in afterschool and summers. We appreciate all of their contributions.

The Charles Stewart Mott Foundation for decades has been a tireless force across America helping thousands of education and community leaders work together to fully utilize their collective learning resources. Their focus is not just 8:00 a.m. to 3:00 p.m., 180 days a year, but afterschool, evenings, weekends, and summers to give more struggling students and their families the "edge to be successful." **This concept is one of the most important education ideas of our time, and the Mott Foundation has made it a priority during challenging financial times when we need to maximize learning supports for more young people.**

Thank you, **Bill White**, the president and CEO of the C.S. Mott Foundation, and thank you, **Gwynn Hughes**, program officer for expanded learning and afterschool. Also, thank you to the Mott Foundation board and to their former colleagues who worked in this area and in community education. Without their leadership and resources, this compendium and many local and state initiatives, as well as the federal 21st Century Community Learning Centers initiative itself and the tens of thousands of local programs serving millions of young people it has supported over the years, would most likely not be a reality.

The College of Charleston's School of Education, Health, and Human Performance, under the leadership of Dean Frances Welch, has supported our national Afterschool and Community Learning Network for the past 11 years, providing matching funding and research and administrative support that included my colleagues, Patty O'Donnell, Sara Perry, Shannon Eggers, and Anja Urbanski Kelley. The College of Charleston's Foundation has also been an important resource in this work.

Collaborative Communications Group has been connecting and convening the afterschool field for more than a decade. As publisher of *Expanding Minds and Opportunities*, Collaborative has again contributed their collective skills, knowledge, and commitment to the field with excellence. Elizabeth Partoyan served as expert advisor and assistant in editing; Sheena Collier and Annie Meyer managed the overall project and myriad details; Christyna Copeland was an extraordinary copy editor through many rounds of review; Bill Glover designed the book with creativity and flexibility for further use; and Terri Ferinde Dunham led and managed the overall production.

Ron Fairchild and **Bob Saffold**, co-principals at the Smarter Learning Group, supported this project in a variety of ways, drawing on their expertise in education program expansion and replication strategy, as well as expanded learning policy, partnerships, and resource development. Bob spent countless hours with the authors and me in editing the content.

FowlerHoffman and their senior strategists, Steve Fowler, Mary Hoffman, and Janelle Cousino, were instrumental in the project from its early conceptualization to interviewing education and afterschool leaders and through the final text review. Their expertise in national system and policy change and consulting work helped immensely.

My parents, Morgan Peterson, who never attended high school, and Florence Hessefort Peterson, who didn't finish high school—and yet who managed to create successful lives, businesses, and a thriving family. Together and without any pressure, but with lots of support, they enabled me to go to college and eventually earn a doctorate. They also gave me the attitude that a "little small town boy (or girl)" can do anything; all it takes is putting your mind and energy into it. They made it possible for me to benefit from many afterschool and summer programs, too.

My wife, Scott, and our five adult children, Terek, Carly, Angie, Buck, and Stacie, have put up with serious interruptions related to "my projects," including this compendium, during weekends, holidays, and evenings for many, many years. Despite their own hectic work and travel schedules, they are always very encouraging, and now our sons- and daughters-in-law (Marsha, Ted, Matt, Ben, and Dominique) put up with this and are supportive, too.

Our grandchildren, John Bennett (JB), Virginia, Morgan, Henry, and Roux provide me with new motivation to keep pushing the envelope for more and better afterschool and summer learning opportunities, as well as quality public schools. With them, I see the value and importance of this combination of learning resources by watching them grow and develop while their parents, like many across America, work long hard hours to make a difference and earn a living.

Richard W. Riley has been a strong leader for better education, from preschool through higher education, for more than a half a century. I have had the honor and privilege to work with him for 8 years when he was governor and another 8 years when he was United States Secretary of Education—and for another 18 years working as a colleague on various joint projects. His inclusiveness and friendly, but always forward-looking, style is something we all should learn from… and I hope our compendium conveys.

Terry K. Peterson
Senior Fellow and Director, Afterschool Network,
College of Charleston

Introduction: The Importance of and New Opportunities for Leveraging Afterschool and Summer Learning and School-Community Partnerships for Student Success

It is a given that today's level of student learning will directly impact our future economic and civic well-being. Yet too often, educators and our public schools, serving almost 50 million students, seem to be under attack, underappreciated, and often underfunded. This is not the way to prepare our nation—and our nation's children— for the future. We need to find a set of strategies and tools both to support them and to accelerate learning.

Among the most promising of such strategies is expanding learning and opportunities for our nation's youth to leverage the power of quality afterschool and summer learning programs and the richly varied and diverse community partnerships that can accompany these programs. While the education improvement toolbox needs to include a number of other important strategies, the sole focus of this compendium, *Expanding Minds and Opportunities: Leveraging the Power of Afterschool and Summer Learning for Student Success*, is on how a growing number of communities across America are successfully and more effectively using some of the available hours children and youth are not formally in school, which equals almost 80% of their time.

Over the past 15 years, there has been a dramatic expansion in the range of engaging learning opportunities available to children and youth through high quality afterschool and summer learning programs. Despite the challenges of the recent economic downturn, this rich array of expanded opportunities for learning is helping millions of America's children and youth have access to experiences and supports that help them succeed. Yet many more such opportunities are needed and wanted across neighborhoods and schools nationwide, while many are still feeling the continuing budget cutbacks from the Great Recession.

Once regarded as mere add-ons, and often disconnected from the regular school day, afterschool and summer programs have steadily grown into enriching learning opportunities for increasing numbers of children and youth.

Once regarded as mere add-ons, and often disconnected from the regular school day, afterschool and summer programs have steadily grown into enriching learning opportunities for increasing numbers of children and youth.

These approaches have evolved into intentional strategies for providing comprehensive educational and developmental learning opportunities. Many quality school-based and community-based afterschool and summer programs have thus now moved from the margins to being a significant part of the education and learning enterprise. These programs have emerged as an opportune and cutting-edge educational approach for rethinking how resources such as time, place, human capital, and financial and material resources can be allocated to support the personalized learning and development of each child, regardless of his/her circumstances.

Yet, with the tight budgets currently confronting families, public agencies, nonprofits, and even foundations, it is worth stepping back to explore whether expanded learning opportunities are making a significant difference in learning and student success. We also need to assess whether there is an adequate infrastructure, not only to make existing opportunities more effective and efficient but also to support their sustainability or expansion—and ultimately to enable state and local leaders to take these sometimes new and different learning opportunities to scale in communities where they are needed and wanted.

This compendium presents an impressive and significant body of work that comprises almost 70 reports, research studies, essays, articles, and commentaries by more than 100 authors representing a range of researchers, educators, policy makers, and professionals in the field, as well as thought leaders and opinion influencers. Collectively, these writings present bold, persuasive evidence that by providing engaging, high quality afterschool and summer learning programs that rely on robust school-community partnerships, expanding learning can generate positive and significant effects on important outcomes related to learning and community/family engagement.

In other words, we can boldly state that there is now a solid base of research and best practices clearly showing that quality afterschool and summer learning programs make a positive difference for students, families, schools, and communities.

Moreover, the nation's largest investment in such opportunities, the annual $1.2 billion 21st Century Community Learning Centers initiative, has also been a resounding success, and has been essential to the movement nationwide. Its addition to the Elementary and Secondary Education Act of 1994 was made possible with bipartisan support in Congress. During the second term of the Clinton administration, the program began to have real and substantial impact as both the president and first lady courageously pushed for rapidly increasing investments. During this period, funding for 21st Century Community Learning Centers grew from $1 million to $1 billion, enabling its scale-up across America. In the years since, Republican and Democratic congressional leaders alike have continued to approve the program's funding level.

Throughout this compendium, case studies and best practice reports show how the 21st Century Community Learning Centers initiative is an important and often critical funding source to local and state afterschool and summer learning programs, as well as to broader educational support initiatives such as community schools and community education. The research findings, best practices, and policy implications presented in this compendium span a wide array of topics and issues germane to learning, development, and educational success. Very importantly, they also lay a solid foundation for considering what must be done further both to improve the quality and to grow the quantity of enriching and engaging opportunities that can support school and lifetime success of many more young people.

Well-designed, quality programs offered to students beyond the school day and year are prime vehicles for providing experiential, hands-on learning opportunities that are often difficult to offer within the constraints of the traditional school day and year.

In the hours after school, on weekends, and during summers, innovative school teachers and community educators are creating enriching activities to expand the minds and open the horizons of young people from all backgrounds—challenging them to dare to try something that stretches them to reach their full potential. Some of these innovative partnerships are supporting students who are struggling to learn core content, helping young people recover credits critically needed for graduation, and breaking new ground by providing innovative ways for middle and high school students to accumulate new credits that will help them on a path to career and college readiness.

Turning "nonschool hours" into "learning hours" requires us to provide learning opportunities that address a broader spectrum of interests and talents possessed by today's youth. We need educators, community organizations, employers, and volunteers not simply to work better together but also to work in new and more productive ways that spark student interest in learning. Afterschool and summer programs throughout the country are, for example, helping schools better fulfill their responsibility to teach students in the most engaging fashion. They are also providing a logical means to bring new community resources to the learning enterprise and to position schools as a hub of learning beyond the typical school day and year. In addition, they are empowering educators and families as facilitators or "orchestrators" of learning—not only in and around the school but also in the broader community.

Visiting high quality expanded learning programs like those presented in this compendium is indeed inspiring. You will see young people meaningfully engaged with each other, as well as with educators, youth development professionals, employers, college students and professors, and volunteers from the community. You will see them participating in activities that encourage inquiry, responsibility, problem solving, solid work habits, creativity, mastery, and a sense of belonging.

The task before us is to work together to invest the will and resources needed to sustain and expand engaging and enriching learning opportunities—anytime and everywhere—so that, regardless of the time or location, young people have access to the supports and opportunities they need to advance their knowledge and skills. Such a collective commitment and effort will place and help keep students on a path to high school graduation as the first rung to achieving economic success and leading successful, fulfilling lives. At the local, state, and national levels, we must continue to build out a solid and sustainable infrastructure and expand strategic partnerships—including the 21st Century Community Learning Centers initiative—to promote high quality, cost-effective, and affordable programs. Included as key elements in this infrastructure are technical assistance, professional development, visionary leadership and stable governance, and strategies and policies that maximize fiscal and human capital.

In a high quality expanded learning experience, you can see youth engaged in a wide variety of activities:

- Writing and acting in the performing arts with local community theater members
- Learning real-life communication skills by taking a stand on a debate team
- Mastering the strategy of chess
- Exploring engineering in a robotics club
- Reading, writing, and illustrating books with a local artist or photographer
- Testing water quality to improve local natural resources with an environmentalist volunteer
- Measuring and using math to design buildings and bridges with local engineers, architects, and employers
- Creating digital games with a graphic designer or composing music with a musician either online or in person
- Apprenticing with a master craftsman
- Teaching younger students in libraries
- Serving as a docent in local museums
- Gardening in the school or community garden and learning to cook their produce
- Getting more fit, eating healthy snacks, and learning about lifetime sports
- Earning high school credit for graduation or preparing for college through partnerships with schools, colleges, employers, or local libraries and museums

This growing infrastructure also includes, and in fact relies on, new strategies for pooling and leveraging resources designed to make a larger impact. For example, the almost 11,000 21st Century Community Learning Centers programs across America involve annually more than 30,000 community partners along with nearly 300,000 families. These partnerships generate significant additional resources to support expanded learning experiences and opportunities for the children and youth served by these programs. So underfunding, diverting funding, or cutting funding for the 21st Century Community Learning Centers program will result not only in diminishing the number of children and youth who can be served but also in the collateral losses of other funding and other resources, including the countless extra "hands and hearts" that greatly exceed any actual budget cut.

Therefore, maximizing the full potential of expanded learning opportunities and partnerships requires a courageous step.

We must venture beyond the notion that learning happens only during the traditional school day and year, when young people are wearing their "student" hats.

Working together, educators, families, community organizations, employers, and volunteers can expand opportunities for continuous and sustained learning in positive, safe, and structured environments.

The basic architecture already exists in many places around the country; thus, our challenge is to figure out how to hardwire this opportunity infrastructure into schools, local and state education agencies, and communities so students and families who need and want quality expanded learning opportunities during the afterschool and summer hours have adequate and appropriate access to them. The articles and authors in *Expanding Minds and Opportunities* offer concrete strategies, approaches, evidence, and best practices to accomplish just that, and even more. I invite you to join us in expanding minds and opportunities by leveraging the power of quality afterschool and summer learning for student success.

ABOUT THE AUTHOR

Terry K. Peterson has a strong background at the local, state, and national levels in education reform, serving as the counselor to the U.S. Secretary of Education, architect of one of America's most comprehensive state improvement efforts, and an expert witness to a dozen states. He currently is a senior fellow at the College of Charleston; serves on 10 education boards (e.g., Alliance for Excellent Education, News Literacy Project, and the Charleston area Engaging Creative Minds), and chairs the national board of the Afterschool Alliance. Peterson has a BS in chemistry and education from the University of Wisconsin and a PhD from the University of South Carolina, with an emphasis in educational research. He was the 2010 Lifetime Education Achievement Awardee from the president and CEO of the C.S. Mott Foundation.

A Focus on Student Success

1

Rhonda H. Lauer
President and CEO, Foundations, Inc.

Ralph R. Smith
Senior Vice President, Annie E. Casey Foundation

The Potential of Quality Afterschool and Summer Learning Programs and 21st Century Community Learning Centers for Supporting School Success

It used to be simple: an elementary education in reading, writing, and arithmetic sufficed for the many; a secondary education sufficed for some; and a postsecondary education sufficed for the very few.

As a nation we began to see that this simple formula was inadequate. We have added the need for knowledge of science, technology, and the arts to our understanding of a basic education, along with the need for the 21st century skills of collaboration and creativity. We have also realized that everyone needs, and is entitled to, this basic education.

We have developed more sophisticated ideas about how to provide universal basic education. We now see the need to provide expanded learning opportunities for children and youth during afterschool hours and summers. We realize that home and community, as well as school, need to be part of a comprehensive plan for helping children and youth learn.

At the same time, we are learning a lot more about the key components that make these expanded learning opportunities work better and more effectively. The articles that follow provide concrete, detailed lessons from research and best practice about how to make afterschool and summer programming more effective in a number of key areas that help young people to be more successful in school and to graduate from high school—the first rung in the ladder leading to full participation in 21st century economic and civic life.

The 21st Century Community Learning Centers initiative has kept pace since its initial authorization in 1994 by incorporating these understandings in its program guidelines (Penuel & McGhee, 2010). In its current form, the program is designed to provide opportunities for academic enrichment, youth development, and family learning (Harris, 2010). The program currently funds about 11,000 centers serving almost 1.7 million children and youth (Afterschool Alliance, n.d.).

In addition, in the decade before the Great Recession hit in 2008, there were efforts by some municipalities, foundations, United Ways, and school districts to provide resources to create and expand learning opportunities in the time after school and during weekends and summers. In the wake of the recession, the growth of this movement has slowed a bit, but there is an expanding chorus of voices calling for more engaged learning time, especially for struggling young people and those in low-income schools and neighborhoods.

With tight budgets, there is more interest in both improving quality and increasing access to expanded learning programs. While not all afterschool and summer programs have fully realized their potential to affect the lives of children and youth in the many ways suggested by the growing body of research in the field, the wealth of new information about what makes programs work well, as well as heightened interest in quality and access to programs, put us in a very positive place to make significant new advances.

The work done over the past decade by our two organizations—Foundations, Inc. and the Annie E. Casey Foundation—has taught us a few lessons about how thoughtful afterschool and summer experiences can make a difference in school success, especially in under-resourced communities and low-performing schools. The recommendations below suggest a few ways to maximize the potential that already resides in the 21st Century Community Learning Centers and in similar local and state initiatives to promote school success.

- **Align in-school and out-of-school learning.** *Afterschool and summer learning programs can do what they do best—offering homework help and hands-on, fun activities—in service to the same standards and objectives that students are expected to meet during the school day. Alignment does not mean doing more of the same beyond the school day and year. It typically specifies arrangements to ensure regular, two-way communication and coordination between teachers and afterschool and summer program providers. Such coordination may take extra effort when 21st Century Learning Centers are located outside of school buildings (Penuel & McGhee, 2010), but it is nevertheless possible, and indeed necessary.*

- **Identify and respond to individual learning needs.** *A key aspect of alignment is focusing out-of-school-time activities on individual students' learning needs. Afterschool and summer programs can usually accommodate more intensive interventions for striving readers—interventions that give striving readers more learning time in more individualized settings outside of the school-day classroom—and can be especially effective in stemming summer learning loss. Providing interventions especially requires close coordination with school-day and school-year programs as to individual students' current academic needs, appropriate materials, and progress. The construction and sharing of individual success plans, to which all pertinent staff contribute, can greatly facilitate this kind of coordination (Foundations, Inc., 2011).*

- **Pay attention to health and school attendance.** *Physical and mental health issues can interfere with attendance and keep students from learning in school-day and out-of-school-time programs, but these problems are often overlooked. Afterschool and summer program staff can share information with other education professionals about students' possible health needs and assist in addressing chronic absenteeism. In this regard, the community-school collaboration that is central to the 21st Century Community Learning Centers should pay more attention to these health and attendance issues, and other school- or community-based initiatives to expand learning should add them to their agendas.*

- **Partner with families.** *Afterschool and summer program staff often have more opportunities than school-day staff to interact and develop positive relationships with families. Out-of-school-time staff can be a critical link between families and the school, not only communicating about school matters but also gathering information about students' interests, coordinating services, and connecting families to each other for support.*

- **Partner with community groups and organizations, and treat school, home, and community as a unified system.** *Children learn wherever they are. To be strategic in helping them get everything they need to succeed in school, the many "educators" in each child's life can join forces. Unlike any other major education initiative, the 21st Century Community Learning Centers initiative requires school-community partnerships, family engagement, and more and varied engaged learning opportunities for young people. As a result, the 21st Century Community Learning Centers initiative invites systems-thinking, in which school, afterschool, and summer-program providers, homes, and the community create a system of supports that takes each partner's unique contributions and makes them add up to an integrated whole that paves the way to school success. Leaders at all levels of 21st Century Community Learning Centers programming should be at the forefront of systems-thinking. It also makes sense for leaders in other afterschool and summer initiatives to incorporate this type of framework in their efforts to help children develop and learn.*

These ideas illustrate and provide additional insights and examples for getting the full power out of 21st Century Community Learning Centers and similar afterschool and summer learning initiatives.

ABOUT THE AUTHORS

Rhonda H. Lauer is president and chief executive officer of Foundations, Inc., a national nonprofit 501(c)(3) organization committed to improving educational experiences for America's most vulnerable children and youth—throughout the day, everywhere they learn. Prior to leading Foundations, she worked in the School District of Philadelphia, one of the nation's largest, as associate superintendent, principal, administrator, and teacher. She also served as superintendent of the Southeast Delco School District. She tours the country as a speaker and panelist to help inform policy and improve education quality. She received her bachelor's and master's degrees from Temple University.

Ralph R. Smith is senior vice president of the Annie E. Casey Foundation. He also serves as managing director for the Campaign for Grade Level Reading, a national effort to increase rates of third-grade reading proficiency. Previously, he sat on the faculty of the Law School of the University of Pennsylvania and also held a number of senior leadership positions for the School District of Philadelphia, including chief of staff and special counsel. He has served on a number of boards, including Leap Frog Enterprises, Inc.; Nobel Learning Communities, Inc.; Venture Philanthropy Partners; and the Center for Responsible Lending.

REFERENCES

Afterschool Alliance. (n.d.). 21st Century Community Learning Centers federal afterschool initiative. Retrieved from http://www.afterschoolalliance.org/policy21stcclc.cfm

Foundations, Inc. (2011). *Grade level reading: An action framework for school and district leaders.* Moorestown, NJ: Author.

Harris, E. (2010, November). *21st CCLC-funded afterschool programs* (Research Update No. 4). Retrieved from Harvard Family Research Project website: http://www.hfrp.org/publications-resources/browse-our-publications/research-update-4-21st-cclc-funded-afterschool-programs

Penuel, W. R., & McGhee, R., Jr. (2010). *21st Century Community Learning Centers: Descriptive study of program practices.* Menlo Park, CA: SRI International.

Lincoln D. Chafee
Governor, State of Rhode Island

Expanded Learning Opportunities Are Key to Student Learning

All across the country, including my home state of Rhode Island, there is growing recognition that to remain competitive in the global marketplace, we must dramatically broaden our young people's academic skills and knowledge as well as the social and emotional capacity to use their skills and knowledge competently and compassionately. Indeed, our economic security, national security, and overall success as a democracy depend on our ability to educate our youth in ways that connect school learning to real-world experiences.

For over a decade, 21st Century Community Learning Centers have been providing a real-world context to learning and leading-edge learning opportunities in the afterschool hours and during the summer months. Strong, vibrant partnerships have been forged between schools and community agencies through the 21st Century Community Learning Centers initiative to make learning relevant for students. In Rhode Island, these partnerships are playing a critical role in preparing our students for the workforce, college, careers, and success in life.

Last year I had the privilege of visiting the Chillin' and Skillin' Summer Program in Woonsocket, Rhode Island. Chillin' and Skillin' is the summer component of the local school district's 21st Century Community Learning Centers program, reaching over 100 third- to sixth-grade students in one of Woonsocket's most underserved neighborhoods. When I arrived for the visit, I expected to take the typical tour of various classrooms in the school building. Instead, I was taken to a local park where students were observing and identifying various bird species and predicting why they found so many species at that park, but nowhere else in the city. I then witnessed another group of students who were taking water samples at the Blackstone River to test for pollution. Rather than teaching only out of textbooks, Woonsocket teachers and their community partners were making learning relevant for the students, and this hands-on learning allowed students to better understand the concepts explained during the school year. The strong partnership between the Woonsocket School Department and its nonprofit partner, Connecting for Children and Families, provided students with high quality, engaging summer programming that reduced summer learning loss and did all of this in a cost-effective way that made sense for all of the organizations involved.

Woonsocket has also been leading the way in offering high school graduation credits for opportunities taking place outside of the traditional school day. During my visit to Chillin' and Skillin', I also had the opportunity to visit RiverzEdge Arts Project. RiverzEdge and other community-based organizations in the city have been partnering with the high school to create the Woonsocket Expanded Learning Opportunities Initiative. This initiative is designed to provide multiple pathways to graduation for high school students by creating rigorous, individualized, standards-based, student-centered projects that engage teachers, community educators, and students in learning.

In one example of a high quality expanded learning opportunity, two students from Woonsocket High School partnered with an American history teacher and the local Museum of Work and Culture to produce an exhibit for the museum comparing and contrasting the immigrant experience from the late-19th century with the immigrant experience of today. The students researched primary and secondary sources, conducted interviews with current immigrants, learned about curating museum exhibits, and met all of the state's American history standards in order to receive course credit. This experience provided them with a real-world application of their knowledge, allowed them to utilize critical thinking and other life skills, and was made possible through the strong collaborative spirit that exists between Woonsocket schools and community partners such as Connecting for Children and Families, RiverzEdge Arts Project, and the Museum of Work and Culture.

The Chillin' and Skillin' program and the Woonsocket Expanded Learning Opportunities Initiative are just two of the many examples of the great results that we have seen from strong school-community partnerships in Rhode Island and across the nation through the 21st Century Community Learning Centers initiative. Rhode Island currently has 21st Century Community Learning Centers in 56 schools, serving over 13,000 students after the school bell rings. These partnerships ensure that afterschool and summer learning programs reinforce school-day learning and strengthen understanding by making real-world connections for students.

Of vital significance to those of us responsible for the wise use of public resources, research shows that the 21st Century Community Learning Centers initiative is working. Recent surveys conducted by the Rhode Island State Department of Education show that 66% of the teachers of all participating students reported improvement in homework completion and class participation. Moreover, 61% of these students' teachers reported improvements in student behavior. Additionally, a recent study by Public/ Private Ventures found that due to the efforts of the Providence After School Alliance, participation in afterschool programming increased student attendance during the school day by 25% (RI Dept. of Education, 2010). For those who were highly engaged in afterschool programs, there were also improvements in math grades, math achievement test scores, and social and emotional competencies (Kauh, 2011). All of these afterschool benefits positively affect how students perform during the school day while at the same time providing learning opportunities that expand our young people's skills, knowledge, and experiences to equip them to handle these rapidly changing times.

Of equal importance, the 21st Century Community Learning Centers initiative has led to greater collaboration between schools, cities, and community organizations, putting Rhode Island at the forefront of many national education improvement efforts. Chillin' and Skillin' and the Providence After School Alliance are wonderful examples of the many summer programs that are creating strong collaborations between schools and community organizations to reduce summer learning loss. Programs across the state have developed an innovative model in which school teachers and community educators cocreate and then codeliver a high quality, hands-on summer curriculum to students. These collaborations have strengthened relationships between schools, community organizations, and in some cases, city departments, and have led to further partnerships during the school year. In Providence, for example, the mayor and superintendent have become advocates and partners in the growth of 21st Century Community Learning Centers programs to help drive a number of youth outcomes—academic, civic, creative, social, and emotional. In addition, an independent evaluation of this summer model by Brown University found it to be replicable in other communities (Laorenza & Whitney, 2010).

21st Century Community Learning Centers collaborations have also resulted in partnerships that have increased the number of pathways that students in Rhode Island have for high school graduation. For the last several years, teams from Woonsocket, Central Falls, and Providence have been working to develop a system in which students receive high school credit for rigorous, student-centered, individualized learning opportunities that occur outside of the traditional school. These learning opportunities require extensive collaboration and coordination between teachers and community organizations, and they are achieving success. In Central Falls, for instance, students who had dropped out of high school have re-enrolled and are currently working toward their diplomas, drawing heavily on these programs. In many cases, these learning opportunities are more rigorous than a traditional class; moreover, they provide students with real-world context for the concepts they are learning.

It is clear that these school-community partnerships benefit student learning and growth and therefore make sense from an educational standpoint. In these trying economic times, these partnerships also make financial sense, often saving school districts and community organizations money. For school districts, partnering with community organizations allows them to provide a service, whether it is a summer program or an afterschool tutoring program, at a fraction of the cost of expanding the school day. In many cases, schools provide in-kind support, such as keeping a building open later or shifting bus schedules to allow for a late bus; in return, students are provided additional academic enrichment. For community organizations, these partnerships allow them to achieve their mission and goals and often provide them with space and resources that they would not otherwise have. Put simply, partnerships make sound financial sense for all parties and, most importantly, they provide students with additional learning opportunities and social and emotional supports after the school bell rings, generating demonstrable results.

When I think about education improvements, I find it implies that something we have tried is not working and that we must continue looking far and wide for the "silver bullet" that will solve the problem. I believe that such an effort is ultimately misdirected. Indeed, when I think about the tools our schools require to adequately prepare our children for a global economy, I look no further than the neighborhoods in which those schools are located. Every school is situated in a neighborhood with a set of community resources and organizations that interact with children every day and provide relevant connections to real-world experiences and future career pathways. The 21st Century Community Learning Centers initiative is proof that strong partnerships between schools and community organizations can lead to solid improvements in learning and significant benefits to children, families, and communities.

To generate the improvements we seek in student achievement, we must remember that learning does not end when the school bell rings and that there are many ways to learn and many ways to teach. School-community partnerships offer a way to ensure that children's learning and personal development does not end when the school day does. Indeed, experiential, inquiry-based learning is reinforced and addressed in new and unique ways in the hours after school and during the summer months. As policy makers, we must strengthen our support of these partnerships. In doing so we will be strengthening our support of our children's academic growth and will ensure that our country remains the leader of the global marketplace.

ABOUT THE AUTHOR

Lincoln D. Chafee is a native of Warwick, Rhode Island, where he served for 4 years on the Warwick City Council and nearly four 2-year terms as mayor. He subsequently served for 7 years as a United States senator. A graduate of Brown University, he was elected in 2010 as the first Independent governor of Rhode Island.

REFERENCES

Kauh, T. J. (2011). *Afterzone: Outcomes for youth participating in Providence's citywide after-school system*. New York, NY: Public/Private Ventures.

Laorenza, E., & Whitney, J. (2010). *Evaluation report: Summer learning project 2009–2010*. Providence, RI: Brown University.

Rhode Island Department of Education. (2010). *The Rhode Island 21st Century Community Learning Center Initiative: Supporting student success for nearly a decade*. Providence, RI: Author.

Danette Parsley
Director, Center for School and District
Improvement Education Northwest

Supporting Mathematics Learning in Afterschool and Summer Learning Programs

It is late afternoon, and fifth- and sixth-grade students at Intermediate School 125 in Woodside, New York, are beating on plastic buckets and hand drums to create fun, rhythmic sounds. However, that is not all they are doing. Their afterschool instructor is also helping them apply and reinforce key mathematics concepts—such as counting, fractions, multiplication, and division—as they keep track of measures to perform percussion routines.

Why do programs, such as the Champions Club After School Program at Intermediate School 125, choose to embed mathematics into their activities? In light of today's strenuous school accountability demands, widespread concern about our nation's ability to compete globally, and high drop-out rates (including disproportionate rates for low-income and minority students), afterschool programs often provide mathematics learning opportunities to support the academic needs of struggling students.

In adding a mathematics component to their core set of activities, programs operating after school and in summer typically have one or more of the following goals in mind:

- *Schools and communities turn to these programs as a resource <u>to raise overall student performance and narrow the achievement gap</u> between high- and low-performing students by providing more individualized learning time through tutoring and other targeted interventions.*

- *Some programs include a mathematics focus to reinforce learning—helping students solidify understandings they develop during the regular school day by engaging with content through different learning modes (e.g., hands-on, interdisciplinary, cross-age, real-world) and during periods when school is not in session, such as the critical summer months when students may be at risk of losing learning gained during the school year.*

- *Finally, some programs incorporate mathematics instruction to accelerate learning, helping students build academic background knowledge they can draw upon as they learn new content in the regular classroom setting.*

Programs typically use a combination of more targeted learning experiences (e.g., direct instruction, tutoring) and enrichment experiences to meet one or more of these purposes.

But do afterschool programs that incorporate a mathematics focus actually lead to improved student outcomes? Early study findings were mixed, and the body of research in this area is still relatively small; however, in recent years a growing number of program evaluations have indicated that participating in well-designed and implemented programs can enhance mathematics test scores and grades, school attendance, and student engagement in learning. Moreover, successful programs tend to have the most significant effects for students most at risk of failing in core subjects, such as math and reading, or dropping out of school (Afterschool Alliance, 2011; Little, 2009).

For the U.S. Department of Education Institute of Education Services (IES) panel recommendations, see *Structuring Out-of-School Time to Improve Academic Achievement* (2009), available at the IES website: http://ies.ed.gov/ncee/wwc/practiceguide.aspx?sid=10

For a robust set of resources to support implementation of the IES recommendations, see the U.S. Department of Education's website Doing What Works: http://dww.ed.gov/Increased-Learning-Time/topic/index.cfm?T_ID=29

Over the last decade, there has been a dramatic increase in the number of schools, districts, and community-based organizations running afterschool and summer learning programs with the goal of improving academic performance (Stonehill et al., 2009). To respond to these programs' need for research-based guidance, the Institute of Education Sciences (IES) convened an expert panel to review existing research on afterschool, summer, weekend, and tutoring programs (Beckett et al., 2009). The panel generated five recommendations for designing, delivering, and evaluating high quality academically oriented programs:

1. Align the out-of-school-time program academically with the school day.

2. Maximize student participation and attendance.

3. Adapt instruction to individual and small-group needs.

4. Provide engaging learning experiences.

5. Assess program performance and use the results to improve the quality of the program.

The following is a discussion of the recommendations as they relate to designing and delivering high quality programs with a mathematics emphasis.

Designing Afterschool and Summer Learning Programs That Address Mathematics

Designing high quality afterschool and summer learning programs with a focus on mathematics requires aligning the program academically without repeating the school day, while maximizing student participation.

To facilitate the communication and collaboration needed to align the program academically with the school day, while maintaining a distinctive programmatic identity and approach, it is important to designate a point of contact for both the out-of-school and regular school-day program. The afterschool program coordinator, who ideally has access to and presence in the school building during day, develops relationships and maintains ongoing communication with regular school day staff. The school staff person designated to coordinate with the out-of-school-time program provides the afterschool coordinator with student data, curriculum materials, and any other information that assists with aligning the program with the school's academic goals and priorities.

Additionally, the afterschool and school coordinators might identify opportunities for collaborative planning and professional development. Finally, they can work together to determine how to strategically use the school's teaching faculty and community-based and business partners to support the program in engaging, hands-on, and personalized ways. Teachers can be recruited to serve as tutors or intervention specialists, mentor new out-of-school-time staff, model instructional strategies, and collaboratively plan enrichment activities to include the mathematics concepts and skills for which students need the most support. Community organizations and business partners can serve as tutors and mentors, help plan and facilitate real-life and practical math problem solving activities, and demonstrate how math and math "talk" are critical in the work world.

Ensuring that the afterschool program aligns with the school day is an important strategy, but alignment alone is insufficient for improving mathematics performance if the students who need the program the most do not take advantage of it. To help maximize student attendance and participation, schools should promote the programs widely using a variety of communication mechanisms; address the needs and preferences of students and parents, including issues of transportation, location, hours of operation, and programmatic interests; and offer enrichment and recreational activities in addition to mathematics instruction.

> Designing high quality afterschool and summer learning programs with a focus on mathematics requires aligning the program academically without repeating the school day.

Ohio

Glover Community Learning Center's Akron After School Program is aligned to the regular school day mathematics curriculum, uses intervention assistance teams to identify struggling students for participation, provides targeted math and reading interventions,

For more information about Glover Community Learning Center, see its profile at Doing What Works: http://dww.ed.gov/Increased-Learning-Time/Align-Instruction/profiles/?T_ID=29&P_ID=75&sID=307

and maximizes attendance by allowing students to choose from among a variety of engaging enrichment classes where they enhance their mathematics and other subject-area knowledge through project-based learning. The afterschool program coordinator plays a critical role in ensuring alignment with the school day and uses regular updates about student needs from school-day teachers to tailor afterschool instructional activities. For example, conversations with different teachers led to a priority focus of supporting fifth-grade students with solving math story problems. To further enhance alignment, school-day and afterschool instructors are provided collaboration time to exchange ideas and information about students. All afterschool instructors are encouraged to participate in professional development sessions with school-day teachers, and many school-day teachers serve as afterschool instructors.

Providing Tailored and Engaging Afterschool and Summer Mathematics Learning Experiences

Recommendations 3 and 4 from the IES panel (above) focus specifically on instructional delivery. Programs should provide targeted, intentionally designed learning experiences that are engaging, active, and maximize the flexibility that out-of-school environments offer to meet specific learning needs. The IES panel did not generate content-specific instructional recommendations. Another project, however, previously funded by the U.S.

Afterschool Programs Multiply Math Skills

A Peace Corps water project in Panama receives virtual assistance from an unlikely source: an afterschool program in rural Washington State. Meanwhile, afterschool program participants elsewhere in Washington are learning to build bridges, engineer wind farms, and design robots.

The Northwest Learning and Achievement Group (NLA), which directs these programs, has been highly successful in utilizing the time beyond school to accelerate student achievement. Each afternoon session begins with tutoring and supervised homework time with math teachers then moves to online math tutorials and interactive group projects. Perhaps surprisingly, organizers have cut back on the afterschool time dedicated to homework in part because they found that providing students more innovative outlets to hone their math skills had a larger positive impact on test scores.

In addition to working with a Peace Corps volunteer, NLA programs utilize community resources, including arts and cultural organizations, city and local governments, environmental programs, and parks and recreation departments. Today, more than 2,000 students attend NLA afterschool programs, 80% of whom are eligible for free or reduced-price lunch. Through quality afterschool programs, these students are expanding their horizons while demonstrating impressive gains in their classroom behavior, homework completion, and standardized test scores.

Department of Education—the National Partnership for Quality Afterschool Learning—identifies promising practices for a variety of content areas, including mathematics, as part of a multiyear study of 21st Century Community Learning Centers-funded programs showing gains in student achievement (National Partnership for Quality

 For information, additional resources, and program examples to support use of the math practices, see SEDL's National Center for Quality Afterschool website: http://www.sedl.org/afterschool/toolkits/about_toolkits.html?tab=math

Afterschool Learning, n.d.). The recommended mathematics practices include the following:

1. Finding Math – use of engaging, everyday situations to bring math to life

2. Math Centers – small-group stations that allow students to work independently or collaboratively on problem-solving tasks at their own pace

3. Math Games – fun activities that develop targeted math strategies and skills

4. Math Projects – learning experiences that extend beyond one lesson that allow students to deepen mathematical knowledge and skills through their own authentic investigations

5. Math Tools – use of pictures, rulers, symbols, technology, and concrete materials to problem solve

6. Math Tutoring – one-on-one or small-group work on specific math skills

7. Family Connections – methods for engaging family and community support and enthusiasm for math in out-of-school time

The project team identified three overarching strategies that should accompany implementation of any of these practices to increase the level of rigor and student engagement with these learning experiences. First, afterschool and summer learning programs should encourage problem solving by providing students opportunities to creatively generate strategies for solving intriguing mathematics problems on their own. Second, program activities should be designed to develop and support math talk by providing ample opportunities for students to communicate ideas to each other. Math talk helps students clarify their thinking, construct meaning, and develop reasoning skills while providing afterschool and summer learning facilitators with informal assessment data they can use to make instructional adjustments and provide targeted feedback. Finally, activities should emphasize students working together to draw on each others' knowledge and deepen learning.

> Math talk helps students clarify their thinking, construct meaning, and develop reasoning skills while providing afterschool and summer learning facilitators with informal assessment data they can use to make instructional adjustments and provide targeted feedback.

These crosscutting strategies for supporting afterschool and summer mathematics learning align nicely with several of the new Common Core State Standards (CCSS) for mathematics. Almost all states have adopted these or similarly rigorous learning goals designed to prepare students to succeed in college and the workforce. The CCSS articulate expectations for math content in addition to mathematical practices, or "habits of mind," such as making sense of and persevering in solving problems, reasoning abstractly and quantitatively, and constructing viable arguments.

With the relative flexibility afterschool and summer programs have with time and structuring activities, they can be perfect environments for fostering these mathematics habits of mind and an invaluable resource as schools and districts plan for transitioning to the CCSS.

For video clips of Purple Sage Elementary School staff members using the recommended practices of Math Centers and Math Games, see the National Center for Quality Afterschool: http://www.sedl.org/afterschool/toolkits/math/pr_math_centers.html

http://www.sedl.org/afterschool/toolkits/math/pr_math_games.html

··

Texas

The afterschool program staff at Purple Sage Elementary School in Houston, Texas, are in ongoing communication with classroom teachers to identify the mathematical concepts they should reinforce through engaging experiences that are different than the school day. At times they focus directly on these concepts. For example, they might have students choose from a variety of center-based math games where one small group of students works to deepen their understanding of and practice applying the concept of equivalent fractions using fraction dominos. Instructors emphasize critical thinking skills through high-level, open-ended questioning, encouraging students to connect math concepts to other familiar ideas and find creative solutions to problems. During other times, mathematics learning is intentionally embedded into other engaging activities, such as incorporating the application of a variety of basic mathematics concepts (e.g., odd and even numbers, factors, multiples) into a competitive group tag activity.

Opportunities for Improving Mathematics Achievement

Afterschool and summer learning programs not only provide additional time but also different modes for supporting, reinforcing, and even accelerating mathematics learning. Communication, collaboration, and coordination between what happens during the school day and what happens in the afterschool or summer learning environment are all critical elements for ensuring successful program outcomes.

In addition, leaders of afterschool and summer learning programs and their regular school day partners who want to enhance math learning and interest should:

- intentionally infuse mathematics content into everyday problems by using math games and centers, incorporating the use of math tools, and constructing authentic project-based learning opportunities;

- provide targeted tutoring assistance; and

- engage families, communities, and businesses to expand students' mathematics learning opportunities through meaningful partnerships.

ABOUT THE AUTHOR

Danette Parsley, director of the Center for School and District Improvement at Education Northwest, has extensive experience providing technical assistance at the local, state, and regional levels in various aspects of systemic school and district improvement, including afterschool teaching and learning practices. She currently serves as co-principal investigator for two federally funded projects to design and evaluate academically oriented afterschool and summer learning programs for high school students. Parsley served on the expert panel that developed the Institute of Education Sciences practice guide *Structuring Out-of-School Time to Improve Academic Achievement*.

REFERENCES

Afterschool Alliance. (2011). *Evaluations backgrounder: A summary of formal evaluations of the academic impact of afterschool programs*. Retrieved from http://www.afterschoolalliance.org/Evaluations%20Backgrounder%20Academic_08_FINAL.pdf

Beckett, M., Borman, G., Capizzano, J., Parsley, D., Ross, S., Schirm, A., & Taylor, J. (2009). *Structuring out-of-school time to improve academic achievement: A practice guide* (NCEE 2009-012). Retrieved from http://ies.ed.gov/

Council of Chief State School Officers. (2011). *Connecting high-quality expanded learning opportunities and the Common Core State Standards to advance student success*. Washington, DC: Author. Retrieved from http://www.ccsso.org/

Little, P. M. (2009). *Supporting student outcomes through expanded learning opportunities*. Retrieved from Harvard Family Research Project website: http://www.hfrp.org/out-of-school-time/publications-resources/supporting-student-outcomes-through-expanded-learning-opportunities

National Partnership for Quality Afterschool Learning. (n.d.). *Afterschool training toolkit*. Retrieved from SEDL, National Center for Quality Afterschool website: http://www.sedl.org/afterschool/toolkits/index.html

Stonehill, R. M., Little, P. M., Ross, S. M., Neergaard, L., Harrison, L., Ford, J., . . . Donner, J. (2009). *Enhancing school reform through expanded learning*. Naperville, IL: Learning Point Associates. Retrieved from http://www.learningpt.org/

Paul E. Heckman
Associate Dean, Professor, and Co-Director of CANDEL (Capital Area North Doctorate in Educational Leadership), School of Education, University of California, Davis

Carla Sanger
Founding President and Chief Executive Officer, LA's BEST After School Enrichment Program

How Quality Afterschool Programs Help Motivate and Engage More Young People in Learning, Schooling, and Life

As we move into the second decade of the 21st century, knowledge in all fields has expanded and yielded developments far beyond the imagined world of science fiction writers just 20 years ago—consider, for example, the iPhone and iPad, tablet computers, and the Android operating system. Even more amazing is the *access* that these and other devices allow to the vast amount of information and knowledge that exists today, as well as the *rapidity* with which that information and knowledge will continue to expand in the near future.

In this context, *how* we learn, especially as young people, matters. While children cannot possibly hope to acquire more than a fraction of the sum total of human knowledge, they should be involved in experiences that are most likely to help them learn and benefit from our extensive and ever-expanding knowledge base.

Background Research

New insights from cognitive and neuroscience research into how children acquire knowledge should be inspiring dramatic new strategies and structures for learning in schools and other educational settings—unfortunately, this is often not the case. There are glimmers of hope, however, in the afterschool arena, especially in conjunction with efforts undertaken in the last decade through the 21st Century Community Learning Centers initiative. Today, there are great examples of these insights that are being incorporated into afterschool practice, enhancing student engagement and creating the conditions that will lead to a greater likelihood that students will stay in school and graduate on time (Mahoney, Parente, & Lord, 2007; Wang & Holcombe, 2010).

Research on Learning

Unlike earlier views of individual capacity—"some have it, some do not"—current research suggests a continuously learning mind, one that is plastic and adaptive into late adulthood and that has enormous capacity for storing memories and knowledge, unless serious brain damage has occurred. Even then, the brain's plasticity asserts itself, as the heroic Gabrielle Giffords has demonstrated so well (Sacks, 2010).

Because individuals are learning continuously from infancy, they acquire insights about themselves and the world around them that influences the way they make sense of their daily interactions and the circumstances they confront. Moreover, prior knowledge forms the foundation for any new learning.

Recent research about learning has also identified intellectual curiosity and interest as essential for learning and intellectual development. Interest and curiosity are the basis for motivating the "hungry mind" (Stumm, Hell, & Chamorro-Premuzic, 2011). The more a student exhibits curiosity, which is rooted in interest, the more he or she can focus on, bring effort to, and engage in meaningful tasks. This aspect of learning, while underutilized in many educational settings, has great potential and has been incorporated into quality afterschool and youth development programs.

Additionally, research also illuminates the importance of caring social relationships and the contributions that those relationships make to learning (Shonkoff & Philips, 2000). Human beings exist in a world with other people. They are "hardwired to connect" (Commission on Children at Risk, 2003). Meaningful relationships with others matter to children, youth, and adults and to their learning.

The research on belonging in educational contexts is relatively new, and the direction of causality has not been definitively established. Nevertheless, many correlational studies have shown that students who report caring and supportive interpersonal relationships in school have more positive academic attitudes and values and are more satisfied with school. They are also more engaged in academic work, and they attend school more and learn more (National Research Council and Institute of Medicine, 2004).

This means that children and the adults with whom children interact in educational settings must have and avail themselves of opportunities to demonstrate that they care about each other in meaningful ways. In that process, children can more easily take risks, explore, express themselves, and learn.

Research on Afterschool and Summer Learning

The general trends in the research literature about quality youth development, afterschool, and summer learning programs show the relationship between the reported engagement and motivation of children and youth and positive outcomes like school and program attendance and positive academic gains in reading and math, even when attendance is low (Hirsch, Mekinds, & Stawicki, 2010).

These general trends in the research literature about the positive consequences of quality afterschool and youth development programs are nicely summed up by the National Research Council's report *Community Programs to Promote Youth Development* (2002). That volume expounds on the important qualities of educational activities that will likely engage children and youth in their learning, such as active construction of knowledge; disciplined inquiry; relevance of material being studied to the student and his or her community culture; regular feedback on progress; opportunities to rethink work and understanding; recognition of and use of students' knowledge, interests, and dispositions; and students working together and tutoring each other. Children will be more likely to work well with each other and with their teachers when the adults demonstrate care and high regard for them.

In their meta-analysis of the research literature about afterschool, Durlak, Weissberg, and Pachan (2010) found that " . . . participants demonstrated significant increases in their self-perceptions and bonding to school, positive social behaviors, school grades and levels of academic achievement, and significant reductions in problem behaviors." Moreover, "there were significant increases in youths' self-perceptions, bonding to school, positive social behaviors, school grades, and achievement test scores. Significant reductions also appeared for problem behaviors."

This and other research suggests that when designing afterschool and summer learning programs, community and education leaders must understand that disaffected and underserved children and youth will only attend noncompulsory educational programs if the program fosters high student engagement—that is, if students remain active, stay focused, and experience enjoyment throughout their participation in the program (Huang, Gribbons, Kim, Lee, & Baker, 2000; Shernoff, 2010; Wang & Holcombe, 2010). Students' engagement requires developing program designs and activities that, at least in the minds of students, stands in stark contrast to the experiences of boredom, distraction, and apathy that typically characterizes their experiences with conventional academic tasks and/or settings (Mahoney et al., 2007). As a consequence, much of the design effort undertaken by program leaders should focus on creating and fostering highly engaging social settings/environments that will maintain student attendance and participation with the program each day.

Support for Practice That Works

Many of these research findings have influenced one of the most important funding streams in this country developed to create vibrant learning environments for children after school: the 21st Century Community Learning Centers initiative. Through the funding requirements of this federal program, public schools partner with community-based organizations to create programs designed to connect students to their homes, schools, and communities. These programs have had more independence, leverage, and flexibility within school systems than most categorical programs had ever experienced before in the history of public education. High quality 21st Century Community Learning Centers programs emphasize creativity, crusade for fresh ideas, continuously energize and motivate staff, and combat any tendency toward bureaucratization.

LA's BEST, like a number of other high quality programs, welcomes the responsibility for training what is primarily a young staff with limited background knowledge and experience in working with children. Most staff members reside within 2 miles of the schools in which they work, and collectively, they more closely reflect the ethnicity and daily experiences of the children who are enrolled in the program. LA's BEST works to build a common understanding and common language about how children learn and what motivates them to learn. This helps create the kinds of learning environments that promote engagement and support the development of trusting, meaningful relationships.

Unlike the regular school-day program, based on predetermined curricula developed by those living far away from the neighborhoods served, programming in LA's BEST is developed at each site, starting with a focus on the students and their interests. Activities in program areas of enrichment, recreation, and nutrition are created based on the interests, curiosities, and even fears of the students. At the same time, the program at each site also complements and expands skills in literacy and numeracy that, in turn, support learning during the regular school day.

Distinctive youth development values are infused within the program culture at LA's BEST. All staff are encouraged and expected to embrace the principle "Nothing we do is more important than the effect it has on the child." Afterschool programs like LA's BEST have the luxury, for example, of not having to be on page 10 of any textbook by Tuesday at 4:00 p.m. If a planned activity does not have the respectful engagement of students, staff members are expected to change the activity. LA's BEST staff members at each site receive training to deliver engaging learning activities and to "monitor and adjust" as needed. Each site is assigned two itinerant support staff, who conduct frequent site visits to monitor program implementation. These traveling staff members also assist staff in achieving activity performance goals through the steps of *inquiry, observation, assessment, debriefing,* and *planning.* Traveling staff, generally more experienced than site-based staff, communicate clear, concise, and observable indicators of high quality practices at each step. Additionally, consistent collaboration and communication by site staff with principals, teachers, and other regular school-day personnel promote tighter alignment of program efforts in support of enhanced student learning.

Additionally, LA's BEST works annually with more than 100 community-based organizations to respond to children's interests and needs by providing opportunities to engage in seasonal sports and games, experience the visual and performing arts, participate in science and math activities, learn how to use new technologies, and acquire information about ways to improve health and nutrition.

The LA's BEST program is a clear and compelling example of a program that reflects quality engagement features. There are other programs that, similarly, have developed and enacted programs to engage youth deeply and meaningfully. Robert Halpern (2009) describes several apprenticeship programs involving young people in various settings, such as schools; youth-serving organizations; and arts, civic, and other cultural institutions. In these programs youth engage in meaningful "real world" activities related to the professional, artistic, and civic work that reflect their career interests. In such an "apprentice-like" relationship, the young person interacts with and learns alongside the adult, who has expertise in the particular area of interest. The student gains knowledge, skills, and habits of mind from the planned activities, social interaction, and performances undertaken with the adult(s).

In his Presidential Address at the Meetings of the Society for Research on Adolescence in 2010, Reed Larson describes a number of youth-serving programs involved in a study he is conducting. Each of these programs seeks meaningful engagement of youth in consequential efforts in which they can make a difference in their own lives and in their community. Larson shares the reflections of one student about the events: "I wasn't super interested. . . [but when] I found out a lot of stuff about the schools, what they were doing, I was like 'Hey, that's wrong!' because that [had] happened to me." He then described becoming "really into it, really psyched" (Larson, 2011, p. 325).

Evidence of Success for LA's BEST

Through its long-time collaboration with UCLA's National Center for Research on Evaluation, Standards and Student Testing (CRESST), LA's BEST has more independent, longitudinal evaluation data and anecdotal results than any program of its kind in the country. Research has found, for example, that students in LA's BEST are 20% less likely to drop out of school than students who do not participate in the program (Huang, Kim, Marshall, & Perez, 2005). LA's BEST students are also 30% less likely to commit juvenile crime compared to peers not in the program (Goldschmidt, Huang, & Chinen, 2007).

Recommendations and Conclusion

Successful afterschool and summer programs should incorporate the following principles:

1. Young people should be actively encouraged to share what is real to them.

2. High quality, effective programs should work to forge strong connections between students and staff, reinforce connections between new knowledge and old, and strengthen connections between what a child already knows how to do and what he or she would like to learn.

3. These programs should support the strengthening of life skills, such as resourcefulness, grit, and resiliency that are critical to a child's whole development.

Ultimately, this site-based, personalized approach to children's learning and engagement after school will generate positive outcomes that are observed not only within the context of the afterschool program itself but during the regular school day as well.

ABOUT THE AUTHORS

Paul E. Heckman is associate dean, professor, and co-director of CANDEL (Capital Area North Doctorate in Educational Leadership) in the School of Education at University of California, Davis. His areas of expertise and research interest include curriculum theory and change; educational ecology of communities; educational leadership; school restructuring; organizational arrangements and structures; and educational change and invention in urban communities, schools, and afterschool programs.

Carla Sanger is the founding president and chief executive officer of LA's BEST After School Enrichment Program. Sanger has been a specialist in children's education policy and advocacy for more than 40 years in the public and private sectors. Over the course of her career, she has been a public school teacher, curriculum writer, supervisor of day care services for the state of New Jersey, executive director of LA Child Care & Development Council, president of the California Children's Council and co-chair of the California State Department of Education Task Force on School Readiness.

REFERENCES

Commission on Children at Risk. (2003). *Hardwired to connect: The new scientific evidence for authoritative communities.* New York, NY: Institute for American Values.

Durlak, J. A., Weissberg, R. P., & Pachan, M. (2010). A meta-analysis of after-school programs that seek to promote personal and social skills in children and adolescents. *American Journal of Community Psychology, 45,* 294–309.

Goldschmidt, P., Huang, D., & Chinen, M. (2007). *The long-term effects of after-school programming on educational adjustment and juvenile crime: A study of the LA's BEST after-school program.* Washington, DC: U.S. Department of Justice.

Halpern, R. (2009). *The means to grow up: Reinventing apprenticeship as a developmental support in adolescence.* New York, NY: Routledge.

Hirsch, B. J., Mekinds, M. A., & Stawicki, J. (2010). More than attendance: The importance of after-school program quality. *American Journal of Community Psychology, 45*(3–4), 447–452.

Huang, D., Gribbons, B., Kim, S. K., Lee, C., & Baker, E. (2000). *A decade of results: The impact of LA's BEST after school enrichment program on subsequent student achievement and performance.* Los Angeles, CA: UCLA Center for the Study of Evaluation.

Huang, D., Kim, K. S., Marshall, A., & Perez, P. (2005). *Keeping kids in school: An LA's BEST example—A study examining the long-term impact of LA's BEST on students' dropout rates.* Los Angeles: National Center for Research on Evaluation, Standards, and Student Testing (CRESST), University of California–Los Angeles.

Larson, R. W. (2011). Positive development in a disorderly world. *Journal of Research on Adolescence, 21*(2), 317–334.

Mahoney, J., Parente, M., & Lord, H. (2007). After-school program engagement: Links to child competence and program quality and content. *The Elementary School Journal, 107,* 385–404.

National Research Council and Institute of Medicine. (2002). *Community programs to promote youth development.* Washington, DC: The National Academies Press.

REFERENCES (CONTINUED)

National Research Council and Institute of Medicine. (2004). *Engaging schools: Fostering high school student's motivation to learn.* Washington, DC: The National Academies Press.

Sacks, O. (2010). *The mind's eye.* New York, NY: Knopf.

Shernoff, D. J. (2010). Engagement in after-school programs as a predictor of social competence and academic performance. *American Journal of Community Psychology, 45,* 325–337.

Shonkoff, J. P., & Philips, D. A. (Eds.). (2000). *From neurons to neighborhoods: The science of early childhood education.* Washington, DC: The National Academies Press.

Stumm, S., Hell, B., & Chamorro-Premuzic, T. (2011). The hungry mind: Intellectual curiosity is the third pillar of academic performance. *Perspectives on Psychological Science, 6,* 574–588.

Wang, M., & Holcombe, R. (2010). Adolescents' perceptions of school environment, engagement, and academic achievement in middle school. *American Educational Research Journal, 47*(3), 633–662.

Betsy Brand
Executive Director, American Youth Policy Forum

Andrew Valent
Program Associate, American Youth Policy Forum

The Potential of Career and College Readiness and Exploration in Afterschool Programs

A high school diploma used to be enough to get by in the job market, but this is no longer the case. A Georgetown University study found that the percentage of jobs in the United States that require some form of postsecondary education will reach a projected 63% by 2018, up from 28% in the early 1970s (Carnevale, Smith, & Strohl, 2010). This trend is being driven by the increasingly complex global labor market that requires more advanced levels of math, science, and language arts proficiency.

Tony Wagner from Harvard University argues that in addition to higher levels of basic skills, students need certain 21st century skills for success in a knowledge economy, such as critical thinking, collaboration, communication, creativity, adaptability, imagination, and entrepreneurism. Yet he laments that these skills are noticeably underemphasized in instruction and assessments within American schools and that youth have few opportunities to develop such skills in school settings (Wagner, 2010).

High schools are increasingly focused on ramping up student performance in basic academic skills—certainly a laudable goal. Many schools are not able, however, to provide opportunities during the school day for all students to learn about college and career options or to develop vital 21st century skills. Students from higher socioeconomic backgrounds can more easily access learning opportunities through networks of family, friends, and other options, but economically disadvantaged youth often have little access to these opportunities and services. Many business and civic groups were pleased when President Obama announced a national goal of having the largest share of college graduates in the world by 2020; consequently, we must redouble our efforts to ensure that all young people are prepared for success in both college and careers. Afterschool and summer learning programs can help us meet this goal.

Many afterschool and summer learning programs expose youth to the importance of college by taking them on visits to college campuses, working with students and families to identify prospective colleges, providing assistance in the college application process, helping families navigate the financial assistance jungle, and providing encouragement and support to students who do not see themselves as college material. These activities, which many high schools do not have the time and resources to provide, are key to helping students become college ready and make a successful transition into college (Bowles & Brand, 2009; College Track, 2012b; Herrera, Linden, Arbreton, & Grossman, 2011; Seftor, Mamun, & Schirm, 2009).

Other afterschool and summer learning programs provide youth with opportunities to learn about careers, participate in internships or work experiences, participate in community service projects, or earn stipends for work. Employers are often key partners with afterschool programs in providing work-based learning or apprenticeship-type experiences. These activities are important for youth who have little exposure to careers or who are unfamiliar with the workplace, again, since activities of this nature are rarely scheduled into the regular school day (Afterschol Alliance, 2009; Bowles & Brand, 2009; Halpern, 2008; Hirsch, Hedges, Stawicki, & Mekinda, 2011; Moran, n.d.; Pearson & Fabiano, 2006).

Afterschool and summer learning programs also provide engaging learning opportunities for youth by connecting learning to careers, college, and other future plans. In many classrooms, students do not learn how to apply their knowledge (Casner-Lotto, 2006). They learn content from a theoretical standpoint, divorced from the real world and rarely placed in the context of how the information or knowledge can be used to solve actual problems. In contrast, many afterschool and summer learning programs excel in providing opportunities for youth to develop these types of skills and abilities by encouraging them to work in teams, design and implement complex projects rooted in real-world challenges, undertake community service, and serve in internships or apprenticeships (Afterschool Alliance, 2009; Bruschi & Clewell, 2008; Chi, Snow, Goldstein, Lee, & Chung, 2010).

The evidence base strongly supports deploying afterschool and summer programs and partnerships to develop students' readiness skills for enrolling in postsecondary education and for joining the workforce; yet many education, community, and higher education leaders have not taken the necessary steps to tap the significant potential of such a strategy. The specific examples shown below clearly demonstrate what is possible in real-life situations and communities.

Examples That Show What Is Possible

What follows are descriptions of several exemplary afterschool and summer learning programs that provide youth with opportunities to learn about postsecondary education and careers and develop employability skills. The programs profiled below include Upward Bound Math-Science, Citizens Schools, and Project Exploration.

....

Upward Bound Math-Science

Upward Bound Math-Science is a college access program, funded by the U.S. Department of Education TRIO program, that has an afterschool and summer component. The program was designed to provide disadvantaged high school students with skills and experiences that prepare them for success in a 4-year college and help them succeed in a math or science career field. Grants are given to 2- and 4-year colleges and universities to provide programs during the school year and summer. School-year programs include supplemental academic instruction and enrichment activities such as faculty-assisted experiments, seminars with outside speakers, and field trips. The 6-week summer program includes an intensive focus on math and science instruction and exposure to life in college, including residency in college dorms. All programs include activities such as preparation for college entrance exams, information on postsecondary opportunities, and assistance completing college applications and understanding financial aid opportunities. A 2007 evaluation of Upward Bound Math-Science showed improved high school grades in math and science among participants and a greater likelihood of majoring in math or science and completing a 4-year degree in math or science (Olsen et al., 2007). The latest evaluation showed that all participants benefited from an increased likelihood of earning a postsecondary certificate or license. Among participants with the lowest initial educational expectations, it found an increased likelihood of receiving Advanced Placement honors or core academic credits in high school and greater chances of enrolling in and completing some type of postsecondary program (Seftor et al., 2009).

....

Citizen Schools

Citizen Schools, funded in part with 21st Century Community Learning Centers funds and based in Boston, partners with public middle schools to provide structured expanded learning opportunities for educational enrichment, career exposure, and high school and college preparation to students in grades 6–8 during and after school. The program incorporates academic support, apprenticeships with adult volunteers in a variety of fields, and a community explorations curriculum that brings the community into the classroom and the classroom to the community. Students participate in experiential learning projects, referred to as apprenticeships. These learning experiences are led by volunteer community members and employers, who set goals, focus on academic support, and teach leadership skills. Students build 21st century skills, such as communication, collaboration, data analysis, effective reasoning, and problem solving, and they create and present a final product to share what they have learned with families, teachers, public officials, community members, and business leaders. Citizen Schools also takes eighth graders on college visits, where students visit classes, attend social events, and engage in other guided activities that provide a concrete awareness of college life. An evaluation of Citizen Schools found increased levels of student engagement and achievement, higher attendance and course pass rates, lower suspension rates, a positive impact on English and math course grades, and an increased propensity to select a rigorous high school (Pearson & Fabiano, 2006).

....

Project Exploration

Project Exploration is a nonprofit organization that provides science education to underrepresented groups, particularly females and minorities. The Project provides over 300 Chicago Public School youth access to free afterschool and summer science programs that spark an interest in science, motivate youth to pursue science-related careers, and ensure that they are equipped for such careers. Participants benefit from hands-on programming, authentic fieldwork, leadership development, and long-term relationships with educators through ongoing mentorships. Programs include a 3-week summer fieldwork immersion program where participants take classes on anatomy, geology, and paleontology and conclude with a week-long paleontology field expedition. Students also can fulfill high school community service graduation requirements by serving as docents for science exhibits at local museums. Project Exploration also offers science programs for girls where science exploration is combined with leadership development through hands-on science activities and interactions with female science role models. A 10-year retrospective review found that Project Exploration participants benefited from higher high school graduation rates, higher 4-year college enrollment and completion rates, a greater likelihood of majoring in a science field, and greater employment rates in science-related professions. The study also found that participants had an increased science capacity and that meaningful engagement in a community of practice with strong relationships supported peer learning and helped students envision careers in science (Chi et al., 2010).

These afterschool and summer learning programs help young people think about their futures, learn some of the skills needed to be successful in postsecondary education and the workplace, and draw connections between classroom learning and the real world through structured learning experiences. All of them rely on strong partnerships among schools, community-based organizations, colleges, and/or employers that enhance and strengthen their programs. These partnerships also help youth connect with caring adults who can provide advice and support about career and college pathways.

Recommendations and Conclusion

Afterschool and summer learning programs can and should help youth be prepared for college and careers, but many do not explicitly include it as an emphasis. Here are some recommendations along with examples of programs addressing the issues.

First, afterschool and summer learning programs can intentionally focus on helping youth explore, set goals, and prepare for postsecondary education. One program that helps youth explore and prepare for postsecondary education is College Track, a national nonprofit that partners with high schools and local community-based organizations and offers college preparatory activities to almost 1,200 underserved youth afterschool and during the summer. Activities include college tours, academic advising, enrichment workshops, ACT and SAT preparation, summer writing institutes focused on the college application process, and guidance on college entrance and financial aid (College Track, 2012a).

Second, programs can create partnerships with employers to help youth learn about and experience careers first-hand through work-based learning, apprenticeships, or internships. The Youth Astronomy Apprenticeship Program, through collaboration between the MIT Kavli Institute for Astrophysics and Space Research, the Smithsonian Astrophysical Observatory, the Timothy Smith Network, and local afterschool providers in the Boston area, fosters science learning among urban teenage high school students and prepares them for professional competitive opportunities. In the program, equal effort is put into pursuing science learning for academic enrichment and in stressing the link between employable skills and the skills developed in science and other professional fields. During the summer apprenticeship program, youth participate in paid positions, working with scientists and science educators from MIT and Harvard. An evaluation showed that youth who participated in these programs increased their commitment to science and demonstrated improved leadership and a greater understanding of astronomy and scientific concepts (Norland, Foutz, & Krabill, 2009).

Third, programs can develop engaging, relevant, and age-appropriate programming for youth that connects their academic studies with hands-on, project-based, experiential, and collaborative work, set in the context of real-world challenges. The Build San Francisco Institute, a partnership between San Francisco Unified School District, the nonprofit Architectural Foundation of San Francisco, and several business and community partners, began 15 years ago as a 6-week summer mentorship program for students interested in design, construction, architecture, and engineering. This collaboration then grew into an integral partnership with San Francisco Unified School District that offers a half-day high school program, complete with fully accredited courses in architectural design and urban studies, mentorships with two dozen major San Francisco firms and civic agencies, and up to 15 units of high school credit (approved for CA State University admission) per semester (Architectural Foundation of San Francisco, n.d.).

Fourth, programs can ensure that youth have opportunities to develop 21st century skills. In New York City and Washington, DC, Global Kids focuses on digital literacy and civic participation through in-school, out-of-school, and online work so that youth can succeed in school, participate effectively in the democratic process, and achieve leadership in their communities and on the global stage. The nonprofit program receives funds from and partners with several corporations, foundations, and government institutions. Thousands of students study global issues, develop local connections, and work in peer education, social action, digital media, and service-learning. Through its various activities, Global Kids has an explicit focus on engaging students in 21st century skills such as problem solving, critical thinking, and cross-cultural communication (Global Kids, n.d.).

These recommendations and examples make clear that afterschool and summer learning programs can develop strong partnerships with K–16 education institutions, employers, museums, and community-based and youth-serving organizations in order to create stronger connections to college and careers. Given their prevalence in communities across the country and their ability to be flexible and responsive to community needs, afterschool and summer learning programs are well positioned to provide youth, particularly underserved youth, with opportunities to be college and career ready. If America is going to be more competitive in the future, we need to capitalize more aggressively on these opportunities.

For More Information

For Tony Wagner's recommendations on essential skills that are currently needed in classrooms see http://www.tonywagner.com/resources/rigor-redefined

For more information on Upward Bound Math-Science see http://www2.ed.gov/programs/triomathsci/index.html

For information on how Citizen Schools aligns resources among multiple partners see http://www.citizenschools.org/school-partners/expectations/

For information on Project Exploration's youth programs, resources, and links to various projects see http://www.projectexploration.org/programs.htm

ABOUT THE AUTHORS

Betsy Brand is the executive director at the American Youth Policy Forum, where she identifies policies and practices that lead to positive outcomes for the nation's young people. Brand has worked in education and youth development in several capacities, including in the U.S. Congress and the U.S. Department of Education as the assistant secretary in the Office of Vocational and Adult Education.

Andrew Valent, program associate at American Youth Policy Forum, researches and helps organize professional learning events on a variety of education policy issues with a particular emphasis on afterschool and expanded learning opportunities.

REFERENCES

Afterschool Alliance. (2009). *Afterschool innovations in brief: Focusing on older youth.* Retrieved from http://www.afterschoolalliance.org/documents/Afterschool_In_Brief_09_FINAL.pdf

Architectural Foundation of San Francisco. (n.d.). Build San Francisco Institute. Retrieved from http://www.afsf.org/program_buildsf.htm

Bowles, A., & Brand, B. (2009). *Learning around the clock: Benefits of expanded learning opportunities for older youth.* Washington, DC: American Youth Policy Forum.

Bruschi, B., & Clewell, B. C. (2008). *Final summative evaluation report: Girls Incorporated Thinking SMART program.* Indianapolis, IN: Girls Incorporated National Resource Center.

Carnevale, A. P., Smith, N., & Strohl, J. (2010). *Help wanted: Projections of jobs and education requirements through 2018.* Washington, DC: Georgetown University Center on Education and the Workforce.

Casner-Lotto, J. (2006). *Are they really ready to work? Employers' perspectives on the basic knowledge and applied skills of new entrants to the 21st century U.S. workforce.* Retrieved from http://www.p21.org/storage/documents/FINAL_REPORT_PDF09-29-06.pdf

Chi, B., Snow, J., Goldstein, D., Lee, S., & Chung, J. (2010). *Project Exploration: 10-year retrospective program evaluation summative report.* Berkeley, CA: University of California Berkeley Lawrence Hall of Science.

College Track. (2012a). About. Retrieved from http://www.collegetrack.org/main/content/view/13/129/

College Track. (2012b). Results. Retrieved from http://www.collegetrack.org/main/content/section/18/212/

Global Kids. (n.d.). About Global Kids. Retrieved from http://globalkids.org/#/about-global-kids

Halpern, R. (2008). *The means to grow up: Reinventing apprenticeship as a developmental support in adolescence.* New York, NY: Routledge Taylor & Francis Group.

Herrera, C., Linden, L., Arbreton, A., & Grossman, J. (2011). *Testing the impact of Higher Achievement's year-round out-of-school-time program on academic outcomes.* Retrieved from http://www.ppv.org/ppv/publications/assets/332_publication.pdf

Hirsch, B. J., Hedges, L. V., Stawicki, J., & Mekinda, M. A. (2011). *After-school programs for high school students: An evaluation of After School Matters* [Technical report]. Retrieved from http://www.sesp.northwestern.edu/docs/publications/19023555234df57ecd0d6c5.pdf

Moran, N. (n.d.). *Evaluation report*: October 2006–August 2007. Washington, DC: Urban Alliance Foundation.

Norland, E., Foutz, S., & Krabill, M. (2009). *Youth astronomy apprenticeship: An initiative to promote science learning among urban youth and their communities—Summative evaluation.* Retrieved from http://epo.mit.edu/resources/YAA-SummativeEvalRpt-2009v3.pdf

Olsen, R., Seftor, N., Silva, T., Myers, D., DesRoches, D., & Young, J. (2007). *Upward Bound Math-Science: Program description and interim impact estimates.* Retrieved from U.S. Department of Education website: http://www2.ed.gov/rschstat/eval/highered/upward-math-science/complete-report.pdf

Pearson, L., & Fabiano, L. (2006). *Preparing students in the middle grades to succeed in high school: Findings from Phase IV of the Citizen Schools Evaluation.* Washington, DC: Policy Studies Associates.

Seftor, N., Mamun, A., & Schirm, A. (2009). *The impacts of regular Upward Bound on postsecondary outcomes 7–9 years after scheduled high school graduation: Final report.* Princeton, NJ: Mathematica Policy Research.

Wagner, T. (2010). *The global achievement gap: Why even our best schools don't teach the new survival skills our children need—and what we can do about it.* New York, NY: Basic Books.

Carol H. Rasco
President and CEO, Reading Is Fundamental

Judy B. Cheatham
Vice President, Literacy Services, Reading Is Fundamental

Sarah H. Cheatham
Research Assistant, Reading Is Fundamental

Earl Martin Phalen
CEO, Reach Out and Read, and Founder,
Summer Advantage USA

Using Afterschool and Summer Learning to Improve Literacy Skills

America's literacy rates remain a national challenge, and fourth-grade reading scores tell the story. An analysis of 2011 National Assessment of Educational Progress (NAEP) fourth grade reading scores reveals that two-thirds of fourth graders were not "proficient" readers, including 36% who scored *below* "basic." Disaggregating the data sheds light on more disturbing findings: 58% of African Americans, 54% of Hispanics, and 52% of American Indian/Alaska Natives scored below "basic." For low-income children, *more than four out of every five scored less than "proficient,"* including 54% who scored below "basic" (National Center for Education Statistics, 2012).

Children who do not become proficient readers by fourth grade are on a trajectory for a wide array of negative consequences in school and in later life. According to the National Research Council (1998), "academic success, as defined by high school graduation, can be predicted with reasonable accuracy based on third grade reading skills." Researchers at Yale University recently concluded that three-quarters of the students who are poor readers in third grade remain poor readers in high school and are far more likely to drop out than their peers (Shaywitz et al., 1997).

The root causes of the literacy crisis in the United States are well documented and multifaceted. A number of studies underscore that reading success—or failure—starts at home. By age 3, children from low-income families have a listening vocabulary only one-third the size of their more affluent peers (Afterschool Alliance, 2011), and they have significantly less access to print. Neuman (2009) found that there was only one book title for every 300 children in low-income neighborhoods. With less access to high quality early care and pre-kindergarten programs, these children may hear as many as 30-million fewer words than do their middle-income peers before reaching kindergarten, impeding such important precursors to literacy as vocabulary acquisition and language development.

In addition, many low-income students miss too much instructional time as a result of chronic absenteeism in the early grades. As many as 25% of low-income students in urban school districts are chronically absent in kindergarten and first grade (Chang & Romero, 2008). When the school year ends, low-income students experience significant learning losses during the summer (See Heyns, 1978; Allington & McGill-Franzen, 2003; Luftig, 2003). Cooper, Nye, Charlton, Lindsay, and Greathouse (1996), for example, found that, on average, low-income students lose more than 2 months of reading performance every summer during their elementary school years.

However, most children—even the most vulnerable—can achieve the benchmark of reading proficiency by the end of third grade. Recent research delineates how people learn to read and provides best practices for teaching reading, via decades of work from the National Institute for Child Health and Development, the National Reading Panel, and others. Mounting evidence suggests that *afterschool and summer learning programs can play a vital role* in improving literacy outcomes for children. Reading enrichment, tutoring, and social-emotional development programs, combined with parent involvement and books and materials of high quality, are producing results that close achievement gaps (Storch & Whitehurst, 2001; Kim & White, 2008; Wilkins et al., 2012).

The Promise of Afterschool and Summer Learning Programs

One example of a successful summer learning program that has demonstrated significant improvement in reading achievement is Summer Advantage USA (www.summeradvantage.org). One of only two scientifically validated summer learning programs in the nation, this 5-week program combines rigorous morning academics with engaging afternoon enrichment activities. Since its inception in 2009, the program has served over 10,000 youth nationwide and has been offered by a number of 21st Century Community Learning Centers programs across several states. Youth (dubbed "scholars") who participate in the Summer Advantage program experience over *2 months of growth in reading skills*, as well as 2 months in math skills.

Summer Advantage attributes its consistent literacy gains to several key programmatic elements that support the literacy development of its scholars: (1) hiring exceptional educators and offering small-group ratios; (2) providing 2 hours of reading and writing instruction each morning, Monday through Thursday; (3) using a rigorous, research-based curriculum; (4) incorporating a multicultural leveled library into each classroom that speaks to the real interests of the scholars; and (5) providing pre-program professional development for program staff that focuses on child development and constructing engaging instruction. These program characteristics—sustained time, access to appropriate print, scaffolded materials, and staff development—are found in similar programs that result in reading gains (e.g., Kim & White, 2008; Wilkins et al., 2012).

Of course, unlike Summer Advantage, many summer and afterschool programs are not explicitly designed to "teach" reading as such; therefore, they may not typically have personnel and/or the expertise to take on such a task. Appropriate interventions can, however, still be effectively used by program staff to help students maintain or enhance their reading skills. The key is to design the *right kind* of summer and afterschool programs as delineated by research. Afterschool and summer learning programs can, in fact, easily infuse reading into activities that children and youth enjoy. So, in addition to strengthening reading skills with well-designed and explicit instructional interventions, these programs can serve to link children's interests with literacy development by simply getting them to read more broadly, consistently, and intensively in pursuit of their interests (Afterschool Alliance, 2011).

The Importance of Getting to Know Students and Being *Explicit* About Their Learning

Because afterschool and summer programs may have students for a short term, Vanderbilt professor Anita Conn notes that the staff "dive into a preplanned 'program' without taking the necessary time to ascertain individual skills levels and target instruction to each student's needs" (personal interview, 18 September 2011). Afterschool and summer program staff should make it a *priority* to find out about students' backgrounds, communities, home lives, and first languages/language spoken at home. Programs can then provide a learner-centered focus, targeting each student's needs, unique struggles, and potential resources.

Consider this scenario: An afterschool tutor reading *The Little Engine That Could* to a group of K–third graders discovered that not one child knew what an engine was. The tutor stopped, created the schema through pictures and acting out, and *then* proceeded with the story. Comprehension requires that readers know English letters, sounds, and print conventions—but also the *meanings* of words! The tutor recognized and addressed the lack of vocabulary knowledge in her audience: She asked, in pre-reading, what a little engine was; when she saw that nobody knew, she explained and then continued with the story. She targeted her "instruction" based on her informal "assessment" of what her audience did and did not know.

Coordination With Classroom Teachers

Certainly, to the greatest extent possible, afterschool and summer program staff should coordinate their programming with learning in the classroom, either to reinforce it or pre-teach it, and then provide additional opportunities for children to process, to practice, to extend, and to reflect upon the experience. If, for example, the state focuses on state history in fourth grade, the summer or afterschool enrichment activities might involve field trips to local historical sites or guest speakers who present interesting,

Urban Arts Partnership – New York City

Urban Arts Fresh ED and Fresh Prep are two great examples of programs tailored to the interests and backgrounds of their target student demographics. They use hip-hop as a way of developing critical literacy, critical thinking, and test prep skills among youth in New York City. These programs also explore the use of hip-hop as a tool to increase students' synthesis of information, analytics of texts, and performance on standardized assessments.

educational activities that set a context, a background, for learning. When children return from the field trip, or after the speaker talks, staff should be explicit about the experience: "Where did we go? Why? Who lived there? What happened there? What did you learn? Anybody learn any new words? Was our trip interesting? Why? Let's write about it in our journals/write a story for our parents/draw a picture/write the new words on our word list." In this informal discussion and activity, children have an opportunity to engage metacognitively, to recount concretely their experience, to add to their knowledge base, and to add to their vocabulary repertoire.

By contrast, misalignment of in-school, afterschool, and summer program learning goals and objectives creates missed opportunities. Consider the case of an at-risk child. He learned short "a" words (c-an, D-an, p-an) in the regular classroom, consonant blends (br-own, bl-own) in the resource room, and colors (red, blue, brown) in his afterschool program. His homework? Memorize spelling words containing the short "a" sound: bat, man, can, ran, and, hand. His day revealed two missed opportunities for someone else to reinforce what was going on in the classroom.

Other Ways to Encourage Literacy

Even if a particular afterschool or summer program's mission is not specifically to teach reading or to teach the subskills involved, staff still can encourage literacy. Program leaders and staff should ensure that books are available and accessible. A reading corner for children, with many, varied, interesting books and lots of comfy pillows, is invaluable.

In addition to books at the program site, regular visits to the public and school libraries are always a good activity for children and their families. Many libraries provide free or inexpensive resources for summer reading programs. In her groundbreaking study, Barbara Heyns (1975) found that the library, more than any other public institution, contributes to the intellectual growth of children over the summer. Some parents have never been in a library and have never checked out a book; staff can explain the concept of the lending library, reassuring parents that it is okay to let children read library books, as opposed to putting those books away to "protect" them. Story time at the library also provides a nice model for how to read to children.

Importance of Parent Involvement

Finally, afterschool and summer programs should work intentionally to increase and enhance parent involvement. Numerous studies and anecdotal evidence have demonstrated the importance of parent and family involvement in reading (see Fan & Chen, 2001, for a meta-analytic review); however, to create an environment that values the parent as the child's first teacher, programs must be flexible and accommodating. "Business as usual" may need to be modified, scheduling open houses or parent information sessions at different times. Staff should share details about the program and suggest specific ways that parents can support their child's learning offered at multiple times to accommodate parents' schedules. The goal is to empower parents to model and encourage literacy activities, to go to the library, to talk with their children all the time, to tell their own stories.

In communicating with parents, staff should provide and solicit ideas for activities. For example, "literacy activities" can be as simple as reading the back of the cereal box together every morning for 10 minutes during breakfast. Reading Is Fundamental (www.rif.org) and other websites contain a treasure trove of suggested storytime activities.

Program staff should communicate frequently and consistently with the family, but they should make sure that they communicate in such a way that the parent actually receives and understands the message. To that end, staff should closely re-examine the kinds of communications they send to parents. Obviously messages from program staff should not patronize; but messages should, nevertheless, be short and simple. Though program staff would never intend this consequence, many adult new or nonreaders are intimidated by a wall of text. Research indicates that many parents do not think they have the skills to encourage the literacy efforts of their children (Cook-Cottone, 2004), and if staff send home text that parents have no chance of reading, programs have unwittingly verified the parental fears.

On family nights, programs should provide models, help, and multiple opportunities for parents to observe and participate in literacy activities. Translators may be needed, and staff planners should ensure that lots of pictures are associated with text. The bottom line is that programs should help parents understand how important they, as parents, are to the literacy development of their children. Some programs communicate with parents weekly by phone, text, or postcard. Some programs teach parents how to do reading assessment. As Karen Mapp says in frequent presentations, "Parent involvement goes beyond the bake sale!"

Conclusion

Summer and afterschool programs have a great potential to help close the gap in achievement among at-risk populations and to enlist more partners for improved reading and literacy because of their community and family connections.

Serious programs should do their homework to ensure top quality in programming that enhances literacy for children of all ages and levels of achievement. Research abounds on best practices and their foundational philosophical underpinnings. Careful planning on the front end, parent communication and involvement, on-going assessment, and best practices throughout should help many more summer and afterschool programs, leading to increased reading achievement, higher literacy rates, more families of readers, and more literate communities across the country.

For More Information

Reading Is Fundamental (RIF) is the nation's oldest and largest children's literacy nonprofit: www.rif.org

RIF's extensive collection of expertly designed, scaffolded reading guides and activities for parents, educators, and community coordinators is available at www.rif.org/mbc.

ABOUT THE AUTHORS

Carol H. Rasco, president and CEO of Reading Is Fundamental (RIF), has taught sixth grade, served as a counselor for elementary and middle school students, and worked in the Arkansas Governor's Office as the director of policy while serving as the liaison to the National Governors' Association. In the Clinton White House she served as the Assistant to the President for Domestic Policy and directed the America Reads Challenge under Education Secretary Richard W. Riley. After working for the College Board in government relations, Rasco assumed her current position at RIF in November 2001.

Judy B. Cheatham joined RIF in January 2011 as vice president of literacy services. She previously served as the Jefferson Pilot Professor of English at Greensboro College, as well as the coordinator of the Modern Languages and Literatures division and director of the Master of Arts in TESOL program. Featured speaker, presenter, educator, and author or co-author of four books on tutoring children and adults, since 1986, she has trained tens of thousands of tutors, teachers, volunteers, and parents across the country, having served on President George H.W. Bush's Goals 2000 task force as well as on the national board of Literacy Volunteers of America.

Sarah H. Cheatham is a graduate student at Georgetown Law School, specializing in public interest/education law. A Benjamin N. Duke scholar at Duke University with majors in Russian and Linguistics, she holds a master's degree from Peabody College, Vanderbilt University, and served as an intern at Reading Is Fundamental during the spring/summer 2012.

Earl Martin Phalen is the CEO of Reach Out and Read and founder of Summer Advantage USA. Reach Out and Read is a national nonprofit that works through 12,000 pediatricians and in partnership with 4 million parents to ensure that all children, regardless of income, arrive at kindergarten ready to learn and excel. Phalen grew his former organization, BELL, from a community service project educating 20 children to a $27M national nonprofit educating 15,000 scholars annually. Phalen graduated from Yale University and Harvard Law School.

REFERENCES

Afterschool Alliance. (2011). *Literacy in afterschool: An essential building block for learning and development* (Issue Brief No. 53). Washington, DC: Author.

Allington, R. L., & McGill-Franzen, A. (2003). The impact of summer setback on the reading achievement gap. *The Phi Delta Kappan, 85*(1), 68–75.

Chang. H. N., & Romero, M. (2008). *Present, engaged, and accounted for: The critical importance of addressing chronic absence in the early grades.* Retrieved from http://www.nccp.org/publications/pdf/text_837.pdf

Cook-Cottone, C. (2004). Constructivism in family literacy practices: Parents as mentors. *Reading Improvement, 41,* 208–216.

Cooper, H., Nye, B., Charlton, K., Lindsay, J., & Greathouse, S. (1996). The effects of summer vacation on achievement test scores: A narrative and meta-analytic review. *Review of Educational Research, 66,* 227–268.

Fan, X., & Chen, M. (2001). Parental involvement and students' academic achievement: A meta-analysis. *Educational Psychology Review, 13,* 1–22.

Heyns, B. (1978). *Summer learning and the effects of schooling.* New York, NY: Academic Press.

Kim, J. S. & White, T. G. (2008). Scaffolding voluntary summer reading for children in grades 3 to 5: An experimental study. *Scientific Studies of Reading, 12,* 1–23.

Luftig, R. L. (2003, May). When a little bit means a lot: The effects of a short-term reading program on economically disadvantaged elementary schoolers. Paper presented at the American Educational Research Association, Chicago.

McKinsey & Company. (2009). *The economic impact of the achievement gap in America's schools.* Retrieved from http://mckinseyonsociety.com/downloads/reports/Education/achievement_gap_report.pdf

National Center for Education Statistics. (2011). *The nation's report card: Reading 2011.* Retrieved from http://nces.ed.gov/nationsreportcard/pdf/main2011/2012457.pdf

National Research Council. (1998). *Preventing reading difficulties in young children.* Washington, DC: National Academy Press.

Neuman, S. B. (2009). *Changing the odds for children at risk: Seven essential principles of educational programs that break the cycle of poverty.* Westport, CT: Praeger.

Share Our Strength. (2011). *Facts on childhood hunger: Annual, national-level statistics.* Retrieved from http://www.strength.org/pdfs/2011-childhood-hunger-facts.pdf

Shaywitz, B. A., Shaywitz, S. E. Fletcher, J.M., Push, K. Gore, J. Constable, R., . . . Lacadie, C. . (1997). The Yale Center for the Study of Learning and Attention: Longitudinal and neurobiological studies. *Learning Disabilities, 8,* 21–29.

Storch, S. A., & Whitehurst, G. J. (2001). The role of family and home in the literacy development of children from low-income backgrounds. *New Directions for Child & Adolescent Development, 2001*(92), 53–72.

Wilkins, C., Gersten, R., Decker, L. E., Grunden, L., Brasiel, S., Brunnert, K., & Jayanthi, M.. (2012). *Does a summer reading program based on Lexiles affect reading comprehension?* Washington, DC: US Department of Education, National Center for Education Evaluation and Regional Assistance.

Natalie Lucas
Jennifer Kobrin
Co-Directors, Center for Afterschool and Expanded
Learning, Foundations, Inc.

Well-Designed Homework Time as a Quality-Building Aid in Afterschool

If any children are peering over your shoulder as you read these lines, hide the next sentence from them.

The evidence that homework aids student achievement is inconclusive (Center for Public Education, 2007).

Yet, for many students, not completing homework on time, or completing it incorrectly, can leave them at a serious disadvantage as they try to progress successfully through school. It is also important to note that well-designed homework, instead of just "throwing worksheets at students," is more likely to have merit and can be a positive connection between school and afterschool programs. Combining well-designed homework with other academic enrichment activities in afterschool can provide a well-rounded package of expanded learning opportunities that contribute to school success and positive youth development.

Homework has maintained a role as a traditional component of the education system over many generations, although it has not been totally proven to be effective as a tool for improving students' learning. A battle waged in recent decades over the value of homework did not come to a definitive conclusion, leaving both proponents and opponents with research they can cite to support either side of the debate[1]. It appears that the presence of homework serves more to forestall a decline in performance (Morrison, Storino, Robertson, Weissglass, & Dondero, 2000) rather than to advance achievement; however, making homework completion just one element of a broader, comprehensive afterschool program enhances its value.

---

1. See, for example, Ramdass & Zimmerman (2011), Cooper, et. al. (2006), Marzano (2003), for research that supports the use of homework. For research that is critical of homework, see Kohn (2006), Bennett & Kalish (2006), and Kralovec & Buell (2000).

Despite the conflicted research base, school policies continue to mandate and teachers continue to assign homework. This reality is where afterschool programs must position themselves, regardless of any personal opinions on homework. The general charge of an afterschool program is to help students succeed in school; and if homework is required by the school, then many afterschool programs see homework support as part of that charge. Going a step further is to encourage staff buy-in and enthusiasm for a program culture that embraces homework time as useful and important, rather than a bore and a chore for all involved.

This commitment to productive homework time can be bolstered by a program's recognition that well-designed homework, as part of a broader afterschool initiative, not only can provide benefits to youth but also serve to reinforce some of the desired—and often required—yet hard-to-come-by program goals: (a) homework is a natural link between afterschool and school, (b) homework is a promising bridge between afterschool and families, (c) homework supports principles of youth development that are central to afterschool programs, and (d) homework help can be a hook to engage students in expanded learning and broader opportunities.

Supporting the School Day and Connecting With Teachers

Homework serves as a natural point of connection between school-day staff and afterschool staff, whose roles are parallel yet often isolated. Many school-day teachers do not ask for help from afterschool, or even do not picture the potential for afterschool programming to aid in school-day goals. The practitioner who takes the first step to building relationships with school-day staff can demonstrate that program practices, such as homework support or tutoring, are working toward the same outcomes the school-day teachers hope to achieve.

Once this common understanding has been reached, the relationship can be maintained through intentional and sustained communication. A regular schedule of check-ins via phone or e-mail or in person should be established. Tools such as a homework contract or a homework completion tracking document allow both sides to stay up-to-date without adding additional strain on job responsibilities. By using such tools and scheduling regular check-ins, afterschool staff can more readily ask school-day teachers for help with students' more difficult assignments. In a time when 89% of students stress about homework (Met Life, 2007) this communication builds trust that makes students more confident in the program's ability to be helpful and meet student needs.

In rural Missouri, for example, the West Plains R-7 Before and After School Education program utilizes the regular school day homework planner to track student assignments and facilitate information sharing between afterschool staff and teachers. The planner includes space for both groups to sign and record relevant information each day. The program director also takes advantage of the school district's data system to track student achievement, routinely meeting with teachers when students fall behind. This real-life example illustrates the kind of collaboration and mutual support that many afterschool programs have found to be a critical ingredient in boosting student achievement.

Opening up the avenues of communication between school and afterschool was the focus of a pilot project conducted by the University of Pittsburgh's Office of Child Development during the 2010–2011 school year. This project, funded by the Heinz Endowments, was a partnership with Pittsburgh Public Schools and five local afterschool program providers. The partnership developed a set of communication strategies based on research that indicates that formal communication between teachers and afterschool providers supports quality homework time in the afterschool setting.

Linking together on homework can even open the door to more substantive school-afterschool collaborations—one of the hallmarks of quality afterschool programs.

Easing the Pressure Off Families

Students are not the only ones whose stress levels rise with homework; in today's society, with more single parents and more dual-income families, the demands of home life leave little time for parents to offer homework help. Most parents want their children to do homework, and they see the importance of connecting with what their children are doing in school, but dinner time, chores, and leisure activities compete with homework time. An overload of homework also competes with sleep, which suffers as a result for students, not just their overtired parents (Dudley-Maring, 2003).

By providing a structured and supportive space for homework time, afterschool programs can become an ally of busy parents. This program role again opens up an opportunity for communication, in this case with families. The tools mentioned above, such as the homework contract, can include families as participants, and informal conversations about homework can reassure parents that their children are completing assignments, indicate what is left to be done at home with bigger projects or additional assignments, and provide a sought-after link by proxy from the parent to the school day. Through this link, an afterschool program kindles homework's role as a cornerstone to facilitating family-to-school communication as it contributes to parents' understanding of what school expectations are and offers direction for how they can support their children (Perlman & Redding, 2011).

For example, the East Allen Family Resource Center in New Haven, Indiana, requires all staff to speak with parents who come to pick up their students in the program and share information about their students' progress with homework. "We really love the parents who choose to pick up their students from the school. It provides such a wonderful opportunity for parents to see what their child is doing, the environment that is provided for them, and have face-to-face time talking with staff," notes the program director. To reach parents who may not be able to pick up their children in person, staff routinely make phone calls to students' homes to discuss student achievement.

In considering homework support as one component of a family involvement plan, an afterschool program is again making strides in the direction of program quality.

Using Homework Time to Enhance Youth Development

Within the body of evidence that exists about homework, studies have shown that homework does play a role in building skills that equip young people to be more efficient and motivated students and prepare them for 21st century careers. By completing homework, students gain soft skills such as greater self-direction, self-discipline, organization, and more independent problem solving (Protheroe, 2009).

In four charter high schools in Philadelphia, Pennsylvania, such skills are coupled with homework time in deliberate lessons taught through "mini clinics" by Foundations, Inc.'s Prep Zone Plus afterschool program. Mini clinics are quick (lasting about 20 minutes), relevant, and engaging lessons that address a variety of study skills and life skills, from reading for meaning to budgeting to selecting colleges. For students who complete their homework early or need extra assistance with certain skills, the mini clinics provide a robust but palatable lesson. Students feel that they are getting more for their time and gaining skills that will be useful as they progress toward college, careers, and independent life.

From its experience of operating homework-based afterschool programs over the past decade, Foundations has learned that a substantive way to improve homework time and other elements of afterschool is to listen to young people in afterschool settings and solicit and use feedback from school-day teachers, administrators, and parents.

Going Beyond Homework

Quality afterschool programs, even homework-based ones, build out engaging learning opportunities that go beyond homework and offer value-added programming. Often after homework time ends, students attend their choice of enrichment clubs (for example, robotics, chess, art, music, cooking, service learning) to round out their afterschool experience. Research shows that afterschool programs with multifaceted programming are more likely to achieve the greatest academic gains (Pearson, Russell, & Reisner, 2007).

Starting in 2011 and continuing through 2012, the Boys and Girls Clubs of Indianapolis has been working to go beyond homework and infuse academics into regular club programming. Through a grant from the Lilly Endowment, and a partnership with the Center for Afterschool and Expanded Learning at Foundations, Inc., Boys and Girls Clubs of Indianapolis has focused on creating a sustainable approach to academically-focused enrichment across seven sites. Staff receive ongoing training on topics such as planning hands-on activities linked to academic standards, project-based learning, STEM, and literacy in out-of-school time. In turn, staff are supported by leadership teams to implement meaningful enrichment activities into a range of existing programming, from art projects to basketball tournaments.

The enrichment opportunities offered on top of homework support help students see how they can apply what they're learning to real-life situations, build confidence through the mastery of new talents or completion of significant projects, and understand the connections between what they are doing now and their future possibilities.

Conclusion and Recommendations

Relationships with the school day, connections to families, youth development practices, and using the attraction of completing homework to engage students in expanded learning and broader opportunities are enhanced with a positive approach to homework.

Below are a number of key recommendations to make homework a positive component of quality afterschool programs:

- *Set up systems for communication between afterschool instructors and school-day teachers that keep everyone up to date. Do the same with families.*

- *Create a physical environment that encourages homework completion—include quiet space with individual desks for assignments that require deep concentration, bigger tables for study groups to gather, couches for catching up on reading, and a resource area with reference materials.*

- *Build in opportunities for youth choice. Do some students study better when they can listen to music through headphones? Can students seek help from peers or adults? Can they choose which assignment they want to work on first?*

- *Keep homework time active, even when all the assignments are done. Offer short, self-directed activities such as brain teasers, board games, or activity centers that students can enjoy while still reinforcing some academic and 21st century skills . . . not just worksheets.*

- *Sometimes the best homework help is just directing students to the right resources they can employ to answer a tricky question. Refrain from giving them the answer; instead, empower them to find it on their own.*

- *Be aware of families' homework preferences. Some families want their students to complete as much homework as possible in the afterschool program; others may want to work with their children on some assignments at home, too.*

- *Keep groups fluid, not static. Depending on the students, the assignments, and the day, change grouping arrangements frequently.*

- *Expand your own view of homework as a positive element of expanded learning. Remember that you are a role model, and students may adopt your attitude toward homework.*

If afterschool programs—and their school partners—use these recommendations, dogs all across the country can experience fewer stomachaches from the proverbial eating of the homework.

For More Information

SEDL Afterschool Training Toolkit – Homework
http://www.sedl.org/afterschool/toolkits/about_toolkits.html?tab=homework

Homework Sharing Tool (You for Youth web portal)
http://y4y.ed.gov/Content/Resources/DCID20110713104426.pdf

TASC Resource Brief
https://www.century21me.org/staticme21/academ_achiev/Research%20on%20Homework%20Help.pdf

What Research Says About the Value of Homework: Research Review
http://www.centerforpubliceducation.org/Main-Menu/Instruction/What-research-says-about-the-value-of-homework-At-a-glance/What-research-says-about-the-value-of-homework-Research-review.html

Homework Time, Afterschool Style
Homework Time, Afterschool Style. (2009). Mt. Laurel, NJ: Foundations, Inc.

Homework Zone Program Pack
Homework Zone Program Pack. (2009). Mt. Laurel, NJ: Foundations, Inc.

ABOUT THE AUTHORS

As co-directors at the Center for Afterschool and Expanded Learning, Foundations, Inc., **Natalie Lucas** and **Jennifer Kobrin** design and implement technical assistance for schools, afterschool programs, and community-based organizations. Their frequent interactions in the field keep them current with the distinct challenges and opportunities facing administrators, educators, students, and parents. As a former Teach for America corps member, Lucas taught middle school science and focuses on the Center's Science, Technology, Engineering, and Math (STEM) initiatives. Kobrin has a background in working with English language learners and focuses on language, literacy, and culture.

REFERENCES

Center for Public Education. (2007). *Key lessons: What research says about the value of homework.* Retrieved from http://www.centerforpubliceducation.org

Dudley-Marling, C. (2003). How school troubles come home: The impact of homework on families of struggling learners. *Current Issues in Education, 6(4).* Retrieved from http://cie.asu.edu/volume6/number4/index.html.

Morrison, G. M., Storino, M. H., Robertson, L. M., & Weissglass, T., & Dondero, A. (2000). The protective function of after-school programming and parent education and support for students at risk for substance abuse. *Evaluation and Program Planning, 23,* 365–371.

MetLife, Inc. (2007). *MetLife survey of the American teacher: The homework experience. A survey of students, teachers and parents.* New York, NY: Author.

Pearson, L. M., Russell, C. A., & Reisner, E. R. (2007). *Evaluation of OST programs for youth: Patterns of youth retention in OST programs, 2005–06 to 2006–07.* Washington, DC: Policy Studies Associates.

Perlman, C. L., & Redding, S. (2011). *Handbook on effective implementation of School Improvement Grants.* Lincoln, IL: Center on Innovation & Improvement.

Protheroe, N. (2009). Good homework policy = Good teaching. *Principal, 89*(1), 42–45.

Hedy N. Chang
Director, Attendance Works

Phyllis W. Jordan
Vice President, the Hatcher Group

Building a Culture of Attendance: Schools and Afterschool Programs Together Can and Should Make a Difference!

The leaders of SHINE (Schools and Homes in Education) Afterschool Program recently resolved to improve the school-day attendance for the students at their 21st Century Community Learning Centers in rural Pennsylvania. The program reached out to parents, offered incentives to students, and carefully tracked attendance data provided by the schools.

The results: a school attendance rate significantly higher than similar programs nationally, improved communications with parents, and a remarkable collaboration with school teachers that could prove a model for out-of-school-time programs.

"They look at us as an extension of their work," director Jeanne Y. Miller said of the five public and four parochial schools where SHINE operates. "I think we're building the mindset that we're part of what they do."

Research has long shown that good afterschool programs can improve school-day attendance (Huang, Gribbons, Kim, Lee, & Baker, 2000; Welsh et al., 2002). The sense of belonging, the connection to caring adults, and the academic enrichment that afterschool provides can make children more likely to go to school. Often though, improved attendance is a by-product of good programs, rather than a stated goal. SHINE's experience in rural Pennsylvania, as well as an innovative approach used in Baltimore (discussed below), shows what can happen when afterschool programs take an intentional approach to reducing chronic absence.

Defining the Need

Like afterschool programming, efforts to reduce school absences are animated by the need to provide students more time on task in quality learning environments. Children on the edge of failure, in particular, can experience an academic boost if they make it to school every day and spend a few extra hours in enriching activities after school. Right now, however, too many vulnerable children are suffering academically because they miss too much school.

Also, many vulnerable youth do not have access to quality afterschool programs. For example, when states hold a competition for 21st Century Community Learning Centers grants, they typically have two to three times more school and community groups applying than there are monies available to fund, leaving many neighborhoods and young people without afterschool programs (O'Donnell, 2013).

Nationwide, one in 10 kindergarten students misses nearly a month of school every year. For many low-income students, chronic absence in kindergarten can translate into poor academic performance throughout elementary school (Chang & Romero, 2008). By sixth grade, poor attendance is a proven indicator of whether a child will drop out of high school, regardless of economic background (Balfanz, Herzog, & MacIver, 2007). By ninth grade, missing excessive amounts of school can predict the likelihood of dropping out with more accuracy than past test scores (Allensworth & Easton, 2007).

> Afterschool programs are particularly well positioned to make a difference. In addition to providing good programming, afterschool leaders can help schools partner with parents and build good attendance habits.

Unfortunately, many families and schools do not recognize they have a problem with attendance because they do not look at the data in the right way. Schools typically measure average daily attendance and truancy (unexcused absences). They do not pay attention to the total number of days each child misses in excused and unexcused absences. Research shows that when a student misses 10% of school days for any reason, or about 18 days, negative effects begin to appear in his/her academic performance (Chang & Romero, 2008). Chronic absenteeism can also affect the rest of the class by inducing the teacher to repeat old material rather than moving forward.

This is a problem that can be fixed. Throughout the country, schools and communities have been able to reduce absenteeism when they monitor attendance data and work together to identify and address barriers that keep children from getting to school every day. Afterschool programs are particularly well positioned to make a difference. In addition to providing good programming, afterschool leaders can help schools partner with parents and build good attendance habits. After all, many parents are more likely to see an afterschool provider at the end of the day, not a teacher.

Notably, attendance is an area of focus in the federal 21st Century Community Learning Centers initiative, which funds afterschool and summer learning opportunities in almost 11,000 low-income sites across America. At the end of the year, sites are required to submit data to state education officials, including school-day attendance data for participants in the afterschool program. Local afterschool leaders could be using these data gathered during the school year—both the in-school attendance data and afterschool attendance data—to make improvements in afterschool programming and to enhance partnerships with schools, families, and other child- and family-focused community organizations in order to address poor attendance.

Connecting With Families and Schools

Administered by Lehigh Carbon Community College, SHINE starts its attendance outreach with parents. The program operates across 430 square miles in Pennsylvania's Carbon and Schuylkill counties and draws from a population largely of low-income students—all of them referred for academic reasons, many of them chronically absent. When families sign up for the afterschool program, providers visit the home to get to know the parents and children. Parents must also sign a contract stressing the importance of attending school and the afterschool program. SHINE sends a midyear letter reinforcing the message.

> Analysis of this data shows that the more students attend SHINE, the better they do in school and the more regular their attendance.

When students do not come to school, they cannot come to SHINE after school. For students who do improve their school-day attendance, SHINE offers rewards: a visit to the "treasure chest" for younger students, gift certificates for others. Parents, too, are entered in monthly drawings for gas cards, family dinners, or trips to Walmart.

It is the interaction with the schools, however, that is key to SHINE's approach. The afterschool providers receive report cards and attendance reports from school teachers every 9 weeks. Providers also track attendance for the afterschool program and submit this data, along with the school district information, to an evaluator.

Analysis of this data shows that the more students attend SHINE, the better they do in school and the more regular their attendance. Specifically, the data show that 88% of the SHINE students had satisfactory school-day attendance. Altogether 78% of the SHINE students improved their academic performance and 96% were promoted to the next grade.

ENCORE! Improving Attendance in Vermont

When the final bell rings in the North Country district schools, more than 1,000 children stay on for fun and engaging learning opportunities through the ENCORE afterschool program. ENCORE takes an intentional approach to attendance by requiring that students attend the regular school day in order to participate in their program. The program also focuses on relationship building between students and their teachers: ENCORE sites are based in their schools, and 90% of the afterschool staff are regular-day employees. This emphasis on strengthening relationships makes young people feel valued, which has led to increased attendance. Regular ENCORE attendees miss 2 less days per year than nonregular attendees.

The ENCORE afterschool program serves students in grades K–8 and provides hands-on and community-based learning approaches not traditionally available during the school day. For example, for fourth grade students studying the history of Vermont, ENCORE devised a program that took students into their communities to learn about the rich history firsthand. ENCORE also introduced a garden program where students learn to plant, cultivate, and care for their gardens while learning the importance of good nutrition. ENCORE also offers creative opportunities, including music, theater, and dance.

Reflecting the Research

SHINE's results echo numerous research studies that have confirmed the role afterschool programs play in improving school-day attendance. Most recently, a 2011 study of the AfterZone program in Providence, Rhode Island, showed that middle school students participating in the program had an absence rate 25% lower than their peers. What's more, the improvement in attendance increased with the amount of time in the program (Kauh, 2011).

A 2009 study of seventh and eighth grade students at 10 Boys & Girls Clubs across the country found that those attending afterschool programs skipped school fewer times, increased school effort, and gained academic confidence; moreover, the first two outcomes cited above increased as the number of days attending afterschool programs increased (Arbreton, Bradshaw, Sheldon, & Pepper, 2009). In many cases, improved school-day attendance is an unexpected bonus. Some programs, such as SHINE and the Baltimore effort discussed below, have begun taking a more intentional approach.

Making It Intentional in Baltimore

Baltimore has made improved attendance a top priority for the city's school district and has engaged the city's child welfare, health, and transit agencies, as well as foundations and church groups, to bring students back to school. Afterschool programs play a key role. The Family League of Baltimore City, which handles the city's out-of-school-time contracts, identifies increased school-day attendance as a key outcome for providers. It prioritizes service to neighborhoods based on chronic absence rates, among other factors. It explicitly asks programs to recruit and enroll students with poor attendance records rather than push out students who might bring down program numbers. It also requires each provider to outline a plan for reducing chronic absence in its application for funds.

The Family League's data show that afterschool is making a difference. At all age levels, students in their programs are less likely to be chronically absent and more likely to be good attenders (missing fewer than 5 days) than the general school population. This holds true, even though the students in these programs are more likely to be living in poverty than the general school population. (For more information, see http://www. flbcinc.org.)

Taking Action

In response to the need to bring nationwide attention to the problem of chronic school absenteeism, Attendance Works was established as a national and state initiative in 2010 to promote better policy and practice around school attendance. The organization works to examine the causes, consequences, and potential responses to missing extended periods of school, starting in the early grades.

Building upon the experience of pioneering programs as well as emerging research, Attendance Works recommends schools and afterschool programs work together in the following ways:

1. **Build a strong culture of attendance in the school and the afterschool program.** Strategies can include establishing a clear policy about the importance of attendance, offering incentives and other motivating activities, and analyzing attendance data to identify areas that need improvement.

2. **Target students with at-risk levels of absence for recruitment and engagement in afterschool programming.** Especially for students who are just beginning to have problematic attendance, the extra support of afterschool may be just what they need.

3. **Share data on program and school attendance.** Such data sharing is critical for identifying students in trouble, regardless of when they are experiencing an attendance problem, and evaluating the impact of program participation on in-school attendance.

4. **Combine resources to engage families around the issue of attendance.** Together, school and afterschool staff can educate parents and students about the importance of going to school every day, as well as solicit their perspectives about the barriers to attendance and how they could be overcome.

5. **Make better use of attendance data reported annually for 21st Century Community Learning Centers.** Program staff should collect and review in-school and afterschool attendance data throughout the year to identify students with chronic absence who might need additional support and to determine if any afterschool classrooms are challenged with large numbers of students with poor attendance. An unusually high level of poor attendance could suggest a lack of engaging afterschool activities, an unresolved problem with bullying affecting all the students in a class, or a problem with the facilities that is creating an unsafe or unhealthy classroom environment. Poor attendance can be an early warning sign that intervention is needed in order to maintain a high quality program.

Attendance Works has a valuable Tools and T.A. section that contains a self-assessment tool to help afterschool programs reflect upon their approach to improving school-day attendance, as well as flyers in English and Spanish to help educate parents about the importance of regular attendance for their children's academic success (http://www.attendanceworks.org/). To see an example of a professional development program aimed at strengthening the capacity of afterschool providers to improve school-day attendance, visit the website of the Maryland Out of School Time Network: http://www.mdoutofschooltime.org/Attendance.html.

Leveraging the power of afterschool programs to reduce chronic absence is especially important now given the economic challenges facing communities and schools and the growing number of students at risk of academic failure and dropping out. By having an impact on attendance, afterschool programs can clearly demonstrate how they benefit students and schools and better justify their own funding.

ABOUT THE AUTHORS

Hedy N. Chang is the director of Attendance Works, a national and state-level
aimed at advancing student success by addressing chronic absence. She has spe
two decades working in the fields of family support, family economic success, educ
and child development, having previously served as a senior program officer at the
Evelyn and Walter Haas Jr. Fund and as co-director of California Tomorrow, a nonprof
committed to drawing strength from cultural, linguistic, and racial diversity. Chang is
the co-author of the seminal report *Present, Engaged and Accounted For: The Critical
Importance of Addressing Chronic Absence in the Early Grades*, as well as numerous
other articles about student attendance.

Phyllis W. Jordan is vice president at the Hatcher Group, a public affairs and
communication firm that connects nonprofits and foundations to policymakers and the
media. She has held editorial positions at the *Washington Post* and the *Los Angeles
Times* and covered education, local government, social services, health care, and
military affairs for a variety of other newspapers. Jordan has a master's degree in
journalism from the University of Missouri and a bachelor's degree in English and
history from Sweet Briar College in Virginia.

REFERENCES

Allensworth, E. M., & Easton, J. Q. (2007). *What matters for staying on-track and graduating in Chicago public high schools: A close look at course grades, failures, and attendance in the freshman year.* Chicago, IL: University of Chicago, Consortium on Chicago School Research.

Arbreton, A., Bradshaw, M., Sheldon, J., & Pepper, S. (2009). *Making every day count: Boys & Girls Clubs' role in promoting positive outcomes for teens.* Retrieved from http://www.ppv.org/ppv/publications/assets/295_publication.pdf

Balfanz, R., Herzog, L., & MacIver, D. J. (2007). Preventing student disengagement and keeping students on the graduation path in urban middle-grades schools: Early identification and effective interventions. *Educational Psychologist, 42*, 223–235.

Chang, H., & Romero, M. (2008). *Present, engaged & accounted for: The critical importance of addressing chronic absence in the early grades.* New York, NY: National Center for Children in Poverty.

Huang, D., Gribbons, B., Kim, K. S., Lee, C., & Baker, E. L. (2000). *A decade of results: The impact of the LA's BEST after school enrichment initiative on subsequent student achievement and performance.* Los Angeles, CA: UCLA Center for the Study of Evaluation, Graduate School of Education & Information Studies.

Kauh, T. J. (2011). *AfterZone: Outcomes for youth participating in Providence's after-school system.* Retrieved from http://www.wallacefoundation.org/knowledge-center/after-school/evaluations/Pages/AfterZone-Outcomes-for-YouthParticipating-in-Providences-Citywide-After-School-System.aspx

O'Donnell, P. (2013). *The demand and need for 21st Century Community Learning Centers across America: Unmet and growing.* Manuscript submitted for publication.

Welsh, M. E., Russell, C. A., Williams, I., Reisner, E. R., White, R. N., Winter, N., & Pearson, L. (2002). *Promoting learning and school attendance through after-school programs: Student-level changes in educational performance across TASC's first three years.* Retrieved from http://www.tascorp.org/content/document/detail/1436

Jay Smink
Retired Executive Director, National Dropout Prevention Center, Clemson University

A Proven Solution for Dropout Prevention: Expanded Learning Opportunities

A successful student in the 21st century is expected to graduate from high school; be prepared for the workforce, additional postsecondary education, or military service; and be able to participate in society as a productive, engaged citizen—one who votes, pays taxes, and serves on juries when called. Yet nearly 25% of America's youth do not complete high school on time, and in low-income communities, the rate of dropping out is much higher than the national average (Stillwell, 2010). These young people consequently lack many of the basic skills needed for future success.

The anecdotal reasons provided by students for dropping out of school, both before and after they actually leave school, are well documented and have been consistent for more than a decade. Most of the reasons focus on students' dissatisfaction with school policies and practices. In addition, students in high-risk circumstances (such as poverty) demonstrate a high disengagement with school, sometimes starting very early in elementary school or even before enrolling in school. Generally, these are the most common reasons provided by students:

- *I didn't like school.*
- *I didn't like the teachers.*
- *I didn't see the value in the schoolwork I was asked to do.*
- *I had family issues.*

The research literature, moreover, is convincing regarding a broad range of risk factors associated with dropping out of school. A review of this research by the National Dropout Prevention Center (NDPC) at Clemson University has identified an extensive set of risk factors organized into four domains (Hammond, Linton, Smink, & Drew, 2007):

A. Individual Factors (referring to the student)

- *Lacks future orientation*
- *Low academic achievement levels*
- *Low attendance*
- *Special learning needs*

B. Family Factors

- *Low socioeconomic status*
- *Low expectations for schooling*
- *Mobility of family*
- *Language and literacy levels*

C. School Factors

- *Lack of alternatives for learning opportunities*
- *No individual learning plans for students*
- *Unfair behavior and disciplines issues*
- *Retention policies*

D. Community Factors

- *Lack of community involvement*
- *Lack of support for schools*
- *High levels of violence and drug abuse*
- *Few recreational facilities*

Unfortunately, there is no "silver bullet" to reduce the persistent and unacceptably high dropout rate across America. While a range of strategies is needed to improve the high school graduation rate, one especially promising tool is that of quality afterschool and summer learning programs. These programs routinely incorporate strategies that complement and align well with effective, research-based dropout prevention programs. The purpose of this article is to illustrate how afterschool and summer learning programs and dropout prevention initiatives can be integrated in order to generate increased school attendance, continued student academic gains, and improved behavioral patterns, all leading to increased graduation rates.

Research Supporting Complementary Strategies: Expanded Learning Opportunities and Dropout Prevention

Longstanding research by the NDPC has identified 15 effective strategies to reduce the dropout rate, one of which is specifically providing afterschool opportunities (Smink & Schargel, 2004). An added advantage is that afterschool and summer learning opportunities delivered through strong school-community partnerships can readily incorporate many other effective dropout prevention strategies identified in the research.

To show this confluence of potential, it is valuable to compare the match between several of the dropout prevention strategies and the common elements of quality, comprehensive afterschool and summer programs.

To gain a nationwide perspective on this potential, it is valuable to review the offerings and elements of the largest nationwide funding source for afterschool and summer learning, the federally funded 21st Century Community Learning Centers initiative. While the specific services provided to youth vary across communities to match local needs, programs funded through this initiative commonly include a focus on mentoring, tutoring, counseling for substance abuse and violence prevention, community service, recreation activities, and youth leadership activities, all of which are associated with effective dropout prevention programs.

Comparing directly a number of the key dropout prevention strategies against the core elements of the 21st Century Community Learning Centers afterschool and summer programs makes it clear that well-designed and well-implemented afterschool, summer learning, and dropout prevention programs align very closely (See Table 1).

....

Table 1. The match between recommended dropout prevention strategies and required or recommended offerings in 21st Century Community Learning Centers.

Recommended Dropout Prevention Strategies	Required or Recommended Offerings in 21st Century Community Learning Centers
School-community collaboration	YES
Family engagement	YES
Mentoring/tutoring	YES
Service learning	YES
Active learning	YES
Professional development	YES
Educational technology	YES
Individualized instruction	YES
Career and technical education	YES for older youth

Another important comparison of the potential of quality afterschool and summer programs is to study the results of afterschool programs leading to school success against the findings of early warning factors linked to dropping out of school.

Research finds that quality afterschool programs can positively affect a number of key school success factors. In a meta-analysis, Durlak, Weissburg, and Pachan (2010), for example, analyzed more than 60 studies of afterschool programs that include emotional, social, and academic development components. They found that those programs meeting quality criteria demonstrated a positive impact in many key areas:

- *School grades*
- *School attendance*
- *Self-perception*
- *Reduction in problem behaviors*
- *Academic achievement (test scores)*
- *Positive social behavior*
- *School bonding*

Further, assessments by classroom teachers of students participating in 21st Century Community Learning Centers programs reveal results similar to those of Durlak et al. These teacher assessments have found that participating students demonstrated improvement in these areas:

> . . . it is very apparent that the student success factors associated with quality afterschool programs and 21st Century Community Learning Centers directly address the predictive factors associated with dropping out of school . . .

- *Greater homework completion*
- *Better school attendance*
- *Better grades*
- *More positive engagement*
- *Less misbehavior*
- *Improved test scores (Learning Point Associates, 2012).*

When this research on the positive impacts of quality afterschool and summer programs is compared with the research on what is needed to help young people stay on a path to high school graduation, it is very apparent that the student success factors associated with quality afterschool programs and 21st Century Community Learning Centers directly address the predictive factors associated with dropping out of school (see Table 2).

Table 2. Predictive factors of dropping out of school matched against the impact of quality afterschool and 21st Century Community Learning Centers.

Predictive Factors Of Dropping Out	Impact of Quality Afterschool From Meta-analysis by Durlak et al.	Results from 21st Century Community Learning Centers
Failing grades in reading and/or math	Improved grades in reading and math	Better grades in reading and math
Poor attendance	Improved school attendance	Better school attendance
Misbehavior	Reduction in problem behaviors	Less misbehavior
Very low test scores	Improved academic achievement (test scores)	Increased test scores
Lack of effort/motivation	Positive social behavior	More positive engagement
Not engaging in class or school work	More positive school bonding	Greater homework completion

The meta-analysis from over 60 studies by Durlak et al. and the many years of data from the 21st Century Community Learning Centers paint a clear picture that quality afterschool and summer programs can have a positive impact on the early warning indicators for students with a high potential for dropping out of school and not graduating.

Real Life Lessons Learned: Afterschool and Summer Learning Programs, Including 21st Century Community Learning Centers Programs

There are many different program objectives for afterschool and summer programs and for community-based learning centers in the context of school-community partnerships across the nation. Basically, these programs are designed in whole or in part to deliver academic programs, provide additional supports, find ways to inspire young people to stay engaged in learning, and/or offer enrichment opportunities to students and sometimes to other family members, as well.

In light of the research discussed above, expanded learning programs, including 21st Century Community Learning Centers, can be designed and implemented in such a way that they can purposefully include dropout prevention strategies and other quality elements that will have positive effects on student success. What follows are several examples of noteworthy programs:

- *The Colorado MESA program in Denver, Colorado, is a premier educational resource and experiential program serving students throughout high school. MESA's mission is to increase the number of economically disadvantaged and at-risk students who graduate from high school fully prepared for postsecondary education in engineering, math, science, computer science, business, and other math and science-based fields. Hands-on activities, team building, and mentoring help build social and literacy skills. Field trips to colles, universities, and industry sites, as well as engineering and science-related design challenges, excite students, sharpen their skills, and increase their awareness of career opportunities (Afterschool Alliance, 2009).*

- *RiverzEdge Arts Project in Providence, Rhode Island, is an art and leadership program where high school students work with artists in fine and commercial arts. They guide youth to create art, and they run an arts enterprise in an environment that stresses hands-on learning, teamwork, mutual respect, responsibility, and workplace discipline. Participants build self-awareness and work skills by creating and selling products and services in the competitive arts and business markets, developing their creative voice, and preparing them for the job market. One hundred percent of participants go on to graduate high school in a city with a 34% dropout rate (Afterschool Alliance, 2009).*

- *Funded by a 21st Century Community Learning Centers grant, EduCare is the afterschool provider at seven Los Angeles School District high schools. EduCare's programs are designed to give students the opportunity to develop their unique abilities, build relationships, and find relevance in their educational experience. Program activities are unique to each school and include homework assistance and tutoring, academic enrichment, structured fitness classes, and performing and fine arts activities. The 2011 graduation rate for students participating in EduCare afterschool programs over the course of 4 years of high school was 90%, as compared to 60% for nonparticipating students. School attendance and standardized test scores also significantly improved (EduCare Foundation, 2011).*

These examples illustrate the growing evidence that some of the predictive factors associated with dropping out of school can be successfully addressed in part through quality afterschool and summer programs and 21st Century Community Learning Centers.

Conclusion: Maximizing the Combined Power of Expanded Learning Opportunities and Dropout Prevention Programs

The lessons learned from both successful 21st Century Community Learning Centers programs, as well as other quality afterschool and summer learning programs, and successful dropout prevention programs should serve as the standard for all new or revised programs designed to increase high school graduation rates. Programs should provide students with these opportunities and supports:

- *Engage actively in the strategies found in both types of program environments.*
- *Acquire extra critical thinking skills as well as basic skills.*
- *Develop positive attitudes.*
- *Keep on track to progress successfully through each step of the education pipeline (for example, maintain passing grades, develop regular attendance habits, stay out of trouble, bring up very low test scores).*
- *See a real and direct connection to jobs, careers, and/or 2- to 4-year colleges.*

Programs should also use these strategies:

- *Engage community organizations and schools as collaborators in time beyond the typical school day (e.g., afterschool, weekends, summers) to help more students succeed.*

- *Involve families outside the traditional school day, both in their own learning and supporting their child(ren)'s success.*

- *Deploy quality standards linked to successful programming and results. (See, for example, Durlak et al., 2010; Huang & Dietel, 2011)*

Although virtually any student could benefit from expanded learning opportunities and school-family-community partnerships, those students in high-risk situations or struggling in school will tend to benefit the most from quality expanded learning opportunities, especially those programs that implement intentional strategies geared to helping students graduate from high school. Now is the time to tap the potential of quality afterschool and summer learning programs—especially those embracing the vision of the 21st Century Community Learning Centers initiative—in support of a nationwide commitment to increasing America's high school graduation rate.

For More Information

Hirsch, B., Hedges, L., Stawicki, J., & Mekinda, M. (2011, June). *After-school programs for high school students: An evaluation of After School Matters*. Evanston, IL: Northwestern University.

Kochanek, J.R., Wraight, S., Wan, Y., Nylen, L., and Rodriguez, S. (2011). *Parent involvement and extended learning activities in school improvement plans in the Midwest Region*. (Issues & Answers Report, REL 2011-No. 115). Washington, DC: U.S. Department of Education, Institute of Education Sciences, National Center for Education Evaluation and Regional Assistance. Regional Education Laboratory Midwest.

Farbman, D. (2011). *Learning time in America: Trends to reform the American school calendar*. Boston, MA: National Center on Time and Learning & Education Commission of the States.

The Wallace Foundation. (2008). *A place to grow and learn: A citywide approach to building and sustaining out-of-school time learning opportunities*. New York: Author.

The Wallace Foundation. (2011). *Think outside the clock*. New York: Author.

Valladares, S. and Ramos, M. (2011). *Children of latino immigrants and out-of-school time programs* (Research-to-Results Brief, # 2011-30). Washington, DC: Child Trends.

Websites

www.wallacefoundation.org
www.afterschoolalliance.org
www.summerlearning.org
www.childtrends.org
www.timeandlearning.org
www.dropoutprevention.org

ABOUT THE AUTHOR

Jay Smink served as executive director of the National Dropout Prevention Center at Clemson University for 24 years and was awarded professor emeritus in the College of Health, Education, and Human Development. His career also included classroom teaching in public schools, leadership positions in state agencies, and he held research and administrative positions in the national career and technical education center at The Ohio State University. Smink is the co-author of the best-selling book *Helping Students Graduate.*

REFERENCES

Afterschool Alliance. (2009, July). *Afterschool: A high school dropout prevention tool* (Issue Brief No. 38). Retrieved from http://www.afterschoolalliance.org/issue_38_DropoutPrevention.cfm

Durlak, J. A., Weissberg, R. P., & Pachan, M. (2010). A meta-analysis of after-school programs that seek to promote personal and social skills in children and adolescents. *American Journal of Community Psychology, 45*, 294–309.

EduCare Foundation. (2011). After school programs. Retrieved from http://educarefoundation.com/wp-eduntent/uploads/EduCare-Foundation_HS_2010-2011.pdf

Hammond, C., Linton, D., Smink, J., & Drew, S. (2007). *Dropout risk factors and exemplary programs.* Clemson, SC: National Dropout Prevention Center, Communities In Schools.

Huang, D., & Dietel, R. (2011). *Making afterschool programs better* (CRESST Policy Brief No. 11). Los Angeles, CA: University of California.

Learning Point Associates. (2012). Profile and Performance Information Collection Center [Online data collection system]. Retrieved from http://ppics.learningpt.org/ppicsnet/public/default.aspx

Smink, J., & Schargel, F. P. (2004). *Helping students graduate: A strategic approach to dropout prevention.* Larchmont, NY: Eye on Education.

Stillwell, R. (2010). *Public school graduates and dropouts from the Common Core of Data: School year 2007–08* (NCES 2010-341). Retrieved from National Center for Education Statistics website: http://nces.ed.gov/pubs2010/2010341.pdf

Taliah Givens
Former Program Director, Council of Chief State
School Officers

Building Mastery of the Common Core State Standards by Expanding Learning With Community Stakeholder Partnerships

The development of the Common Core State Standards (Common Core) marks a major turning point in the history of the U.S. public education system. The Council of Chief State School Officers (CCSSO) and the National Governors Association Center for Best Practices coordinated a state-led, multiyear effort to create the standards in collaboration with teachers, school administrators, and experts from across the nation. The Common Core (http://www.corestandards.org) addresses three leading concerns in our nation's fight for education reform: an inadequate number of students prepared for college and careers, a lack of equity in academic expectations across and within states, and the inability to compare results across states. The Common Core provides clearly defined and consistent standards that represent the knowledge and skills students should acquire within their K–12 education in English language arts and mathematics. These standards are intended to serve as a framework to prepare our children for college and to compete in the global workforce. Through widespread adoption in 45 states and the District of Columbia, educators, administrators, and parents can ensure consistent expectations and support for students, regardless of their zip code.

The Common Core is the "what," not the "how." Although we have accomplished a great deal since 2010, there is still a mountain to climb to ensure successful implementation, assessment, and student mastery of the Common Core. CCSSO has prioritized implementation by providing advocacy, communications, and technical resources to state education agencies through its Implementing the Common Core Standards (ICCS) Collaborative (http://www.ccsso.org/Resources/Programs/The_Common_Core_State_Standards_Initiative.html). The organization is also involved with two consortia of states committed to developing and sharing comprehensive assessment instruments aligned with Common Core: the Smarter Balanced Assessment Consortium (SMARTER) and the Partnership for the Assessment of Readiness for College and Careers (PARCC).

There are also various other stakeholder groups that are playing significant roles in helping students actualize their potential through the standards. Among these significant stakeholders are expanded learning educators across every state, including leaders in local 21st Century Community Learning Centers programs, who are providing before- and afterschool, weekend, and summer programs. These expanded learning opportunities are an essential component to help students master the Common Core.

- *They support teachers and administrators with additional resources both within and outside the school. These resources provide the necessary student learning supports to help ensure that more students master the rigorous content.*

- *They allow students to go deeper in their learning and development to become college and career ready. Often the flexibility in afterschool and summer programs encourages more active and hands-on learning, with direct connections to workforce and college access opportunities.*

- *They promote student engagement and effective learning habits that are important for students to successfully progress toward on-time graduation. College and career readiness typically necessitates a broad set of skills and dispositions that afterschool and summer learning can help encourage, reinforce, and perhaps even help deliver with community, workforce, and college partners.*

With the effects of devastating state cuts in education, coupled with high drop-out rates as well as high numbers of college students needing remediation courses upon entering postsecondary institutions (Lee, Rawls, Edwards, & Menson, 2011), our schools have been forced to face the reality that they cannot increase student achievement alone. There is a need to coordinate sustainable, cost-effective resources for schools to ensure mastery of the Common Core.

Researcher Robert Balfanz (2010) has shown that student achievement is not fully academic in nature. Challenges can include decreased engagement, academics or poverty. Schools may find a critical need for a "second shift" of human resources to support students in overcoming these challenges and achieving educational goals.

Afterschool and summer learning programs are designed to resource this "second shift." Through partnerships, these programs work directly with schools, teachers and parents. Districts can design a comprehensive system of support to ensure that students are completing homework, receiving adequate tutoring, maintaining consistent attendance, and receiving appropriate physical and/or social-emotional supports for their academic achievement. Some students may even be able to recover course credit, accumulate new course credits, or explore career and college options through afterschool and summer learning partnerships with colleges, employers, or youth organizations.

An expanded learning educator, with a clear understanding of the math concepts students are studying within the context of the Common Core, is uniquely situated to provide targeted opportunities for students to deepen their learning by applying new concepts through enrichment activities. More time and attention is accorded the skills espoused by the Common Core, increasing the students' likelihood to understand the underlying concepts and acquire key skills that enable them to demonstrate their competency (CCSSO, 2011).

Many afterschool and summer learning programs are well positioned to support learning practices and conditions that accelerate the "habits of mind," which represent the capacities and practices students should exhibit while learning the Common Core, including the following:

English/Language Arts Capacities of a Literate Individual

- *Demonstrate independence.*
- *Build strong content knowledge.*
- *Respond to the varying demands of audience, task, purpose, and discipline.*
- *Comprehend as well as critique.*
- *Value evidence.*
- *Use technology and digital media strategically and capably.*
- *Come to understand other perspectives and cultures.*

Mathematical Practices to Master Grade-Level Standards

- *Make sense of problems and persevere in solving them.*
- *Reason abstractly and quantitatively.*
- *Construct viable arguments and critique the reasoning of others.*
- *Model with mathematics.*
- *Use appropriate tools strategically.*
- *Attend to precision.*
- *Look for and make use of structure.*
- *Look for and express regularity in repeated reasoning.*

Afterschool and summer learning programs provide an extended platform on which students can build their expertise in these habits. Expanded learning programs typically use experiential learning strategies that include activities that cater to students' academic needs and their particular areas of interest. Such activities are offered in the form of extracurricular arts, STEM, civic/cultural, or athletic programs; service learning; internships; apprenticeships; mentoring; dual college enrollment; and virtual learning. These programs begin through early-childhood education opportunities. They include partnerships with community-based organizations, corporate and local businesses, state and local government agencies, arts and science organizations, higher education institutions, and faith-based communities. In essence, through expanded learning programs, the community becomes the 21st century classroom.

States and districts can structure frequent and robust opportunities for teachers, principals, and expanded learning program staff to learn and work together. As states are rolling out their implementation plans for districts, they should introduce their afterschool professionals to the standards alongside teachers and principals. This expanded learning workforce will be tutoring and mentoring, designing STEM enrichment projects and activities, leading literacy classes, teaching digital media and photography, and coaching drama, dance, debate, and journalism clubs. How powerful would it be if these adult staff and volunteers were paired with teachers and administrators in regularly scheduled collaborative sessions on what students will be learning? How powerful would it be if expanded learning staff and volunteers used their planned activities as a platform for students to demonstrate their deeper understanding of a math or English language arts standard? What if all of this learning was shared across the implicit boundaries between teachers and expanded learning providers, thereby building a comprehensive and cohesive alignment between the adults who are educating and supporting all students?

> In essence, through expanded learning programs, the community becomes the 21st century classroom.

We are starting to see these essential collaborations take shape:

- *In Wisconsin, district and local expanded learning programs are connecting with school curriculum online and directly with teachers. They include current and retired teachers on their staff to facilitate effective engagement with schools and the academic content students are learning (Holsted, 2012).*

- *The Massachusetts Afterschool Partnership has worked with a leading arts curriculum publisher and the Massachusetts Cultural Council to develop an out-of-school-time arts curriculum called "Creative Minds." This curriculum lists the math core standards that are embedded in each activity (Topal, 2011).*

- *The Georgia Afterschool Investment Council published their revised "afterschool quality standards" to include intentional alignment to the Common Core (Georgia Afterschool Investment Council, 2011).*

- *The New Jersey State Afterschool Network (NJSACC), in cooperation with the New Jersey State Department of Education, completed a statewide pilot training program on the Common Core for afterschool program leaders. Training sessions focused on how to align student activities and curriculum with the Common Core.*

We are also seeing this type of collaboration between state education agencies and the statewide afterschool networks in Oregon, Rhode Island, Utah, South Dakota, New Mexico, North Carolina, and New Hampshire. It is becoming an effective mechanism to deploy Common Core training to local expanded learning program providers, especially

21st Century Community Learning Centers grantees. A recent commentary by the Forum for Youth Investment highlights the unique role program leaders can play in communicating about the Common Core to help schools build stronger relationships with families and the community (Devaney & Yohalem, 2012).

The Common Core is a catalyst to build a transformative education system that provides unique learning experiences for students while leading them to high scholastic achievement. However, it will take investment from all stakeholders, including expanded learning leaders, to develop the comprehensive supports our students, and schools, will need to achieve mastery.

ABOUT THE AUTHOR

Taliah Givens is a former program director at CCSSO where she led the expanded learning opportunities work within CCSSO's Innovation Lab Network and across CCSSO's strategic initiatives, ensuring its effective integration into the education landscape. Her public sector career in education, youth development, and association management began at Jobs for America's Graduates – DC, Inc. and the Association for Information Systems, which was preceded by her experience as an optical and systems engineer. Givens holds a master's in public administration from Baruch College, CUNY as a 2006 National Urban Fellow to the Xcel Energy Foundation, as well as bachelor's degrees in both computer engineering and electrical engineering technology from Georgia Tech and Alabama A&M University respectively.

REFERENCES

Balfanz, R. (2010, November). *Making persistently low-achieving schools places for learning: What states can do*. PowerPoint presentation to Council of Chief State School Officers Annual Policy Forum, Louisville, KY.

Council of Chief State School Officers (CCSSO). (2011). *Connecting high-quality expanded learning opportunities and the Common Core State Standards to advance student success*. Washington, DC: Author.

Devaney, E., & Yohalem, N. (2012). *The Common Core Standards: What do they mean for out-of-school-time?* (Out-of-School Time Policy Commentary No. 17). Washington, DC: Forum for Youth Investment.

Georgia Afterschool Investment Council. (2011). *Georgia afterschool quality standards*. Atlanta, GA: Author.

Holsted, J. (2012). *Making the connection: Next generation learning & expanded learning opportunities*. Washington, DC: Council of Chief State School Officers.

Lee, J. M., Rawls, A., Edwards, K., & Menson, R. (2011). *The college completion agenda 2011 progress report*. New York, NY: College Board Advancement and Policy Center.

Topal, C. W. (2011). *Creative minds*. Cambridge, MA: Davis.

Steven D'Agustino
Director of Online Learning, School of Professional
and Continuing Studies, and Director, Center For
Professional Development, Fordham University

Providing Innovative Opportunities and Options for Credit Recovery Through Afterschool and Summer Learning Programs

Credit recovery refers to efforts undertaken to allow students to earn high school Carnegie units needed for graduation. Credit recovery permits students to make up courses that they have previously failed due to excessive absences, inability to grasp the content, or other factors associated with academic failure.

Credit recovery programs take various forms, ranging from retaking a course in an alternative time or setting (before school, after school, in night school, or during the summer) or through an alternative methodology (via an approved project that satisfies course requirements or through online learning). Generally, students are eligible to enroll in credit recovery programs if they have met the "seat time" requirements for a course needed for graduation but have failed to meet the end-of-course standards required to receive credit; that is, if they have attempted to take the course and failed, rather than taking it for the first time.

Online credit recovery programs are increasingly prevalent due to the pressure felt by school districts to improve graduation rates through the No Child Left Behind Act coupled with the increase in educational technology in schools and the growth in providers of online course content aligned with state education standards.

Among states reporting dropout data to the U.S. Department of Education in 2006, 26.8% of public high school students do not graduate with a regular diploma 4 years after starting ninth grade. The report also shows that students from low-income families were roughly 10 times less likely to complete high school between 2006 and 2007 than were students from high-income families. In October 2007, approximately 3.3 million civilian non-institutionalized (meaning those not committed to an institution) 16- through 24-year-olds were not enrolled in high school and had not earned a high school diploma or alternative credential (Cataldi, Laird, & KewalRamani, 2009).

Failure to obtain a high school diploma has severe consequences. The annual median income of a male over the age of 24 without a high school diploma is approximately $27,000. By contrast, a similar individual with a high school diploma earns almost $37,000 annually (Sable, Gaviola, & Hoffman, 2007). High school dropouts also face higher rates of imprisonment; those without high school diplomas are more likely to end up incarcerated than those who complete high school successfully (Harlow, 2003). The financial and social costs stemming from high school failure and high dropout rates in the United States are enormous when considering the loss of income and productivity and the costs of incarceration and rehabilitation. It has been estimated that dropouts cost the nation billions of dollars annually (Ou & Reynolds, 2010).

Promising Practices for Credit Recovery

As the need for credit recovery programs has become more apparent and urgent, districts have begun to look toward advances in instructional technology as a solution. Unfortunately, many obstacles prevent students in need of credit recovery from taking advantage of the flexibility and convenience of online learning, including a lack of computer skills (Oliver et al., 2007) and the self-regulation skills required for independent study (Cavanaugh, Gillan, Kromrey, Hess, & Blomeyer, 2004). Moreover, those students most in need of credit recovery—those in urban environments and those living in poverty—often do not have access to technology, or they attend schools with poor technology infrastructure, making online learning frustrating and impractical. Students are therefore more likely to drop out from and fail online courses than they are from traditional face-to-face courses (Roblyer, 2006).

Hybrid courses—that is, online courses that include in-person interactions—lead to greater academic success and student retention (Cavanaugh et al., 2004). As a result, students who require credit recovery in order to graduate and who attempt to get back on track academically through an online intervention appear to experience higher levels of success in a blended environment. Also, as Cavanaugh et al. (2004) noted, "online learning has the unique capability for immersing students in information and communication technologies (ICT) beyond the traditional classroom." Developing ICT skills is especially important for students who do not have regular and meaningful access to learning opportunities that integrate technology in their traditional classrooms.

Credit Recovery in Afterschool and Summer Learning Programs

Afterschool and summer learning programs supported by 21st Century Community Learning Centers funding are especially well-suited for online, asynchronous credit-recovery efforts. These programs typically employ a variety of innovative instructional techniques, offering a nontraditional approach to student learning that differs from regular school-day instruction and that incorporates a specific emphasis on youth development. In the particular case of credit recovery programs offered by 21st Century Community Learning Centers and other similar afterschool and summer programs funded by other sources, the youth development focus includes helping students set and achieve academic goals, developing students' confidence in their ability to acquire credits and progress to graduation (self-efficacy beliefs), and also developing and refining students' self-regulation skills required for independent study.

Successful 21st Century Community Learning Centers afterschool and summer programs, as well as other similar afterschool and summer programs, typically employ alternative systems to monitor student behavior, progress, and achievement. They also seek to provide curricula and activities that are relevant, enjoyable, and flexible, especially with regard to high school students. Notably, afterschool and summer learning programs that offer credit recovery are essentially asking students to engage in academic activities during their free time, in the same disciplines in which these students have experienced failure. This creates a significant challenge; however, it is the *nontraditional* nature of 21st Century Community Learning Centers afterschool and summer programs that enables them to attract and retain students.

By jettisoning typical barriers to student achievement, online credit recovery learning management systems allow students to interact directly with the instructional content. For example, the content of the course and the pace of the instructor are not controlled by the teacher, but by the student. Students can therefore progress at their own pace, without the teacher as gatekeeper. The student can also repeat sections of content, test out of others, and avoid the issues that often arise in classrooms related to management and discipline. Also, these afterschool and summer programs empower students to take control of their own learning. Unlike regular school-day progams, afterschool and summer programs are voluntary. Students can opt out, and this power gives the students a sense of agency—another important program goal for high school students.

In short, as a result of their innovative practices and nontraditional approaches, 21st Century Community Learning Centers afterschool and summer programs are especially well suited for technologically mediated credit recovery because (1) they are attended by students who are voluntarily present, (2) they are staffed by professionals who bring a youth-development (rather than a narrow, academically-focused) approach to student progress, and (3) they do not replicate the structures and oversight mechanisms of traditional day school programs.

Examples From the Field

In light of mounting national urgency to increase graduation rates and reduce dropout rates, education practitioners and advocates alike are giving increased attention to the potential of afterschool and summer learning programs to provide additional resources and supports needed by students who are at-risk of dropping out. The following programs explicitly target potential dropouts with a set of focused strategies, including credit recovery, aimed at helping these students alter their trajectory so that they achieve success in school and persist until they graduate.

Fordham University's 21st Century Community Learning Centers program is conducted on the university campus after school and during the summer and is designed explicitly to provide opportunities and supports for credit recovery for at-risk high school students. The program uses an online learning management system, PLATO, to help students earn credits in academic subjects and make progress toward graduation. Supported by licensed teachers and Fordham University undergraduate mentors, as well as a licensed social worker, participants receive one-on-one guidance in note taking, Internet research, and study skills. Students are also invited to visit university events and college classes and to eat dinner regularly in the campus cafeteria with their undergraduate mentors. Parents and adult family members of participating students can take free classes in workforce development, technology, and English skills, and they can take other workshops provided through partnerships with local community-based organizations. Over the course of the latest reporting period, 250 students recovered 539 high school credits. Of the 256 students enrolled during the 2010–11 academic year, 175 (68%) earned a total of 346.5 credits. Of the 134 students enrolled for credit recovery during the summer leading up to the 2010–11 school year, 106 (79%) earned a total of 192 credits (New York State Dept. of Education, 2011).

The Seminole County (Florida) Public Schools Midway Safe Harbor Center operates the "Last Best Chance" program—a credit-recovery initiative that engages highly qualified teachers and tutors to provide intensive intervention to students who are at risk of dropping out of school because of low performance and repeated behavioral reprimands. Students are also matched with community mentors to promote positive relationships and continuous support for academic success. Moreover, the initiative includes a character education component, designed to foster cooperation and communication with others. Activities focus on the development of appropriate verbal skills that enable participants to effectively communicate needs without verbal aggression or bullying.

Habitat for Humanity of North Idaho and Post Falls High School have combined to create a cooperative apprenticeship program called Learn to Earn in Hayden, Idaho. Students get hands-on experience and earn school credits by working on Habitat for Humanity construction sites. Students pick up skills in all phases of a construction project, are able to apply their work experience toward earning their diploma, and make contacts in the construction field with the potential for employment after graduation (Afterschool Alliance, 2009).

Students in need of credit recovery at Blair High School in Pasadena, California, have found success through the BlairLEARNS program. The grades 7–12 school offers a rich assortment of afterschool programs, from cutting-edge technology to sports to academic support and credit recovery. As a result, the school's on-time graduation rate is up 28% since 2004. In 2007, more than a third of the graduating class participated in the credit recovery program (Afterschool Alliance, 2009).

Recommendations

- **Strong partnerships with feeder schools/day program.** *A successful credit recovery program sponsored by community-based afterschool partners depends upon close collaboration with feeder schools. These partnerships will enable the afterschool credit recovery program to identify students who are struggling in the traditional classroom setting and who, in the judgment of teachers and counselors, can thrive in an afterschool program with an academic focus. Also, feeder programs can provide support for afterschool partners by encouraging students to persist in attending the afterschool program, by taking note of any positive effects that participation in credit recovery has on students' current academic performance (like behavior and attendance), and perhaps most importantly, by ensuring that all requirements for credit have been completed.*

- **Flexible scheduling.** *Since afterschool credit recovery programs focus on adolescent learners, flexible scheduling is imperative. Especially for nontraditional high school students who may have children of their own, family responsibilities, or jobs, afterschool credit recovery programs need rolling enrollment and flexible policies for arrival and departure.*

- **Family involvement.** *Communication with the home is essential for afterschool programs, and credit recovery is no exception. Parents or caregivers must be informed about the importance of their child's recovering credits and progressing towards graduation. Family involvement includes communicating about attendance and academic progress, as well as celebrating success by notifying the family when a credit is recovered. Successful programs also offer courses for parents and adult family members in workforce development and technology.*

- **Ongoing staff development.** *Since many credit recovery programs in afterschool settings rely on learning management systems, staff development in technology is essential. Also, staff must learn new ways of interacting with students that differ distinctly from traditional relationships between teachers and students. The very presence of students in afterschool credit recovery programs is evidence that traditional school-based approaches have not been successful for these students, so alternative methods of instruction and interaction are needed. Each program will have somewhat different specific professional development needs; however, staff development around emerging cultural, technological, and instructional issues is imperative.*

- **Effective evaluation strategies.** *Tightly coupled with the need for ongoing staff development is the need for regular and systematic evaluation to identify strengths and weaknesses of the program. All constituent groups invested in the program should be part of the evaluation, including students, families, feeder school staff, and program staff. Importantly, the evaluation should include, if possible, assessment of the instructional environment of students' school-day classes so that program refinements can be made, based in part on those findings.*

- **Strong technological infrastructure.** *If the credit recovery program depends on technology, the technical infrastructure must be solid and reliable. Nothing will undermine a program's reputation among students faster than technology that does not work. This requires a commitment of funding and staff.*

- **Postsecondary focus.** *Experiences of post-high school life are essential motivating factors for academically at-risk high school students. Successful credit recovery programs offer students support in postsecondary preparation and planning, including visits to colleges; assistance with college essays, applications, and financial aid forms; and sponsorship of workforce development workshops that improve interview skills and support resume writing.*

- **Youth development emphasis.** *Successful credit recovery programs incorporate a youth development emphasis that essentially permeates the program culture. This helps students feel that staff members are invested in their future, provides authentic opportunities for student agency and leadership, and helps create and maintain meaningful relationships between staff and students. These relationships often take the form of mentoring by successful program completers or volunteers from local colleges and the community.*

Conclusion

As a result of their innovative and nontraditional approaches to student learning—freed from the constraints of regular school-day and school-year programs—21st Century Community Learning Centers afterschool and summer programs have been able to embrace credit recovery programs that are highly engaging for high school students who have struggled academically. These programs typically employ online learning management systems along with in-person support, and freed from the constraints of regular school-day and school-year programs, they allow students to accumulate credits at their own pace, thereby empowering them to take control of their learning.

As a result, credit recovery through engaging afterschool and summer learning programs, like those supported by the 21st Century Community Learning Centers initiative, offer many struggling high school students the opportunity to experience academic success, often for the first time—and these successes typically carry over into their regular school-day classes. This creates a major "win" for all stakeholders involved: the students and their families, their high schools and communities, and of course, these highly-innovative afterschool programs themselves.

Additional Program Examples

The following examples are drawn from Afterschool Alliance Issue Brief #39: *Afterschool: Providing a Successful Route to Credit Attainment and Recovery* (August 2009).

- **Prep Zone** *in Philadelphia, Pennsylvania, is an innovative high school afterschool program that offers students the opportunity to earn credit during afterschool time for substantial projects that apply classroom learning to real-world situations. The program includes rigorous coursework, development of an entrepreneurial project and business plan, and culminates in levels of competitions where the students can win grants and computers.*

- **EVOLUTIONS (EVOking Learning & Understanding Through Investigations of the Natural Sciences)** *is a free program at the Yale Peabody Museum of Natural History in New Haven, Connecticut, that serves underrepresented, inner city older youth. Students earn academic credit at their schools for participating in a program revolving around science career awareness/literacy, college preparation and transferable skills development. Students design and construct their own museum exhibition and produce DVDs that teach state science standards to elementary students. They also go on a 2- to 3-day college visitation trip and visit another museum in the region, all free of charge. One component of the program provides students with paid opportunities as trained interpreters of museum resources. The local school district provides free transportation in the form of free city bus passes, allowing for greater access by the students most in need.*

- **Hallways to Learning** *in Kewanee, Illinois, used the results of a student survey to design their program. Students indicated what their interests and goals were, and they now have the opportunity to participate in a cardio club, a jazz ensemble, a writing club, culture club, film club and book club. Woven throughout the curriculum is a credit retrieval program that helps students graduate with their peers.*

ABOUT THE AUTHOR

Steven D'Agustino is director of online learning for the School of Professional and Continuing Studies, director of the Center for Professional Development, and adjunct professor in the Department of Communications and Media Management in the Gabelli School of Business, Fordham University. He has overseen the implementation of a number of grant-funded programs to provide access to technology to historically underserved urban populations funded through 21st Century Community Learning Centers, Title IID No Child Left Behind, and the American Recovery and Reinvestment Act.

REFERENCES

Afterschool Alliance. (2009). *Afterschool: Providing a successful route to credit attainment and recovery* (Issue Brief No. 39). Retrieved from http://www.afterschoolalliance.org/issue_39_CreditAttainment.cfm

Cataldi, E. F., Laird, J., & KewalRamani, A. (2009). *High school dropout and completion rates in the United States: 2007 compendium report* (IES 2009-064). Retrieved from http://eric.ed.gov/PDFS/ED506561.pdf

Cavanaugh, C., Gillan, K. J., Kromrey, J., Hess, M., & Blomeyer, R. (2004). *The effects of distance education on K–12 student outcomes: A meta-analysis*. Naperville, IL: Learning Point Associates.

Dessof, A. (2009). Reaching graduation with credit recovery: Districts provide the latest programs to help failing students succeed. Retrieved from http://www.districtadministration.com/viewarticle.aspx?articleid=2165

Harlow, C. (2003). *Education and correctional populations*. Retrieved from Bureau of Justice Statistics website: http://bjs.ojp.usdoj.gov/content/pub/pdf/ecp.pdf

Chris Smith
Executive Director, Boston After School & Beyond

Carol R. Johnson
Superintendent, Boston Public Schools

Achieving, Connecting, Thriving: Afterschool and Summer Learning in Collaboration With Schools

Too many young people struggle in school and need more targeted and engaging learning opportunities to succeed. Afterschool and summer programs provide such opportunities to learn and grow, both in a formal school setting and in the community beyond the school walls. For low-income families, however, such programs are in short supply and are typically inaccessible for a variety of reasons (for example, high cost; lack of transportation; or the use of different programming schedules for children of various ages, making coordination of child care difficult).

Research supports what educators and parents have long known: strong afterschool and summer programs produce results for children and youth. There is growing evidence that quality afterschool programs make a positive difference in the areas that contribute to school success—higher attendance, better grades, and improved behavior (Huang et al., 2007; Goerge, Cusick, Wasserman, & Gladden, 2007; Vandell, Reisner, & Pierce, 2007; Durlak & Weissberg, 2007). There is substantial evidence that summer learning loss is a serious problem that disproportionately affects low-income students (Alexander, Entwisle, & Olson, 2007; McCombs et al., 2011). Equally compelling is the mounting evidence that quality programs can stem, or even reverse, summer learning loss and prepare young people to begin the next grade ready to learn and build upon their previous success (Borman, Goetz, & Dowling, 2009; Cooper, Charlton, Valentine, & Muhlenbruck, 2000).

Unfortunately, in the search to find the "silver bullet" for American education, afterschool and summer learning are often considered optional and, in a time of tight budgets, frequently pitted against each other in competition for scarce resources. A more productive approach is to explore afterschool and summer learning as complementary strategies that can combine to strengthen instruction during the regular school year. Understanding and leveraging this connection will enable greater numbers of students to experience academic and developmental success.

Community organizations increasingly have the "people power" to help more young people keep up, catch up, and get motivated to stay in school and learn. These organizations often find it difficult, however, to link their services to struggling students or schools, and vice versa. How can we better harness these expanded learning opportunities to stimulate students' interest and success? What would a well-coordinated, integrated, and sustainable system of afterschool and summer supports look like?

This paper explores how Boston is working to connect afterschool and summer learning, uniting schools and community partners to help more young people achieve, connect, and thrive. Other similar efforts are also emerging across America. Several will be cited near the end of the article, but many more are needed to meet the demand.

A Vision for an Integrated Learning System

Under the leadership of Mayor Thomas M. Menino, Boston has doubled the number of young people in afterschool programs over the past decade. The 21st Century Community Learning Centers program has been a vital source of funding for this expansion in Boston. Recently, major funding from other public and private sources has also been invested in these programs. As a result, nearly every elementary and middle school in the district now offers its students some form of afterschool program. More than 700 organizations offer over 1,700 afterschool and summer programs for Boston's children. This proliferation of programs and community partnerships brings extraordinary potential to address students' academic and social-emotional needs and to stimulate their interests and motivation.

Afterschool and summer learning programs are critical to supplementing instruction and meeting the educational and developmental needs of our young people. They help provide students with the knowledge, skills, and experiences that are critical to success in school, college, careers, and life. They bring resources and approaches that no one school, or even school district, could provide on its own. Moreover, they are generally cost effective when compared to other models because they can take advantage of a wide array of school and community resources that often are underutilized in the afterschool hours and during the summer.

Boston stands as one example of a district that is creating a unified and integrated learning system that addresses the whole child, throughout the whole day and the whole year. This system embraces a comprehensive approach to student learning, drawing on the strengths of a variety of community partners, from sports and the arts to social justice, leadership, and environmental education.

A Framework for School-Community Collaboration

In order to align school, afterschool, and summer, we developed a common vision and shared vocabulary for the skills that students need to succeed in school, work, and life. Boston stakeholders are uniting around a framework to support the implementation of this vision. Derived from the best of the youth development field and afterschool program providers themselves, the Achieving-Connecting-Thriving Framework is informing how schools and community organizations collaborate.

This framework highlights the skills that research from a number of fields, including education and developmental psychology, suggests are important for success in school, college, and 21st century careers.

- *"Achieving" is about self-management skills—the skills necessary to succeed academically, including critical and creative thinking, flexibility, and planning—that help students master an objective or complete a task.*

- *"Connecting" is about relationship skills—including teamwork, communication, and respect—that help students form supportive, positive relationships.*

- *"Thriving" is about perseverance skills—including drive, efficacy, self-awareness, and self-regulation—that help students maintain the effort required to become successful.*

These skills must be nurtured in supportive environments, and afterschool and summer programs represent a valuable opportunity in this area. Successful partner organizations have the ability to provide these skill-building experiences, and their capacity stems from their flexibility in staffing, use of time, and even location. For example, through the Boston Summer Learning Project (which involves selected Boston schools and community partners), students take advantage of the city's broad array of resources, including leading universities, cultural institutions, and natural spaces.

Afterschool and summer programs activate academic content through hands-on, project-based learning. These experiences allow students to apply academic content in tangible ways and to build background knowledge they may have been lacking. They can make learning and school feel more relevant to a student, helping both students and adults answer the age-old question, Why do I have to know this? At the same time, students' interests and aspirations are stimulated by better access to the world around them, and new contexts and styles of working strengthen relationships with adults and with peers.

Collectively, afterschool and summer programs engage and motivate students, build community, and allows teachers and youth development staff to work together focused on the needs of young people. The persistent achievement gap is all too often an access gap because students and families are not sure how to easily find the resources they need. Furthermore, the variety of approaches allows schools and community organizations to test new ideas and understand what works and what needs to be adjusted. Information of this sort is valuable to policy makers, funders, school leaders, and parents.

This kind of learning happens best as part of a citywide agenda, rather than school by school or nonprofit by nonprofit. Boston's partnership agenda is driven by an approach that is student centered, standards aligned, and results focused. The Boston Public Schools and Boston After School & Beyond, an intermediary that catalyzes partnerships among schools, city agencies, community groups, and philanthropy, coordinate strategies at the district level. Funders recognize the power of collaboration, evidenced by the Boston Opportunity Agenda's commitment to summer learning as part of cradle-to-career strategy.

Other cities across America are also working to forge stronger connections and alignment among schools, afterschool, and summer learning. Interested readers should explore how the following cities are making better use of time, partnerships, and public and private funding streams:

- *The Providence After School Alliance (www.mypasa.org) and Nashville After Zone Alliance (www.naza.org), which are structuring geographic hubs of learning and development focused on middle school students*

- *The After-School Corporation (TASC) in New York City (www.tascorp. org), which is expanding the school day, drawing a variety of financial and community resources*

- *After School Matters in Chicago (www.afterschoomatters.org), which is providing high school students with apprenticeships to develop marketable skills*

- *Big Thought in Dallas (www.bigthought.org), which is making "imagination part of everyday learning" by integrating the arts with education*

What's Next?

A full decade into the 21st century, it is well understood that responsibility for educating children cannot reside with just one sector of society, especially if we are to realize our national potential on the global stage. Schools cannot do it alone—and neither can parents. Even together, schools and parents are not necessarily equipped to overcome the pernicious effects of poverty. To develop our students to their full potential, we must harness talent and resources from across multiple sectors—from schools and community organizations to businesses and institutions of higher education. But schools and community organizations cannot work in isolation. The systems must be aligned and the learning goals in schools must be reinforced at home and in the community.

As federal policy makers look to reauthorize the Elementary and Secondary Education Act, they should recognize that the achievement, connection, and opportunity gaps are inextricably linked. Low-income students fall behind their higher-income peers because they do not have access to the same opportunities, many of which afterschool and summer programs can provide. Also, these students often do not have regular connections to community organizations and resources that can help them learn, set goals, and develop aspirations. Public policy should promote nimble, flexible, and cost-effective approaches that help school districts work closely with community partners to address the specific needs of students in targeted ways.

As we build on more than a decade of growth and success in afterschool and summer learning, we look forward to advancing this agenda and addressing the challenges that face all of us. For example, how do we make sure there is equitable distribution of these programs? How do we ensure program quality and connect students with the opportunities that best meet their specific needs and interests? How do we ensure that they serve students who could benefit most, including English language learners and those with disabilities? How do we create sustainable and affordable partnership models?

The answers to these challenges are well within reach. Working together, school districts and their nonprofit partners are establishing citywide agendas that merge the best of afterschool and youth development with public education. Funding opportunities for strategies to expand learning and development are in short supply. That is why municipal and school district leadership must work together. Intermediaries also can play a pivotal role in leveraging and coordinating resources and organizations to link school, afterschool, and summer learning strategies.

Limited funding also means that the 21st Century Community Learning Centers program remains an essential resource, perhaps now more than ever. It is the only large-scale funding source for expanding learning afterschool and during the summer that catalyzes school-community partnerships and family engagement around a locally designed agenda of learning improvement. It is critical to realizing our vision of an integrated learning system that applies the strengths of schools and community partners—after school and during the summer—in ways that build the skills necessary for school, work, and life.

Local school, community and municipal leaders can take a number of actions to grow and improve expanded learning opportunities after school and during the summers:

- *Set community goals under which various partners can organize themselves, play to their strengths, and measure progress. In Boston, the Superintendent's Acceleration Agenda has been adopted by private funders and community partners.*

- *Establish a regular venue where coordinated strategies are devised and implemented across sectors with monitoring to ensure mutual accountability. Boston Mayor Thomas Menino appointed a Partnership Council, managed by Boston After School & Beyond, for this purpose.*

- *Build a data system that catalogues opportunities, allows parents and other caring adults to find appropriate program matches for students, and supplies information for analysis of the afterschool sector.*

- *Document the lessons learned between schools and partners, as well as across sectors, to maximize quality and build on success.*

ABOUT THE AUTHORS

Chris Smith is executive director of Boston After School & Beyond, a citywide intermediary dedicated to increasing learning opportunities for Boston's youth by aligning school, afterschool, and summer efforts. Prior to joining this organization in 2008, Smith led partnership, policy, and measurement strategies in the areas of K–12 education, high school and college completion, and workforce development for the Boston Private Industry Council and for the U.S. Department of Education.

Carol R. Johnson has served as superintendent of the Boston Public Schools since 2007, having been appointed by a unanimous vote of the Boston School Committee after a national search. Under her leadership, the 57,000-student district has focused on closing achievement and access gaps as well as graduating all students prepared for college and career success. Johnson previously served as superintendent in Memphis, Tennessee, and Minneapolis, Minnesota.

REFERENCES

Alexander, K. L., Entwisle, D. R., & Olson, L. S. (2007). Lasting consequences of the summer learning gap. *American Sociological Review, 72*(2), 167–180.

Borman, G. D., Goetz, M. E., & Dowling, N. M. (2009). Halting the summer achievement slide: A randomized field trial of the KindergARTen summer camp. *Journal of Education for Students Placed at Risk, 14*, 133–147.

Chaplin, D., & Capizzano, J. (2006). *Impacts of a summer learning program: A random assignment study of Building Educated Leaders for Life (BELL)*. Retrieved from Urban Institute website: http://www.urban.org/publications/411350.html

Cooper, H., Charlton, K., Valentine, J. C., & Muhlenbruck, L. (with Borman, G. D.). (2000). Making the most of summer school: A meta-analytic and narrative review [Monograph]. *Monographs of the Society for Research in Child Development, 65*(1), 1–118.

Durlak, J. A., & Weissberg, R. P. (2007). *The impact of after-school programs that promote personal and social skills*. Retrieved from Collaborative for Academic, Social, and Emotional Learning website: http://casel.org/publications/the-impact-of-after-school-programs-that-promote-personal-and-social-skills/

Goerge, R. M., Cusick, G. R., Wasserman, M., & Gladden, R. M. (2007). *After-school programs and academic impact: A study of Chicago's After School Matters* (Issue Brief No. 112). Retrieved from Chapin Hall Center for Children website: http://www.chapinhall.org/research/brief/after-school-programs-and-academic-impact

Huang, D., Coordt, A., La Torre, D., Leon, S., Miyoshi, J., Pérez, P., & Peterson, C. (2007). *The afterschool hours: Examining the relationship between afterschool staff-based social capital and student engagement in LA's BEST* (CSE Tech. Rep. No. 712). Los Angeles, CA: University of California, National Center for Research on Evaluation, Standards, and Student Testing (CRESST).

McCombs, J. S., Augustine, C. H., Schwartz, H. L., Bodilly, S. J., McInnis, B., Lichter, D. S., & Cross, A. B. (2011). *Making summer count: How summer programs can boost children's learning*. Retrieved from RAND Education website: http://www.rand.org/pubs/monographs/MG1120.html

Vandell, D. L., Reisner, E. R., & Pierce, K. M. (2007). *Outcomes linked to high-quality afterschool programs: Longitudinal findings from the study of promising afterschool programs*. Retrieved from University of California-Irvine website: http://www.gse.uci.edu/childcare/pdf/afterschool/PP%20Longitudinal%20Findings%20Final%20Report.pdf

Lisa Pray
Associate Professor of the Practice
Vanderbilt University, Peabody College

Supporting English Language Learners in School and in Afterschool and Summers

The number of school-age children entering U.S. schools speaking little or no English has grown exponentially in the last 10 to 15 years. From the 1997–98 school year to the 2008–09 school year, the number of English language learners (ELLs) enrolled in public schools increased from 3.5 million to 5.3 million (National Clearinghouse for English Language Acquisition, 2011). In tandem with these demographic increases, No Child Left Behind accountability measures have spotlighted significant lags in achievement of ELLs in critical academic areas, including reading and mathematics (Garcia & Frede, 2010). ELL student achievement continues to lag behind non-ELL student achievement at all socioeconomic levels, but this gap is most acute for students at the lowest socioeconomic levels (Garcia & Frede, 2010).

Understanding and closing this persistent achievement gap requires a multifaceted approach to supporting ELLs in school and beyond the school day and year. This article focuses on one promising approach: afterschool and summer learning programs specifically designed to support the linguistic, cultural, and academic needs of students who are learning English as an additional language. On balance, participation in afterschool, summer learning, and other community-based programs has been associated with improved academic achievement and improved linguistic and social development of ELLs (Tellez & Waxman, 2010; Hirsch, 2011). Moreover, helping ELL students improve their English not only supports their success in school but also can benefit all students in a school.

The body of research on the general benefits of afterschool and summer learning programs is robust and encouraging. Those students who regularly attend well-structured afterschool and/or summer learning programs demonstrate higher rates

> ... participation in afterschool, summer learning, and other community-based programs has been associated with improved academic achievement and improved linguistic and social development of ELLs.

of attendance in school, have fewer discipline referrals, are more prepared for the academic rigors of school, and demonstrate increased achievement in core academic areas such as mathematics, science, reading, and language arts (Martin, et al., 2007; Farmer-Hinton, Sass, & Schroeder, 2009; Huang & Cho, 2009).

Generally, afterschool and summer learning programs are most successful when they are structured to offer (1) homework support, including specific study skills and motivational strategies structured to complement the school curriculum; (2) staff members who share the same linguistic and cultural backgrounds as the students; and (3) constructive ways to include parents and other family members in the program (Huang & Cho, 2009; Wong, 2010; David, 2011; Rodriguez-Valls, 2011). When serving ELLs, each of these features must be designed to boost the English language development of students, a complex process that is inherently social and best developed through varied and authentic learning opportunities. Authentic learning opportunities consist of activities that intrinsically motivate students to learn and are directly tied to students' linguistic and cultural background and interests (Weisburd, 2008; Wong, 2010; Rodriguez-Valls, 2011). Each of the above aspects of successful afterschool and summer learning programs is described below, specifically with regard to implications for serving ELLs.

Homework Support

Afterschool and summer learning programs can help students negotiate the complicated task of keeping up with grade-level academic content while concurrently developing their English proficiency, thus reducing the gaps in academic achievement between ELLs and their native English-speaking peers. The strongest programs complement and extend school activities and programs. School curricula, however, are bound by district or state-level mandates that often impose isolated learning tasks and tight time constraints. Curricula for afterschool and summer learning programs serving ELLs should include a greater number of project-based learning activities and greater amounts of time to focus on the activities. These projects are more personally meaningful to ELL students and offer opportunities for authentic uses of language and support of students' culture. As Hirsh (2011) reports, such activities and projects allow "positive aspects of youth culture to flourish," including "strong relationships, spontaneity, creativity, expressiveness, engagement with music, knowing how to have fun, and idealism."

Students, teachers, and administrators alike recognize the value of high quality afterschool and summer learning programs. Litke (2009) surveyed and interviewed culturally and linguistically diverse students who attended afterschool programs and found that the students placed great value on having the extra time after school to complete homework assignments, work one-on-one with teachers, engage in a structured review of homework, and review for tests.

Quality Staff With Connections to the Community

Afterschool and summer learning programs have been shown to promote positive relationships among students, school personnel, and members of the community (Anderson-Butcher, 2010). For example, the highly acclaimed program in Los Angeles, LA's BEST, intentionally recruits instructional staff from the school neighborhood. Students relate more with mentors from their neighborhood because they share the same or similar cultural and linguistic backgrounds. LA's BEST has demonstrated long-term positive effects on attendance, academic achievement, and lowered drop-out rates in high school (Huang & Cho, 2009; Anderson-Butcher, 2010; Sanger, 2011).

Programs in Chicago, Los Angeles, and New York also staff programs with adults from the same or similar neighborhoods who share students' linguistic and cultural backgrounds. These staff members help students cope with stressors that are part of the shared experience of living in the same community. They also help young people develop the knowledge, attitudes, and skills needed to navigate the complexities of society (Farmer-Hinton, et al., 2009; Wong, 2010; Hirsch, 2011; Sanger, 2011). One positive consequence of recruiting staff directly from the school's surrounding community is that the afterschool/summer learning staff members often develop long-term careers in education and fill critical administrative and instructional roles within the school. As a result, the faculty and administrative pools more accurately reflect the cultural and linguistic backgrounds of the students they serve (Sanger, 2011), helping all students broaden their learning opportunities and experiences.

Connections With Parents

Well-designed afterschool and summer learning programs can assist immigrant families in navigating complex U.S. school structures through culturally relevant understandings of the community (Wong, 2010). These understandings are critical to developing a "funds-of-knowledge" approach in which the cultural and linguistic strengths that students and their families bring to the learning environment are recognized and supported. Such afterschool programs allow for language-rich educational opportunities and authentic learning activities that enhance the instruction provided during the regular school day.

Rodriguez-Valls (2011) found positive parent partnerships in an afterschool cooperative in which parents and their children practiced reading strategies together as they read books in Spanish and English. Participants (including parents and children alike) became keenly aware of how they could leverage their Spanish literacy skills to develop their knowledge of English, realizing that "their knowledge in both languages was an asset to reading their world with biliterate eyes." Building parents' English skills helps both them and their children be more successful.

In addition, afterschool programs can be deliberately constructed to pass along to children a connection to their heritage culture and language by providing a place for children to share their ethnic values, identity, and friendships. Such programs are designed to teach students more about their native language, relying on parental and community support, along with appropriate teaching methodology and materials, to help children become bilingual in their heritage language and English. Siegal (2004) examines such a program in Arizona in which Japanese parents started an afterschool program, assisted in staffing the program, and created the curriculum to ensure that their children maintain the language and traditions of Japan. In a global economy, knowing English and another language or two is a tremendous asset for Americans of all backgrounds.

Participants (including parents and children alike) became keenly aware of how they could leverage their Spanish literacy skills to develop their knowledge of English, realizing that "their knowledge in both languages was an asset to reading their world with biliterate eyes."

Recommendations and Conclusion

Afterschool and summer learning programs are playing a larger and more significant role in addressing the academic, linguistic, and social needs of ELL children and their families. If the programs are designed and staffed by members of the community that reflect children's linguistic and cultural backgrounds and that complement the school curriculum, the likely result will be gains in ELL academic achievement.

The most effective programs leverage ELL students' bilingual abilities, while assisting with homework, recruiting staff from the local community, and engaging parents. Since English language acquisition is an active process requiring frequent, purposeful interaction with English content, the most useful afterschool activities will be meaningful and closely tied to real objects and enterprises in the students' world to provide a concrete context for words and ideas. To the extent possible, activities and support should be provided to bridge the students' primary language, while simultaneously giving students authentic opportunities and encouragement to practice responding in English. In addition, program leaders should vary the style and medium of communication whenever possible. Spoken directions should also be written, for example, and gestures should accompany oral language. Students will more likely engage in these activities that take into account their previous cognitive, social, and cultural and linguistic experiences.

For More Information

The following websites offer resources for developing effective afterschool and summer learning programs targeting the needs of English language learners.

Afterschool Alliance gathers and disseminates information about effective afterschool programs. Articles range from general recommendations to summations of current research describing how programs can support ELLs. For articles related to English learners, see http://www. afterschoolalliance.org/issue_49_ELLs.cfm

Center for Applied Linguistics provides a comprehensive range of research-based information, tools, and resources related to language acquisition and culture. http://www.cal.org/

Institute of Educational Sciences, What Works Clearinghouse reports on empirically validated practices that support the literacy of English language learners. Their website provides a helpful, cohesive guide entitled "Effective Literacy and English Language Instruction for English Learners in the Elementary Grades." http://ies.ed.gov/ncee/wwc/findwhatworks.aspx

National Clearinghouse of English Language Acquisition provides many resources for ELL teachers and program administrators including resources for parents (written in six languages), resources for program developers, synopses of useful teaching strategies, and other useful guides. http://www.ncela.gwu.edu

A Snapshot of Programs Supporting English Language Learners

- *Community Lodgings in Alexandria, Virginia, serves homeless and low-income families by providing transitional housing as well as career counseling and budget mentoring for parents. Their Youth Education Program, funded through the 21st Century Community Learning Centers initiative, provides academic assistance, a safe alternative for gang influence, and a focus on avoidance of at-risk behaviors. Community Lodgings serves a population that is entirely low-income and 82% Latino, including many ELLs. Middle school students in the program for 2 years or more passed their and English SOL tests by a rate 10% higher than their Hispanic peers.*

- *Latin American Youth Center (LAYC) in Washington, DC, serves a predominantly Latino population, including many ELL students. LAYC's varied multilingual afterschool program offerings include educational enhancement, social services, workforce investment, art and media, as well as advocacy. In the 2008–09 school year, 58% of elementary students receiving regular tutoring through LAYC's Americorps partnership increased either their language arts or math grade by a full letter grade over the course of the year, and 31% increased both math and language arts grades by a full letter grade.*

- *Montana Migrant Education Program in Helena, Montana, serves children of migrant workers who have changed school districts within the past 3 years to accommodate a parent seeking temporary or seasonal employment; 70% of its participants are ELLs. Montana Migrant Education Program focuses on academic achievement and self-esteem building for students who are disadvantaged in education by language barriers, poverty, and a migratory lifestyle. During its 2010 summer program, 79% of participants improved in reading by an average of 11%, and 99% of participants improved in math by an average of 20%.*

- *The CORAL Program in California is intentionally structured to create strong relationships among students and between students and staff. Staff members are often young adults who share a cultural and linguistic background with the students, and they often capitalize on that connection to create multicultural, multilingual learning opportunities. Staff members also use their knowledge of students' languages and cultures to create high quality literacy lessons that provide students an opportunity to share their own experiences, family backgrounds, languages, and cultures and to deepen their understanding of, and connection to, a variety of cultures. English learners participating in CORAL achieve academic gains in equal measure to other children in the program—suggesting that CORAL offers a promising approach to strengthening literacy skills in the afterschool hours.*

Reference: Afterschool Alliance: Issue Brief #49: *English Language Learners: Becoming Fluent in Afterschool* (2011)

ABOUT THE AUTHOR

Lisa Pray is an associate professor of the practice of English language learners at Vanderbilt University, Peabody College. Her research interests include understanding second language acquisition in the context of educating English language learners, special education of culturally and linguistically diverse students, and assessment of English language learners. Pray received her PhD from Arizona State University.

REFERENCES

Afterschool Alliance. (2011). *English language learners: Becoming fluent in afterschool* (Issue Brief No. 49). Retrieved from http://www.afterschoolalliance.org/issue_49_ELLs.cfm

Anderson–Butcher, D. (2010). The promise of afterschool programs for promoting school connectedness. *The Prevention Researcher, 17*(3), 11–20.

David, J. L. (2011). After–school programs can pay off. *Educational Leadership, 68*(8), 84–85.

Farmer-Hinton, R. L., Sass, D. A., & Schroeder, M. (2009). What difference does an hour make? Examining the effects of an afterschool program. *Planning and Changing, 40,* 160–182.

Garcia, E. E., & Frede, E. C. (2010). *Young English language learners: Current research and emerging directions for practice and policy.* New York, NY: Teachers College Press.

Hirsch, B. J. (2011). Learning and development in after-school programs. *Phi Delta Kappan, 92*(5), 66–69.

Huang, D., & Cho, J. (2009). Academic enrichment in high–functioning homework after-school programs. *Journal of Research in Childhood Education, 23,* 382–392.

Litke, E. (2009). After the bell rings: Student perceptions of after–school. *Teachers College Record, 111,* 1954–1970.

Martin, D., Martin, M., Gibson, S. S., & Wilkins, J. (2007). Increasing prosocial behavior and academic achievement among adolescent African American males. *Adolescence, 42,* 689–698.

National Clearinghouse of English Language Acquisition. (2011). *The growing number of English learner students* 1998/99–2008/09. Retrieved from http://www.ncela.gwu.edu/files/uploads/9/growingLEP_0809.pdf

Rodriguez-Valls, F. (2011). Coexisting languages: Reading bilingual books with biliterate eyes. *Bilingual Research Journal, 34*, 19–37.

Siegel, S. Y. (2004). A case study of one Japanese heritage language program in Arizona. *Bilingual Research Journal, 28*, 123–134.

Téllez, K., & Waxman, H. C. (2010). A review of research on effective community programs for English language learners. *The School Community Journal, 20*(1), 103–119.

Tung, R., Diez, V., Gagnon, L., Uriate, M., Stazesky, P., de los Reyes, E., & Bolomey, A. (2011). *Learning from consistently high performing and improving schools for English language learners in Boston Public Schools.* Retrieved from http://scholarworks.umb.edu/cgi/viewcontent.cgi?article=1156&context=gaston_pubs

Weisburd, C. (2008). Gaining a voice after school. *Education Week, 27*(25), 28–29.

Wong, N-W. A. (2010). "Cuz they care about the people who goes there": The multiple roles of the community–based youth center in providing "youth(comm)unity" for a low–income Chinese-American youth. *Urban Education, 45*, 708–739.

Kara N. Smith
Project Consultant/Trainer,
Kids Included Together (KIT)

Mary M. Shea
Project Consultant/Trainer,
Kids Included Together (KIT)

Providing Access to Training and Resources to Afterschool and Summer Learning Professionals to Promote Full and Meaningful Inclusion for All Children

A growing number of parents of children with disabilities, as well as the regular classroom teachers who work with their children, are recognizing the value of including these children in afterschool and summer learning programs. Such programs often provide more natural environments where children with disabilities can experience joyful learning and develop genuine friendships with same-age peers without disabilities.

While there is not yet nearly enough access to summer and afterschool programs for children with disabilities, programs that provide expanded learning opportunities are reporting notable increases in the enrollment of children who require some type of accommodation or support. As a result, the need has never been greater for afterschool and youth development professionals to have access to resources that will support them in successfully welcoming and making accommodations for students with disabilities or special needs, including those with learning differences or those who exhibit challenging behaviors.

Extensive research has been conducted on the benefits of training afterschool and summer learning providers. The relationship between high quality professional development and child and youth success in programs that extend beyond the school day has been well documented in the literature (Bouffard & Little, 2004).

With 15 years of providing support to afterschool and summer programs, Kids Included Together (KIT)—a national nonprofit organization—has witnessed major cultural transformations in afterschool and summer learning programs when staff begin to recognize and acknowledge the value of inclusive programs. The process for staff is often described as a journey: The first step involves adopting a philosophy of inclusion followed by learning the skills and best practices to include all children meaningfully. By receiving high-quality professional development on inclusion and accommodations, staff will better the lives of children, families, and programs, and they will even see a positive change in their own lives. It is vital, however, that the training and resources are research based and validated to ensure that caregivers are receiving the most effective professional development possible.

KIT has recently conducted a series of efficacy and validity studies to generate evidence that its training and resources lead to the full and meaningful inclusion of children with disabilities in out-of-school-time programs. It was KIT's expectation that validating its services and strategies would help promote their implementation throughout the country and overseas, with an eye towards allowing more children of *all* abilities to be fully included in expanded learning programs worldwide. These studies found that there is a statistically significant positive relationship between KIT's partnership with an organization and the beliefs, attitudes, practices, policies, and relationships with families within those organizations (Smith, 2011).

> Providers reported that they felt more comfortable including children with disabilities, felt more supported when including children of all abilities, were more likely to partner with families to ensure the success of their children, and were implementing accommodations in the program on a daily basis (Smith, 2011).

In a large-scale needs assessment, KIT collected data from caregivers in expanded learning programs in four different regions of the country. After an analysis of the data, a number of themes emerged. KIT established that, in general, caregivers did not feel prepared to include children with disabilities, they were unsure what types of accommodations to utilize in the program, and they were unsure how to communicate with parents and families about challenges their children were having in the program. After 1 year of participating in KIT training and utilizing KIT, however, providers reported that they felt more comfortable including children with disabilities, felt more supported when including children of all abilities, were more likely to partner with families to ensure the success of their children, and were implementing accommodations in the program on a daily basis (Smith, 2011).

Unfortunately, the same barriers that exist in the delivery of traditional in-school professional development also exist in the expanded learning field, including restricted budgets, a lack of necessary resources, time and geographical constraints, and inflexibility in caregivers' demanding schedules. To ensure that all caregivers have access to training, KIT has developed a program to combat those barriers. KIT has adopted a blended learning style that allows caregivers to access training at a time and in a way that is most appropriate for them.

Studying in more depth the KIT delivery system can provide strong clues for afterschool and summer learning intermediaries and professional development providers regarding the range of learning opportunities and supports needed to improve professional practices. KIT delivers research-based professional development through face-to-face training, eLearning modules, webinars, print materials, KIT Support Center phone calls and e-mails, and one-on-one assistance. When participants complete live trainings, eLearning modules, or webinars, they are eligible to receive continuing education units (CEUs). KIT's National Training Center on Inclusion is an authorized provider of CEUs through the International Association for Continuing Education and Training.

KIT trainers travel both domestically and overseas to deliver 2-hour face-to-face trainings to afterschool and summer learning staff. Prior to the visit, an inclusion specialist discusses the needs of the program with a director and determines the training that will best meet the needs of the staff. Trainings are interactive, include a great deal of movement, and allow for collaboration between participants.

KIT also offers training modules through interactive, self-paced online modules that are designed to take about 30 minutes to complete. KIT tracks participant progress on the eLearning modules and provides certificates for completion of the "Opening Doors to Inclusive Programs" series. Completers can, in addition, receive CEUs for the successful completion of the four core modules.

Research has revealed that the benefits of KIT's training and resources extend well beyond the expanded learning program itself (Smith, 2011). For example, communication is a key component of all of KIT's professional development. Caregivers are provided training on communicating with parents, teachers in the child's school, and other caregivers that work with the child. One communications tool that has been found to be effective is a "Communication Journal for Parents and Providers." This tool is designed to facilitate communication between program staff and parents of children with disabilities who exhibit challenging behavior. Caregivers implement accommodations for a specific child in the program; when the accommodation is found to be successful, the provider documents it in the communication journal and sends it home to share with parents. The journal supports consistency, celebrates successes, and encourages collaboration and trust between the home and the caregivers.

In presenting at more than 20 state afterschool and 21st Century Community Learning Centers conferences, KIT has often been the only organization providing assistance and support for inclusion and accommodation. While KIT welcomes more organizations working in this important area, we are also pleased with comments from afterschool providers who have participated in our training. The following comments help frame how providers have found KIT's training to be helpful.

From a staff member from a large provider that runs 21st Century Community Learning Centers in San Diego County, as well as other afterschool and summer learning programs:

After I attended a KIT training this summer, I realized that you have to be willing to accommodate every child with a positive attitude. Taking the time to know the children and know what the children like to do and incorporating it in the program can make them feel connected.

From another staff member from the same San Diego provider:

KIT trainings over the summer helped me understand that accommodations such as visual rest spots in the classroom can improve the outcome of behavior in some of my students. I like that all the information is applicable to my work area and I truly learn and enjoy KIT trainings.

From the director of United Youth Theater in Hartford, Connecticut:

There are so many misconceptions around disabilities, and too many people approach inclusion with a formulaic, often misguided, approach to this is how things "should" be done. KIT and NTCI help partners move away from those things. They not only "get inclusion" but they understand the behaviors, strategies, and best practices that can help their partners make inclusion a reality.

The most regularly noted benefit of KIT's training and resources, however, are the clear, easily communicated recommendations for accommodations in the expanded learning time environments, whether classrooms, stages, or outdoor spaces. Commonly suggested recommendations for including all children in the program include the following: The most regularly noted benefit of KIT's training and resources, however, are the clear, easily communicated recommendations for accommodations in the expanded learning time environments, whether classrooms, stages, or outdoor spaces. Commonly suggested recommendations for including all children in the program include the following:

- *Staff should become more intentional and skilled observers by documenting what environmental influences impact a child's learning or behavior, e.g., ratios, the physical, sensory and/or social-emotional environment.*

- *Staff should ensure attention to transitions and use appropriate tools to support transitions, as well as provide visual supports to increase comprehension and processing.*

- *Staff should be intentional and clear about behavioral expectations for children with challenges; however, they also should consistently and descriptively reinforce appropriate behaviors every time a child complies with direction or a staff request.*

- *Rather than assign a single, dedicated staff member to support a child with special needs, KIT recommends that staff who are inclusion facilitators design accommodations that will naturally include several other staff peers, thereby changing staff-to-child ratios, as well as modeling respectful interactions between children with and without disabilities.*

- *That said, program staff and leadership should also be cognizant of shifting caregivers throughout the day, particularly in a summer learning program. This limits consistency and predictability, which can be particularly difficult on young children or youth who might be more emotionally vulnerable.*

Conclusion

Providing training and resources to program staff ensures that children with and without disabilities have an equal opportunity to participate in expanded learning and recreational opportunities. Although there is a great deal of support for children with disabilities during the school day, similar supports should be available in the expanded learning field so that this group of children can take advantages of the benefits of afterschool and summer learning and enrichment opportunities. It is imperative, therefore, that afterschool and summer programs both reach out to include children with disabilities and provide the professional development for their staff to make these essential learning opportunities engaging and effective for all children and youth.

The professional development experiences offered by KIT have generated overwhelmingly positive responses from afterschool and summer learning professionals who have participated. With the new empirical evidence validating the efficacy of KIT's training and resources (Smith, 2011), it is imperative that KIT and others like them disseminate resources and communicate trainings to afterschool and summer learning programs across the nation. By arming all caregivers with the tools necessary to fully and meaningfully include children with disabilities, the field can ensure that all children have the opportunity to benefit from expanded learning opportunities in their communities.

For More Information

Additional information and recommendations on including children with disabilities can be found at www.kitonline.org. You will also gain access to KIT's eLearning modules, online instructional videos, sessions from KIT's National Training Center on Inclusion, and a variety of other resources.

ABOUT THE AUTHORS

Kara N. Smith began her career working as a high school history teacher and tennis coach. Her subsequent work has included providing professional development training and conducting evaluations of large-scale, federally funded grants. She has presented research findings at numerous conferences and has published articles in various educational research and online technology journals. She holds a doctorate from Boston College in educational research, measurement, and evaluation.

Mary M. Shea has served in nearly every professional capacity at Kids Included Together (KIT) over the past 14 years. She currently serves as an organizational and leadership consultant and regularly represents KIT at regional and national conferences. She has keynoted at several conferences and has published articles in a number of professional journals. Shea holds a doctoral degree in education sciences and leadership studies from the University of San Diego.

REFERENCES

Bouffard, S., & Little, P. M. D. (2004). *Promoting quality through professional development: A framework for evaluation* (Issues and Opportunities in Out-of-School Time Evaluation Brief No. 8). Cambridge, MA: Harvard Family Research Project.

Smith, K. (2011). *Organizational integration: How KIT is promoting collaboration and results within organizations.* Retrieved from http://www.kitonline.org/html/about/documents/HowKITisPromotingCollaborationandResultsWithinOrganizations.pdf

Expanding Skills and Horizons

2

Gene R. Carter
Executive Director and Chief Executive Officer, ASCD
(formerly the Association for Supervision
and Curriculum Development)

The Importance of Educating and Developing Many Aspects of the "Whole" Child

Each second we live is a new and unique moment of the universe, a moment that will never be again. And what do we teach our children? We teach them that two and two make four and that Paris is the capital of France. When will we also teach them what they are?

We should say to each of them: do you know what you are? You are a marvel. You are unique. In all the years that have passed, there has never been another child like you . . .

You may become a Shakespeare, a Michelangelo, a Beethoven. You have the capacity for anything. Yes, you are a marvel.

- Pablo Casals

Imagine a conversation about learning. In many places and situations the conversation would quickly change from "learning" to "achievement on standardized tests." In others, it would shift from learning to teaching. But in far too few cases would it remain on "learning"—the one concept that specifically and unequivocally draws our thoughts to the child as he or she exists now and as he or she will exist in the future. To be clear, achievement is not the same as learning. And, as any educator willing to tell the truth will admit, neither is teaching.

Learning is what prepares young people for meaningful citizenship, employment, postsecondary education, and active participation in a global society. It is developmental and experiential. It is not restricted to time or space, adult qualification or status, intent or accident. Learning is the only thing that matters. And children do learn. The question we must ask ourselves is whether they learn that which we believe will help them succeed.

> Learning is the only thing that matters. And children do learn. The question we must ask ourselves is whether they learn that which we believe will help them succeed.

At ASCD, we believe, and decades of research confirm, that certain conditions maximize children's opportunity to learn. We have committed through our Whole Child Initiative to ensuring that each child, in each school, in each community is healthy, safe, engaged, supported, and challenged. Joined by more than 60 partners across the spectrum of education associations, recreation and health organizations, arts, history, civics, and other content-based nonprofits in the United States and beyond, we have called on educators, families, community organizations, and policy makers to change the conversation from one of "schooling" to one of "learning" and to take definitive action to realize a vision for the whole child that currently only exists on paper.

We seek nothing less than to revolutionize the way children learn. This means during the typical school day, as well as by including engaging expanded learning opportunities in afterschool, weekends, and summers as part of that equation, especially for struggling students.

For too long, in too many schools, young people have been provided a learning experience that so undermotivates, undereducates, underprepares, and underincludes that they are left reaching for remedial preparation for the careers, further education, and civic participation they seek. In the worst situations, young people are neither healthy nor safe, neither engaged nor supported, and certainly not challenged.

In others, schools with seemingly healthy school cultures (little bullying, supportive staff-student relationships, wraparound supports for families, etc.) fail to hold high expectations for each child and instead create an environment of academic pity that fails to prepare even graduates for meaningful career, college, and civic next steps. In still others, the emphasis on academic rigor, rote memorization, and test preparation is so disproportionate that students experience high levels of social-emotional stress. This leads to a disconnection from school and the community and creates boredom in a culture of repetition from school that can extend into afterschool, weekend, and summer activities if we do not design and deliver expanded learning opportunities so they are more engaging, more personalized, more enriching, and include school-community collaboration and family involvement. Rather than a broadening of learning, more of the same only longer will leave increasing numbers of young people unprepared for anything beyond the world of multiple-choice exams. We can and must do better both during the regular school day as well as in quality expanded learning programs after school and during the summer, which are typically less hampered by too much of the educational system's "red tape" that regulates the typical day and year.

In the current system, of course, children learn. They learn that only some kinds of kids make it. They learn that art and physical education are "special." They learn that creativity is for free time. They learn that information, skills, interests, and opinions are irrelevant if they are not on the test and that scores define their worth. This needs to change during the regular school day if we are to be successful, but afterschool and summer programs through school-community partnerships can also can be a good source of arts and creative learning, physical fitness and health, engagement in hands-on science, learning about the world, using digital learning to expand horizons—all building on and expanding the school day and the very essence of learning.

While the United States continues to pursue a regimen of "if at first you don't succeed, do the same thing longer or fire everyone involved" thinking, the rest of the world seeks opportunities to stimulate creativity, critical thinking, content application, and joy in the learning process. They intentionally and strategically move away from the standardized testing that serves as the North Star of the U.S. system of educational reform and find new options to provide seamless experiences from home to school to after school to work to life.

What if we closed the believing-doing gap that leads us to believe that each child should be healthy, safe, engaged, supported, and challenged, while we simultaneously pursue actions that defeat exactly that purpose? What if, instead, each child entered school healthy and learned about and practiced a healthy lifestyle? What if each child learned in an environment that was physically and emotionally safe for children and adults? What if broad learning, and not narrow multiple-choice tests, allowed her to be actively engaged in learning—in school, after school, on weekends, and during breaks—that connected her both to school and to the community? What if he had access to personalized learning unbound by time and space, supported by qualified, caring adults? What if they all were challenged academically and prepared for success in college or further education and for employment and participation in a global economy? What if the flexibility of afterschool, weekend, and summer programs were leveraged to directly connect more young people, particularly those who are struggling, to see and experience careers and learn about college?

> While the United States continues to pursue a regimen of "if at first you don't succeed, do the same thing longer or fire everyone involved" thinking, the rest of the world seeks opportunities to stimulate creativity, critical thinking, content application, and joy in the learning process.

We can make this vision of a system focused on learning the reality for each child. Together we can eliminate the barriers of time, money, geography, role, and expertise to ensure that each child is healthy so that she may learn in pace with her development. By expanding learning opportunities after school and in summers, we can ensure that each child is safe—academically, emotionally, and physically—so that he may participate in active, authentic, experiential learning opportunities. We can engage students in aligned learning from content area to content area, learning venue to learning venue that reflects their interests and opinions and connects them in meaningful ways to the communities in which they live. We can surround children with adults in a variety of school and community-based roles who conscientiously and consciously attend to the model they provide, the relationship they foster, and the expectations they hold. We can change the conversation from schooling to learning and challenge the very definition of success by raising the bar of performance for ourselves as educators, organizations, and citizens.

Now is the time to move toward the leading edge of learning in expanded opportunities afterschool, summers, weekends and through school-community partnerships. I invite you to leap; to take bold action; to revolutionize the way you learn, teach, and lead so that each child among us learns each day that he or she is a marvel.

ABOUT THE AUTHOR

Gene R. Carter is a veteran educator with experience as a private and public school teacher, public school administrator, superintendent of schools, and university professor. He is active in community, business, and civic organizations. He assumed his position of executive director and CEO of ASCD (formerly the Association for Supervision and Curriculum Development) in 1992.

Milton Chen
Senior Fellow, Th
Educational Fou

The Rise of *Any Time, Any Place, Any Path, Any Pace* Learning: Afterschool and Summer as the New American Frontier for Innovative Learning

Pause for a just a second. . . . Take a moment to think about the sheer number of fundamental changes and major trends that have affected our students, families, and education over the past decade.

Some might acknowledge that we're lucky to be living in a unique time in history—a time in which global, social, and economic forces in the early 21st century have rewritten the rules we lived by in the 20th century, in politics, economics, and now education, globally. Others might see these changes as challenging, perhaps even frightening.

Regardless of your perspective, these changes are dramatically changing what our students and their families face in order to be equipped to live, learn, and succeed in the 21st century. New types of learning opportunities, partnerships, and time and space configurations are emerging. The wave of the future is evident in new and expanded options for learning after school, over the weekend, and during the summer through new school-family-community partnerships.

We have crossed over what was once a distant horizon, barely a glimmer in a futurist's eye. A new landscape of learning is coming into sharper focus. As NYU lecturer and author Clay Shirky (2009) says in his marvelous TED talk, "The moment we're living through is [seeing] the largest increase in expressive capability in human history." Everyone—notably in our younger generation—can now be a producer of knowledge and not just a consumer of someone else's version of it. Today's learners were born digital and are used to having the world of information at their fingertips and in their pockets.

2010 may mark the first year of the 21st century in education, when we crossed the chasm between the analog and digital worlds in education. Educators and policy makers in the United States and abroad are embracing a new willingness to think differently

education, what I call the Thinking Edge of innovation in schools (Chen, 2010). Today, we can see, much more clearly than even 3 years ago, how learning can occur any time, any place, any path, any pace." Schools and homes continue to be important places for learning, but not exclusively.

Many education experts, such as Bob Wise from the Alliance for Excellent Education, Michael Levine from the Joan Ganz Cooney Center at Sesame Workshop, and Alexis Menten of the Asia Society, understand the importance of the "third learning space," the many places where students learn in ways not bounded by the schedule of the school day, the limitations of the four classroom walls, or the location of one's home. These places include afterschool programs, museums, science centers, libraries, parks, and anywhere students can connect with the Internet and their "learning partners."

> The real issue behind the achievement gap is an "experience gap": students living very narrow lives within a tight social and geographic network.

The real issue behind the achievement gap is an "experience gap": students living very narrow lives within a tight social and geographic network. The expansion of their "experience portfolio" requires more learning time and contact with more caring adults who can show them the wider world. These are strengths of afterschool programs that leverage time during afternoons, evenings, weekends, and summers.

President John Hennessy of Stanford University has described its model students as "T-students" (Auletta, 2012): students who not only have a tremendous breadth of interests, knowledge, and skills, but also an impressive depth of knowledge in a particular domain. A T-shaped education should start early, giving our youngest students the broadest possible exposure to many learning experiences and places, spanning the arts, history, literacy, sports, and the STEM disciplines, creating the long, horizontal part of their T. Social/emotional learning should be a vital platform for developing persistent, confident, and collaborative learners. Through these varied experiences, students are more likely to discover their true passion that can lead to deep expertise, the vertical part of that T.

Taking project-based and place-based learning to its ultimate expression, students can now pursue personalized, passion-based learning. This should be the goal of a 21st century education: to find one's passion and develop it. While traditional schooling offers limited courses and extracurriculars that do not map fully onto students' many interests, afterschool programs can expand their options and help them locate more experiences and mentors in their communities and online.

Two recent examples of the power of the "third learning space" come to mind. I joined a team from the California Afterschool Network in a site visit to an afterschool program at an elementary school in San Jose. We were using the visit to inform our thinking about a website that would offer training and activities for STEM education. We observed 4th-graders, organized in small teams, in animated conversations about the best way to build a "marble roller coaster" using a marble and foam tubes, doing hands-on physics and engineering. What impressed me most was how quickly, once given the goal of the activity and the materials, these young students were able to design, test, and improve their roller coasters—and how much they enjoyed it.

I also recently participated in an evening videoconference with a group of high school students near San Francisco at the Redwood City Peapod Academy, whose partners include the Black Eyed Peas, Adobe Youth Voices, and the International Education & Resource Network (IEARN). The American students, largely Latino, spoke with two separate groups of boy and girl students in Pakistan during their morning, quickly learning about cultural values that prohibit girls from traveling and limitations on broadband Internet access.

I told the Pakistani students that I was honored to witness this exchange, since it was my first time speaking with students there. When Osama bin Laden was taken there weeks later, I'm certain all of those present that evening thought of those students and how more online student exchanges like it could contribute to a more peaceful world.

The rise of the afterschool and summer learning movement continues to be a bright spot in the new landscape of American education. Often delivered through school-community partnerships, the programs encompassed by this movement help to engage and broaden students' experiences from their lives in school or at home. This is a distinctly American invention, fueled by the commitment and perseverance of thousands of local educators and a broad spectrum of nonprofit, public, and private partners. Some may try to rein in this innovative movement to make learning look more like that offered during a typical 20th-century school day, but that would be a move in the wrong direction in light of global, social, and economic forces prevalent in the early 21st century. The afterschool and summer learning movement is a key driver of break-the-mold efforts to provide children with any time, any place, any path, any pace learning opportunities and is thus on the leading edge of the future of education.

But . . . let's keep this a secret from policy makers in Finland and Singapore. If they understand the types of creative learning going on in this "third learning space," they will create these places and programs for every child in their countries. On the other hand, perhaps we should learn a lesson from them and scale the innovations we've "Made in America" to every child here.

ABOUT THE AUTHOR

Milton Chen is senior fellow and executive director, emeritus, at The George Lucas Educational Foundation in the San Francisco Bay Area (edutopia.org). He also serves as chairman of the Panasonic Foundation and the education committee of the National Park System Advisory Board. Chen's 2010 book, *Education Nation: Six Leading Edges of Innovation in Our Schools*, was selected as a top book of the year by the American School Board Journal.

REFERENCES

Auletta, K. (2012, April 30). Get Rich U. *The New Yorker*. Retrieved from http://www.newyorker.com/reporting/2012/04/30/120430fa_fact_auletta

Chen, M. (2010). *Education nation: Six leading edges of innovation in our schools*. San Francisco, CA: Jossey-Bass.

Shirky, C. (2009). How social media can make history [Video file]. Retrieved from http://www.ted.com/talks/clay_shirky_how_cellphones_twitter_facebook_can_make_history.html

Bob Wise
President, Alliance for Excellent Education
and Former Governor, West Virginia

Terri Duggan Schwartzbeck
Senior Policy Associate, Alliance for
Excellent Education

Technology Makes Learning Available 24/7: Digital Learning in Expanded Learning Spaces After School and During the Summertime

- Students in a shopping mall office space, retaking courses they previously failed

- A group of inner-city students producing a high-quality music video that features poetry, sociology, and urban development

- Teens participating in nationwide arts events while developing graphic design skills or learning video gaming technology

- Students gathering to compete in robotics competitions

- A school district increasing student achievement over the summer while tightening its budget

These are all examples of how digital learning can have a powerful impact on the lives of students outside the regular classroom. Such opportunities are increasingly within reach for schools, districts, and communities.

The need for these opportunities is great. The future of the American economy increasingly depends upon students graduating from high school ready for college and a career. Momentum is building to expand learning time for students to help meet these challenges, but most efforts have been focused on elementary and middle school students. Meanwhile, many of the nation's high school students are still struggling. Schools now have an opportunity to accelerate the pace of improvement by taking advantage of the learning opportunities offered by the effective use of technology in afterschool, weekend, and summer learning environments and by building new or better partnerships with community organizations, employers, and 2- and 4-year colleges.

Almost three out of ten students fail to graduate from high school within four years, and the number of over-age, under-credited students continues to plague American secondary education. There are many reasons why students drop out: boredom, lack of motivation, pregnancy, or the need to work (Alliance for Excellent Education, 2010). Even among those who do graduate from high school, only about one in four students is deemed college-ready in all four tested subjects on the ACT, and one in three students will need to take at least one remedial course at the postsecondary level. Together, these challenges have significant implications for the nation's economy (ACT, 2011; Bureau of Labor Statistics, 2011).

Despite ongoing efforts to improve public K–12 schooling, this lack of progress is not entirely surprising. The American high school experience, despite enormous changes in the global economy and advances in technology, has remained largely the same over the last 50 years. Schools are still confined to the 180-day school year and the 6-hour school day. At the same time, dwindling budgets have become commonplace in most states and districts.

Multiple forces are converging to create a significant opportunity to influence education powerfully within the next 2–3 years. The technology available for instruction continues to improve, while the cost of that technology continues to decrease. More and more students today are digital natives, already accustomed to the rapid feedback, collaborative nature, and ease of use of many digital technologies. Schools are ramping up for the online assessments linked to the Common Core State Standards adopted by most states (Alliance for Excellent Education, 2012). Additionally, recent federal regulatory trends are freeing states and districts to innovate with greater freedom and flexibility. To accelerate the pace of progress, every institution focused on the education of youth should have a comprehensive strategy for the effective use of digital learning tools to improve career and college readiness or risk continued stagnation.

Successful Technology Strategy Elements

Leaders looking to expand learning opportunities through technology and digital learning should begin with a strategic review of their goals, challenges, and current settings. There is no one right solution or strategy, and the effective use of digital learning outside the regular classroom can look very different in various learning environments. It is also critical that leaders focus on the instructional needs of students first and then look at the ways in which technology can be used as a tool to meet those needs. Local and state education leaders need to redefine their roles in order to function as "orchestra conductors of learning." They should tap the rich array of available and reliable community, business, and college partners to deliver and support digital learning during the afterschool hours, weekends, and summers, rather than rely exclusively on a single instrument for delivering instruction—the traditional school (that is, the traditional 6 hour school day, the 180-day school year, and school spaces) that has defined and constrained formal learning opportunities for children and youth for generations.

Expanding learning time is a key strategy for schools and districts desiring to be more innovative and economically efficient in how they structure and deliver teaching and learning. The idea of anytime, anyplace learning has especially strong potential for high school students, whose unique needs and challenges are often best met outside the traditional high school structure. Consequently, school and community leaders should consider a range of options for expanding learning time.

Summer programs

Summer is a critical time for districts hoping to make progress in closing the achievement gap. Summer learning loss is well documented, and many districts struggle to fund or support summer learning programs. Technology can make these programs more accessible and affordable. At Rawlins High School, in the rural town of Rawlins, Wyoming, students have access to many summer school options through a blended-learning program in which they spend some time in the school and some time participating in the courses online. Because of the reduced costs to the district, Rawlins is able to provide access to many more courses for the same total price while keeping at-risk students on track for graduation (Alliance for Excellent Education, 2011).

Walled Lake Consolidated School District, in Oakland County, Michigan, has been implementing a one-to-one laptop program (one laptop per student) since 1999. The district began offering summer school programs online in 2008, starting with 300 students. This approach has helped the district cut per-student summer school costs nearly in half. The program utilizes a blended approach, with an online course combined with biweekly face-to-face interactions with a teacher (U.S. Department of Education, 2012).

Afterschool programs

There are also many examples of the successful use of technology-based learning programs that operate during the hours after school. In Wichita, Kansas, the school district operates dropout recovery centers in which students can take computer-based courses in office spaces in local malls and community centers and on high school campuses. Licensed teachers are onsite, and the hours are flexible. Credit recovery centers located inside high schools serve students who have fallen behind but not yet dropped out by allowing them to take courses after school. The cost of these centers is just one-third of the district's per-pupil expenditure (Mackey, 2010). Another center, LifeSkills, of Orange County, Florida, is a public charter school located in a shopping center. Many of LifeSkills' students had dropped out or were failing when they came to the center. Students advance based on demonstrated competency. Many of these students hold jobs and, therefore, need a flexible school schedule; the school's design and technology meet that need (Wise, 2011).

The Thurgood Marshall Academy for Leadership and Social Change is a Harlem middle school. As a member of The After-School Corporation's (TASC's) network of expanded learning time schools, the academy partners with the Abyssinian Development Corporation (ADC) to expand the learning day by 3 additional hours. Terrance Roumph, a math teacher, uses the Khan Academy's online video library to provide students with interactive practice exercises, immediate assessment, and feedback after 3:00 p.m. Students view tutorial videos and practice at their own pace while they review the day's concepts and preview the next day's topics. Embedded assessment and tracking components provide the teacher with immediate feedback, allowing him to plan face-to-face interventions with students. Thanks to the school's shared staffing with the ADC, Roumph is joined by an AmeriCorps member, who helps students with everything from logging on to socio-emotional issues. Roumph also found that using online tutorials engages parents and guardians, who log on to help their children at home and track their progress (Curry & Jackson-Smarr, 2012).

Expanding the times during which high school students can access learning can promote college and career readiness through increased time for core academic subjects, more personalized and customized learning, and on-call tutoring services. Some school districts have also found that when they implement one-to-one technology initiatives or bring-your-own-device programs, supported by adequate Internet access and learning management systems that are available 24 hours a day, they are effectively lengthening the school day. In Forsyth County, Georgia, Chief Technology Officer Bailey Mitchell found that the district's bandwidth use increased dramatically during the afterschool hours and in the evenings as students logged on to the district learning system to continue their work (Mitchell, 2012).

Expanded Learning Time at a Crossroads

The research supporting the use of technology in expanded learning time is still in its infancy because the pace of technological innovation is so rapid; however, an analysis of multiple high-functioning afterschool programs shows that students in technology-rich programs attend for longer amounts of time, and that staff in those programs receive more professional development and have higher expectations for their students. Additionally, technology-based programs are more likely to present material in relevant and engaging ways (Huang et al., 2010). An analysis of one technology-based literacy program, Scholastic's "Read 180," shows that computer-based programs can be successfully implemented in out-of-school settings with proper planning and accommodations (Hartry, Fitzgerald, & Porter, 2008).

Expanded learning programs now stand at a crossroads. Over the next 2 years, as states work to implement college- and career-ready standards along with online assessments, there are opportunities for expanded learning programs after school and during summers to step up and partner with communities, 2- to 4-year colleges, schools, and states to provide strategic, integrated, and powerful learning opportunities. It is imperative that schools and communities come together to develop plans and action steps for how they can not only better utilize technology to accelerate the pace of improvement, but also do so outside of the traditional classroom—after school, during the summer, and in ways that make learning truly a 24/7 experience.

ABOUT THE AUTHORS

Bob Wise is president of the Alliance for Excellent Education, a national policy and advocacy organization that works to promote high school transformation to make it possible for every child to graduate prepared for postsecondary learning and success in life. Wise has become one of the nation's strongest leaders in promoting the effective use of technology, college- and career-ready standards, and high expectations for high school graduation rates. He is former governor of West Virginia and chairs the National Board for Professional Teaching Standards.

Terri Duggan Schwartzbeck is a senior policy associate at the Alliance for Excellent Education, where her areas of focus include digital learning, connecting in-school and out-of-school learning, and rural education. She coordinates a wide range of webinars, social media efforts, and works on the Alliance's Digital Learning Day campaign. She has a master's degree in public policy from Harvard University's John F. Kennedy School of Government.

REFERENCES

ACT. (2011). *The condition of college and career readiness 2011*. Retrieved from http://www.act.org/research/policymakers/cccr11/index.html

Alliance for Excellent Education. (2010). *Fact sheet: High school dropouts in America*. Retrieved from http://www.all4ed.org/files/GraduationRates_FactSheet.pdf

Alliance for Excellent Education. (2011). *Digital learning and technology: Federal policy recommendations to seize the opportunity—and promising practices that inspire them*. Retrieved from http://www.all4ed.org/files/DigitalLearning.pdf

Alliance for Excellent Education. (2012). *The digital learning imperative: How technology and teaching meet today's education challenges*. Retrieved from http://www.all4ed.org/files/DigitalLearningImperative.pdf

Bureau of Labor Statistics. (April 8, 2011). College enrollment and work activity of 2010 high school graduates. Retrieved from http://www.bls.gov/news.release/archives/hsgec_04082011.pdf

Curry, J. S., & Jackson-Smarr, R. (2012). *Where the kids are: Digital learning in class and beyond*. New York, NY: The After-School Corporation.

Hartry, A., Fitzgerald, R., & Porter, K. (2008). Implementing a structured reading program in an afterschool setting: Problems and potential solutions. *Harvard Educational Review, 78*(1), 181–210.

Huang, D., Cho, J., Mostafavi, S., Nam, H., Oh, C., Harven, A., & Leon, S. (2010). *What works? Common practices in high functioning afterschool programs across the nation in math, reading, science, arts, technology, and homework—A study by the National Partnership. The afterschool program assessment guide* (CRESST Report 768). Los Angeles: University of California, National Center for Research on Evaluation, Standards, and Student Testing (CRESST).

Kober, N., & Stark Rentner, D. S. (2011). *Strained schools face bleak future: Districts foresee budget cuts, teacher layoffs, and a slowing of education reform efforts*. Washington, DC: Center on Education Policy.

Mackey, K. (March 2010). *Wichita Public Schools' Learning Centers: Creating a new educational model to serve dropouts and at-risk students*. Retrieved from http://www.inacol.org/research/docs/WichitaCaseStudy.pdf

Mitchell, B. (2012, February 1). Leadership and innovation: BYO technology (B. Wise, Interviewer) [Video webcast]. Retrieved from http://www.digitallearningday.org/news-and-events/eventmap/archives/dldwebcast/

U.S. Department of Education, Office of Educational Technology. (2010). *Transforming American education: Learning powered by technology*. Retrieved from http://www.ed.gov/sites/default/files/netp2010.pdf

Wise, B. (April 18, 2011). Seeing how high tech works with high touch [Blog post]. Retrieved from http://www.all4ed.org/blog/seeing_how_high_tech_works_high_touch

Michael H. Levine
Executive Director, Joan Ganz Cooney
Center at Sesame Workshop

Rafi Santo
Graduate Research Assistant, Indiana University

Upgrading Afterschool: Common Sense Shifts in Expanded Learning for a Digital Age

The days when summer and afterschool learning programs that only offered "safe custodial care" were considered fine are thankfully behind us. Tectonic social changes—including demographic shifts that have placed most women with school-age children in the labor force, research breakthroughs in the learning sciences and in socio-emotional and brain development, and daunting national achievement worries—have all converged to place a major new emphasis on the quality of a child's learning experiences throughout the typical school day, after school, weekends, and across the year, including summers.

Over the past decade the C. S. Mott Foundation, the Wallace Foundation, the MacArthur Foundation, and others have conducted groundbreaking programmatic and research initiatives to expand learning time after school and during the summer. These initiatives have defined "a new day for learning" (Herr-Stephenson, Rhoten, Perkel, & Sims, 2011; Time, Learning, and Afterschool Task Force, 2007). The recent convergence of scholarly research, program development efforts, and policy advocacy work have all pushed in the direction of a fresh "ecological" framework for learning that nests more responsibility in the nonschool hours. This "mind shift" has been helpfully characterized by scholars at the National Science Foundation's Learning in Formal and Informal Environments (LIFE) Center as the "life-long, life-wide, and life-deep" approach to learning (Banks et al., 2007). Such a shift characterizes a natural progression in how we should think about learning in the 21st century.

It is now broadly understood that expanded learning programs can and must be much more than "graham crackers and basketball"—that is, they can play a critical role in young people's lives. But what does a real mind shift look like? Currently, there exist dramatically different visions of the desired outcomes of expanded learning time programs. One vision is that afterschool and summer learning programs should be aligned with current education reform efforts—high-stakes testing, narrow accountability, and the Common Core State Standards that are directed at just two subjects. Another view—and the one we argue for here—is that expanded learning-time programs should exist as part of the larger ecology of a young person's 21st century existence. This ecology is framed by the digital, interconnected world in which we all live and should, therefore, incorporate systemic links between what are now disparate venues of learning. Thus, we place great priority on youth participation and productivity in learning opportunities that burnish their civic and collaborative skills through the creative, evolving digital technologies so ubiquitous in the world.

Research shows that the past decade's focus on accountability and high-stakes testing is leading to a more intensive emphasis on reaching all children, but it is inadvertently resulting in a curriculum for many low-income children that is narrower, fragmented, and oriented towards "direct instruction" instead of student-driven inquiry (Au, 2007). The Common Core, while arguably a strong baseline for student learning in the United States, are rightfully being criticized for a weak emphasis on 21st century competencies like creativity, collaboration, and communication (Partnership for 21st Century Skills, 2010), as well as for a narrow focus on only reading and math.

A New Vision for Learning

Expanding learning-time programs that focus with all good intentions on remediation and tutoring, but that extend traditional school structures into afterschool time, may experience weak attendance and missed opportunities because these efforts are too often disconnected from the rich learning lives of today's youth. The Kaiser Family Foundation's "Generation M" research and the qualitative work of Mimi Ito and colleagues (2009) document the explosion of interest in digital technologies that allow youth not only to "media multitask," but also to explore, create, and share knowledge around their personal interests and across many knowledge domains. We believe that these experiences can be significantly leveraged and augmented in expanded learning-time environments.

We advocate another vision for out-of-school-time organizations—one that positions young people as creators, makers, and innovators. Our vision will allow youth to go deep into 21st century learning by focusing on *knowledge production* with the technologies pervasive in our world. Youth are increasingly doing incredible things through their engagement with digital media. For example, in online multiplayer games, they are collaborating with sometimes hundreds of people around the world to tackle complex challenges in the form of dragons to be slain. In fan communities, they write and rewrite favorite books like *Harry Potter*, extending plotlines and creating alternate endings, all the while engaging in rigorous feedback and revision processes that English teachers would admire.

Key Principles for Program Design

There are several outstanding models of innovation in the expanded learning-time domain that suggest a set of key principles to guide afterschool and summer learning leaders in designing new, digitally savvy, and integrated learning environments. The principles offered below are based on an examination of three exemplary innovators in expanded learning time: the YouMedia network, spearheaded by the Chicago Public Library; Global Kids, an afterschool leadership organization based in New York City; and the Computer Clubhouse network, which was developed originally by the MIT Media Lab and now includes approximately 100 community centers in over 20 countries (Kafai, Peppler, & Chapman, 2009).

1. **Provide technological infrastructure that supports media design and production.** Providing access to technology is essential, of course, but this should be seen only as a first step. Programs should ensure that access to the Internet is relatively unrestricted, that files and programs can be downloaded, and that youth have ways to save personal work and access it using any computer. These elements are all essential to creating a space in which design and production activities with media can promote robust learning. Additionally, program developers should ensure that production-and design-oriented software and hardware are available. At the Computer Clubhouse, and in over 3,000 "Club Tech" centers operated by the Boys and Girls Clubs, software is available that supports computer programming, game design, graphic design, and audio and video production; moreover, hardware, such as video cameras, sound recording equipment, and digital cameras, can be checked out at some centers.

2. **Create a culture of sharing meaningful media creations.** Some of the most important learning outcomes associated with digital media are tied to creating, sharing, and getting feedback from peers on projects that youth care about. This can happen through gallery showings, performances, screenings, "critique" sessions, and the creation of localized online spaces in which youth can review and comment on each others' work. In 2009, Global Kids co-founded Emoti-Con, the annual New York City youth media and technology festival that brings together hundreds of youth from across the city to exhibit their digital creations in a public forum, get critiques from both peers as well as professionals, and connect with a larger community of media creators. These kinds of meaningful contexts for sharing work encourage youth to go deep and develop expertise through iteratively improving their projects.

3. **Provide skilled mentors to support and respond to youth interests.** Adults, as always, have important roles to play in afterschool and summer learning programs. In connected, expanded learning programs, adults often provide mentoring around technology use and promote good citizenship practices associated with new media use and production. At YouMedia, skilled artists serve as mentors, leading workshops on specialized topics and helping youth organize projects around emerging interests. These highly skilled adults provide youth with role models and powerful images of engagement in expert practice and mastery of fundamental skills needed to do well in school and in life.

4. **Create mixed-age spaces.** One of the key aspects of 21st century learning environments is that they feature participants of many ages that have a range of experiences, backgrounds, and areas of expertise. Schools typically maintain the increasingly outmoded practice of grouping children by age, while most other successful learning environments leverage the strengths of mixed-age populations. At the Computer Clubhouse, groups diverse in age and experience ensure that participants can sometimes be learners and sometimes be leaders, with reciprocal benefits accruing on both ends of those relationships.

5. **Design spaces to build relationships!** Peer relationships matter most in effective expanded learning communities. Youth will rarely persist in an activity or remain a member of an organization if they do not form strong relationships to peers or mentors. YouMedia's model incorporates both unstructured time for developing such relationships, as well as a conducive physical space in which youth can hang out, socialize, and develop bonds.

Recommendations for Extended Learning Practice and Policy in Afterschool and Summer Programs

In a digital age in which technology is a central part of kids' lives, leaders in the expanded learning-time movement need to embrace a "mind shift" so that the United States can make dramatic progress by building a system of expanded digital learning, one based on pragmatic changes that acknowledge the ways learning is happening in the 21st century. In the next 5 years we recommend the following priority areas for expanding learning investments:

1. **Modernize places in every community.** With the goal of creating a new expanded digital learning road map in every community, each of the nation's 21st Century Community Learning Centers should undertake its own "digital learning inventory" to determine what is currently being done to advance digital learning in local afterschool and summer programs. These inventories should identify the funds that are currently available, the barriers to using new resources for digital learning in these programs, and the capacity of local partners to contribute tools that are needed for technology-based innovations.

2. **Create professional learning communities.** Youth-serving professionals are too often behind the curve when it comes to understanding the capacities of new media for learning. They should look to models of new online professional communities that are forming across key professional associations and networks, such as the National Writing Project (NWP), Consortium of School Networking (CoSN), and city-based affiliations like the Hive Learning Networks. The expanded learning community should take up the challenge of creating a digitally savvy mentors corps to identify a cadre of capable leaders who can train and support youth-serving professionals, based on a blueprint for teachers offered by Levine and Gee (2011).

3. **Build capacity and awareness.** A cadre of pioneering expanded learning organizations has already begun program development work around anytime, anywhere learning, including Think Together in California, the Digital Youth Network in Chicago, the Digital On-Ramps initiative in Philadelphia, the Kids and Creativity Coalition in Pittsburgh, and numerous others mentioned throughout this article. They are updating or creating new program materials and projects on digital media and expanded learning themes. We should support these leaders with research and development funds to document successes and failures, invite them to national conferences to share these, and use their models as the focus of the advocacy work of state afterschool networks to expand quality programs for a digital age.

Future investments in local program capacity can be advanced by recruiting champions for expanded digital learning, including governors, mayors, businesses interests in economic development, as well as chief state school officers, state boards, school districts, and influential nonprofit partners. Policy leaders, in particular, can (1) support initiatives that expand broadband availability in all of the federally funded 21st Century Community Learning Centers and in state and locally-funded afterschool sites; (2) encourage robust experimentation with digital platforms that allow expanded learning organizations to collaborate, share practices, and connect experiences that kids are having at various expanded learning sites; and (3) support pilot experiments in up to 10% of the 21st Century Community Learning Centers that focus on integrating evolving technologies.

Over the next 5 years, major innovations in digital technologies and learning are not only possible, but almost inevitable. Investment in educational technologies by venture capital is at a 20-year high (Ash, 2012), and many cutting-edge community educators are fashioning ways to connect the learning happening on youth's own time to what is happening in school and in out-of-school environments. Expanded learning time initiatives, including afterschool and summer programs, should help lead our nation out of its narrow educational mindset by promoting communities in which children and youth are positioned as "makers and creators," based on what they are passionate about. By unlocking new opportunities for "modern" learning, we can drive a pragmatic mind shift that will generate great benefits for our nation.

For More Information

- YouMedia – YouMedia.org
- Global Kids – GlobalKids.org
- Computer Clubhouse – ComputerClubhouse.org
- Club Tech of the Boys and Girls Club of America – myclubmylife.com/clubtech
- TASC's Where the Kids Are – tascorp.org/content/document/detail/3656/
- Digital Youth Network – DigitalYouthNetwork.org
- Common Sense Media's Digital Citizenship Curriculum – www.commonsensemedia.org/educators/curriculum

ABOUT THE AUTHORS

Michael H. Levine is the founding director of the Joan Ganz Cooney Center at Sesame Workshop, an action research and innovation institute devoted to harnessing the potential of digital media to advance young children's learning and development. Previously, Levine oversaw Carnegie Corporation of New York's groundbreaking work in early childhood development, educational media, and primary grades reform, and was a senior advisor to the New York City Schools Chancellor, where he directed dropout prevention, afterschool, and early childhood initiatives. Levine is a frequent adviser to the White House, the U.S. Department of Education, PBS, and the Corporation for Public Broadcasting.

Rafi Santo is an educator, researcher, technologist and activist currently pursuing his doctorate in the learning sciences at Indiana University. His research and professional interests focus on the intersection of new media, educational design, interest driven learning, and online participatory cultures with a particular eye towards how to leverage these areas to create greater equity and democratization in society. He specializes in the design and implementation of digital learning projects and in understanding innovation in the education sector.

REFERENCES

Au, W. (2007). High-stakes testing and curricular control: A qualitative metasynthesis. *Educational Researcher, 36*(5), 258–267.

Ash, K. (2012, February 1). K–12 marketplace sees major flow of venture capital. *Education Week, 31*(19).

Banks, J., Au, K., Ball, A., Bell, P., Gordon, E., Gutiérrez, K. D., . . . Zhou, M. (2007). *Learning in and out of school in diverse environments.* Retrieved from http://life-slc.org/docs/Banks_etal-LIFE-Diversity-Report.pdf

Herr-Stephenson, B., Rhoten, D., Perkel, D., & Sims, C. (2011). *Digital media and technology in afterschool programs, libraries, and museums.* Retrieved from mitpress.mit.edu/books/full_pdfs/Digital_Media_and_Technology_in_Afterschool_Programs.pdf

Ito, M., Baumer, S., Bittanti, M., Boyd, D., Cody, R., Herr-Stephenson, B., . . . Tripp, L. (2009). *Hanging out, messing around, geeking out: Kids living and learning with new media.* Cambridge, MA: MIT Press.

Kafai, Y. B., Peppler, K., & Chapman, R. (Eds.). (2009). *The Computer Clubhouse: Creativity and constructionism in youth communities.* New York, NY: Teachers College Press.

Levine, M., & Gee, J. (2011, September). *The digital teachers corps: Closing America's literacy gap* (Policy Brief). Retrieved from Progressive Policy Institute website: http://www.progressivepolicy.org/2011/09/policy-brief-the-digital-teachers-corps-closing-america%E2%80%99s-literacy-gap/

Partnership for 21st Century Skills. (2010). Statement from Ken Kay, President of P21, on the Common Core State Standards Initiative [Press Release]. Retrieved from http://www.p21.org/events-aamp-news/press-releases/918-statement-from-ken-kay-president-of-p21-on-the-common-core-state-standards-initiative

Time, Learning, and Afterschool Task Force. (2007). *A new day for learning.* Retrieved from http://www.newdayforlearning.org/docs/NDL_Jan07.pdf

Nicholas C. Donohue
President and CEO, Nellie Mae
Education Foundation

The Promise of Extended Learning Opportunities: New, Powerful, and Personalized Options for High School Students

As we prepare our communities and our nation for a future that is increasingly complex and global, our education system—a relic of a bygone era—must shift dramatically to ensure that all of our citizens can thrive in the 21st century. New models are emerging that may help move our educational system from the "one-size-fits-all" practice we have known it to be, to a design that might well be described as an orchestra. This image of a well-tuned and aligned orchestra conjures up notions of coordination, variety, and harmony—with many parts of the system "in concert" with each other.

One model that is showing particular promise in this regard provides high school students with access to well-facilitated, high-quality, real-world experiences in which they can acquire essential, complex skills and knowledge by studying, collaborating, and doing.

A case in point: Andy is a high school student with an interest in exploring a career in health care. He spent some of his school year in an internship under the guidance of an infection control nurse on-site at a regional medical center, learning how diseases spread and what to do about it. As part of his "coursework," Andy helped design, organize, manage, and analyze results from a study on hand washing as a way of limiting contagion. The study consisted of close observations of doctors, nurses, and staff and the development of an original benchmarking system to monitor the effectiveness of hand-sanitizing stations within the facility.

With guidance from teachers and an on-site mentor, Andy gathered, synthesized, analyzed, and compared his local data to Centers for Disease Control (CDC) data and then developed a set of findings. He then presented his research to the medical center's Infection Control Board—staffed by certified experts in the field.

This would be an exciting opportunity for a college student, let alone someone in high school. What makes it even more valuable is that it is credit-bearing. With the support of rigorous assessment processes, students like Andy can now have these powerful experiences while doing something that "counts" in addition to, and in some cases instead of, time spent sitting—and mostly listening—in a classroom. In Andy's own words, "I think this was a very powerful learning experience. I practiced a lot of working skills . . . including my presentation skills . . . self-direction and critical thinking . . . (and) graphing and map skills. This internship really brought my learning together."

In addition to Andy's own obvious appreciation of this kind of learning experience, evaluation and research findings validate that these kinds of efforts are worthy and feasible. New research from neuroscience suggests that these types of engaging experiences contribute to the ongoing development of the brain and a literal strengthening of its synapses. Contrary to earlier notions that significant brain development is limited to the preschool years, we now know that the very nature of learning activities themselves as we experience them throughout our lives—their complexity, their relevance, their vitality—have a positive result on exercising and strengthening our brains in ways that help us do similar tasks. Doing, it turns out, helps prepare us to do better (Hinton, Fischer, & Glennon, 2012).

Youth development research also reminds us that the higher the relevance and interest quotients, the stronger the motivation. We know that tapping learner motivation is a key to persistence and success. Combining classroom instruction with hands-on learning experiences facilitated by community mentors gives us another way of aligning education with what we know about young people and how they learn best (Halpern, 2012).

More good news is that the kinds of skills and knowledge that are developed through these complex, applied real-world experiences are consistent with what employers want and what global competition demands. "Organize, research, analyze, synthesize, write, and present are all words that describe the challenges of Andy's work. These are not 'soft skills'; they make up the 'new basics' to which we must attend if we are to adequately prepare our society for the future" (Rennie Center, 2010).

The evaluation of this type of learning opportunity tells us that Andy and his peers enjoy this kind of learning and want more of it. Teachers, while challenged at first, will eventually embrace these approaches with the right support. Designing and delivering real-world learning with community mentors allows teachers to tap their own creative juices by developing learning opportunities, demonstrating their expertise about content, and exercising their professional judgment concerning performance. Evaluation also tells us that the credits earned are worthy in terms of the strength of learning they represent (Zuliani & Ellis, 2011).

Evaluation results also point to the many challenges that come with this work. Teaching in a classroom is hard enough; developing criteria for a credit-worthy experience in a real-world setting and setting the thresholds that signify proficiency are even more difficult—particularly since most educators who are currently in the workforce were not trained for such 21st century experiences (Zuliani & Ellis, 2011).

While we refer to the type of expanded learning opportunities described above as "ELOs," they link teachers and community mentors more intensively and are often much more robust and engaging than other programs that use the same term. As effective and supportive as the ELO efforts described here are, they currently only exist in small patches across the country. However, there are many possibilities for enriching the way we currently extend learning through creating and strengthening school-community partnerships and simultaneously deploying teachers and hands-on-learning with mentors.

How do we bring such efforts to scale so that ELOs are not just high quality add-ons to traditional school practices, but so they find their way to eventually defining educational practices more fully? What are the barriers to doing so? Seat-time requirements known as "Carnegie Units" may stand in the way of making ELOs a creditable norm. High stakes assessment rarely focus on the complex skills and knowledge that define high quality ELOs. If dollars follow the learner instead of supporting the classroom directly, will school budgets shrink even further? The public policy and practice challenges are daunting. Yet the political, educational, cultural, and economic tides may be turning in the direction of these ELO-like approaches.

The advent of the Common Core State Standards—a nearly universally adopted set of learning standards in the United States—is a step forward for those who seek a greater and better focus on complex skills and knowledge within applied settings. The development of next-generation assessments will also allow for more performance information than bubble filling provides. While far from perfect, these two improving aspects of standards and assessment—more amenable outcomes and better measures—are more aligned with what ELOs need to be successful.

From an economic vantage point, school is not getting any cheaper and the window is wide open for more cost-effective approaches to learning. While ELOs at scale have costs associated with them, the returns on investment in terms of retention, lower drop-out rates, and levels of skill attainment make them an attractive option to educators and taxpayers.

Culturally, technology is bringing such terms as customization and personalization into our social and business lexicon. Witness the advent of the PC, playlists, Amazon.com, Netflix, and the ubiquitous smartphone. In education, this wave of change has resulted in an explosion of tech-driven educational opportunities that is accelerating as fast as the appetite of younger, tech-savvy educators for modern ways of teaching. The burgeoning field of K—12 online learning that now defines some of our nation's largest stand-alone "school districts" is proof of technology's impact. How long will it be before modularization of educational opportunities gathers steam and squeezes out traditional school designs, much as iTunes has replaced CDs and record albums?

These exciting developments reinforce the notion that we are fast moving to a time when educators, parents, guardians, and/or students will be able to package learning based on need and interest—if they can afford it. If the attractiveness and quality of ELOs continue to grow, these inventive approaches will find learners who want to prepare for their future and who will stay authentically engaged as they do so.

The opportunity for out-of-school-time, afterschool, summer learning, and extended- learning time providers is enormous; however, infighting currently defines much of this relationship. Maybe it is time to call a truce in the name of survival—or even move to a self-interested collaboration.

> These exciting developments reinforce the notion that we are fast moving to a time when educators, parents, guardians, and/or students will be able to package learning based on need and interest.

Leaders in these various movements could, for example, work together to design new types of learning modules and other learning opportunities that could be used in a variety of settings beyond the school day and school year. They could also work together to advocate for enhanced public funding to support ELOs, including freeing up funds that support existing federal programs (like Title I) so that ELOs are an allowable expenditure; enlarging the funding pool from the state (for example, creating a state innovation fund for credit-worthy expanded learning time); or increasing federal sources (for example, increasing the 21st Century Community Learning Centers funding).

One way forward in terms of deep collaboration is modeled in New Hampshire. As part of the evolution of ELOs in the Granite State, Learning Studios (developed through a partnership with the National Commission on Teaching and America's Future) are sprouting up, staffed jointly by teachers and afterschool providers. In these labs, students engage in real-world challenges in workplace settings.

At one Learning Lab, managed by Lebanon High School in the middle of the state, students identify problems to solve, make a plan to solve the problems, enlist community experts, identify specific learning outcomes that align with academic standards, and then execute their plan. Their projects, presentation, and videos are screened and discussed. The effort is linked to the emergence of new school accountability designs so the work "counts" and credits may be awarded.

Bullying, student-teacher relationships, and academic favoritism are some of the topics chosen by students. Researching, writing, collaborating, and making a solid argument are some of the student outcomes that are assessed.

This year in Providence, Rhode Island, 35 students have been actively engaged in a pilot initiative off-campus that involves a community-based ELO connected with the Providence Public Schools' (PPS) Juanita Sanchez Educational Complex. The management structure of this effort is a model for inter-sector collaboration, with some interesting implications for how all sides think about available funds. As part of the pilot process, the director of the school's 21st Century Community Learning Center has worked closely with the Providence After School Alliance, or PASA (a long standing community entity that coordinates out-of-school-time work in the city), and school staff who have been coordinating and advancing the ELO initiative with students, faculty, and community partners.

The center director considers ELOs to be a connected part of the center's program at the school and has helped recruit students to take part in the ELO pilot. For the coming school year, the director has asked PASA to provide technical assistance to other 21st Century Community Learning Centers program providers to help guide them on developing eligible, standards-aligned programs that PPS could approve to be future credit-bearing ELOs. Additionally, the center director is encouraging programs from the ELO pilot to apply for grant funding through the existing pool of federal 21st Century Community Learning Centers funds in order to further connect the ELO initiative with the school's effort.

The director of expanded learning, who works jointly at PASA and PPS, has been working with district leadership to plan an expansion of the ELO initiative to other schools, in which the relationship with 21st Century Community Learning Centers will again be a hallmark of the initiative. PASA and PPS view these federal resources as part of a braided funding strategy, along with federal Title I, School Improvement Grants, and private funding, to support community-based staff who lead ELOs. These community partnerships are an essential component of the high school ELO work in Providence.

Furthermore, the collaborative work of the Providence out-of-school-time community already connects a number of high quality 21st Century Community Learning Centers programs and providers serving high school youth. In addition to the Juanita Sanchez Educational Complex program, many of the providers—including many of the 12 who are part of the ELO pilot—also provide programming through 21st Century Community Learning Centers structures at other high schools. This cross-fertilization of programs through this network will allow for an easier and faster replication of the ELO strategy at the new partner high schools in the coming academic year.

These and other stories tell us that there are more than enough opportunities, intelligence, experience, and talent to move ahead to collaborative work on a new learning ecosystem. 21st Century Community Learning Centers providers have a long, solid history of responding to market demands. Those programs serving high school students could right now begin to provide more high quality, real-world learning that links creative teachers and community mentors. School folks have long experience with standards and higher stakes assessments. Their leadership in meeting the challenges of the Common Core would be invaluable.

. . . there are more than enough opportunities, intelligence, experience, and talent to move ahead to collaborative work on a new learning ecosystem.

Why not work together on the development of rigorous, interesting, and credit-worthy ELOs? As the location and time for learning becomes more varied, we should develop high quality ELOs that "blend" virtual experiences with rich student/teacher/mentor relationships. In these and many other ways, ELO designs become better, and natural allies find common ground.

The only thing standing in the way of a potentially historic collaboration is the deep commitment on both sides to sustaining themselves; however, in a wired, hyper-connected, ever-changing world, a joint reinvention for these education sectors is absolutely necessary. So, instead of modeling the losing battle between newspapers and magazines fighting for disappearing "eye-balls," these educational players could be more like fierce collaborators developing our education industry's "new media," finding ways to keep the customer engaged—and willing to pay.

The opportunity to move into this new learning time and space is enormous for the range of groups working on expanding learning, afterschool programs, summer initiatives, and out-of-school-time efforts by extending real-life learning through school-community partnerships. ELO work provides a true "sweet spot" for collaboration and learning from each other. Partners can develop low-cost, sustainable options that engage struggling students and better connect real-world, hands-on learning in the community with modern educational expectations. Such efforts can also involve families more in their students' successes.

The risks are considerable, but the rewards and opportunities are far greater. Just ask Andy and his peers.

ABOUT THE AUTHOR

Nicholas C. Donohue, president and CEO of the Nellie Mae Education Foundation, is leading efforts to reshape New England's public education systems to be more equitable and more effective for all learners. Previously, Donohue was a special master at Hope High School in Providence, where he oversaw implementation of the Rhode Island Commissioner of Education's order to reconstitute the school. Before his tenure at Hope High School, Donohue was commissioner of education in New Hampshire.

REFERENCES

Halpern, R. (2012). *It takes a whole society: Opening up the learning landscape in the high school years.* Quincy, MA: Nellie Mae Education Foundation. Retrieved from http://www.nmefoundation.org/getmedia/747d8095-748b-4876-a3dd-ebc763796e1d/358NM-Halpern-Full

Hinton, C., Fischer, K. W., & Glennon, C. (2012). *Mind, brain and education.* Retrieved from http://www.studentsatthecenter.org/sites/scl.dl-dev.com/files/Mind%20Brain%20Education.pdf

Rennie Center for Education Research & Policy. (2010). *A new era of education reform: Preparing all students for success in college, career and life.* Cambridge, MA: Author.

Zuliani, I., & Ellis, S. (2011). *New Hampshire extended learning opportunities: Final report of evaluation findings.* Hadley, MA: University of Massachusetts Donahue Institute.

Lucy N. Friedman
President, TASC

Reinventing the Learning Day: How ExpandED Schools Blend the Best of School and Afterschool Through Community Partnerships

The traditional school calendar was designed for life a century ago, when Americans could thrive and be successful without even earning a high school degree. Today disadvantaged students, and those who are poorly served by conventional public schools, need better learning opportunities—and more of them—that capitalize on the best assets of their schools, communities, and families. By partnering with community organizations, schools can give students more time and a wider range of opportunities to learn by broadening school faculty to include a mix of certified teachers, teaching artists, and role models such as AmeriCorps members. We can help 21st century learners prepare to succeed in the information age by using more learning hours to engage, support, and challenge all students more effectively.

> ExpandED Schools offer at least 35% more learning time at 10% of the cost of the school day.

ExpandED Schools, developed by TASC, offer a promising model for educators and communities to reinvent the learning day. The model incorporates research-based practices that have been found effective in improving students' school attendance, attitudes and achievement. Each school partners with an experienced youth-serving community organization to expand the conventional school day by approximately 3 hours to match parents' working hours. By partnering with their communities, schools can draw on a blend of education and youth development funds. This is a cost-effective way to expand learning opportunities, even in difficult economic times. In fact, ExpandED Schools offer at least 35% more learning time at 10% of the cost of the school day. Families are valued partners in establishing a shared vision for student success and planning the redesign of their schools.

This article will lay out the rationale for this approach, provide examples of effective practices within TASC's ExpandED Schools national demonstration project, and offer resources for getting started.

Rationale

Starting in 2008, TASC supported a pilot of the ExpandED Schools model (formerly called Expanded Learning Time/New York City) that grew over 3 years to include 17 New York City public elementary and middle schools. This informed the design of a subsequent 3-year national demonstration of 11 ExpandED Schools currently operating in New York, Baltimore, and New Orleans. This initiative builds on the broad evidence base of effective afterschool programs and successful charter schools in order to offer an active, balanced learning day.

TASC afterschool programs get positive results. TASC developed a quality model for school-based afterschool programs that are operated by a community partner, such as a YMCA or community development corporation. Programs are designed to serve hundreds of children in a school and offer a variety of enriching activities.

From the beginning, in 1998, TASC encouraged parents to get involved. TASC staff quickly discovered that a child's afterschool program was a natural entry-point to a school for parents. Parents could communicate with afterschool staff during dismissal about their child's progress. Many afterschool programs encouraged parents to volunteer, to participate in parent-and-child literacy and science events, and to join in parent workshops. In collaboration with the New York State Afterschool Network, TASC developed an afterschool quality checklist for parents.

Research has shown that TASC afterschool programs increase student achievement and school attendance and improve students' likelihood of high school graduation. (Russell, Mielke, Miller, & Johnson, 2007; Reisner, White, Russell, & Birmingham, 2004). In particular, Reisner et al. (2004) conducted a large-scale, longitudinal evaluation of TASC-model programs. The results revealed that participants had greater gains in their math standardized scores and maintained a higher rate of school attendance than nonparticipating peers. Middle school participants had significantly higher attendance rates in the ninth and tenth grades (Reisner et al., 2004). Researchers also found that length of time enrolled in TASC programs and number of days attended were significant correlates of educational outcomes (Reisner et al., 2004). Students who were eligible for free lunch, English language learners, and special education students who attended TASC programs regularly performed significantly better on math standardized scores than matched nonparticipants. In addition, highly engaged black and Hispanic participants showed greater gains over nonparticipants than did white and Asian participants in math achievement. Overall, students who participated in TASC-model programming for at least 2 years and attended at least 60 days of programming experienced the greatest gains on math standardized test scores relative to matched nonparticipants. Together, these findings provide evidence that TASC programs helped to close the achievement gap between students of high and low socioeconomic status and between students of different racial groups in New York City (Reisner et al., 2004).

Thousands of children and youth continue to be served by the TASC afterschool programs. TASC provides schools and community partners with technical assistance and professional development to support continuous improvement.

ExpandED schools offer a new learning model with community partners. TASC began testing a school-improvement model in 2008 in New York City elementary and middle schools. The goal of the 3-year pilot was to build partnerships between schools and community organizations to provide all students with a well-rounded education that would help them grow into adults who can innovate, create, and think for a living. The pilot schools incorporated into expanded school days the best of what afterschool programs have to offer, including the adult mentorship of community educators who fortify students against the stresses and hardships of poverty. They differed from schools with afterschool programs by treating the hours between the time students arrived and roughly 6:00 p.m. as one unified learning day. They encouraged teachers and their partners to set goals jointly and build curriculum and activities around each individual school community's needs and student and family interests.

Pilot schools innovated in several ways, including

- *teaming teachers with artists to integrate arts into other academic subjects;*

- *having AmeriCorps members do small-group academic interventions with students before 3:00 p.m. and lead enrichments afterwards; and*

- *offering joint planning time and professional development for teachers and community educators.*

Close examination of the impact of these reform elements in schools prepared TASC for the next phase of work—a more ambitious, fully-integrated national demonstration of what can be achieved with more time, balanced curricula, an expanded school labor pool, and the coordination of education and youth development funding streams. Now, in 11 ExpandED Schools, partners are customizing additional learning time and opportunities to the needs of their students.

All ExpandED Schools embrace these four core elements: (1) more time for balanced learning, (2) school-community partnerships, (3) engaging and personalized instruction, and (4) a sustainable cost model of $1,600 per student at scale. The model is designed to serve whole schools, with the potential of phase-ins through whole grades.

Parents play a crucial role. For example, if a neighborhood lacks safe spaces for children to play outdoors, parents can advocate for devoting time and resources to rigorous physical activity. Parent involvement is an ongoing process. Schools survey parents and students throughout the year and use their feedback to adapt staffing and curriculum.

Evidence

TASC contracted Policy Studies Associates and Abt Associates to conduct an evaluation of its 3-year pilot of TASC Expanded Learning Time/New York City. The study found that 85% of teachers reported that the expanded time had improved participants' learning, and 67% of teachers reported that nonparticipants gained from the presence of expanded learning in the school. Schools also increased fidelity to the model over the course of the pilot. Higher fidelity schools demonstrated greater student outcomes. In schools implementing the model with high fidelity, there was a positive and statistically significant effect of expanded learning time on math achievement in Year 3 and attendance in all 3 years (Policy Studies Associates & Abt Associates, 2012).

Additionally, these schools outperformed their city peers on New York State English language arts and math exams. The two schools that implemented the model with the greatest fidelity (including offering the program to all students by Year 3) produced impressive results. At Young Scholars' Academy for Discovery and Exploration, which partners with University Settlement (a New York City settlement house), the percentage of third, fourth, and fifth graders achieving proficiency increased by 26 percentage points in English language arts between 2009–10 and 2010–11, compared to 3.3 percentage points citywide, and 17.3 percentage points in math, compared to 2.6 percentage points citywide. At Thurgood Marshall Academy Lower School, which partners with Abyssinian Development Corporation, the percentage of students in grades 3–5 achieving proficiency increased by 13.1 percentage points in English language arts, compared to 3.3 percentage points citywide, and by 18.5 percentage points in math, compared to 2.6 percentage points citywide (NYC Department of Education, 2012).

> 85% of teachers reported that the expanded time had improved participants' learning, and 67% of teachers reported that nonparticipants gained from the presence of expanded learning in the school.

According to parent surveys in 2010–11, 93% of parents at Thurgood Marshall Academy and 96% at Young Scholars' Academy agreed their child's school offers a wide enough variety of courses and activities to keep them interested, compared to 84% of parents citywide. The survey also found that 96% of parents at Thurgood Marshall Academy and 97% at Young Scholars' Academy agreed their child was learning what he or she needed to succeed, compared to 91% citywide (NYC Department of Education, 2011).

ExpandED Schools Success Stories

The most successful partnerships team teachers with community educators in classrooms before and after 3:00 p.m.

- The principal at PS 188 in Lower Manhattan was concerned that social studies was getting squeezed out of the regular school day schedule. Teachers now collaborate with teaching artists hired through Educational Alliance, the school's community partner, to explore social studies through the arts in the expanded day. Together they deliver a rich curriculum that incorporates art forms such as drama and painting. As an example, fifth grade students who were studying government worked with a drama coach to stage mock elections.

- Fannie C. Williams, a K–8 school in New Orleans, re-opened 2 years after Hurricane Katrina. The school partners with Vietnamese Initiatives in Economic Training (VIET) to expand the learning day. Teachers and community educators continuously share data to identify students struggling with reading and math and target them for small group interventions. VIET community educators lead students in targeted skill-building activities.

- Strong collaboration is also evident at Young Scholars' Academy. When Principal Danika LaCroix was assigned to reconstitute a failing Brooklyn elementary school, she vowed to give her students as rigorous and broad an education as children get in more affluent neighborhoods. The school divided 3 extra hours among intensive math, English, and enrichment experiences chosen by students and parents, including dance and robotics. While community staff members work alongside teachers with small groups of students who need intensive instruction in math and literacy, students who are more advanced do homework with help from community staff.

Recommendations

- *School districts or schools and community organizations that are interested in expanding learning time and opportunities should start by assessing their readiness. Learnings from quality afterschool programs and strong community-school partnerships should inform their efforts.*

- *Schools that are considering more time as a turnaround strategy should partner with strong community organizations. By blending their resources and coalescing as teams, they can educate the whole child at a cost public funding can sustain. Schools and their community partners should involve families in school redesign and ongoing feedback to sustain progress.*

- *When thinking about increasing learning time, schools and their partners should assess gaps in the curriculum and identify student interests in order to ensure a well-rounded curriculum that deeply engages students and leads to higher achievement. More time will neither yield better results nor engage students more deeply unless it is used well.*

- *Schools should consider expanding the learning day to 5:30 or 6:00 p.m. to match parents' working hours and give students a third meal.*

- *Schools should track students' progress in attendance, grades, and behavior as well as academic achievement. Students who are chronically absent, fail math or science, or have significant behavior problems during the elementary and middle grades are at highest risk for dropping out of high school.*

For More Information

www.expandedschools.org

Is Your District Ready to ExpandED? A System-Level Readiness Tool
This tool was designed for school districts, cities, and intermediaries to assess their readiness to implement the core elements of ExpandED Schools. A school-level tool is also available.

Three Ways to Expand Learning
These schedules show how ExpandED Schools in Baltimore, New Orleans and New York City have re-engineered time and resources to an expanded school day.

A Fiscal Map for Expanded Learning Time (ELT)
TASC developed this fiscal map, analysis, and set of policy recommendations in an effort to (1) show how many sources of funding schools and community partners can bring to expanded learning approaches—29 at the federal level alone—and (2) highlight for policymakers who control one or more of these funding streams just how complex this picture is.

ABOUT THE AUTHOR

Lucy N. Friedman is the founding president of TASC, a nonprofit organization dedicated to giving all kids expanded learning opportunities that support, educate, and inspire them. Under her leadership, TASC has helped 442,000 kids, supported 528 public schools, partnered with 369 community and cultural organizations and colleges, and trained 21,000 community members to work in schools. She holds leadership positions in organizations including the Afterschool Alliance, the Coalition for Science After School, the New York State Afterschool Network, and the Collaborative for Building After-School Systems.

REFERENCES

New York City Department of Education. (2011). 2011 NYC school survey. Retrieved from http://schools.nyc.gov/Accountability/tools/survey/2011

New York City Department of Education. (2012). New York City results on the English language arts (ELA) & math tests, grades 3–8. Retrieved from http://schools.nyc.gov/Accountability/data/TestResults/ELAandMathTestResults

Policy Studies Associates & Abt Associations. (2012). *Education of ExpandED, TASC's national demonstration to expand learning time.* Unpublished report.

Reisner, E. R., White, R. N., Russell, C. A., & Birmingham, J. (2004). *Building quality, scale, and effectiveness in after-school programs.* Washington, DC: Policy Studies Associates.

Russell, C. A., Mielke, M. B., Miller, T. D., & Johnson, J. C. (2007). *After-school programs and high school success: Analysis of post-program educational patterns of former middle-grades TASC participants.* Washington, DC: Policy Studies Associates.

Anita Krishnamurthi
Director of STEM Policy, Afterschool Alliance

Ron Ottinger
Executive Director, Noyce Foundation

Tessie Topol
Senior Director for Strategic Philanthropy &
Community Affairs, Time Warner Cable

STEM Learning in Afterschool and Summer Programming: An Essential Strategy for STEM Education Reform

Science, technology, engineering, and math (STEM) skills are increasingly necessary to navigate an ever-more complex world and a globalized economy. There is tremendous energy and momentum to improve these skills among our citizens and students so they can participate fully in contemporary society and the modern economy.

> Afterschool and summer programs all over the United States are offering engaging, hands-on STEM learning programs that are not only getting children excited about these topics, but also are helping them build some real-life skills and proficiencies.

Yet most strategies and policies for reforming STEM education focus on what happens during the school day. While schools are absolutely essential for learning, we must acknowledge that children spend less than 20% of their waking hours in schools each year, and some persuasively argue that school is not where most Americans learn most of their science anyway (Falk & Dierkling, 2010).

Hence, efforts to improve and increase STEM education opportunities must include programs that take place during the afterschool hours and the summer. Despite the need for many more quality afterschool and summer programs, more than 8 million young people already attend afterschool programs (Afterschool Alliance, 2009).

In addition, there is a sizeable infrastructure of programming and support (for example, the 21st Century Community Learning Centers initiative and the California Afterschool and Safety Program) focused especially on serving young people from groups that are typically

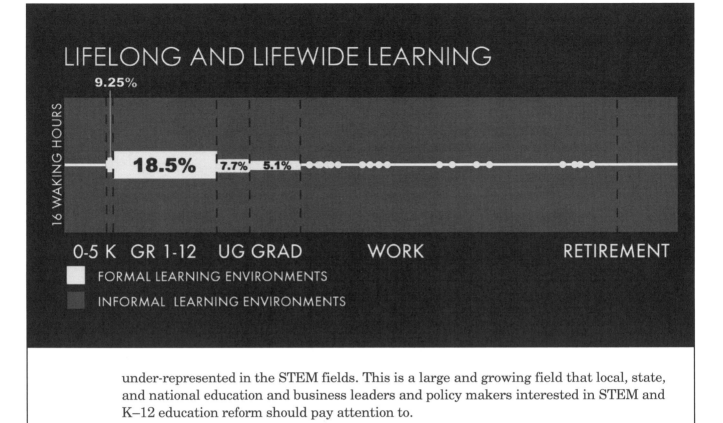

LIFELONG AND LIFEWIDE LEARNING

9.25%

16 WAKING HOURS

18.5%   7.7%   5.1%

0-5 K   GR 1-12   UG GRAD   WORK   RETIREMENT

☐ FORMAL LEARNING ENVIRONMENTS

☐ INFORMAL LEARNING ENVIRONMENTS

under-represented in the STEM fields. This is a large and growing field that local, state, and national education and business leaders and policy makers interested in STEM and K–12 education reform should pay attention to.

Afterschool and summer programs all over the United States are offering engaging, hands-on STEM learning programs that are not only getting children excited about these topics, but are also helping them build some real-life skills and proficiencies. There is mounting evidence that demonstrates the impact of these settings. A recent analysis of evaluation studies of several afterschool STEM programs showed that high quality programs can lead to increased interest and improved attitudes toward STEM fields and careers, increased STEM knowledge and skills, and increased likelihood of pursuing STEM majors and careers (Afterschool Alliance, 2011b).

Evidence of STEM Benefits From Afterschool

● **4-H** (nationwide) – 71% of 4-H science participants say science is now one of their favorite subjects, and 59% say they would like to have a job in a science field.

● **ACE Mentor Program** (nationwide) – 66% of program alumni (mostly from minority communities) are studying Architecture, Construction, or Engineering or working in one of these fields.

● *FIRST* (nationwide) – Participants learn a wide variety of skills, ranging from technical to teamwork and presentation skills, in this program focused on robotics. 89% of alumni go on to college.

● **TechBridge** (Oakland, CA) – This girls-only program enjoys great success, with more than 80% of participants reporting improved problem-solving, computer, and technical skills.

The impact of these types of expanded learning programs and extracurricular activities is also reflected in improvements in academic performance, as noted in the research cited by many other authors in this compendium. Other recent research also reveals the importance of out-of-school-time settings for STEM education. Tai, Liu, Maltese, and Fan (2006) found, for example, that early engagement with STEM fields was crucial and that a professed interest in STEM careers by eighth grade was a more accurate predictor of getting a science-related college degree than were the math or science test scores for average students. Thus, early encouragement of elementary and middle school students in STEM fields can be very effective in influencing their choice of college majors. Additionally, Wai, Lubinski, Benbow, and Steiger (2010) found that students who had more opportunities to participate in STEM learning (including beyond the classroom) were more likely to follow STEM career pathways and excel in them.

Afterschool programs are well placed to deliver on these needs by not only providing additional time to engage in STEM topics but also by doing so in a manner that is different from school and that engages different types of learners. These programs can also be very effective in improving access to STEM fields and careers among populations that are currently greatly underrepresented – women, African Americans, and Hispanics (Beede et al., 2011a; Beede et al., 2011b)—helped in part by the fact that African American and Hispanic children participate in afterschool programs in greater numbers (Afterschool Alliance, 2009).

Promising Trends in Afterschool STEM Learning

Afterschool programs are no strangers to STEM programming. STEM-rich institutions, such as museums and universities, as well as youth groups such as 4-H, Girls Inc., Girl Scouts, etc., that have deep roots in their communities, have been offering afterschool STEM programs for many decades. What has changed in the past decade is that they have renewed and deepened their commitment and that the average afterschool provider has also become interested in offering such opportunities to the children they serve. The only federal funding source exclusively dedicated to afterschool and summer learning programming, the 21st Century Community Learning Centers initiative, is now emphasizing STEM as a priority area for its grantees. Indeed, the importance of this key funding source cannot be overstated, as it is essential for providing the basic programs and infrastructure that many other STEM-focused partners can tap into to expand learning opportunities for students.

Funding from this federal initiative has significantly leveraged additional resources for STEM programming. For example, the Noyce Foundation is a private philanthropic foundation that invests heavily in afterschool STEM learning through innovative partnerships. A C. S. Mott Foundation-Noyce Foundation collaboration currently is active in 16 states and will continue to expand among the nation's growing number of state afterschool networks, which are supported by the Mott Foundation. Also Noyce is investing in "Project LIFTOFF," an initiative to develop and nurture afterschool STEM systems in 10 Midwestern states. This initiative has led many school districts to combine their foundation funding with their 21st Century Community Learning Centers funding to offer exceptionally high quality afterschool STEM opportunities.

In 2011, the Nebraska 21st Century Community Learning Centers program received a NASA Summer of Innovation grant to launch Nebraska BLAST! This is a 4-year collaborative initiative that brings together STEM content specialists with teachers and afterschool staff from schools that receive funding through the 21st Century Community Learning Centers initiative. This effort will provide high quality STEM training to staff of all of Nebraska's 21st Century Community Learning Centers programs and will give thousands of Nebraska youth the opportunity to engage in exciting, hands-on STEM experiences through their local program.

As schools, communities, and parents negotiate how to provide additional learning opportunities for their children and youth, afterschool and summer programs that work closely with schools provide a model to meet this need. Research shows that afterschool programs that are well aligned with the school day and have strong community ties have optimal benefits for kids (Afteschool Alliance, 2011a).

The corporate sector is also getting deeply involved in afterschool STEM education. Change the Equation is a nonprofit organization that was formed to help companies with their STEM education-related philanthropy. Most of the philanthropic investments of these companies focus on the "informal education" arena, which includes afterschool.

> Nebraska BLAST! will provide high quality STEM training to staff of all of Nebraska's 21st Century Community Learning Centers programs and will give thousands of Nebraska youth the opportunity to engage in exciting, hands-on STEM experiences.

For example, in 2009, Time Warner Cable (TWC) decided to focus the majority of its philanthropic resources on a single cause. The result was Connect a Million Minds (CAMM)—a 5-year, $100 million cash and in-kind commitment to inspire students to engage in math and science learning. To bring this commitment to life, TWC supports *FIRST* (For Inspiration and Recognition of Science and Technology), a robotics organization with a model proven to engage young people in STEM learning also funded by 21st Century Community Learning Centers programs in areas across the country. On a national level, TWC also partners with the Coalition for Science After School to provide the "Connectory," a free, online resource that makes it easy for parents and teachers to find informal STEM learning opportunities. In addition, TWC brings the impact of CAMM to its local markets by supporting *FIRST* teams and competitions, science museums, and other nonprofit organizations that are engaging kids in STEM.

Several *FIRST* teams have also utilized 21st Century Community Learning Centers funding with great success. The Camdenton R-III Afterschool Science, Engineering and Robotics program in rural Missouri receives funding from the 21st Century Community Learning Centers initiative and has leveraged that to great effect. Their team has won several awards, including the regional competition that has allowed them to go to the finals for 2 years in a row. The Safe Harbor Before and After School Program in Michigan City, Indiana, which has received 21st Century Community Learning Centers funds for many years, worked with the Indiana Afterschool Network and the Indiana Department of Education to develop a *FIRST* Robotics team in 2012. The team won the All Star Rookie award in the Midwest and went to the national championship.

Recommendations

It is becoming clear that there is a great need—and a prime opportunity—to tap the potential of afterschool and summer learning programs to serve an urgent national priority to enhance STEM education. Deliberate action by all key stakeholders is required, however, to help afterschool and summer programs fully realize this potential and become strategic—and integral—partners in STEM education.

Federal and state education policies must ensure, in particular, that afterschool and summer programs are included in STEM education policy initiatives if this to become a sustainable, long-term practice (Krishnamurthi, 2012; Afterschool Alliance, 2012).

In addition, the afterschool field must also adopt several strategies to become effective partners in STEM education:

- *Afterschool programs must deliberately commit to offering STEM learning opportunities and then prioritize and allocate resources to provide professional development in STEM programming areas to staff.*

- *Afterschool intermediary organizations and large networks must widely promote existing high quality curricula to avoid wasting scarce resources on developing new programs and curricula.*

- *The field must reach consensus around youth outcome indicators and adopt them widely so that programs have a clear vision of their goals and role within the STEM education ecosystem. A local- or state-level hub is often a necessity for disseminating information and coordinating professional development efforts and other STEM programming needs for afterschool. This may include seeking partnerships with STEM-rich institutions, such as science museums and universities, as well as other science and math hubs in many states.*

- *Meaningful STEM learning that extends beyond one-shot experiences are necessary. Afterschool and summer programs must pay close attention to offering regular, consistent programming in STEM topics. Furthermore, wherever possible, programs must offer a continuum of STEM learning experiences that extend into middle and high school in order to derive maximum impact from their STEM programming.*

Employers and professionals in STEM fields who would like to engage in afterschool programs might find it helpful to familiarize themselves with the landscape of afterschool STEM in their region before getting started. As with any new community, the afterschool field has its own culture and philosophy, and it is important to be aware of the issues before delving into it.

- *A good place to start is to seek out the Mott-funded statewide afterschool network in the state, the national Afterschool Alliance, the local afterschool consortium, or the National Girls Collaborative Project and other similar networks to find out about existing efforts and partnership needs.*

- *Large afterschool providers, such as local and state 21st Community Learning Centers programs, 4-H, Boys and Girls Clubs, Girls Inc., the YMCA, as well as afterschool coordinators within school districts, are all good places to get started at a local level.*

- *Additionally, businesses wishing to get involved in supporting afterschool and summer STEM programming might find the guidelines suggested by Change the Equation in their "Design Principles for Effective Philanthropy" (n.d.) useful. Public-private partnerships could also greatly advance the systems-building effort required to support STEM learning in afterschool by focusing on content-related professional development, evaluation studies, and other technical assistance. An example of such a public-private partnership is that between the Mott Foundation and the Department of Education around the 21st Century Community Learning Centers. Recently, the Noyce Foundation has partnered with the Mott Foundation to support some of the Statewide Afterschool Networks in their STEM efforts, further leveraging the investments. Many other partnership opportunities are available with the state afterschool networks and local and state 21st Century Community Learning Centers programs.*

Afterschool and summers programs have emerged as essential partners in improving and increasing STEM education opportunities for our children and youth. They are often overlooked but have a big and growing infrastructure and interest in STEM. Your involvement and leadership is needed to capitalize on it.

For More Information

- **Afterschool Alliance** – http://www.afterschoolalliance.org/STEM – This website provides information on resources for programs as well as ways for STEM professionals to get involved in afterschool.

- **Coalition for Science After School** – http://afterschoolscience.org/ – This organization has several resources, including a guide to science activities and curricula (look under the Program Resources tab).

- **Connect a Million Minds Connectory** – http://connectamillionminds.com/ connectory.php – This resource allows you to search by zip code for activities and resources for afterschool programs.

- **Statewide Afterschool Networks** – http://www.statewideafterschoolnetworks. net/ – The Statewide Afterschool Networks work with a broad range of partners to foster partnerships and policies to develop, support and sustain high quality afterschool and expanded learning opportunities for children and youth.

ABOUT THE AUTHORS

Anita Krishnamurthi is director of STEM policy at the Afterschool Alliance. She leads the Alliance's efforts to advance policies, research, and partnerships so children and youth can have rich STEM education experiences in their afterschool programs. She worked at the National Aeronautics and Space Administration (NASA) for 6 years. Before joining NASA, Anita was a program officer at the National Academy of Sciences. Anita's formal training is as an astrophysicist,

Ron Ottinger is the executive director of the Noyce Foundation and is leading the foundation's initiatives in informal and out-of-school-time science, focusing on field-building efforts that are marrying afterschool and science. These efforts include strategies to scale quality out-of-school science programming nationally within the Mott State Afterschool Networks, the urban Collaborative for Building After School Systems, 4-H, the Afterschool Alliance, National Afterschool Association, and National Summer Learning Association.

Tessie Topol is senior director for strategic philanthropy & community affairs at Time Warner Cable. In this role, she is responsible for the company's community giving and engagement strategy and leads its signature philanthropy program, Connect a Million Minds™, a 5-year, $100 million cash and in-kind initiative to inspire the next generation of STEM innovators.

REFERENCES

Afterschool Alliance. (2009). *American after 3pm: The most in-depth study of how America's children spend their afternoons*. Retrieved from http://www.afterschoolalliance.org/AA3_Full_Report.pdf

Afterschool Alliance. (2011a). *Evaluations backgrounder: A summary of formal evaluations of afterschool programs' impact on academics, behavior, safety and family life*. Retrieved from http://www.afterschoolalliance.org/documents/EvaluationsBackgrounder2011.pdf

Afterschool Alliance. (2011b). *STEM learning in afterschool: An analysis of impact and outcomes*. Retrieved from http://www.afterschoolalliance.org/STEM-Afterschool-Outcomes.pdf.

Afterschool Alliance. (2012). *Afterschool programs as partners in STEM education: Policy recommendations*. Retrieved from http://www.afterschoolalliance.org/Alliance_STEM_Policyasks_FINAL.pdf

Beede, B., Julian, T., Khan, B., Lehrman, R., McKittrick, G., Langdon, D., & Doms, M. (2011a). Education supports racial and ethnic equality in STEM [Executive summary]. Retrieved from U.S. Department of Commerce, Economics and Statistics Administration website: http://esa.gov/Reports/education-supports-racial-and-ethnic-equality-stem

Beede, B., Julian, T., Langdon, D., McKittrick, G., Khan, B., & Doms, M. (2011b). Women in STEM: A gender gap to innovation. Retrieved from U.S. Department of Commerce, Economics and Statistics Administration website: http://esa.gov/Reports/women-stem-gender-gap-innovation

Change the Equation. (n.d.). Design principles for effective STEM philanthropy. Retrieved from http://changetheequation.org/design-principles-effective-stem-philanthropy

Falk, J. H., & Dierkling, L. D. (2010). The 95 percent solution. *American Scientist, 98*, 486–493.

Krishnamurthi, A. (2012, June 15). [Letter to Joan Ferrini-Mundy, Leland Melvin, and Michael Feder]. Retrieved from http://www.afterschoolalliance.org/stem/AfterschoolAlliance_CoSTEM_recommendations.pdf

Tai, R. H., Liu, C. Q., Maltese, A. V., & Fan, X. (2006). Planning early for careers in science. *Science, 312*, 1143–1144.

Wai, J., Lubinski, D., Benbow, C. P., & Steiger, J. H. (2010). Accomplishment in science, technology, engineering, and mathematics (STEM) and its relation to STEM education dose: a 25-year longitudinal study. *Journal of Educational Psychology, 102*(4), 860–871.

Alexis Menten
Director, Afterschool and Youth Leadership
Initiatives, Asia Society

Evie Hantzopoulos
Executive Director, Global Kids

Learning for a Complex World: Expanding Global Learning in Afterschool and Summers

Leaders in the afterschool and summer learning fields are increasingly in agreement on a single, fundamental belief: High quality afterschool and summer programs should focus on providing what young people need to be successful in school and in life. Exemplary programs seek to fill the gaps between school, community, and home in ways that not only keep kids on track, but also help them get ahead and become contributing members of society. Furthermore, the type of learning provided by high quality afterschool and summer learning programs is designed to be hands-on, experiential learning that engages youth in personally meaningful topics and pursuits while simultaneously reinforcing core knowledge and skills. This article will describe how high quality, cutting-edge programs can incorporate all of these core principles and strategies and, in addition, do it within a *global learning framework*, thereby providing enhanced relevance and meaning for youth in our rapidly changing world.

When considering what young people need to be successful in both college and career, those in the business community (Committee for Economic Development, 2006; New Commission on the Skills of the American Workforce, 2008) and the higher education community (Reimers, 2006; Reimers, 2009) alike emphasize that knowledge of the wider world, the skills to innovate and navigate in multiple contexts, and the dispositions to make a positive impact are critical. The complex mix of knowledge, skills, and dispositions that makes up *global competence* is no longer only required for specific university majors or certain careers—and it can no longer be for elite students only. Global competence is critical for all students, from all backgrounds, to be able to collaborate and compete effectively in the global 21st century (Darling-Hammond, 2010). Building global competence is an especially powerful tool for broadening students' skill sets, interests, and capacity for learning, especially in underserved and marginalized communities.

> Building global competence is an especially powerful tool for broadening students' skill sets, interests, and capacity for learning, especially in underserved and marginalized communities.

By using the world as a context for learning, afterschool and summer programs can help youth explore meaningful and relevant content while developing the academic skills and other competencies they need to succeed as citizens of the 21st century. The process by which young people develop global competence needs to become an essential approach for all education programs, both in school and out of school. Global learning provides the opportunity for experiential, interdisciplinary learning that deeply engages youth and that more tightly links schools, communities, and families around a focus on global issues and topics that have local and personal connections.

Defining Global Competence

The Council of Chief State School Officers recently partnered with the Asia Society to convene a national task force that defined global competence as *the capacity and disposition to understand and act on issues of global significance*. Globally competent students are able to:

1. **Investigate the world** beyond their immediate environment, framing significant problems and conducting well-crafted and age-appropriate research.

2. **Recognize perspectives**, others' and their own, articulating and explaining such perspectives thoughtfully and respectfully.

3. **Communicate ideas** effectively with diverse audiences, bridging geographic, linguistic, ideological, and cultural barriers.

4. **Take action** to improve conditions, viewing themselves as players in the world and participating reflectively (Boix Mansilla & Jackson, 2011).

In the push to focus on standardized tests, however, these four domains of global competence are often addressed as an afterthought, or they are seen as the natural byproduct of a good education. In fact, the types of knowledge and skills required to achieve global competence can be *foundational* to—not simply a result of—disciplinary and interdisciplinary inquiry. In this article, we demonstrate how schools and afterschool programs can integrate global learning as the foundation for a comprehensive approach to crafting curriculum, facilitating instruction, and embedding authentic assessment.

Promising Practices in Global Learning

The four domains of global competence described above provide a ready lens for embedding globally significant content and contexts into afterschool programming. The key is to consider how the global context adds meaning to the knowledge and skills reflected by state standards for student achievement or other learning goals. Rather than treat global competence as an "add-on," afterschool and in-school educators can use the four domains described above as a framework for student engagement and learning.

In terms of curriculum, global competence has clear implications for the content and topics that educators and students in school and in expanded learning programs choose to explore in the course of teaching and learning. In *Educating for Global Competence*, Boix Mansilla and Jackson (2011) write that globally significant topics generate deep engagement, demonstrate clear local-global connections and visible global significance, and invite genuine disciplinary or interdisciplinary exploration:

> *Topics can be deemed significant on multiple grounds: breadth, uniqueness, immediacy, consequence, urgency, ethical implications. Some topics matter because they affect a large number of people on the planet (e.g., climate change). Others may be significant because they demand urgent global solutions (e.g., girls' rights to education, global health and security) or because they directly affect students' lives (e.g., migration in local neighborhoods). Clarity about why a topic matters underlies all quality instruction (p. 56).*

Classroom teachers and community educators in afterschool and summer programs must consider how best to guide student learning on globally significant topics. As described above, the four domains of global competence expect learners to investigate the world, recognize perspectives, communicate ideas, and take action. This framework is designed to promote engaged and active inquiry and can serve as a guide for structuring instruction that promotes global learning. When applied to significant content and topics, the framework offers a powerful tool for guiding student learning both within and across disciplines.

Clearly, the type of learning that global competence requires cannot be assessed via a simple multiple choice test. Educators can assess student progress and achievement by creating learning opportunities that require students not only to acquire knowledge and skills but also to apply them to complex problems in novel situations. A variety of performance-based assessments, such as presentations, performances, exhibitions, and action projects, provide critical information to the staff about where students are on their journey towards global competence. In addition, and perhaps more importantly, more authentic assessments with real-world audiences motivate repeated practice and drive student engagement towards mastery.

> When afterschool programs use global learning as the foundation for curriculum, instruction, and assessment, they are able to connect with school subjects across the disciplines while continuing to ground learning in the core principles of youth development.

Global Learning in Out-of-School Time

When afterschool programs use global learning as the foundation for curriculum, instruction, and assessment, they are able to connect with school subjects across the disciplines while continuing to ground learning in the core principles of youth development. One outstanding example of how afterschool programs can infuse youth leadership and development principles within a global education and civic engagement curriculum is provided by Global Kids. Global Kids offers a number of globally oriented education programs to youth during the school day, after school, and during the summer at school sites across New York City and Washington, DC, as well as online.

Four key strategies undergird all Global Kids programs: global education, civic engagement, leadership development, and college/career readiness. The curriculum is designed as a series of 1.5- to 2-hour workshops, each focused on a global issue. The workshops incorporate active learning in the form of small-group work, games, role-playing, and the use of media and technology to bring issues to life. The goal is to engage youth participants in interactive activities and ensure they are actively sharing knowledge and discussing and debating the issues at hand. In planning the curriculum, staff members first identify a set of core learning outcomes and competencies, which include content, skills, and experiences. Then taking into account youth input on what they want to learn, Global Kids staff map out a series of themes for the year and assign each theme to a staff member to develop, according to his/her expertise and interest.

> The workshops incorporate active learning in the form of small-group work, games, role-playing, and the use of media and technology to bring issues to life.

Although workshops are the core components of the organization's approach, Global Kids also incorporates field trips, guest speakers, and other elements to help youth engage with critical issues. Youth across all programs are required to take action by developing and implementing substantive peer-education projects—including workshops, movie screenings and discussions, mini-conferences, and educational theater pieces—as well as social action and service projects. A recent youth-driven Global Kids campaign involved local, national, and international engagement on climate change, including the participation of five students at the United Nations Rio +20 Earth Summit in Brazil in June 2012.

Afterschool programs in more rural communities can also take a global approach to connecting youth development with academic achievement. At the Newfound Regional High School in Bristol, New Hampshire, a federally funded 21st Century Community Learning Centers program has become an afterschool International Club that offers students expanded learning opportunities (ELOs) to earn high school credit. The afterschool director works with the teachers to build their capacity to develop student-driven performance assessment tasks connecting global competencies with course competencies. The student-driven International Club decided to lead an international project monthly for the entire school. The students design the project, identifying the competencies they are targeting and the means by which these competencies will be assessed.

In Milledgeville, Georgia, the High Achievers Program has incorporated a global learning focus by creating a structure for programming, staffing, and partnerships that would support the development of global competences in youth from age 6 to 18. During this year-round expanded learning program, youth in grades 9–12 learn about different countries and cultures that are linked to current events and that have connections to the United States. These youth participate in the Peace Corps World Wise Schools curriculum and Skype with Peace Corps volunteers living abroad. Students compare what they are learning about global issues with issues that affect them in their community. These youth are then hired to serve as camp counselors for younger students, ages 6–12, who attend global-themed camps held over spring break and during the summer. During the Global Spring Break Camp, high school youth help their younger peers explore a different country each day, while during the Global Summer Camps, students explore a different country each week. The High Achievers Program relies on strong community partnerships for its success. The program works closely with the Georgia College and State University at Milledgeville. College interns gain required experiential learning hours by working with the high school students throughout the year to identify global topics, issues, and examples that the students then research and convert into activities for the spring break and summer camps for younger children. International faculty and students from the college visit the program throughout the year to talk about their native cultures as well.

For More Information

The following websites provide additional resources on global competence and global learning in afterschool programs:

- Expanding Horizons: Developing Global Learning in Out-of-School Time
  www.asiasociety.org/expandedlearning

- CCSSO EdSteps Project: Global Competence
  http://edsteps.org/

- Educating for Global Competence: Preparing Our Youth to Engage the World
  http://asiasociety.org/files/book-globalcompetence.pdf

- Global Kids
  www.globalkids.org

Recommendations for Getting Started

The Asia Society provides technical assistance to afterschool and summer programs across the nation, including many statewide afterschool networks, that are seeking to incorporate a focus on global education. Drawing on its capacity-building work, the Asia Society offers the following recommendations to help afterschool and summer programs consider how best to integrate a global learning approach to help youth become globally competent:

1. **Form partnerships** with local businesses, nonprofits, and universities, many of which have global connections and resources to help you get started—and can help you spread the word and build local interest and support.

2. **Create clear learning goals** that combine disciplinary knowledge and skills embedded in state or local student achievement standards with the four domains of global competence: Investigate the World, Recognize Perspectives, Communicate Ideas, and Take Action. See the CCSSO EdSteps website for a matrix of global learning outcomes: http://edsteps.org/CCSSO/DownloadPopUp.aspx?url=SampleWorks/Matrix_Print_Apr8.pdf

3. **Design curriculum around globally significant topics** that have local and personal connections within your community and student populations. Consider long-term projects as well as the shorter 1–2 hour workshop format that Global Kids employs.

4. **Foster active and engaged inquiry** by using the four domains of global competence defined by the Asia Society and the CCSSO taskforce to structure student learning.

5. **Embed authentic assessments** that enable to students to apply and demonstrate their learning through performances for real-world audiences.

ABOUT THE AUTHORS

Alexis Menten directs Asia Society's Expanding Horizons initiative, which provides technical assistance and professional development to national, state, and local expanded learning programs and afterschool intermediaries. She also leads the Society's Proficiency-Based Pathways work, which is implementing a performance-based assessment system for global competence in four high schools in Colorado, Texas, and New Hampshire. Menten joined Asia Society in 2005 after several years in Central Asia and the Middle East.

Evie Hantzopoulos became executive director of Global Kids in 2010, after serving as its director of programs/deputy director since 1996. Over the years, she has helped oversee the development, supervision, and expansion of GK's global education, youth leadership, and social action programs in New York City and Washington, DC, public schools. She also spearheaded the writing of Teen Action, a service-learning curriculum grounded in GK methodology for the New York City Department of Youth and Community Development. Hantzopoulos is a member of the Council on Foreign Relations.

REFERENCES

Boix Mansilla, V. & Jackson, A. (2011). *Educating for global competence: Preparing our youth to engage the world.* Council of Chief State School Officers' EdSteps Initiative and Asia Society Partnership for Global Learning. Retrieved from http://asiasociety.org/files/book-globalcompetence.pdf

Committee for Economic Development. (2006). *Education for global leadership: The importance of international studies and foreign language education for U.S. economic and national security.* Retrieved from http://www.eric.ed.gov/PDFS/ED502294.pdf

Darling-Hammond, L. (2010). *The flat world and education: How America's commitment to equity will determine our future.* New York, NY: Teachers College Press.

New Commission on the Skills of the American Workforce. (2008). *Tough choices or tough times.* National Center on Education and the Economy. Retrieved from http://www.skillscommission.org/wp-content/uploads/2010/05/ToughChoices_EXECSUM.pdf

Reimers, F. (2006). Citizenship, identity and education: Examining the public purposes of schools in an age of globalization. *Prospects, 36*(3), 275–294.

Reimers, F. (2009). "Global competency" is imperative for global success. *Chronicle of Higher Education, 55*(21), A29.

Stewart, V. (2007). Becoming citizens of the world. *Educational Leadership, 64*(7), 8–14.

Suarez-Orozco, M., & Qin-Hilliard, D. (Eds.). (2004). *Globalization: Culture and education in the new millennium.* Berkeley & Los Angeles, CA: University of California Press.

Gigi Antoni
President/CEO, Big Thought

Rickie Nutik
Executive Director, Young Audiences of Louisiana

Amy Rasmussen
Executive Director, Chicago Arts Partnerships
in Education

Reversing Learning Loss Through the Arts in Afterschool and Summers

In the religion of "being-a-kid," few times are as sacrosanct as the free hours after school and during the summer. Unfortunately for parents, educators and policy makers, it is not an easy task to convince students to put down the PlayStation and focus on learning in their time off—yet the advantages of doing so are widely regarded as critical in determining academic success. Previous studies (e.g., Alexander, Entwisle, & Olson, 2007; Cooper, Nye, Charlton, Lindsay, & Greathouse, 1996) show that when students, especially those from low-income households, are not provided educational opportunities in the vast amount of time that they are not in the traditional classroom, they lag behind their peers in reading and math and are less likely to graduate from high school.

Nonprofits across the nation have been testing the hypothesis that integrating creative activities like dance, theater, music, and visual arts with core academics in the context of afterschool and summer learning programs not only reverses these troubling trends but actually helps students invest in and seek out learning, motivated by interesting, yet rigorous, educational experiences.

This article describes the academic, social, and societal benefits of creative summer and afterschool programming from the viewpoint of three successful nonprofits: Chicago Arts Partnerships in Education (CAPE), Young Audiences of Louisiana, and Big Thought in Dallas, Texas. Each emphatically supports the inclusion of enrichment in extended day programs. Collectively, their experiences suggest four foundational principles for more effective afterschool and summer programming.

Why the Arts?

James Catterall (2009) demonstrates that children who participate in the arts succeed academically, socially, and cognitively in his formative longitudinal study, *Doing Good and Doing Well by Doing Arts*. In fact, the students Catterall studied showed marked gains, as compared to their peers, in most behavioral and academic areas when they maintained their involvement in the arts over the years. For most non-arts advocates, this information raises the question *why?*

Creative programs inherently offer unique environments for learning, but in afterschool contexts these benefits are especially pronounced. For instance, students who enter into formal learning with developmental or social obstacles possess the same potential as their peers and often flourish when barriers to learning are minimized or removed. An English language learning student might struggle to complete assignments in language arts or mathematics but can, just like his or her peers, paint a picture of family or master chords on the guitar by watching an instructor. The arts offer an entry point to reintroduce learning as something positive and equitable.

For Young Audiences of Louisiana, executive director Rickie Nutik has observed that students who feel displaced or dispirited in traditional classrooms or settings often find a place to shine and excel outside of the classroom, equipping them with the self-esteem to push themselves intrinsically and find the motivation to work harder. This desire is particularly useful for helping students discover activities that they cherish—or as author Peter Benson (2008) describes it, helping students' "spark." Kids who find their deepest passions in an academic setting are inspired from within to achieve, both as a student and as a person. Dr. Benson found that the creative arts are consistently one of the top activities that imbue intrinsic motivation in children.

> The arts offer an entry point to reintroduce learning as something positive and equitable.

For all students, high- and low-achieving, focusing on the arts after school and during the summers can maximize the pivotal in-school hours between 8:00 a.m. and 3:00 p.m. Students in Chicago Public Schools attend school for less than 6 hours a day for 170 days per year (as compared to 7 hours a day for 180 days a year in Houston, for example), which means that educators often do not have the time available to go beyond basic learning. Teachers' minutes are stretched and often dictated by strict testing guidelines. Amy Rasmussen, executive director at Chicago Arts Partnerships in Education (CAPE), believes that afterschool providers like hers are invaluable in not just lengthening the lessons taught during school, but in *strengthening* them.

Organizations like CAPE, Young Audiences of Louisiana, and Big Thought identify the concepts that students struggle with during the school day and use the afterschool time to expand students' exposure and understanding of core curriculum. A student unable to master fractions might understand them in a dance context, learning through active, tangible quarter steps and half turns. Since 2007, CAPE has studied creativity through observable indicators, demonstrating that students participating in creative programming report that they are better able to understand core curriculum principles when they are explained through creative activities. In one case study, a teaching artist and language arts teacher co-created curriculum combining photography with lessons on tone, a key concept measured by the English Advanced Placement Test. Of 19 students participating, 17 agreed that they believed the curriculum helped them understand tone and other literary devices in a deeper, more meaningful way (Paradis, 2011).

> A student unable to master fractions might understand them in a dance context, learning through active, tangible quarter steps and half turns.

The President's Committee on the Arts and the Humanities (2011) describes these kinds of outcomes in terms of "habits of mind" that create agile and flexible ways of thinking. America has entered a Steve Jobs era of success: the minds that can innovate are the minds that will find success. Unlike 50 years ago, there is not a skill or knowledge set that will not require updating, remodeling, or improving. Today's students will have to adapt to dynamic technologies and rapidly changing industries in practically every job that they encounter in the 21st century economy.

What Do We Know About How to Make Programs Effective, Engaging, and Successful?

To begin deciphering the ingredients of success in arts and creative learning in afterschool and summer programs, the Chicago Arts Partnerships in Education in Chicago, Young Audiences of Louisiana, and Big Thought in Dallas analyzed what they learned and what strategies and approaches might have implications for others. All three organizations

- *possess decades of arts and education program delivery and coordination experience;*

- *research and evaluate curriculum, professional development, and arts integration techniques;*

- *document the academic, social, and societal benefits of creative summer and afterschool programming; and*

- *support the inclusion of enrichment in extended day programs and in the school day.*

To make these opportunities happen "on the ground" in multiple locations across Louisiana, Chicago, and Dallas, they build bridges among parents, schools, instructors, cultural institutions, school districts, and city resources.

An analysis of their experiences and history of success suggests the following four foundational principles as the basis for more effective afterschool and summer programming:

1. **The arts in an afterschool and summer learning context naturally advance quality teaching and learning. When students and teachers have wider parameters in how and where to carry out curriculum, the learning environment flourishes.**

Students in Big Thought's Thriving Minds Summer Camps, in cooperation with the Dallas Independent School District (Dallas ISD), visited a variety of city cultural and educational institutions as part of their summer learning in 2010–11. Students traveled to a nature conservatory, for instance, where they took pond samples and then drew or diagrammed the creatures they found to tie in with their science classes. Some also visited a historic district and spoke with an architect to understand the significance of buildings in their own neighborhoods. In all cases, students were exposed to distinctive lessons that lent themselves to high-impact learning opportunities.

High-impact learning is demonstrated by students when they freely offer ideas, show an active interest in making better or more creative choices, and work with the teacher to discover principles instead of memorize facts. At this level, students work towards higher grades, better answers, and intrinsic goals. The chart below provides an analysis of the increased positive influence of Big Thought programs on students' learning opportunities in the summer. Assessed across a 4-year observational period, these opportunities are arranged along a scale of lowest impact learning (insufficient) to highest impact learning (advanced). Through a citywide commitment to creative learning, the number of Dallas participants who moved out of the "less than basic" learning designation to reach basic, proficient, or advanced increased by 22 percentage points.

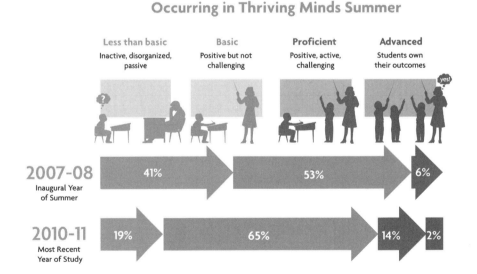

Percentage of High-Impact Learning Occurring in Thriving Minds Summer

Creating Quality. (n.d.). Summer learning - student benefits. Retrieved from http://www. creatingquality.org/Home/SummerLearning/BenefitsforStudents.aspx

The increase in high impact learning has meant that students in Dallas classrooms are beginning to catch up with their peers on standardized tests. For instance, after participating in Thriving Minds Summer Camps with greater high-impact learning, students' scores rose dramatically in only one year. Participants in grades 3 through 5 who significantly trailed their peers in 2010 saw scores on the 2011 state reading assessment rise 7 percentage points, while math scores improved more than 10 percentage points (Big Thought, 2011).

2. **Educators who seek to work with afterschool and summer providers are often the crème-de-la-crème, having chosen to participate explicitly because they have the energy and desire to reach children better. These attributes are particularly useful when general classroom teachers and artists team up.**

The classroom instructors and teaching artists bring complementary paradigms that both types of professionals typically find highly valuable. In the case of Chicago Arts Partnerships in Education, the organization began by examining the needs of each school to tailor programs that were most effective.

CAPE planned with the schools themselves, asking a variety of questions about the programs currently in place and determining where important connections could be made through the arts. The organization interviewed teachers and administrators to determine what kinds of integration points they needed help with, such as social studies, math, or other core subjects. CAPE's studies (DeMoss & Morris, 2002; Paradis, 2011) of the effectiveness show extensive buy-in from teachers and artists, with 91% integrating academics and with 94% of elementary students saying this made "learning fun."

In fact, the students did more than have fun—they showed gains in affective connections to core subjects. The arts consistently engaged all students in complex and analytical cognitive processes, including those students who typically struggle with academic content. No such gains were associated with traditional instructional experiences.

3. **As many of us have experienced, a trip to the principal's office was not generally positive as a child and remains similarly unappealing as an adult. Too often, parents are called in to the school when there's a problem. With afterschool and summer programs, they are called in when their children are doing something positive and excelling.**

Rickie Nutik explains that parents in New Orleans find afterschool and summer programs less intimidating and more flexible, encouraging them to take a more active role in their child's education. As a result, Young Audiences of Louisiana has employed a parent engagement specialist so that parents willing to help are met in the middle by the convening organization.

This success mirrors the formative work that Big Thought has done to determine what keeps parents distant from the learning process. In 2003, Big Thought began interviewing hundreds of families and found that an overwhelming majority indicated that two major barriers are lack of information (communicated in both Spanish and English and in a timely manner) and lack of transportation. By marketing and providing buses for family outings, celebration events, school-based recitals, or parent-teacher meetings, nonprofits can play a catalytic role as connectors and conveners.

In fact, many afterschool and summer learning programmers have begun to offer English classes for English language learning parents or workshops for those interested in financial literacy or parenting courses to become better all-around caregivers.

4. **Thanks to the 21st Century Community Learning Centers grants provided by the United States Department of Education, nonprofits like Chicago Arts Partnerships in Education, Big Thought, and Young Audiences of Louisiana are expanding relationships with local organizations beyond the "usual suspects."**

For instance, Chicago Arts Partnerships in Education not only partners with dance and theater companies to carry out afterschool programs, they also partner with family/social service organizations that provide emotional and developmental supports to children and families.

> Arts and creative education nonprofits can take the lead in providing these valuable programs and services, using what they know best—how to spark the interests of children through exciting curriculum and instruction.

In fact, many newly formed partnerships stemmed from the interest of a non-arts organization. Young Audiences of Louisiana found that the 21st Century Community Learning Centers grants magnetized nonprofits in the area that had been interested in reaching children in valuable ways but that had struggled to find the right partner or mechanisms to operationalize the work. Some willing partners simply lacked funding, thus giving the 21st Century Community Learning Centers grants powerful leverage. The 21st Century Community Learning Centers initiative, in fact, is the only nationwide major federal education program that requires community-school partnerships to expand learning opportunities in afterschool and summers.

Moreover, 21st Century Community Learning Centers grants can also act as a catalyst to garner the attention of additional funding sources. The afterschool and summer areas have only just begun to enter the consciousness of many donors, major and minor. In order to facilitate dynamic and effective programming, it will take braided funding from multiple sources, as well as an array of partnerships, to design, deliver, and integrate creative activities. Ultimately the complexities of funding, designing, and implementing these programs are outweighed by the potential to dramatically affect student behavior, academic achievement, and development.

Conclusion

By placing the arts at the center of afterschool and summer learning time, arts organizations will respond to the overwhelming demand by civic leaders, parents, and educators for high quality, creative, expanded learning opportunities for children and youth.

With sustained financial support from the 21st Century Community Learning Centers initiative and other similar state and local afterschool and summer funding streams, arts and creative education nonprofits can take the lead in providing these valuable programs and services, using what they know best—how to spark the interests of children through exciting curriculum and instruction.

School, community, and parent leaders should reach out to their arts, cultural, and creative organizations and businesses to explore how they can systematically work together to integrate and infuse the arts into their expanded learning opportunities in the summers and afterschool. Furthermore, schools can incentivize these partnerships and creative teaching and learning by using their Title I, Title II, and local funds in new but entirely permissible ways—thereby maximizing their impact and leveraging other resources.

The beneficiaries will not just be arts organizations and participating schools but the children themselves—a goal that can unite us all.

ABOUT THE AUTHORS

Gigi Antoni, president/CEO of Big Thought, has more than 20 years of experience as a nonprofit executive, consultant, and speaker, both nationally and internationally. She was named a Champion of Change by the White House and received the National Arts Leadership Award by the National Guild for Community Arts Education

Rickie Nutik is the executive director of Young Audiences New Orleans. She has worked on behalf of Louisiana children for over 25 years to inspire, empower, and unite children and communities through education, arts, and culture. She also serves on several community boards, including the Mayor's Advisory Committee on Youth and Families.

Amy Rasmussen serves as executive director of Chicago Arts Partnerships in Education, where she has guided the organization through unprecedented growth as a partner to Chicago Public Schools in implementing and sustaining arts programs. Rasmussen was named a Champion of Change for Arts Education by the White House in July 2011.

REFERENCES

Alexander, K., Entwisle, D., & Olson, L. (2007). Lasting consequences of the summer learning gap. *American Sociological Review, 72*, 167–180.

Benson, P. L. (2008). *Sparks: How parents can help ignite the hidden strengths of teenagers.* San Francisco, CA: Jossey-Bass.

Big Thought. (2011). [Summer learning report 2011]. Retrieved from http://www.bigthought.org/Portals/BT/PDFs/summercamp_2011.pdf

Catterall, J. S. (2009). *Doing well and doing good by doing art.* Los Angeles, CA: Imagination Group/I- Group Books.

Cooper, H., Nye, B., Charlton, K., Lindsay, J., & Greathouse, S. (1996). The effects of summer vacation on achievement test scores: A narrative and meta-analytic review. *Review of Educational Research, 66*, 227–268.

DeMoss, K., & Morris, T. (2002). *How arts integration supports student learning: Students shed light on the connections.* Retrieved from Chicago Arts Partnerships in Education website: http://www.capeweb.org/wp-content/uploads/2011/05/support.pdf

Paradis, L. (2011). *[Measuring] the seen and unseen: How the veteran units foster student creativity.* Retrieved from Chicago Arts Partnerships in Education website: http://www.capeweb.org/wp-content/uploads/2011/11/VETs-report-1011.pdf

President's Committee on the Arts and the Humanities. (2011). *Reinvesting in arts education: Winning America's future through creative schools.* Retrieved from http://www.pcah.gov/sites/default/files/PCAH_Reinvesting_4web_0.pdf

Sam Piha
Founder and Principal, Temescal Associates

David Sinski
Chief Officer of Strategy and Innovation,
After School Matters

Connecting Older Youth to Success Through Afterschool

Many people assume that since high school youth have outgrown daycare and have ready access to academic programs and extracurricular activities provided by the typical comprehensive high school, they have everything they need to succeed. One only has to look, however, at the high numbers of disconnected youth, as well as the high number of dropouts and the expressed concerns of the business community, to accept that many young people are not prepared to enter the workforce and join in as full participants in our nation's democracy.

Making the Case

Adolescents are at a time in their lives where they are experiencing a number of key developmental tasks that afterschool and summer learning programs have the opportunity to address. Robert Halpern (2009) describes these tasks, as follows:

- *Older youth begin to seek experiences that involve more complex tasks, and they start to assert control over their lives and communities. They also need to balance their preoccupation with self versus a commitment to others.*

- *Teenagers resist being dependent upon and controlled by another, while they also know they must navigate the adult world and create their role in it.*

- *Young people are forging a sense of identity and finding their voice as individuals who can positively influence others. They want to demonstrate real accomplishment, and they yearn for recognition of their achievements.*

While afterschool programs serving older youth are not new, there is growing recognition that they are critical for helping young people grow into well-rounded, successful adults.

Evaluations of 22 afterschool and summer programs done by the American Youth Policy Forum (AYPF) in 2009 found that older youth who participated in expanded learning opportunities demonstrate positive outcomes across a range of indicators, including improved academic success, career preparation, and social and emotional development (Bowles & Brand, 2009).

For some older youth, the regular school day can be too narrowly focused and not long enough to provide adequate access to the types of developmental activities that they want and need. While afterschool programs serving older youth are not new, there is growing recognition that they are critical for helping young people grow into well-rounded, successful adults. Adolescents need access to structured opportunities that offer greater autonomy and meaning. That said, due to competing demands for teenagers' time (such as hobbies, team sports, work, and social interests), activities provided by afterschool programs must be relevant to their wants and needs (Temescal Associates, 2009).

Research has shown that expanded learning opportunities are highly successful in improving young people's academic performance, college and career preparation, social and emotional development, and health and wellness (Bowles & Brand, 2009). Evaluations of 22 afterschool and summer programs done by the American Youth Policy Forum (AYPF) in 2009 found that older youth who participated in expanded learning opportunities demonstrate positive outcomes across a range of indicators, including improved academic success, career preparation, and social and emotional development (Bowles & Brand, 2009).

Promising Practices

Two large-scale afterschool and summer programs for older youth, one across California and one across Chicago, provide a learning laboratory for the field to identify what strategies and structures are most effective. Additionally, what makes these programs so instructive is that they are supported by different funding streams, are led and coordinated by different types of organizations, and were initiated at different levels—one at the state level primarily using federal funds and one at the local level primarily using local funds. Yet, their examples should be helpful to anyone interested in engaging older youth in afterschool and summer learning.

....

California

In California, over 50% of the state's 21st Century Community Learning Centers funding is dedicated to afterschool programs for high school age youth. These 5-year grants are currently supporting 345 high schools programs that serve nearly 55,000 youth. The following examples illuminate essential characteristics of effective local programs guided and supported by this key state-directed initiative known as the After School Safety and Education Program for Teens (ASSETs).

Engaging, Active, and Meaningful Learning Opportunities

Successful programs that serve older youth foster active, hands-on learning. For example, Balboa High School Afterschool program in San Francisco offers project-based learning clubs that allow participants to engage in hands-on activities, including woodworking, digital media arts and animation, and computer programming and troubleshooting.

Quality programs for teenagers often help them prepare for their future in the workforce. The Los Angeles After School All-Stars program, for example, exposes older youth participants to different career options in its Career Exploration Opportunities Initiative. Participants meet with local business owners, community leaders, and role models through in-person interviews and field trips to workplaces and business schools. Students have had the opportunity to interview chefs at the Culinary Institute and take a design class at the Sketchers headquarters, where they were able to design their own sneakers.

> Balboa High School Afterschool program in San Francisco offers project-based learning clubs that allow participants to engage in hands-on activities, including woodworking, digital media arts and animation, and computer programming and troubleshooting.

Community Involvement

Afterschool programs need to build relationships with organizations within the community in order to offer young people a bridging experience to the real world (Temescal Associates, 2009). For example, the program at McLane High School in Fresno, California, partners with a number of businesses and community organizations, such as GAP, Chic Shoes, Macy's, Mary-Kay, Bloomingdale's, the NFL, and other organizations, in order to provide in-kind donations, workshops, and speaking engagements covering topics such as self-esteem and healthy relationships.

Link to the School Day and Use of School Personnel

Successful afterschool programs must have a strong partnership with school site leaders. This partnership must be based on a shared vision of how they will support young people (Temescal Associates, 2009). The Blair LEARNS high school afterschool program in Pasadena, California, has had success in a number of areas, including recruitment and retention, improved school day attendance, and student achievement. This could not have been possible without the strong relationship between the program's director and the school principal. The two meet regularly and engage school counseling staff to share student performance data, including grades, test scores, attendance, and behavior/discipline. A large percentage of Blair LEARNS participants take advantage of the credit recovery option, and the school increased its on-time graduation rate by over 28% between 2003 and 2007. Of 155 on-time graduates in 2009, 84 relied on credits recovered in afterschool (Forum for Youth Investment, 2009).

Chicago

After School Matters targets high school teens in underserved neighborhoods who attend schools struggling with high drop out rates and low graduation rates. In 2011, After School Matters offered more than 900 programs across Chicago, engaging more than 15,000 teens. Partners included 60 high schools, more than 100 community-based organizations, the Chicago Park District, the Chicago Public Library, and various departments within the City of Chicago. Financial support for these opportunities is provided by a variety of sources, including government funding from the city of Chicago and the state of Illinois, partner support from the schools and parks, and contributions from corporations, foundations, and individuals.

After School Matters core programs are apprenticeships in which teens develop their career readiness capacities while learning marketable skills from industry professionals. The programs keep teens safe and connected to caring adults. A recent study by Northwestern University's School of Education and Social Policy found that teens participating in After School Matters showed more positive youth development and less problem behavior and exhibited a stronger sense of connection to their school, as well as a stronger perceived value of school and academics (Hirsch, Hedges, Stawicki, & Mekinda, 2011).

Some of the key strategies that make After School Matters successful include

- *hands-on, project-based activities in five content areas: arts, communications, sports, science, and technology;*

- *instructors with professional backgrounds in their content area;*

- *an annual professional development conference for instructors and ongoing youth-work training on concepts from the Youth Program Quality framework developed by the David P. Weikert Center for Youth Program Quality (http://www.cypq.org/);*

- *incentives, such as service learning credit, program awards or stipends, transportation support, end-of-year celebrations, food, field trips, guest speakers, and master classes taught by industry experts;*

- *formalized meetings with school leadership to review program success metrics and reinforce roles;*

- *simple introductory telephone conversations with parents to encourage full teen engagement in programming; and*

- *authentic learning that connects teens to the world outside of their school and neighborhood.*

Recommendations for Practitioners Within Schools and Within Communities

While the origination and funding sources of the afterschool and summer learning programs across California and in Chicago described above are different, the lessons learned are similar and consistent regarding how to make these programs work effectively. Based on those findings, here are some key recommendations:

- *Successful programs develop strong partnerships with community-based organizations and the school administration. This includes hiring staff members who develop strong working relationships with principals and key school personnel. Collaboration with community partners is also essential.*

- *In order to be competitive with older youth's interests and developmental needs, programs must offer a blend of structured activities, informal social time, opportunities to develop skills, and the chance to build close relationships with adults and peers. Older youth are also motivated to join programs that provide academic credit, college and job preparation, internship opportunities, and stipends for participation.*

- *Gathering youth input on program planning and offerings is crucial to engaging and retaining older youth.*

- *Successful programs should have strong adult leaders and skilled staff who are able to relate to older youth and are more expert in their subject matter than those who work with younger children.*

Capture Their Hearts and Their Minds Will Follow

Thanks to a partnership with NASA, students in the rural community of Santa Rosa, Texas, have created a community on Mars that was not only scientifically sound but also one they'd want to be a part of. Focused back on Earth, students toured the city's courthouse and met with a federal magistrate, whose personal story gave the teenagers a better understanding of how current coursework relates to future careers.

The "ACE" (Afterschool Centers on Education) program serves 300 students ages 12 to 18. It has a holistic approach that focuses on strengthening science, technology, engineering, mathematics, and arts skills. By blending in the arts, abstract thinking is increased and lets students explore creative ideas while also learning math and science. Thanks to extensive community partnerships, students are introduced to a range of careers through field trips and interactions with local leaders.

According to a survey of district teachers, 80% reported an increased rate of homework completion and 84% reported an overall improvement in academic performance for participating students. In the past year, 100% of seniors in the program graduated. By creating engaging and meaningful learning opportunities in partnership with the community the ACE program is truly living its motto "Capture their hearts and their minds will follow."

For More Information

There are a number of resources that provide best-practices recommendations for afterschool practitioners:

- **High School Field Resources** (http://www.temescalassociates.com/resources/hsresourcesfield.asp), developed by Temescal Associates, provides articles, written interviews, case studies, and other resources for high school workers.

- **Learning in Afterschool & Summer** (http://www.learninginafterschool.org/), developed by Temescal Associates, calls on afterschool to promote young people's learning by incorporating five key learning principles. It provides a number of resources for high school afterschool program leaders, including videos, research, literature, current developments in the afterschool field, a regularly updated blog, and much more.

- **Beyond Expectations: The Power of High School Afterschool** is a video that provides a number of best practices and recommendations for high school afterschool programs. It is available to watch or order at http://www.temescalassociates.com/video/beyondexpectationsweb/beyondexpectationswatch.htm.

- **After School Matters** (http://www.afterschoolmatters.org/) offers more detailed background on After School Matters, its programming, and related research.

ABOUT THE AUTHORS

Sam Piha is the founder and principal of Temescal Associates, a firm that provides consulting in education, youth development, and afterschool programs. He began his career in 1975 as a classroom teacher and a family therapist before directing afterschool programs at the regional and national levels. He has been a long-time advocate for and trainer on high school afterschool programs.

David Sinski is chief officer of strategy and innovation for After School Matters in Chicago. He has worked in youth development for over 25 years, starting first as a counselor to teenage runaways and their families and then working with immigrant families as they struggled to support teens at risk of psychiatric hospitalization. More recently he has held administrative positions and has currently served in leadership capacities at After School Matters. He has been active in building coalitions of providers and intermediaries and has great interest in nurturing learning communities regarding serving older youth.

REFERENCES

Bowles, A., & Brand, B. (2009). *Learning around the clock: Benefits of expanded learning opportunities for older youth*. Retrieved from http://www.temescalassociates.com/documents/resources/highschool/AYPF_ELOs_w-cvr.pdf

Forum for Youth Investment. (2009, April). *After-school grows up: Helping teens prepare for the future* (Out-of-School Time Policy Commentary No. 14). Retrieved from http://www.temescalassociates.com/documents/resources/temescal/OSTPC14.pdf

Halpern, R. (2009). *The means to grow up: Reinventing apprenticeship as a developmental support in adolescence*. New York, NY: Taylor & Francis.

Hirsch, B., Hedges, L., Stawicki, J., & Mekinda, M. (2011). *After-school programs for high school students: An evaluation of After School Matters*. Retrieved from http://www.sesp.northwestern.edu/docs/publications/19023555234df57ecd0d6c5.pdf

Temescal Associates. (2009). *Bedrock to rooftop: Building successful high school afterschool programs*. Retrieved from http://www.temescalassociates.com/documents/model/Bedrock_to_rooftop.pdf

Crystal Weedall FitzSimons
Director of School and Out-of-School Time
Programs, Food Research and Action Center

Daniel W. Hatcher
National Healthy Out-of-School Time Advisor,
Alliance for a Healthier Generation

Creating Healthier Environments: Strategies and Examples for Afterschool and Summer Programs, Including 21st Century Community Learning Centers

Afterschool and summer programs, especially those supported by the federal 21st Century Community Learning Centers initiative, can play an important role in improving the health and nutritional well-being of our nation's children. Too many children are not at a healthy weight—one-third of school children in our country are overweight or obese (Ogden, Carrol, Kit, & Flegal, (2012). Too many also experience food insecurity—one-fifth of all children live in households that are struggling to put food on the table (Coleman-Jensen, Nord, Andrews, & Carlson, (2011).

As will be discussed below, obesity and hunger have a negative impact on student achievement. There are, however, accessible and affordable strategies to address these problems that are well suited to the design of afterschool and summer programs. Implementing these strategies helps support the broader goal of many afterschool and summer programs, especially those supported by the 21st Century Community Learning Centers initiative, to improve student achievement among children attending high-poverty schools.

The negative impact of obesity and hunger on student achievement is well documented. Children who are overweight or obese have poorer academic performance, more behavioral problems, and higher rates of school absenteeism (Bethell, Simpson, Stumbo, Carle, & Gombojav, 2010; Krukowski et al., 2009; Taras & Potts-Datema, 2005; BeLue, Francis, & Colaco, 2009; Geier et al., 2007; Mustillo et al., 2003). Children experiencing hunger have lower math scores and are more likely to repeat a grade (Alaimo, Olson, & Frongillo, 2001). They are more likely to be hyperactive, absent, and tardy, and more likely to display behavioral and attention problems more frequently than other children (Murphy et al., 1998).

Some of the children attending 21st Century Community Learning Centers programs and similar programs are likely to be experiencing both obesity and food insecurity (that is, the inability to afford and/or access enough nutritious food for a healthful life). Obesity negatively affects both males and females, as well as all racial and age groups, but low-income children and food-insecure children may be at even greater risk (Eisenmann, Gundersen, Lohman, Garasky, & Stewart, 2011; Singh, Saipush, & Kogan, 2010; Townsend & Melgar-Quinonez, 2003). Child obesity is linked to limited access to healthy and affordable foods, limited opportunities for physical activity, greater availability of fast food restaurants (especially near schools), and greater exposure to food-related marketing (Larson, Story, & Nelson, 2009; Powell, Slater, & Chaloupka, 2004; Kumanyika & Grier, 2006). Those who are food insecure and suffer periods of even moderate deprivation may also overeat when food does become available, resulting in chronic ups and downs in food intake that can contribute to weight gain (Smith & Richards, 2008).

Strategies to Reduce Hunger and Combat Obesity

The key strategies that afterschool and summer programs can use to combat obesity are to serve healthy meals and snacks, improve the nutritional and physical environment, offer nutrition education, and provide physical activity. Similarly, the key strategy to reducing hunger is to provide children with the nutritious meals and snacks that their bodies desperately need, using the federal funding that is available through the afterschool and summer nutrition programs. These strategies, discussed below, ensure that children can continue learning throughout the afternoon or for the duration of a summer program. These strategies also provide an additional sustainable funding source for local 21st Century Community Learning Centers programs and ease the financial burden on struggling families' resources so that their food dollars can stretch further.

> The key strategies that afterschool and summer programs can use to combat obesity are to serve healthy meals and snacks, improve the nutritional and physical environment, offer nutrition education, and provide physical activity.

- **Serving healthy meals and snacks.** *Nutrition research suggests the importance of afterschool and summer programs for obesity prevention. For example, children of mothers working nontraditional hours are at greater risk of becoming overweight and experiencing obesity (Miller & Han, 2008). This supports the need to provide afterschool snacks and suppers to children, especially those from working families. During the summertime, children are more vulnerable to rapid gains in body mass index (BMI), as well as food insecurity, because many of them do not have access to the good nutrition provided by school meal programs available during the school year (von Hippel, Powell, Downey, & Rowland, 2007; Nord & Romig, 2006).*

Afterschool and summer programs should therefore serve meals and snacks that include low-fat milk, fruits and vegetables, lean proteins, and whole grains, and they should make water freely available during the program. Federal dollars are accessible to 21st Century Community Learning Centers and other afterschool and summer learning programs to enable them to serve nutritious meals and snacks to children. Specifically, the Afterschool Meal and Snack Programs[1] and the Summer Nutrition Programs[2] provide funding to purchase food, freeing up resources that can be redirected to support staffing or program activities. Research reveals that on days when school-age children eat federally funded supper at an afterschool program, they have a higher daily intake of fruits, vegetables, milk, and key nutrients such as calcium, vitamin A, and folate, compared to days that they do not (Plante & Bruening, 2004).

- **Improving the nutritional and physical environment.** *Afterschool and summer programs should take a comprehensive approach to creating healthier out-of-school-time environments. For example, the Alhambra Unified School District in California provides monthly staff trainings on fruits and vegetables. This training is supported by weekly meetings of cooking clubs that provide staff with hands-on learning opportunities. The district also encourages staff wellness by sponsoring activities, including health screenings at professional development trainings for out-of-school-time staff, onsite fitness activities (such as Zumba, walking clubs, yoga, etc.), and promoting physical activity opportunities in the community (for example, staff participation in 5K races, free passes to fitness centers).*

  Staff wellness programs not only support employees individually, they benefit students as well and contribute to overall program success. Potential benefits include increased employee retention, improved employee morale, the presence of more healthy adult role models for students, and a more positive community image for program sites.

- **Offering nutrition education and/or physical activity.** *Afterschool and summer programs can offer evidence-based nutrition education classes that are delivered by qualified personnel. Black's Mill Elementary School in Dawsonville, Georgia, for example, implemented an eight-session healthy living curriculum called empowerME4Life to teach children how to eat better and move more. The site has developed a partnership with its local American Taekwondo Association. A representative from the association comes to the site to lead physical activity. Another program of note is that of the Genesee Intermediate School District in Michigan, which offers regular nutrition education and also coordinates a school garden program. In addition to eating a healthy snack after school, children take fresh produce back to their homes.*

---

1. The Child and Adult Care Food Program provides funding to serve meals and/or snacks at 21st CCLCs and other afterschool programs that are located in areas where at least half of the children are qualified to receive free or reduced-price school meals. Programs that are school-sponsored also can receive federal funding for snacks through the National School Lunch Program.

2. The Summer Food Service Program and the National School Lunch Program provide funding to serve meals and snacks during the summer to children at 21st CCLCs or other sites that are located in areas where at least half of the children are eligible to receive free or reduced-price school meals, that serve primarily low-income children, or that serve primarily migrant children.

Looking Ahead: Healthy Out-of-School Time

One of the most exciting recent developments in efforts to improve nutrition and health in afterschool and summer programs is the promulgation of a set of *Standards for Healthy Eating and Physical Activity*[3] by the Healthy Out-of-School Time (HOST) Coalition, a national coalition of leading organizations in the fields of out-of-school time and health and nutrition. The Alliance for a Healthier Generation and the Food Research Action Center provided expertise and guidance to the coalition.

Evidence-based standards have now been crafted for afterschool programs around physical activity, nutrition, and nutrition education. These new program models and standards, coupled with additional funding for programs such as the federal afterschool meal program, have given communities new tools in the quest to keep our kids healthy for life.

The vision for this coalition is to foster health and well-being practices in afterschool programs nationwide, using science-based standards for healthy eating, physical activity, screen time, and social supports for these behaviors including staff, family and child engagement. The evidence-based standards developed by the HOST Coalition, and adopted by the National Afterschool Association, provide an important roadmap for afterschool and summer programs, especially 21st Century Community Learning Centers programs, to address the health and nutritional needs of the children they serve.

Over the past 15 years, funding from the 21st Century Community Learning Centers initiative and other afterschool sources has a created a new space and extra time for caring adults to work with children and youth. It has created what some have called a "new neighborhood" of supports for our children. At the same time this new space has grown across America, concerns have grown about children's health, particularly obesity and hunger. Afterschool and summer programs have risen to this challenge by developing new program approaches that focus on healthy activities and nutrition. Evidence-based standards have now been crafted for afterschool programs around physical activity, nutrition, and nutrition education. These new program models and standards, coupled with additional funding for programs such as the federal afterschool meal program, have given communities new tools in the quest to keep our kids healthy for life. Those tools are now being used in thousands of communities across America. Yet, too many afterschool and summer programs are still not taking full advantage of these new tools and resources that are increasingly available to them to support healthier lifestyles. They could and should actively seek out those in their communities who have an interest in improving children's health and the resources to do so. Conversely, others who are concerned about children's health should assertively reach out to these programs to expand and improve them with healthy eating and healthy activities components. The health of our children—and the health of nation's future—are at stake.

3. http://www.naaweb.org/downloads/resources/HEPAStandards8-4-11final.pdf

For More Information

Alliance for a Healthier Generation, www.healthiergeneration.org, resources for schools, out-of-school time programs, communities, families, doctors and industry on ways to work together to address one of the nation's leading public health threats - childhood obesity.

EmpowerME4Life, www.healthiergeneration.org/teens, a healthy living curriculum from the Alliance for a Healthier Generation—equipping kids with new attitudes, skills and knowledge about eating better and moving more—for life.

Food Research and Action Center, www.frac.org, information on how to participate in the afterschool and summer nutrition programs.

National Institute on Out-of-School Time HOST Coalition, http://www.niost.org/HOST-Program/, resources for Healthy Out-of-School Time.

Afterschool Nutrition in Washington, DC: An Overview of the District's Accomplishments and Opportunities for Growth, http://www.dchunger.org/pdf/afterschool_issue_brief.pdf, an in-depth analysis of the Afterschool Meal Program operated by the District of Columbia Public School's Office of Food and Nutrition Services.

ABOUT THE AUTHORS

Crystal Weedall FitzSimons is the director of school and out-of-school time programs for the Food Research and Action Center (FRAC). At FRAC, FitzSimons oversees FRAC's policy, advocacy, and technical assistance work to increase children's access to the federal school, summer, and afterschool nutrition programs. She holds a BA in philosophy and sociology from Carroll College and a baster of social work from Washington University.

Daniel W. Hatcher is a national healthy out-of-school time advisor for the Alliance for a Healthier Generation. At the Alliance, Hatcher supports community-based organizations to ensure out-of-school-time settings promote the healthy development of all young people. He holds a BA in international relations and a master of public health with a concentration in health education, both from Western Kentucky University.

REFERENCES

Alaimo, K., Olson, C. M., Frongillo, E. A., Jr. (2001). Food insufficiency and American school-aged children's cognitive, academic and psychosocial development. *Pediatrics, 108,* 44–53.

BeLue, R., Francis, L. A., & Colaco, B. (2009). Mental health problems and overweight in a nationally representative sample of adolescents: Effects of race and ethnicity. *Pediatrics, 123,* 697–702.

Bethell, C., Simpson, L., Stumbo, S., Carle, A. C., & Gombojav, N. (2010). National, state, and local disparities in childhood obesity. *Health Affairs, 29,* 347–356.

Coleman-Jensen, A., Nord, M., Andrews, M., & Carlson, S. (2011). *Household food security in the United States in 2010* (ERR-125). Retrieved from http://www.ers.usda.gov/publications/err-economic-research-report/err125.aspx

Eisenmann, J. C., Gundersen, C., Lohman, B. J., Garasky, S., & Stewart, S. D. (2011). Is food insecurity related to overweight and obesity in children and adolescents? A summary of studies, 1995–2009. *Obesity Reviews, 12*(Suppl.), e73–e83.

Geier, A. B., Foster, G. D., Womble, L. G., McLaughlin, J., Borradaile, K. E., Nachmani, J., Sherman, S., Kumanyika, S., & Shults, J. (2007). The relationship between relative weight and school attendance among elementary schoolchildren. *Obesity, 15*, 2157–2161.

Krukowski, R. A., Smith West, D., Philyaw Perez, A., Bursac, Z., Phillips, M. M., & Raczynski, J. M. (2009). Overweight children, weight-based teasing and academic performance. International *Journal of Pediatric Obesity, 4*, 274–280.

Kumanyika, S., & Grier, S. (2006). Targeting interventions for ethnic minority and low-income populations. *Future of Children, 16*(1), 187–207.

Larson, N. I., Story, M. T., & Nelson, M. C. (2009). Neighborhood environments: Disparities in access to healthy foods in the U.S. *American Journal of Preventive Medicine, 36*, 74–81.

Miller, D. P., & Han, W. J. (2008). Maternal nonstandard work schedules and adolescent overweight. *American Journal of Public Health, 98*, 1495–1502.

Murphy, J. M., Wehler, C. A., Pagano, M. E., Little, M., Kleinman, R. F., & Jellinek, M. S. (1998). Relationship between hunger and psychosocial functioning in low income American children. *Journal of the American Academy of Child & Adolescent Psychiatry, 37*, 163–170.

Mustillo, S., Worthman, C., Erkanli, A., Keeler, G., Angold, A., & Costello, E. J. (2003). Obesity and psychiatric disorder: Developmental trajectories. *Pediatrics, 111*(4, Part 1), 851–859.

Nord, M., & Romig, K. (2006). Hunger in the summer: Seasonal food insecurity and the National School Lunch and Summer Food Service programs. *Journal of Children and Poverty, 12*, 141–158.

Ogden, C. L., Carroll, M. D., Kit, B. K., & Flegal, K. M. (2012). Prevalence of obesity and trends in body mass index among US children and adolescents, 1999–2010. *Journal of the American Medical Association, 307*, 483–490.

Plante, M. L. K., & Bruening, K. S. (2004). Supper meal improves diets of children at nutritional risk [Poster session abstract]. *Journal of the American Dietetic Association, 104*(Suppl. 2), 42.

Powell, L. M., Slater, S., & Chaloupka, F. J. (2004). The relationship between community physical activity settings and race, ethnicity, and socioeconomic status. *Evidence-Based Preventive Medicine, 1*(2), 135–144.

Singh, G. K., Siahpush, M., & Kogan, M. D. (2010). Rising social inequalities in US childhood obesity, 2003–2007. *Annals of Epidemiology, 20*, 40–52.

Smith, C., & Richards, R. (2008). Dietary intake, overweight status, and perceptions of food insecurity among homeless Minnesotan youth. *American Journal of Human Biology, 20*, 550–563.

Taras, H., & Potts-Datema, W. (2005). Obesity and student performance at school. *Journal of School Health, 75*, 291–295.

Townsend, M., & Melgar-Quinonez, H. (2003). Hunger, food insecurity, and child obesity. *Food Assistance and Nutrition Research Report, 38.* Washington, DC: U.S. Department of Agriculture, Economic Research Service.

Von Hippel, P. T., Powell, B., Downey, D. B., & Rowland, N. J. (2007). The effect of school on overweight in childhood: Gain in body mass index during the school year and during summer vacation. *American Journal of Public Health, 97*, 696–702.

Wiecha, J., Gannett, E., Hall, G., & Roth, B. (n.d.). (*Standards for healthy eating and physical activity*). Retrieved from National Afterschool Association website: http://www.naaweb.org/downloads/resources/HEPAStandards8-4-11final.pdf

Recent Evidence of Impact

3

Eva L. Baker
Distinguished Professor, Divisions of Psychological
Studies in Education and Social Research
Methodology, UCLA Graduate School of Education
and Information Studies

The Importance of Afterschool Programs in Education Reform Worldwide: Making It Essential in America

As president of the World Educational Research Association, an organization consisting of American, European, Asian-Pacific, Latin American, African, and Indian-subcontinental research associations, I have given invited talks to international groups in 20 countries in the last 3 years. While so much travel is not wise, I have learned much about educational reform—indeed, much more than the usual stories that we have grown accustomed to hearing. We all know by now, for example, that Finnish schools have much independence, that children in many Asian countries have excellent math skills, or that teacher applicants in many countries are of high academic quality, in part because teaching in those countries is a highly respected profession.

Beyond these comparisons that are now very familiar to us, I have learned that places like Korea, Japan, Hong Kong, and Singapore—well-known for their high academic achievements— all have afterschool programs as a common educational option. Afterschool programs are being regulated in some countries; that is, they must close by 11:00 p.m. so that students do not work too hard! There also is some backlash in these nations directed at the extra money that parents pay year after year to enroll their children in these programs. New developments, such as Korea's comprehensive computer-based system, will provide a platform for afterschool activities, including homework help and other options, to engage students deeply in subject matter. Korea is changing its exam structure, as well, to be more oriented to the performance of complex, multistepped tasks. Some of these changes have occurred in a context in which students are also expected to excel in sports, music, and other areas outside the usual U.S. curriculum. Computer systems are in place to support afterschool learning in countries such as Korea, in which broadband connectivity greatly exceeds that in the U.S. and in which afterschool activity is not principally focused on child care.

How are these developments received in the U.S. policy arena, especially in the light of unacceptable U.S. performance on international measures, such as the Programme for International Student Assessment (PISA)? Such findings are primarily, but not completely, attributable to poorer performance by students in poorer communities, and many of these students also come from minority groups. The U.S. has not, in 50-plus years of attempts to solve this problem, found a scalable way to reduce persistent gaps in performance between black and Hispanic students on the one hand and white and Asian students on the other. There has been some movement, but the overall picture remains unacceptable. Without delving into the myriad plausible explanations for the inability of the U.S. (overall) to develop scalable, effective strategies in the context of the regular school day, let us turn back to U.S. afterschool programs.

Afterschool programs in the U.S. are of different types—public, private, tuition-bearing, free—and are conducted in a variety of settings. These programs may attempt to meet multiple goals: keeping students safe; supporting learning and higher academic achievement; providing mentoring by caring adults to support healthy psycho-social development; extending the school day with practice-oriented materials to reinforce concepts and skills taught earlier in the day; and providing social and intellectual enrichment, such as music, dance, artwork, field trips, and service learning opportunities to instill a broader set of values now missed by many schools that focus their attention almost exclusively on accountability needs.

Do afterschool programs implement findings from research and evaluation? Yes, they do, as many are focused on a simple premise: time-on-task aids learning. Student engagement and interest in learning is a key aspect of time-on-task. Quality afterschool and summer programs therefore increase learning time by providing learning opportunities that are more engaging, broadening young peoples' skills and interests. So which learning tasks are used? In the countries ranking highest on the

Highlander Afterschool Program Helps Students Realize Their Full Potential

Students end every week at the Highlander Charter School's Afterschool Program in Providence, Rhode Island, by participating in "Freedom Friday." Through group projects, school assemblies and performances, field trips, and community service, these Fridays introduce students to a variety of social issues—from bullying to homelessness—and encourage critical evaluation and engagement. This is just one of the many ways the Highlander Afterschool Program takes the education of its students beyond the classroom to help them absorb the lessons from the school day and to develop important skills such as leadership, teamwork, and community involvement.

The Highlander Afterschool Program is integrated seamlessly into the regular school day, connecting its activities to the core curriculum, which reinforces school-day skills and provides students the opportunity to learn new ones in a hands-on, inquiry-based, experiential manner. By effectively leveraging the time outside of school, Highlander is improving academic achievement; data shows a direct connection between student participation in afterschool and performance on the New England Common Assessment Placement (NECAP) exam, with students who participate in 90 days or more of afterschool programming showing 20% greater proficiency in both math and literacy.

PISA, there is increasing variety in afterschool activities; these countries no longer emphasize practicing routine test items. Countries such as Singapore, Japan, Malaysia, and South Korea are changing their expectations of students' competencies to include the development of character, identity, an understanding of their role in society, and key affective outcomes, such as resiliency and having high aspirations. In addition, they have embraced so-called 21st century skills and are planning to implement strategies and activities that foster creativity and entrepreneurship within these programs.

Why is this information relevant to us? If we cannot import the cultural context that values schools and teachers and that brings parents into close contact with the schools, we must approximate it and adapt these features to our own setting. The U.S. stagnation in performance levels (Organisation for Economic Co-operation and Development, 2011), in graduation rates (Office of Science and Technology Policy, 2011a), productivity in STEM (Office of Science and Technology Policy, 2011b), and the educational component of the credit downgrade should impel us toward the highest goals for educational reforms. Encouragingly, there is some forward movement. The newly developed Common Core State Standards in mathematics and language arts, soon to be augmented by science, can provide clear benchmarks for attainment, with one caveat: The tests developed to assess attainment must be of high quality in terms of their match to learning, as opposed to employing psychometric approaches that merely assess low-order learning.

Returning to afterschool programs, there is a rapidly growing body of evidence that draws on the explosive growth of the field in recent years. This evidence is somewhat mixed, in part because of the considerable variation in afterschool programs. A substantial and growing number of studies, however, support the significant and positive impact of these programs on students and families in myriad ways. These afterschool programs should therefore be granted the same opportunities, including policy and budgetary supports by political leaders, as are being granted to other, more highly-promoted innovations for which the research evidence is mixed and inconclusive—for instance, value-added teacher compensation.

To recap, little is working well in the U.S. school system for those students who will form the majority of our nation's population within the foreseeable future. Better standards will help, if accompanied by high quality assessments (still an unknown), innovative technology, better teacher training, recruiting of highly qualified teachers, and the like. If the U.S. is to begin to regain its leadership in STEM and in intellectual performance, we must use tools available to us now that fit the purposes we have.

Looking at effective reforms that can be quickly adopted, one obvious strategy is to extend time on task, when the "task" is multifaceted learning of content, 21st century skills, social behaviors, and higher personal and academic aspirations—and not merely more focused, uninspiring instruction on narrow, shallow skills. These multifaceted learning goals can be readily embodied in well-designed afterschool programs.

Independent studies of almost two decades have documented, for example, a set of noteworthy findings for students in the LA's BEST afterschool program. There are similar findings, as well, from quality afterschool programs in California's statewide afterschool initiative and 21st Century Community Learning Centers. These programs have the virtue of point-of-contact operation, ability to adapt rapidly to changing requirements, and the important, but sometime less valued, feature of bringing joy to learning in an exciting, collaborative way. Importantly, these efforts cannot be seen as discretionary. They are essential to a strategy to bring American children back to levels of accomplishment demanded by the future. The following list provides credible research findings that may exceed the evidence base of many other government-supported interventions in two key areas:

Academic Impact

- *Improved test scores (Goldschmidt, Huang, & Chinen, 2007; Huang, Gribbons, Kim, Lee, & Baker, 2000; Huang, Leon, Harven, La Torre, & Mostafavi, 2009; Huang, Leon, & La Torre, 2011; Huang, Leon, La Torre, & Mostafavi, 2008)*

- *Improved school grades (Huang et al., 2011)*

- *Improved school attendance (Huang et al., 2011)*

- *Increased engagement in learning (Huang et al., 2007a; Huang et al., 2000)*

- *Lower dropout rates (Huang, Kim, Marshall, & Perez, 2005)*

Social, Safety, and Family Impacts

- *Provided students safety in dangerous areas (Huang et al., 2004; Huang et al., 2007b)*

- *Strengthened feelings of security by families (Huang et al., 2000)*

- *Bridged the language gap between non-English speaking parents and the school (Huang et al., 2007b)*

- *Improved self-efficacy (Huang et al., 2004)*

- *Made healthier choices in food groups selection and food portions (Huang et al., 2008)*

- *Reduced juvenile crime (Goldschmidt et al., 2007)*

- *Formed productive learner adult relationships (mentors) (Huang et al., 2007a; Huang et al., 2000; Huang et al., 2007b)*

Conclusion

In short, can we name any other reform with this empirical track record and low cost?

Disturbingly, it seems that just as we are learning significantly more from initiatives in the U.S. and abroad about how to maximize and expand learning through engaging afterschool and summer learning opportunities, there are attempts in some states and communities to replace some of these programs with considerably less well-researched alternatives, including some programs and strategies with demonstrably poor results.

Many of these alternatives also appear to be more costly because they do not deploy a collaborative model of school-community-family partnerships. A growing body of evidence suggests that more successful afterschool approaches employ partnerships and collaboration as a core organizing principle. This means, moreover, that that these programs can also be built out, where there is interest, to become more comprehensive community schools, community learning centers, or full-service schools. This simply makes good sense as well, given evidence of their success.

Quality afterschool and summer learning programs have a positive, significant effect on a number of very important aspects of student learning and 21st century skill development. They should be an essential part of the nation's education improvement agenda. Local school districts, municipalities, states, and the federal government should provide the necessary resources to enable more young people to have quality afterschool and summer learning through a collaborative model of school-community-family partnerships.

ABOUT THE AUTHOR

Eva L. Baker is a distinguished professor in UCLA's Graduate School of Education and Information Studies; director of the National Center for Research on Evaluation, Standards, and Student Testing (CRESST); and president of the World Education Research Association. As a congressionally appointed member of the National Council on Education Standards and Testing, Baker was chair of the National Research Council Board on Testing and Assessment from 2000 to 2004. She is also a former president of the American Educational Research Association (2006–2007) and was co-chair of the committee to revise the Standards for Educational and Psychological Testing (1999). Baker is presently involved in the design of technologically sophisticated testing and evaluation systems of assessment in learning environments for both military and civilian education.

REFERENCES

Goldschmidt, P., Huang, D., & Chinen, M. (2007). *The long-term effects of afterschool programming on educational adjustment and juvenile crime: A study of the LA's BEST afterschool program.* Retrieved from http://www.lasbest.org/what/publications/LASBEST_DOJ_Final%20Report.pdf

Huang, D., Choi, K., Henderson, T., Howie, J., Kim, K., Vogel, M., Yoo, S., & Waite, P. (2004). *Exploring the long-term impact of LA's BEST on students' social and academic development.* Los Angeles, CA: University of California, National Center for Research on Evaluations, Standards, and Student Testing (CRESST).

Huang, D., Coordt, A., La Torre, D., Leon, S., Miyoshi, J., Perez, P., & Peterson, C. (2007a). *The after school hours: Examining the relationship between afterschool based staff capital and student engagement in LA's BEST* (CSE Technical Report No. 712). Retrieved from CRESST website: http://www.cse.ucla.edu/products/reports/R712.pdf

Huang, D., Gribbons, B., Kim, K. S., Lee, C., & Baker, E. L. (2000). *A decade of results: The impact of the LA's BEST After School Enrichment Program on subsequent student achievement and performance.* Los Angeles, CA: University of California, National Center for Research on Evaluations, Standards, and Student Testing (CRESST).

Huang, D., Kim, K. S., Marshall, A., & Perez, P. (2005). *Keeping kids in school: An LA's BEST example. A study examining the long-term impact of LA's BEST on students' dropout rates.* Retrieved from http://www.lasbest.org/what/publications/Keeping_Kids_in_School_Exec_Sum.pdf

Huang, D., Leon, S., Harven, A., La Torre, D., & Mostafavi, S. (2009). *Exploring the relationship between LA's BEST program attendance and cognitive gains of LA's BEST students* (CRESST Report No. 757). Retrieved from CRESST website: http://www.cse.ucla.edu/products/reports/R757.pdf

Huang, D., Leon, L., & La Torre, D. (2011). *Supporting student success in middle schools: Examining the relationship between elementary afterschool participation and subsequent middle school attainments.* Retrieved from CRESST website: http://www.cse.ucla.edu/downloads/files/Huang.etal.AERA.paper.pdf

Huang, D., Leon, S., La Torre, D., & Mostafavi, S. (2008). *Examining the relationship between LA's BEST program attendance and academic achievement of LA's BEST students* (CRESST Report No. 749). Retrieved from CRESST website: http://www.cse.ucla.edu/products/reports/R749.pdf

Huang, D., Miyoshi, J., La Torre, D., Marshall, A., Perez, P., & Peterson, C. (2007b). *Exploring the intellectual, social, and organizational capitals at LA's BEST* (CSE Technical Report No. 714). Retrieved from CRESST website: http://www.cse.ucla.edu/products/reports/r714.pdf

Office of Science and Technology Policy. (2011a). *A strategy for American innovation: Securing our economic growth and prosperity.* Retrieved from http://www.whitehouse.gov/sites/default/files/uploads/InnovationStrategy.pdf

Office of Science and Technology Policy. (2011b). *Winning the race to educate our children: Science, technology, engineering, and mathematics (STEM) education in the 2012 budget.* Retrieved from http://www.whitehouse.gov/sites/default/files/microsites/ostp/OSTP-fy12-STEM-fs.pdf

Organisation for Economic Co-operation and Development. (2011). *PISA in focus 2: Improving performance: Leading from the bottom.* Retrieved from http://www.oecd.org/dataoecd/32/53/47271471.pdf

Tony Evers
State Superintendent of Public Instruction
Wisconsin Department of Public Instruction

Quality Afterschool Programs Supported by the 21st Century Community Learning Centers Are Part of the Equation for Education Success in Wisconsin

Each year the Wisconsin Department of Public Instruction (DPI) recognizes schools with low socioeconomic student populations that achieve high rates of proficiency on the Wisconsin Knowledge and Concepts Exam (WKCE) with the Wisconsin School of Recognition award. Many of the schools served by 21st Century Community Learning Centers programs have gone on to receive this prestigious acknowledgement of high achieving school environments, aided by the support the afterschool program provides. This illustrates the importance of the enriched learning environments afterschool programs provide students, particularly students in need of additional learning opportunities.

During the 2009–10 school year, 21st Century Community Learning Centers in Wisconsin served over 47,219 youth attending 188 high-poverty schools. These programs provide academic support and enrichment in core subject areas, such as mathematics and reading, as well as a wide array of youth development opportunities that are otherwise limited during regular school hours. Examples of activities include, but are not limited to, recreation (88%), science (88%), arts (85%), cultural studies (82%), technology (60%), tutoring (46%), leadership development (37%), drug prevention (33%), mentoring (19%), and much more. On average, Wisconsin programs added 495 hours of activities, an equivalent of 74 school days to students' learning time.

Annual performance data revealed that among regular attendees at 21st Century Community Learning Centers, 67% improved their academic performance (see Figure 1), and 62% increased their classroom participation (as reported by teachers). Teachers also reported that many more students were motivated to learn (see Figure 2).

Figure 1. Improvement in academic performance.

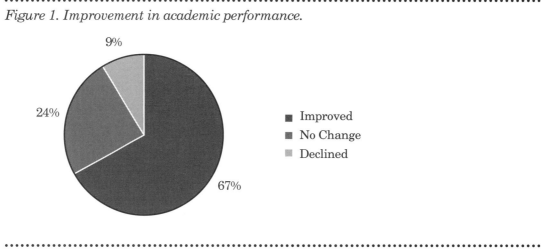

Figure 2. Improvement in coming to school motivated to learn.

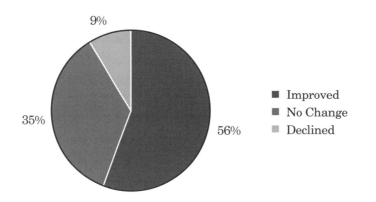

Clearly, students who are engaged in learning hold more promise for success in and outside of the school day. However, these programs do not do it on their own.

In 2009–10, there were 968 community-based partners that contributed to the success of the 21st Century Community Learning Centers. In addition to services, these partners contributed over $3.4 million to support programs. This support is all that much more important as these 21st Community Learning Centers face uncertain future funding and our public schools are challenged to do more with less. Schools in Wisconsin provide some of the best educational experiences in the country, and yet the academic gap is still too wide.

It is for these reasons that our agency will not choose to pursue flexibility for the alternative use of 21st Century Community Learning Centers funds and instead commit ourselves to strengthening the afterschool programs. With the support of high quality learning opportunities before, during, and after school, youth can realize their potential with the skills to be successful 21st century citizens.

Our students continue to learn well beyond the time limits of the school day and year. Supporting and encouraging them to reach their full academic potential requires us to consider additional avenues for providing instructional opportunities. High quality afterschool, before-school, and summer programs will help us achieve the goal of having all children graduate with the knowledge and skills necessary for postsecondary success in college and careers.

Annual performance data revealed that among regular attendees at 21st Century Community Learning Centers, 67% improved their academic performance.

ABOUT THE AUTHOR

Tony Evers was elected Wisconsin state superintendent of public instruction in April 2009. He began his career in 1976 as a classroom educator and has served Wisconsin students, parents, and citizens as an education leader at every level—principal, school district administrator, Cooperative Educational Service Agencies administrator and deputy state superintendent—before his election to the state's highest educational post. Evers earned his bachelor's, master's and doctoral degrees in educational administration from the University of Wisconsin-Madison.

Milwaukee Students Find a Space to Grow in Boys & Girls Clubs

When the school day ends in the city of Milwaukee, thousands of students flock to the 38 local Boys & Girls Clubs for a range of learning opportunities that take them out into the community and deeper into their studies. Milwaukee struggles with some of the highest rates of teen pregnancy, academic underachievement, and childhood poverty rates in the country, but thanks to the Club's focus on academics, members of all ages are seeing important improvements.

For example, the SPARK Early Literacy Initiative, a U.S. Department of Education—Investing in Innovation (i3) Fund recipient program, helps students through grade 3 with their reading proficiency. A UW-Madison randomized-control design study has demonstrated that regularly attending participants demonstrate 35% more literacy growth on the Measures of Academic Progress (MAP) assessment. Meanwhile, the Stein Scholars program helps high schoolers meet the academic demands for graduation and college admission and provides scholarship support for more than 45 graduates annually.

Working with more than 200 organizations in the community, the clubs offer a wide range of other learning opportunities for members—from on-the-job training through the Milwaukee Area Workforce Investment Board to civic engagement projects where members help to beautify their neighborhoods and promote safety in the community.

Deborah Lowe Vandell
Founding Dean, School of Education,
University of California, Irvine

Afterschool Program Quality and Student Outcomes: Reflections on Positive Key Findings on Learning and Development From Recent Research

In my years researching the effects of afterschool programs on children's social and academic outcomes, I have observed the power that high quality programs can have on the learning and development of young people. This paper provides some reflections on selected research from my own study of the field in recent years, which has been deeply informed by that of many others. Since my first study of afterschool programs conducted more than 25 years ago (Vandell & Corasaniti, 1988), I am heartened by the growth in our understanding of the effects of out-of-school time from a virtually unstudied area to abundant and solid evidence on the positive impacts of high quality programs. Whether they are called afterschool, expanded learning opportunities, out-of-school time, or something else, we know from research that these types of opportunities can lead to positive outcomes for children and youth, as well as families, communities, and schools (Durlak, Weissberg, & Pachan, 2011; Eccles & Gootman, 2002; Mahoney, Vandell, Simpkins, & Zarrett, 2009).

As the nomenclature in the field has evolved, so too have my own research lens and lines of inquiry. Through my investigations over the years, I have developed some beliefs about the implications of what we have learned for policy, which I share at the end of this paper. In my estimation, based on years of examination, *high quality* expanded learning programs are essential to the learning process because they provide young people with opportunities to relate to their world in new ways. Strong programs foster an orientation of being open to novel experiences, of being interested in others and the world, of being inquisitive and creative, and, ultimately, of becoming lifelong learners (Larson, 2000; Lerner et al., 2005; Shernoff & Vandell, 2008). As I see it, we have before us today unprecedented opportunities to ensure all expanded learning programs make a difference for children and youth (Vandell, 2012).

A Robust and Growing Research Base and Enhanced Measures of Effectiveness

Continued investment in research and evaluation in the expanded learning field has resulted not only in a robust research base but also in the development of reliable and valid measures of program effectiveness and impact that can be used effectively by practitioners and researchers to improve program quality (Vandell, 2011 September). Assessment tools are being created and refined by the academic and research community, as well as from within the growing local, state, and national infrastructure that promotes and supports high quality afterschool and summer programs. These instruments can be used by expanded learning programs to assess such factors as program quality and attendance; staff beliefs, attitudes, education, and training; staffing patterns, including recruitment and retention; and student performance in specific domains and skills, such as behavior and academic achievement.

> Continued investment in research and evaluation in the expanded learning field has resulted not only in a robust research base but also in the development of reliable and valid measures of program effectiveness and impact that can be used effectively by practitioners and researchers to improve program quality.

The measures my colleagues and I developed for the California Afterschool Outcome Measures Project are examples of the kinds of psychometrically reliable and valid instruments available that assess student outcomes in the areas of skill development and positive behavior change (Vandell, O'Cadiz, Hall, & Karsh, 2012). The set of surveys, which can be administered online, is designed to be completed by students, program staff, and classroom teachers. Student surveys assess areas such as social competencies with peers, task persistence, work habits, and reductions in misconduct. Surveys completed by program staff and classroom teachers include measures of child behavior with other children, social skills with peers, task persistence, and work habits. With these data, programs are able to study changes in their students' behaviors across the school year and to compare these changes to those found in other programs across the state.

In addition, students are able to use the Afterschool Outcome Measures Online Toolbox to report the quality of their experiences at the programs in three key areas—the quality of their interactions with program staff, quality of interactions with peers at the program, and their interest and engagement in program activities—again using well-established instruments with strong psychometric properties. Programs can then use these aggregated reports to assess how they are doing from the perspective of the youth who attend their program.

The Afterschool Outcome Measures Online Toolbox is now being used at more than 1,000 afterschool program sites in California, with plans to double the number of sites using the measures in the next 2 years. It will be important to see if the Afterschool Outcome Measures Online Toolbox can be used by program sites to improve student experiences (and student outcomes).

Of course, valid and reliable measures for researchers and practitioners alike are fundamental to being able to draw conclusions about the quality and outcomes of expanded learning programs. Some of the skills and knowledge that many afterschool programs are designed to promote are, in fact, complex to assess, and research in the field is limited by the inability to use experimental design to identify causal relationships. However, the instruments, approaches, and statistical models currently available do provide us with the ability to make substantive assertions about the correlations between program quality and outcomes for students.

Program Quality and Student Outcomes—Academic, Social, and Behavioral

My recent research, including the Study of Promising After-School Programs (Vandell, Reisner, & Pierce, 2007), the Longitudinal Study of Program Quality (Pierce, Bolt, & Vandell, 2010), and the NICHD Study of Early Child Care and Youth Development (Li & Vandell, 2013; Auger, Pierce, & Vandell, 2013; Lee & Vandell, 2013) reinforces previous studies that the breadth, quality, intensity, and duration of expanded learning programs make a difference in both short-term and enduring effects on student academic, social, and behavioral outcomes (Mahoney, Vandell, Simpkins, & Zarrett, 2009; Vandell, 2012). Based on the evidence, following are key characteristics of high quality expanded learning programs:

- *foster positive relationships between program participants and staff,*

- *build positive relationships among program participants,*

- *offer a blend of academic and developmental skill-building activities,*

- *promote high levels of student engagement,*

- *maintain an orientation toward mastery of knowledge and skills, and*

- *provide appropriate levels of structure as well as opportunities for autonomy and choice (Eccles & Gootman, 2002).*

Other recent studies reveal that positive staff–child relations are important for both academic and socio-behavioral growth. Reading and math grades are associated with positive relationships between program staff and participants, and supportive interactions with nonparental adults are important for facilitating child adjustment. In addition, when dosage is high (that is, students attend expanded learning programs frequently and regularly), research shows that expanded learning programs can be a significant factor in fostering positive academic and social outcomes (Pierce, Bolt, & Vandell, 2010).

Other investigations (Auger, Pierce, & Vandell, 2013; Li & Vandell, 2013; Pierce, Bolt, & Vandell, 2010) that I have conducted with colleagues reinforce the finding that the availability of a diverse array of structured, age-appropriate activities is positively associated with student math grades and classroom work habits, particularly at the elementary level. As students get older and seek more autonomy in their out-of-school activities, research tells us that greater flexibility in programming becomes more important (Vandell, Reisner, & Pierce, 2007).

Some of my research sheds light on the types of activities in expanded learning programs that correlate with various student outcomes. For example, students who participate in the arts have been found to have greater self-efficacy and achievement orientation, as evidenced by their increased time doing English homework and reading for pleasure (Li & Vandell, 2013; Vandell, Pierce, & Karsh, 2011). Additionally, participation in sports seems to be associated with better work habits, self-efficacy, school attachment, and achievement orientation (Vandell, Pierce, & Karsh, 2011).

Social and behavioral outcomes. There is substantial evidence from the current body of research that expanded learning programs promote positive social and behavioral outcomes (Durlak et al., 2010). High quality expanded learning opportunities are linked to gains in social skills with peers, increased pro-social behavior, and reductions in aggression, misconduct (e.g., skipping school, getting into fights), and illegal substance use (Vandell, Reisner, & Pierce, 2007). These opportunities also demonstrate promise because they have been shown to increase student engagement, intrinsic motivation, concentrated effort, and positive states of mind (Larson, 2000; Shernoff & Vandell, 2008). These findings are significant because the social and emotional outcomes that are fostered through high quality afterschool programs lay the psychological groundwork for the kinds of cognitive processes that are required for mastery of academic content knowledge and skills to apply that knowledge.

Academic outcomes. We know from research that engagement in activities that are both fun and that require focus helps develop the competencies needed for academic learning, including concentration, intrinsic reward, and motivation (Shernoff & Vandell, 2007; 2008). For example, in the Study of Promising After-School Programs, students who regularly attended high quality programs demonstrated significant gains in standardized mathematic test scores as well as self-reported work habits (Vandell, Reisner, & Pierce, 2007). This study and other recent research provide a solid basis for three core assertions that should be used to continue to advance the field:

- *Expanding learning programs show promising evidence for helping to close the achievement gap.*

- *High quality afterschool programs have positive long-term effects on school attendance and task persistence.*

- *Expanded learning opportunities have positive cumulative effects on student grades and academic work habits (Vandell, 2011 February).*

Implications for Policy

One of the drivers behind my work is a strong belief that the interdependence of research, practice, and policy is key to increasing positive outcomes for children and youth. As I noted in the opening section of this paper, my research over the years has led me to form some conclusions about the research-practice-policy dynamic. Based on these, I offer the following implications of my research and that of others for practice and policy:

- *Practitioners already have access to reliable and valid measures that can be used to assess program quality.*

- *A next step is to expand awareness in the field of these measures and to increase capacity to use these data to improve program quality and to monitor improvements in youth outcomes.*

- *Practitioners can combine and compare research findings from across studies to determine the factors that fit best with their program contexts and characteristics.*

- *Policy makers must heed the evidence that high quality programs with sufficient dosage have positive impacts on student behavior and academic performance.*

- *Policy makers must set the stage for longitudinal data systems that enable the tracking of program, staff, and student indicators over time.*

- *Policy makers must provide sufficient resources for expanded learning programs to offer both academic activities, such as homework help, as well as enrichment activities, such as sports and arts, that ultimately help students improve academic performance (Vandell, 2010; Shernoff & Vandell, 2008).*

Conclusion

Over the years, I have had the great honor to interact with a wide array of students, practitioners and educators, parents, policy makers, and other researchers in the field of expanded learning. As I reflect on the research and consider its implications for future work, I am encouraged by the growing awareness of the importance of out-of-school time as a critical educational context and by the extent and caliber of the research that is being conducted by scholars in the U.S. and elsewhere.

As we move forward together in this effort, researchers, practitioners, policy makers, and other key stakeholders, such as funders and technical assistance providers, must continue to intersect intentionally to ensure our efforts are aligned and that they inform the efforts of others. We have come a long way in having a growing body of research and evaluation evidence that quality afterschool programs work and make a positive difference. We also know a lot about improving quality. So at the local, state, and federal levels, it is time for us to find the will, energy, and resources to expand quality afterschool programs in the many schools and communities that need and want them—not in another 10 years, but now. In so doing, we will truly be able to leverage the power of expanded learning for student and community success.

ABOUT THE AUTHOR

Deborah Lowe Vandell is a professor of education and psychology and the founding dean of the School of Education at the University of California, Irvine. The author of more than 150 articles and three books, she has focused much of her research on the effects of afterschool and summer programs, extracurricular activities, and unsupervised time on academic and social outcomes on young people from kindergarten through the end of high school. Vandell earned her master's degree in education at Harvard University and received a PhD in psychology from Boston University. She began her career as a kindergarten and second grade teacher. She is a member of the Governing Council for the Society for Research in Child Development and is a Fellow of the American Educational Research Association, the American Psychological Association, and the American Psychological Society.

REFERENCES

Auger, A., Pierce, K. M., & Vandell, D. L. (2013). *Participation in out-of-school settings and student academic and behavioral outcomes*. Manuscript in preparation.

Durlak, J. A., Weissberg, R. P., & Pachan, M. (2010). A meta-analysis of after-school programs that seek to promote personal and social skills in children and adolescents. *American Journal of Community Psychology, 45*, 294–309.

Eccles, J., & Gootman, J. A. (Eds.). (2002). *Community programs to promote youth development*. Washington DC: National Academy Press.

Larson, R. (2000). Toward a psychology of positive youth development. *The American Psychologist, 55*, 170–183.

Lee, K., & Vandell, D. L. (2013). *Understanding the link between substance use and the interaction of the individual and the environment*. Manuscript in preparation.

Lerner, R. M, Lerner, J. V., Almerigi, J. B., Theokas, C., Phelps, E., Gestdottir, S. . . . von Eye, A. (2005). Positive youth development, participation in community youth development programs, and community contributions of fifth-grade adolescents: Findings from the first wave of the 4-h study of positive youth development. *Journal of Early Adolescence, 25*, 17–71.

Li, W., & Vandell, D. L. (2013). *Relating type, intensity, and quality of after-school activities to later academic and behavioral outcomes*. Manuscript in preparation.

Mahoney, J. L., Vandell, D. L., Simpkins, S., & Zarrett, N. (2009). Adolescent out-of-school activities. In R. M. Lerner & L. Steinberg (Eds.), *Handbook of adolescent psychology: Vol. 2. Contextual influences on adolescent development* (3rd ed., pp. 228–269). New York, NY: Wiley.

National Institute of Child Health and Human Development (NICHD) Early Child Care Research Network. (2004). Are child developmental outcomes related to before- and after-school care arrangements? Results from the NICHD Study of Early Child Care. *Child Development, 75*, 280–295.

Pierce, K. M., Bolt, D. M., & Vandell, D. L. (2010). Specific features of after-school program quality: Associations with children's functioning in middle childhood. *American Journal of Community Psychology, 45*, 381–393.

Shernoff, D. J., & Vandell, D. L. (2007). Engagement in after-school program activities: Quality of experience from the perspective of participants. *Journal of Youth and Adolescence, 36*, 891–903.

REFERENCES (CONTINUED)

Shernoff, D. J., & Vandell, D. L. (2008). Youth engagement and quality of experience in afterschool programs. *Afterschool Matters, Occasional Papers Series,* (9), 1–11.

Vandell, D. L. (2009). *California After School Outcomes Measures Project: Phase I.* Submitted to the David and Lucile Packard Foundation and the Afterschool Division of the California Department of Education, University of California, Irvine.

Vandell, D. L. (2010, January). *Afterschool research in 2010: Implications for policy and practice.* Presentation at the 2010 National Network of Statewide Afterschool Networks Meeting, San Diego, CA.

Vandell, D. L. (2011, February). *Impacts and outcomes: What we know about afterschool and expanded learning opportunities.* Presentation at the 2012 Meeting of the National Network of Statewide Afterschool Networks, San Francisco, CA.

Vandell, D. L. (2011, September). *The power of expanded learning opportunities today.* Presentation at the 2011 National Network of Statewide Afterschool Networks Leads Meeting, Washington, DC.

Vandell, D. L. (2012, June). *Expanded learning opportunities can make a difference.* Presentation to the Charles Stewart Mott Foundation Board of Directors, Flint, MI.

Vandell, D. L., & Corasaniti, M. A. (1988). The relation between third graders' after school care and social, academic, and emotional functioning. *Child Development, 59,* 868–875.

Vandell, D. L., O'Cadiz, P., & Hall, V. (2010, August). *California Afterschool Outcome Measures Project: Phase II report.* Submitted to the David and Lucile Packard Foundation and the Afterschool Division of the California Department of Education, University of California, Irvine.

Vandell, D. L., O'Cadiz, P., Hall, V., & Karsh, A. (2012, January). *California Afterschool Outcome Measures Project: Report of the field test.* Submitted to the David and Lucile Packard Foundation and the Afterschool Division of the California Department of Education, University of California, Irvine. Retrieved from http://afterschooloutcomes.org/sites/default/files/caomp_field_test_report_4.13.12.pdf

Vandell, D. L., Pierce, K. M., & Dadisman, K. (2005). Out-of-school settings as a developmental context for children and youth. In R. V. Kail (Ed.), *Advances in child development and behavior* (Vol. 33, pp. 43–77). New York, NY: Academic.

Vandell, D. L., Pierce, K. M., & Karsh, A. (2011). *Study of promising after-school programs: Follow-up report to participating school districts.* Irvine, CA: University of California-Irvine.

Vandell, D. L., Reisner, E. R., & Pierce, K. M. (2007). *Outcomes linked to high-quality afterschool programs: Longitudinal findings from the study of promising afterschool programs.* Report to the Charles Stewart Mott Foundation, Flint, MI.

Vandell, D. L., Shernoff, D. J., Pierce, K. M., Bolt, D. M., Dadisman, K., & Brown, B. B. (2005). Activities, engagement, and emotion in after-school programs (and elsewhere). In H. B. Weiss, P. M. D. Little, & S. M. Bouffard (Eds.), *New directions for youth development: No. 105. Participation in youth programs: Enrollment, attendance, and engagement* (pp. 121–129). San Francisco, CA: Jossey-Bass.

Vandell, D. L., Shumow, L., & Posner, J. (2005). After-school programs for low-income children: Differences in program quality. In J. L. Mahoney, R. W. Larson, & J. S. Eccles (Eds.), *Organized activities as contexts of development: Extracurricular activities, after school and community programs* (pp. 437–456). Mahwah, NJ: Erlbaum.

Heather Weiss
Founder and Director, Harvard Family
Research Project

Fifteen Years of Evaluation of 21st Century Community Learning Centers: A Driver for Program Quality and Capacity in the Field

The agreement by key congressional and administration leaders to significantly increase funding of the landmark federal 21st Century Community Learning Centers legislation between 1997 and 2001 was a powerful signal that afterschool programs and activities were worth significant public investment as part of the nation's efforts to educate and prepare its children for future success. At the same time, the legislation's evaluation requirements and the subsequent emphasis on "scientifically based research" in the 2001 No Child Left Behind Act (NCLB) made it clear that these newly funded programs had to be accountable and prove their public value.

These challenges, including their accompanying performance management and accountability requirements, were powerful drivers for taking data and evaluation seriously in a new field. Addressing these challenges was also a shared priority of the innovative public and private partnership begun in 1998 between the United States Department of Education and the C. S. Mott Foundation. The Foundation's leadership, along with the significant national opportunity that the 21st Century Community Learning Centers initiative afforded for continuing support for afterschool and expanded learning opportunities for children and youth, leveraged subsequent philanthropic investment in evaluation. Without these strategic foundation investments, the afterschool field would not be in the strong position it is in today.

So what has all of this investment in evaluation helped the field achieve in the past 15 years? In 1997 there existed little by way of evaluation of afterschool programs. Since then, the federal investment in the 21st Century Community Learning Centers initiative, along with strategic evaluation investments by others, has built afterschool into a maturing field with demonstrated public value on an array of commonly valued youth outcomes. In this commentary, I offer a brief scan of the state of afterschool evaluation to suggest that the field is, in fact, maturing and has met the evaluation challenge. Quality afterschool programs that are well designed can positively impact areas on which they focus. I also suggest that the field's evolving research and evaluation agenda holds important lessons for other fields.

For me, a mature field in the 21st century positions evaluation and performance management not only to show it delivers valuable public outcomes for youth but also to ensure it can *continue* to attain and be accountable for these outcomes. With respect to the position and role of evaluation, a maturing field has three distinct features: practitioners with a commitment to using information to support continuous improvement, innovation, and accountability; a substantial, high quality, and nuanced research and evaluation base from which to learn and to show the public the value of high quality programs; and a deepening research- and practice-based understanding of how to build the quality programs and activities that continue to deliver their promised outcomes.

> Because the 21st Century Community Learning Centers funding does not support any one model or approach to afterschool programs and activities, the initiative has stimulated the evaluation of a wide array of program models and approaches operating in diverse communities and conditions.

The Harvard Family Research Project has been tracking and synthesizing the results of afterschool evaluations for over a decade. We developed and maintain a national database of afterschool program evaluations for the field (www.hfrp.org/out-of-school-time/ost-database-bibliography). Both the number and quality of the studies in the database and our understanding of the evolution of afterschool evaluation underscore how important the 21st Century Community Learning Centers initiative has and continues to be, not only in funding programs but also in creating and shaping the knowledge base for the afterschool field that can be used by school, community, and afterschool leaders, as well as public and nonprofit funders.

The evaluation of the 21st Century Community Learning Centers programs got off to a rocky start with a federally funded and premature outcome evaluation reporting mixed results in 2003. It was used by some at the federal level to attempt to reduce funding for the program by half; but fortunately, as other evidence was documented and the serious concerns about how this early evaluation was conducted became known, support in Congress and the administration was retained. By being conducted early on in the field's development, despite the study's flaws and because of the reaction of researchers suggesting problems with the study, the process actually helped clarify the role of evaluation and position it to be useful in developing this growing field, hence my assertion that it was premature. In particular, it suggested some programs were effective while others were not, thereby putting a critical and early emphasis not only on assessing outcomes but on understanding program goals and implementation and on determining the factors and conditions necessary to deliver quality and effective services (Evaluation Exchange, 2002).

The 21st Century Community Learning Centers initiative has created incentives for evaluating afterschool programs and has therefore shaped afterschool evaluation in a number of ways. It has funded and stimulated programs to conduct evaluation, reflected in the fact that at least a third of the programs in our database of afterschool programs call themselves 21st Century Community Learning Centers or indicate they receive some of their funding from this source. Because the 21st Century Community Learning Centers funding does not support any one model or approach to afterschool programs and activities, the initiative has stimulated the evaluation of a wide array of program models and approaches operating in diverse communities and conditions.

This decision not to fund a particular approach turns out to have been a wise one, not least because studies show that participation and engagement in afterschool depend on children and youth having choices among programs and access to diverse activities. The large number of 21st Century Community Learning Centers programs and their diversity have also attracted applied developmental researchers using afterschool programs as sites for studying where youth learn and what engages them in learning, thereby enriching the knowledge base of the field (Mahoney, Lord, & Carryl, 2005; Mahoney, Larson, & Eccles, 2005; Durlak, Mahoney, Bohnert, & Parente, 2010).

> Multiyear funding support from the 21st Century Community Learning Centers initiative allows local program sites to test new and creative approaches and incorporate successful ones into their programming …

Multiyear funding support from the 21st Century Community Learning Centers initiative allows local program sites to test new and creative approaches and incorporate successful ones into their programming (see HFRP 21st Century Community Learning Centers Research Updates, 2010, 2012). Multiyear program support also allows flagship leaders in the afterschool field, such as the large, multiprogram, citywide organizations that serve large numbers of children and youth (for example, TASC in New York City and LA's BEST), to attract evaluation support and develop a longer-term evaluation strategy. Their ongoing series of evaluations and partnerships with evaluators are important for the field because they address key questions about the professional training, organizational supports, and other elements of infrastructure and program quality that lead to positive outcomes (HFRP 21st Century Community Learning Centers Bibliography, 2010; Reisner et al., 2007; Huang et al., 2007).

At this point, with federal 21st Century Community Learning Centers and philanthropic support, the afterschool field has a large number of evaluations meeting the criteria NCLB set in 2001 for scientifically based research in education. There are many small, single-site evaluations, as well as large, multi-site evaluations, conducted by a growing national cadre of investigators who are using both experimental and quasi-experimental research designs to assess program outcomes. Having this large set of studies enables meta-analytic syntheses that examine outcomes across an array of programs and that tease out the success factors that enable positive ones (Durlak, Weissberg, & Pachan, 2010). There is also growing convergence across multiple studies on the success factors and elements of quality programs (Little, Weimer, & Weiss, 2008). The afterschool field is in a strong position because it can make evidence-based claims about its public value on an array of commonly valued youth outcomes, such as improved attendance, grades, homework completion, classroom participation, behavior and—depending on the focus—achievement and performance. These programs also contribute to an array of positive developmental outcomes, including socio-emotional skills and healthy behaviors that support learning, and they prevent a number of problem behaviors that are detrimental to school and life success (Little, Wimer, & Weiss, 2008).

Equally important, the afterschool field is benefitting from a steady flow of increasingly nuanced evaluations that have been providing information to address seven key questions that are critically important if it is to continue to grow and provide high quality services. I offer the questions here to invite others into a conversation about what the learning agenda for the field should contain and prioritize:

1. *What works for whom, when, where, and why?*

2. *What doesn't work?*

3. *What are the elements of high quality programs and activities?*

4. *How do the elements work together to achieve the desired youth outcomes?*

5. *What internal program organizational and leadership characteristics and processes are necessary to develop and maintain quality services?*

6. *What policy, funding, and infrastructure supports are necessary for high quality at scale?*

7. *How can and do afterschool programs fit together with schools, digital media, and other learning supports to offer coordinated, accessible, and seamless opportunities?*

Many of the studies addressing the first three questions and some addressing number 4 are available in our searchable database and have been included in meta-analyses and key syntheses of the state of knowledge in the afterschool field (Lauer et al., 2006; Little, Weimer, & Weiss, 2008; Granger, 2010; Durlak, Weissberg, & Pachan, 2010; Durlak, Mahoney, Bohnert, & Parente, 2010). There are fewer research studies and evaluations to address questions 5 through 7. I suggest they are a priority for further research investment in the field and that addressing them will require the kinds of ethnographic and mixed methods work in the following examples.

Hirsch, Deutsch, and DuBois's recent work (2011) exemplifies an important effort to understand the organizational dimension of service quality—an effort that is also being repeated in research across other education and human services domains (Bryk, Sebring, Allensworth, Luppescu, & Easton, 2010; Glisson, 2007; Duggan, 2012; Douglass, 2011). Hirsch (2011) and his colleagues' ethnographic work on three comprehensive afterschool centers examines how multiple organizational characteristics and processes like leadership, a strong focus on positive youth development, organizational climate, staff development and supervision, connections to family and community, and organizational learning all fit together and interact to create quality services that, in turn, move the needle on youth outcomes in a significantly positive direction. Their work is pathbreaking for the field in that it assembles the pieces that other studies have shown are important for quality services and shows how they all work together to create quality youth experiences.

The landscape of learning is rapidly changing, with more use of digital media and a growing emphasis on anywhere, anytime learning, both in and out of school. In this regard, another important new strand of work is being conducted by developmental researchers and ethnographers studying where and how youth use and learn with digital media. Both Baron's (2006) work on self-initiated learning and Ito and colleagues' (2009) studies of how youth use digital media, for example, highlight how youth are seeking opportunities to build important skills across learning environments, as well as how learning in school can lead to learning in afterschool and vice versa. It suggests that youth are actually ahead of institutions in seeking and connecting learning opportunities in and out of school and that they could both help make and benefit from greater connections.

Strategic investments in evaluation research over the past 15 years have yielded significant evidence that 21st Century Community Learning Centers and high quality programs that serve children and youth during the nonschool hours are essential for preparing young people for the future. It also shows what is essential to deliver high quality services that contribute to better learning and developmental outcomes for youth. In 15 years, the afterschool field has built a substantial research and evaluation literature that is serving as a driver for more high quality programs and opportunities around the country. It is also a model for how to invest in research and evaluation for those seeking to invest in building the knowledge base in other new service fields. That said—and as important as the knowledge we already have today is—we have work to do as a field to investigate and uncover findings about more complex aspects of this field from an organizational and systems perspective. The next frontier, in fact, includes more sophisticated research that studies expanded learning opportunities, including the perspective of children and youth themselves, and that reveals optimal ways to support learning processes, program capacity and scalability, and systemic infrastructure building. As this commentary suggests, the afterschool field is "on it."

> Strategic investments in evaluation research over the past 15 years have yielded significant evidence that 21st Century Community Learning Centers and high quality programs that serve children and youth during the nonschool hours are essential for preparing young people for the future.

ABOUT THE AUTHOR

Heather Weiss is founder and director of the Harvard Family Research Project at the Harvard Graduate School of Education. HFRP's mission is to research, document, and evaluate practices, interventions, and policies to promote children's successful development from birth to adulthood. Weiss and her colleagues built an ongoing, accessible, national database of afterschool program evaluations to support the field's quality enhancement, continuous improvement, innovation, and advocacy work.

REFERENCES

Baron, B. (2006). Interest and self-sustained learning as catalysts of development: A learning ecology perspective. *Human Development, 49*, 193–224.

Bryk, A. S., Sebring, P. B., Allensworth, E., Luppescu, S., & Easton, J. Q. (2010). *Organizing schools for improvement: Lessons from Chicago school reform*. Chicago, IL: University of Chicago Press.

Douglass, A. (2011). Improving family engagement: The organizational context and its influence on partnering with parents on formal child care settings. *Early Childhood Research and Practice, 13*(2), 1–20.

Duggan, A. (2012, March). Service is everything: How home visit service delivery impacts family outcomes. *Harvard Family Research Project FINE Newsletter, 4*(1).

Durlak, J. A., Mahoney, J. L., Bohnert, A. M., & Parente, M. E. (2010). Developing and improving after-school programs to enhance youth's personal growth and adjustment [Special issue *American Journal of Community Psychology, 45*, 285–293.

Durlak, J. A., Weissberg, R. P., & Pachan, M. (2010). A meta-analysis of after-school programs that seek to promote personal growth and social skills in children and adolescents. *American Journal of Community Psychology, 45*, 294–309.

Glisson, C. (2007). Assessing and changing culture and climate for effective services. *Research on Social Work Practice. 17*, 736–747.

Granger, R. C. (2010). Understanding and improving the effectiveness of after-school practice. *American Journal of Community Psychology, 45*, 441–446.

Harvard Family Research Project. (2002). Special report on the 21st Century Community Learning Centers program national evaluation. *Evaluation Exchange, 9*(1), 11–15.

Harvard Family Research Project. (2010, November). 21st CCLC bibliography: Evaluations and research studies of out-of-school time programs that receive 21st CCLC funding: Appendix to Research Update No. 4. Retrieved from http://www.hfrp.org/var/hfrp/storage/fckeditor/File/research4appendix.pdf

Harvard Family Research Project. (2010, November). Research update 4: 21st CCLC-funded afterschool programs. Retrieved from http://www.hfrp.org/publications-resources/ browse-our-publications/research-update-4- 21st-cclc-funded-afterschool-programs

Harvard Family Research Project (2012, May). Research update 8: 21st CCLCs—Stable funding for innovation and continuous improvement. Retrieved from http://www.hfrp.org/publications-resources/publications-series/research-updates-highlights-from-the-out-of-school-time-database/ research-update-8- 21st-century-community-learning-centers-stable-funding-for-innovation-and-continuous-improvement

Hirsch, B. J., Deutsch, N. L., & DuBois, D. L. (2011). *After-school centers and youth development: Case studies of success and failure.* New York, NY: Cambridge University Press.

Huang, D., Coordt, A., La Torre, D., Leon, S., Miyoshi, J., Perez, P., & Peterson, C. (2007). *The afterschool hours: Examining the relationship between afterschool staff-based social capital and student engagement in LA's BEST* (CSE Tech. Rep. No. 712). Los Angeles, CA: University of California, National Center for Research on Evaluation, Standards, and Student Testing (CRESST).

Ito, M., Baumer, S., Bittanti, M., Boyd, D., Cody, R., Herr-Stephenson, B., . . . Tripp, L.. (2009). *Hanging out, messing around, and geeking out: Kids living and learning with new media.* Cambridge, MA: MIT Press.

Lauer. P. A., Akiba, M., Wilkerson, S. B., Apthorp, H. S., Snow, D., & Martin-Glenn, M. L. (2006). Out-of-school time programs: A meta-analysis of effects for at-risk students. *Review of Educational Research, 76,* 275–313.

Little, P. M. D., Wimer, C., & Weiss, H. B. (2008). After school programs in the 21st century: Their potential and what it takes to achieve it. *Issues and Opportunities in Out-of-School Time Evaluation,* 10.

Mahoney, J. L., Larson, R. W., & Eccles, J. W. (Eds.). (2005). *Organized activities as developmental contexts: Extracurricular activities, after-school and community programs.* Mahwah, NJ: Lawrence Erlbaum.

Mahoney, J. L., Lord, H., & Carryl, E. (2005). Afterschool program participation and the development of childhood obesity and peer acceptance. *Applied Developmental Science, 9*(4), 202–215.

Reisner, E. R., Vandell, D. L., Pechman, E. M., Pierce, K. M., Brown, B. B., & Bolt, D. (2007). *Charting the benefits of high-quality after-school experiences: Evidence from new research on improving after-school opportunities for disadvantaged youth.* Washington, DC: Policy Studies Associates.

Joseph A. Durlak
Emeritus Professor of Psychology,
Loyola University Chicago

Roger P. Weissberg
NoVo Foundation Endowed Chair
in Social and Emotional Learning,
University of Illinois at Chicago

Afterschool Programs That Follow Evidence-Based Practices to Promote Social and Emotional Development Are Effective

The purpose of this brief is to summarize the findings from our research review, which indicated that afterschool programs that follow four evidence-based practices are successful in promoting young people's personal and social development (Durlak, Weissberg, & Pachan, 2010). While a number of afterschool programs need to change and improve, others have positively improved multiple dimensions of student learning and development. For this reason, the findings from various outcome studies on afterschool programs have led commentators to emphasize that a main focus in research should now primarily be to understand the factors that distinguish *effective* from *ineffective* programs in order to guide future policy and practice (Granger, 2010).

For example, the 21st Century Community Learning Centers initiative is an important large-scale funding stream for afterschool and summer learning in high-poverty schools and neighborhoods across America. Because the Community Learning Centers initiative allows for local design and variation, it should not be surprising that program results vary. Nor should it be surprising that early studies, conducted before the field was informed about promising and evidence-based practices and design, found mixed results. For instance, the large-scale evaluations of the outcomes of 21st Century Community Learning Centers programs serving elementary (James-Burdumy et al., 2005) or middle school students (Dynarski et al., 2004), that is centers that received federal funding through No Child Left Behind legislation, have generated controversy and led to questions regarding the wisdom of federal funding for afterschool programs. These early evaluations failed to detect any significant gains in achievement tests scores, although there were some gains in secondary outcomes such as parental involvement in school and student commitment to work. However,

> So the question should be not whether [these opportunities] should be offered, but rather what research-based design elements should be included to make them and other afterschool programs like them more successful.

researchers have noted several methodological problems in these evaluations that involve the lack of initial group equivalence, high attrition among respondents, low levels of student attendance, and the possible nonrepresentativeness of evaluated programs (Kane, 2004; Mahoney & Zigler, 2006).

There is also the critical issue of treating programs collectively as though they provided the same uniform set of services when this is clearly not the case. While some of these 21st Century Community Learning Centers provided students with intensive small-group instruction or individual tutoring, which has been shown to be an effective approach (Lauer et al., 2006), others provided relatively unstructured homework time, which is not likely to be successful. It is precisely because afterschool programs vary in form, structure, and specific goals that they should be carefully evaluated along these dimensions. There is no question that many young people and their families need and want expanded opportunities such as those funded by the 21st Century Community Learning Centers initiative. So the question should be not whether they should be offered, but rather what research-based design elements should be included to make them and other afterschool programs like them more successful.

Our review included 68 studies in which those attending an afterschool program that had the specific goal of fostering personal and social development were compared to nonparticipating control youth. We did not review programs that focused exclusively on academic achievement. The reviewed programs were drawn from across the country; they operated in urban and rural areas and served school-aged youth between 5 and 18 years old.

We hypothesized that effective programs would use evidence-based practices for enhancing young people's personal and social skills. We were able to identify four practices used in some afterschool programs, but not in others. These four evidence-based practices formed the acronym SAFE and are explained further in our full research report. In brief, our procedures identified whether or not program staff used a step-by-step training approach (S), emphasized active forms of learning by having youth practice new skills (A), focused specific time and attention on skill development (F), and were explicit in defining the skills they were attempting to promote (E). Each of these practices has a strong research base in many skill training studies of youth. The afterschool programs that followed all four recommended practices were called SAFE programs (N = 41) and those that did not were called Other programs (N = 27).

Our findings were clear-cut. SAFE programs were associated with significant improvements in self-perception, school bonding and positive social behaviors; significant reductions in conduct problems and drug use; and significant increases in achievement test scores, grades, and school attendance. The group of Other programs failed to yield significant improvements on any of these outcomes. Table 1 contains the mean effect sizes achieved on these outcomes by SAFE and Other programs.

Table 1. Mean effect sizes on different outcomes for participants in SAFE and Other afterschool programs.

Outcomes	Effect Size	
	Other Programs	SAFE Programs
Drug Use	.03	.16
Positive Social Behaviors	.06	.29
Reduction in Problem Behaviors	.08	.30
School Attendance	.07	.14
School Bonding	.03	.25
School Grades	.05	.22
Self-Perceptions	.13	.37
Academic Achievement (Test Scores)	.02	.20

Note: All of the outcomes associated with SAFE programs but none of the outcomes for Other programs were statistically significant.

Figure 1. Average percentile gains on selected outcomes for participants in SAFE and Other afterschool programs.

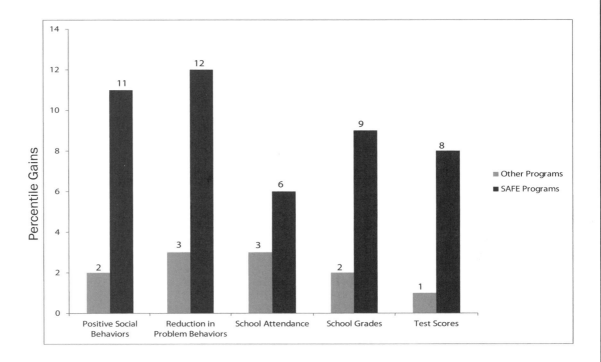

Another way to portray how much of a difference in outcomes is associated with SAFE programs is by calculating an improvement index (Institute of Education Sciences, 2008). The improvement index is a percentile figure that suggests how much change the average youth would demonstrate depending on whether they participate in a SAFE or Other type of program. These percentiles are presented in Figure 1 for some notable outcomes from our review. For example, on average, youth could gain 8 percentiles in standardized test scores, show an increase of 11 percentiles in positive social behaviors (e.g., cooperation, helping others), and show a reduction of 12 percentiles in problem behaviors (e.g., aggression, noncompliance) if they were in a SAFE program. In contrast, participants in Other programs would show very minimal and statistically nonsignificant percentile improvements in each of these categories.

Are such percentile gains worthwhile to participating youth? Of course, it would be preferable if the SAFE program outcomes were higher, but the outcomes for SAFE programs are comparable to those obtained by many other successful youth programs that have been carefully evaluated. For example, in terms of increasing positive social behaviors, reducing problem behaviors and promoting academic achievement, the outcomes for SAFE programs are similar to those achieved by many effective school-based programs designed to improve student academic performance or social adjustment (see Durlak, Weissberg, Dymnicki, Taylor, & Schellinger, 2011). In other words, afterschool programs that follow evidence-based skill training practices are part of the array of worthwhile interventions for youth. Our findings also suggest the possibility of aligning effective interventions during the school day with those occurring after school to maximize the benefits for participating youth.

> . . . policy and funding should be focused on assisting more afterschool programs to develop evidence-based practices that are associated with better outcomes.

The practical implications of our findings are that policy and funding should be focused on assisting more afterschool programs to develop evidence-based practices that are associated with better outcomes. As others have noted, quality matters in afterschool programs, just as it matters in other types of youth services (Hirsch, Mekinda, & Stawicki, 2010; Yohalem & Wilson-Ahlstrom, 2010). Carefully done evaluations can help us understand how quality is manifested in afterschool programs that vary in their structural and operational characteristics and in relation to different participant outcomes. With the knowledge that we now have, we should spend time and energy developing strategies, supports, policies, and funding to expand SAFE afterschool and summer learning programs through the 21st Century Community Learning Centers initiative and similar initiatives where they are needed across America rather than continue to argue whether they make a positive difference.

ABOUT THE AUTHORS

Joseph A. Durlak's major interests are in prevention and promotion programs for children and adolescents. He has been a clinical psychologist in the U.S. Army and on the faculties of Southern Illinois University in Carbondale and Loyola University Chicago, from which he recently retired with the position of emeritus professor of psychology.

Roger P. Weissberg is NoVo Foundation Endowed Chair in Social and Emotional Learning and a LAS Distinguished Professor of Psychology at the University of Illinois at Chicago (UIC). He is also president and CEO of the Collaborative for Academic, Social, and Emotional Learning (CASEL), an international organization committed to making evidence-based social, emotional and academic learning an essential part of preschool through high school education (www.casel.org).

REFERENCES

Durlak, J. A., Weissberg, R. P., Dymnicki, A. B., Taylor, R. D., & Schellinger, K. B. (2011). The impact of enhancing students' social and emotional learning: A meta-analysis of school-based universal interventions. *Child Development, 82*(1), 405–433.

Durlak, J. A., Weissberg, R. P., & Pachan, M. (2010). A meta-analysis of after-school programs that seek to promote personal and social skills in children and adolescents. *American Journal of Community Psychology, 45*, 294–309.

Dynarski, M., James-Burdumy, S., Moore, M., Rosenberg, L., Deke, J., & Mansfield, W. (2004). *When schools stay open late: The national evaluation of the 21st Century Community Learning Centers Program: New findings* (NCEE 2004-3001). U.S. Department of Education, National Center for Education Evaluation and Regional Assistance. Washington, DC: U.S. Government Printing Office.

Granger, R. C. (2010). Understanding and improving the effectiveness of after-school practice. *American Journal of Community Psychology, 45*, 441–446.

Hirsch, B. J., Mekinda, M. A., & Stawicki, J. A. (2010). More than attendance: The importance of after-school program quality. *American Journal of Community Psychology, 45*, 447–452.

Institute of Education Sciences. (2008). *What Works Clearinghouse procedures and standards handbook*. Retrieved from http://ies.ed.gov/ncee/wwc/DocumentSum.aspx?sid=19

James-Burdumy, S., Dynarski, M., Moore, M., Deke, J., Mansfield, W., & Pistorino, C. (2005). *When schools stay open late: The national evaluation of the 21st Century Community Learning Centers Program: Final report* (NCEE 2005-3002). Washington, DC: U.S. Department of Education, Institute of Education Sciences, National Center for Education Evaluation and Regional Assistance.

Kane, T. J. (2004). The impact of after-school programs: Interpreting the results of four recent evaluations. Retrieved from http://www.wtgrantfoundation.org/

Lauer, P. A., Akiba, M., Wilkerson, S. B., Apthorp, H. S., Snow, D., & Martin-Green, M. (2006). Out-of school time programs: A meta-analysis of effects for at-risk students. *Review of Educational Research, 76*, 275–313.

Mahoney, J. P., & Zigler, E. F. (2006). Translating science to policy under the No Child Left Behind Act of 2001: Lessons from the national evaluation of the 21st-Century Community Learning Centers. *Journal of Applied Developmental Psychology, 27*, 282–294.

Yohalem, N., & Wilson-Ahlstrom, A. (2010). Inside the black box: Assessing and improving quality in youth programs. *American Journal of Community Psychology, 45*, 350–357.

Carol McElvain
Director, Afterschool and Expanded Learning,
American Institutes for Research

Building on What We Have Learned About Quality in Expanded Learning and Afterschool Programs: Working Toward the Development of a Quality Indicator System

For almost a decade and half, my colleagues and I at the American Institutes for Research (AIR)[1] (and our predecessor organizations, Learning Point Associates and NCREL) have watched the expanded learning community grow and develop in many positive ways, both its day-to-day practice as well as in its knowledge of what works well and of how to measure what works, particularly in relation to the 21st Century Community Learning Centers initiative. The significant growth in the number, sophistication, and strength of 21st Century Community Learning Centers since 1997 has been quite remarkable: from 10 schools in 1997 to almost 11,000 afterschool and summer learning programs in schools and community centers in every state in 2012–13. These programs are now broadening and deepening learning for almost 1.7 million students, engaging over a quarter-million parents, and coordinating 40,000 school-community partnerships that provide a variety of important academic supports and enriched learning opportunities through afterschool and summer programs.

During this time period, a number of local and state expanded learning initiatives were also launched, and those already underway experienced dramatic growth. Local efforts sprang up nationwide, including on the East Coast, such efforts as the Providence Afterschool Alliance (PASA) and The After School Corporation (TASC) in New York; in the heartland, such efforts as After School Matters in Chicago and STRIVE in Cincinnati; and on the West Coast, such efforts as LA's BEST in Los Angeles and the Partnership for Children and Youth in the Bay Area of Northern California.

1. The author would like to acknowledge the significant contribution of her colleagues at AIR toward the development of this work and their input on this article, particularly Neil Naftzger, Deborah Moroney, Jaime Singer, and Fausto López. Any errors or misstatements are the author's. We are also grateful for the work of Charles Smith and the Weikart Center for Youth Development at the Forum for Youth Investment.

State efforts also were initiated and refined, including in California, which has the largest state effort, the Afterschool Education and Safety (ASES) program based on Proposition 49.

As with any growth, it has not happened without a certain amount of initial growing pains and with significant opportunities to learn and improve. As a training partner in the original incarnation of the 21st Century Community Learning Centers program, continuing on with the development of professional development materials and trainings, including *Beyond the Bell: A Toolkit to Create Quality Afterschool Programs* (Kaplan, McElvain, & Walter, 2005), and in other work supporting the program and its operation, my colleagues and I have had the privilege of a close view of the positive changes and growth in program development and measurement. It is worth stepping back a minute to think back about the magnitude of the growth in and learnings from the 21st Century Community Learning Centers with an eye toward encouraging and supporting further developments in the field in the years ahead.

While the ultimate goal of educational support programs like the 21st Century Community Learning Centers initiative is increased student achievement and student success, such growth is not possible in isolation and is dependent on critical supporting factors.

While the ultimate goal of educational support programs like the 21st Century Community Learning Centers initiative is increased student achievement and student success, such growth is not possible in isolation and is dependent on critical supporting factors. This is where a high quality expanded learning program after school and during the summer can play a pivotal role. Focusing on the end-game of test scores at the end of the school year in just a few subjects in isolation has sometimes left key actors, who either work in or are responsible for programs, in a quandary. Reports about year-end test scores and other outcome measures are often received after the program year has ended. Yet this information is critically needed when the programs are actually operating in order to make key decisions regarding how programs might best serve students and build their improvement efforts.

Studies are clear that high quality afterschool programs structured in a variety of ways bring many positive outcomes for students, including achievement in terms of test scores (Durlak, Mahoney, Bohnert, & Parente, 2010). Furthermore, for almost 10 years, the Profile and Performance Information Collection System (PPICS) has been collecting annual data on all 21st Century Community Learning Centers across the nation, working through their respective state departments of education. More recently several state education departments (for example, those in Texas and New Jersey) have expanded upon the federal PPICS system to collect and analyze more data on the Centers in their states. In these data, teachers report that regular program participants tend to show improved homework completion, class participation, attendance, classroom behaviors, English and math classroom grades, and reading and math achievement scores, with those students who have higher program attendance showing the greatest improvement (Naftzger, Vinson, Manzeske, & Gibbs, 2011; American Institutes for Research, 2012).

This recent knowledge that high quality afterschool programs work and make a positive difference is indeed a "game changer." This means that we should spend much less time arguing about whether quality afterschool programs work and much more time on working to ensure that all programs are effective and to make high quality programs more accessible and scalable.

While empirical research investigating the impact of program quality on youth outcomes is still emerging, it is now generally agreed that in conjunction with youth characteristics, community context, and youth participation, higher levels of program quality promote many robust outcomes, including

- *active youth engagement,*

- *higher attendance in school,*

- *better school grades,*

- *positive social behaviors,*

- *improved homework completion and class participation, and*

- *fewer disciplinary issues to disrupt their learning.*

These are all building blocks to improvement of student achievement (Birmingham, Pechman, Russell, & Mielke, 2005; Black, Doolittle, Zhu, Unterman, & Grossman, 2008; Durlak & Weissberg, 2007; Granger, 2008; Lauer, Akiba, Wilkerson, Apthorp, Snow, & Martin-Glenn, 2006; Vandell, Shumow, & Posner, 2005). Further, many of these outcomes can be measured during the time the afterschool program is operating, so that adjustments can be made both in the school-day program and in the afterschool program to try to improve them.

> In these data, teachers report that regular program participants tend to show improved homework completion, class participation, attendance, classroom behaviors, English and math classroom grades, and reading and math achievement scores, with those students who have higher program attendance showing the greatest improvement.

Our hope is that, in the near future, the field will devote itself and its resources to pursuing the development of consistent measures of these interim indicators of program quality to help programs see where their critical levers of change are to promote high quality programming, both in organization and direct program-level supports.

Other articles in this compendium will focus on what those studies have found, but this article will focus on what the development of a robust program quality indicator system might be able to measure and demonstrate to those who might support the expansion of high quality expanded learning programs afterschool and summers. What we are increasingly trying to accomplish is to provide more real-time indicators and information to the educators and community organizations working in afterschool and summer programs so they can adjust, change, and improve opportunities and programming, as appropriate, at the time they are actually operating and not after the fact. This system builds on the research, evaluation, and quality assessment work that has developed over the past decade and puts it in a context that is both actionable and measurable, with short- and long-term outcomes. It also creates the opportunity for any participant in the delivery of services to see how they play a part in creating positive outcomes.

Based on the Weikart Center's approach to program point of service quality (Smith, Peck, Denault, Blazevski, & Akiva, 2010), we use the following frame to suggest that organizational processes (such as those described in *Beyond the Bell*) are integral for delivery of those services:

The critical point underlying a quality indicator system is that quality indicators focus primarily on *quality implementation* while the program is functioning as opposed to reviewing end-of-the-year information received after the program year has ended. The idea here is to help centers engage with data related to the adoption of quality practices and approaches, help identify strengths and weaknesses relative to these areas, and focus staff reflection on those areas where there are opportunities for growth and further development from a practice standpoint. Based on the research we have seen, we believe that better implementation from a quality perspective will better support the achievement of desired youth outcomes.

It is important to recognize that the development of a quality indicator system is not meant to duplicate or replace existing efforts. We recognize that many states and programs have developed or adopted quality assessment processes that are also reflective of the research on program quality, as well as local context. In contrast, the quality indicator system we are developing is intended to integrate the multiple efforts in place toward achieving high-quality programs that are appropriately reflective of context and best practice. Creating a quality indicator system is intended to emulate the quality improvement practices used in other education and business sectors and is directed toward the end of putting in place best practices that support positive youth outcomes and student success, including achievement.

Quality indicators have a benefit that is twofold. First, they support the integration of continuous quality improvement practices, data collection efforts, and responsibility toward aligning with industry-defined quality standards. Secondly, quality indicators describe valuable data on program processes and support quality practices at the point of service that are purported to promote positive youth outcomes. This information is critical to assessing the relationship between program quality and youth outcomes. The great benefit of a quality indicator system is that it helps develop both formative and summative evaluation and affords the opportunity to use data gathered in ways that are meaningful for program leaders, staff, and participants.

Quality indicators should meet the following criteria:

- *Represent promising, evidenced-based practices that are relevant to the local context and the goals and principles of the program*

- *Be informed by multiple data sources (e.g., PPICS, surveys)*

- *Allow program leaders and staff to make data-driven decisions and provide tools for collaboration and reflection related to organizational processes and program practice*

- *Help programs leaders and staff strive toward alignment with local and national systems of program quality (e.g., state- or organization-developed program quality standards)*

- *Help programs move towards practices that ultimately support positive youth outcomes*

A quality indicator system has multiple practical elements, including staff and leadership surveys, aligned resources for building program quality (i.e., planning tools), optional components of technical assistance (e.g., technical assistance on using data to drive program development), and the quality indicators themselves: staff, partnerships, and practices. Under each domain, there are multiple elements, as indicated in the following figure:

Indicator Domain	Indicator Element
Staff	Staff Recruitment and Retention
	Staff Professional Development
	Opportunities for Staff Reflection and Improvement
Partnerships	School Partnerships
	Community Partnerships
	Family Partnerships
	Youth as Partners
Practices	Practices That Support Implementation Quality
	Academic Skill Building Practices
	Youth Development Practices
	Family Engagement Practices
	Quality Improvement Practices

Critical in this understanding is that high quality programming is comprised of both program-level interactions and the organization of the program itself. Program-level interactions are the ways direct program staff work with their participants. They include elements such as how staff structure activities, the variety of activities they provide, how staff talk to students or provide leadership or develop opportunities for them, and how engaged children are in the activities in which they participate. Organizational elements are comprised of the overarching structure, including the program and its management. Program elements include such things as the adoption of a quality framework; evaluation and monitoring; the process for selecting staff; program partnerships and relationships with families, the schools with which they work, and other stakeholders in the community. Management context elements include opportunities for staff professional development, ongoing staff supervision, and program monitoring and evaluation.

> Programs need a quality framework and a related set of indicators to support high quality programming within all contexts of program operations.

Programs need a quality framework and a related set of indicators to support high quality programming within all contexts of program operations. Developing a system that provides timely, interpretable, and actionable data regarding how programs are functioning from a quality perspective guides ongoing quality improvement efforts. This also gives programs the time and support they need to use data to drive toward higher-quality-related decision making.

The initial goals of a quality indicator system would focus on both short- and longer-term outcomes. Critical to that process is the combination of self-assessment and other data measures to give a better picture to programs and staff about where they are and where they want to head. Implementing a reflective self-assessment process would first raise program awareness of organizational quality indicators, and would also provide a base understanding of how well a program is implementing quality indicators. The self-assessment process is a strategy that is more likely to engage program staff and management in identifying training and professional development needs.

Longer-term goals of a quality indicator system include the following:

- *Programs will see, over time, how they can use the self-assessment process and the data they have developed from ongoing assessment of point-of-service quality to help programs develop yearly quality improvement plans.*

- *Programs receive ongoing support through training and professional development areas targeted for program improvement and in making data driven program decisions.*

- *Programs gain experience and knowledge in using evaluation to inform an ongoing cycle of quality improvement;*

- *Student growth on short term and long term goals are measured to evaluate program impacts.*

Conclusion

Over more than a decade, the expanded learning field has learned and accomplished a great deal. It is now generally agreed that as a result of higher levels of program quality in afterschool and summer learning programs, we are increasingly seeing significant positive and student outcomes. Because of these learnings and positive developments, building a system of program quality indicators is the next logical developmental step in application of what we, as a field, have learned. These indicators have been identified in conjunction with the many implementation studies and evaluations of effective expanded learning programs, as well as from the research and literature spanning multiple fields, including youth development, conditions for effective learning, and effective classroom practices.

Now is the time—and the opportunity is ripe—to use these many learnings to enhance the extensive expanded learning infrastructure for afterschool and summer learning programs that is already in place in just about every state and to strengthen the professional practice of the tens of thousands of individuals who work in them, from schools and from other child- and youth-serving organizations, in just about every community across America.

ABOUT THE AUTHOR

Carol McElvain leads afterschool and expanded learning work at the American Institutes for Research. She provides national leadership on matters of quality, particularly as it relates to school improvement efforts and speaks at numerous conferences and workshops. She is co-author of the seminal afterschool resource *Beyond the Bell: A Toolkit for Creating High Quality Afterschool Programs* and has served as a local school board member.

REFERENCES

American Institutes for Research. (2012). *Texas 21st Century Community Learning Centers: Interim evaluation report.* Retrieved from http://www.tea.state.tx.us/WorkArea/linkit.aspx?LinkIdentifier=id &ItemID=2147506331&libID=2147506324

Birmingham, J., Pechman, E. M., Russell, C. A., & Mielke, M. (2005). *Shared features of high-performing after-school programs: A follow-up to the TASC evaluation.* Washington, DC: Policy Studies Associates.

Black, A. R., Doolittle, F., Zhu, P., Unterman, R., & Grossman, J. B. (2008). *The evaluation of enhanced academic instruction in after-school programs: findings after the first year of implementation* (NCEE 2008-4021). Retrieved from http://ies.ed.gov/ncee/pdf/20084021.pdf

David P. Weikart Center for Youth Program Quality. (2011). *School-age PQA.* Ypsilanti, MI: Forum for Youth Investment.

Durlak, J. A., Mahoney, J. L., Bohnert, A. M., & Parente, M. E. (2010). Developing and improving after-school programs to enhance youth's personal growth and adjustment: A special issue of AJCP. *American Journal of Community Psychology, 45*(3–4), 285–293.

REFERENCES (CONTINUED)

Durlak, R., & Weissberg, R. (2007). *The impact of after-school programs that promote personal and social skills*. Chicago, IL: CASEL.

Granger, R. C. (2008). After-school programs and academics: Implications for policy, practice, and research. *Social Policy Report*, 22(2). Retrieved from After-School Programs and Academics: Implications for Policy, Practice, and Research

Kaplan, J., McElvain, C., & Walter, K. (2005). *Beyond the bell: A toolkit for creating effective afterschool programs* (Rev. 3rd ed.). Naperville, IL: Learning Point Associates.

Lauer, P. A., Akiba, M., Wilkerson, S. B., Apthorp, H. S., Snow, D., & Martin-Glen, M. L. (2006). Out-of school time programs: A meta-analysis of effects for at-risk students. *Review of Educational Research, 76*, 275–313.

Naftzger, N., Vinson, M., Manzeske, D., & Gibbs, C. (2011). *New Jersey 21st Century Community Learning Centers (21st CCLC) impact report 2009–10*. Naperville, IL: American Institutes for Research.

Smith, C., Peck, S. C., Denault, A.-S., Blazevski, J., & Akiva, T. (2010). Quality at the point of service: Profiles of practice in after-school settings. *American Journal of Community Psychology, 45*(3), 358–369.

Vandell, D. L., Shumow, L., & Posner, J. (2005). After-school programs for low-income children: Differences in program quality. In J. L. Mahoney, R. W. Larson, & J. S. Eccles (Eds.), *Organized activities as contexts of development: Extracurricular activities, after school and community programs* (pp. 437–456). Mahwah, NJ: Erlbaum.

Gary Huggins
CEO, National Summer Learning Association

The Promise of Summer Learning

Summer vacation from school is a long-cherished American tradition, associated with images of freedom, relaxation, play, and imagination. But for many low-income youth, summer is actually a time of boredom and atrophy, when academic skills slide and basic needs fulfilled during the school year may not be met. Important knowledge gained during the year is likely to be forgotten, and children also may be left on their own during the day because their parents cannot afford to pay for their basic supervision, much less the engaging learning opportunities, camp activities, and vacations that middle-class children typically take for granted when school is out. In addition, many neighborhoods and communities lack accessible summer learning opportunities.

Most children, regardless of socioeconomic status, lose 2 months of grade-level equivalency in math computational skills each summer (Cooper, Nye, Charlton, Lindsay, & Greathouse, 1996). In addition, low-income children lose more than 2 months in reading achievement, while middle-income peers make slight gains in reading (Cooper et al.). This learning gap widens over time, research from Johns Hopkins University shows, so that by ninth grade, summer learning accounts for two-thirds of the achievement gap in reading between low-income students and their middle-income peers. The same students most affected by summer learning loss were also more likely to drop out of high school and less likely to attend college (Alexander, Entwistle, & Olson, 2007).

Summer learning loss means that, all across our country, teachers must spend a good part of the first 2 months of school on review. In a 2012 survey of 500 teachers in summer learning programs in 15 cities, 66% said it typically takes them at least 3–4 weeks to reteach the previous year's skills at the beginning of a new school year. Another 24% said reteaching takes them 5–6 weeks. (National Summer Learning Association [NSLA], 2012c).

Until all children in a given classroom are offered the same kinds of summer learning experiences, these reteaching estimates are likely to persist. That translates into millions of dollars in public education funding wasted each year.

Ignoring the summer months also wastes incredible opportunities for innovation in instructional approaches and curriculum development during a season that offers great flexibility for students and teachers to pilot new learning models. With the arrival of the Common Core State Standards, school districts will need to harness not only the extra time summer provides but also this space for innovations that can help all students meet higher targets.

Recent research from the RAND Corporation has demonstrated that high quality, engaging, low- or no-cost summer learning programs can prevent summer learning loss and even boost student achievement (McCombs et al., 2011). Voluntary, mandatory, and home-based summer programs all were found to have positive effects, and the benefits endured for 2 years after a student engaged in a summer program.

In order for programs to produce these benefits, they must be of high quality. Research indicates that certain program characteristics are associated with achievement gains. Important quality indicators include the following:

- *Regular student attendance*

- *Individualized instruction*

- *Smaller class sizes*

- *Parent involvement*

- *High quality instructors*

- *Alignment of school year and summer curricula*

- *Inclusion of content beyond remediation*

- *Tracking of effectiveness (McCoombs et al., 2011)*

> Ignoring the summer months also wastes incredible opportunities for innovation in instructional approaches and curriculum development during a season that offers great flexibility for students and teachers to pilot new learning models.

In recent years, some large school districts have started innovative summer learning programs that are adopting more of these characteristics of quality and transforming the remedial summer school model of the past. This kind of sea change is taking place even in the nation's largest school district. After attending a citywide forum on summer learning in 2011, Dennis M. Walcott, chancellor of the New York City Department of Education, and Jeanne B. Mullgrav, commissioner of the New York City Department of Youth and Community Development, joined forces with the Fund for Public Schools to implement the first-ever coordinated summer learning initiative in New York City involving both the schools and community-based organizations. The initiative, called

Summer Quest, provided more than 1,000 children with small-group reading and math instruction, project-based learning, enrichment activities, and field trips through full-day programs.

As part of NSLA's New Vision for Summer School Network, now 24 district members strong and growing, districts like New York City are sharing best practices and learning together with high quality community partners about how to provide summer learning that is both academically challenging and highly engaging for more students. These initiatives often blend public funds from sources such as 21st Century Community Learning Centers initiative and Title I with private philanthropic support and strategic use of partner resources to operate.

One increasing focus for summer learning is on the middle grades, when students are especially vulnerable to achievement dips and other off-track indicators (Bottoms, 2010; NSLA, 2012b). Since 2011, NSLA's Smarter Summers project has brought together nonprofit providers with school district partners and local intermediaries to provide 20,000 slots for middle-school summer learning and build summer learning systems in 10 cities nationally. Beginning in 2012, NSLA funded an additional five school districts—Houston, Oakland, Pittsburgh, Providence, and Duval County (Jacksonville, Florida)—to expand their middle grades summer learning programs.

> NSLA's Smarter Summers project has brought together nonprofit providers with school district partners and local intermediaries to provide 20,000 slots for middle-school summer learning and build summer learning systems in 10 cities nationally.

In addition to providing summer learning opportunities, these initiatives also are providing information about the cost of summer learning loss and the benefits of summer learning programs. Along with data on reteaching skills after summer break, survey results from 2012 included the following:

- *Students in these programs not only avoided summer learning loss, but built on their skills. Rising sixth graders showed as much as 5.5 months' growth in grade level equivalency skills in reading during summer 2012.*

- *Among teachers surveyed, 72% agreed or strongly agreed that the professional development they received during the summer would help improve their school year practices. Ninety-three percent said that teaching in the summer learning program enabled them to build more personal relationships with students, and 88% said summer learning is an important part of the overall plan to support student success in school (NSLA, 2012c).*

In its visits to dozens of summer learning programs each year, NSLA documents numerous effective practices and promising program models. The annual Excellence in Summer Learning Award recognizes some of the best of those programs serving low-income children at little or no cost to their families.

2012 Excellence in Summer Learning Award Winners

Fun in the Sun Initiative (FITS). Drawing on an array of community partners, United Way of Santa Barbara County's Fun in the Sun Initiative (FITS) serves 250 young people ages 7–18 for 7 weeks each summer. The FITS program is designed for participants willing to make a multisummer commitment and offers a daily emphasis on reading and writing. Afternoon enrichment opportunities include activities in science, technology, engineering, arts, math, service learning, and field trips. In 2011, 82% of participants showed gains of 2.1 grade levels in reading comprehension, phonics, and vocabulary skills, according to tests administered at the beginning and end of the program (NSLA, 2012a).

Summer Advantage. In 2012, Summer Advantage in Indianapolis worked with an initiative called Journey World, a program of the Girl Scouts of America (GSA). Scholars took over a "sim city" by being assigned specific functions in the community such as city government, media, commerce, banking, the culinary arts, and a host of other careers. GSA shared learning resources with Summer Advantage students so they could study the careers they would take on in the simulation. These activities were just part of the 2012 Summer Advantage program, in which scholars gained an average of 2.1 months in reading and 4.1 months in math (NSLA, 2012a).

LiFE Sports Camp. Operated through a partnership between the Ohio State University Department of Athletics and the College of Social Work, the free LiFE Sports Camp serves 600 Columbus, Ohio, youth ages 9–15 for 4 weeks each summer, focusing on teaching participants vital life skills and social competence through sports. During the culminating LiFE Sports Olympics, young people develop a team name, team banner, advertisements, posters, family invitations, and radio announcements for the Olympics. In addition, the youth work together to assign roles to their team during the Olympics. In 2011, 74% of the participants reported that they were interested in going to college because of LiFE Sports (NSLA, 2012c).

Conclusion

As part of a multiyear evaluation commissioned by the Wallace Foundation, RAND researchers have been studying the challenges and best practices associated with the work of six school districts that have committed to offering summer learning programs to large numbers of struggling elementary students (Augustine, 2012). Based on early lessons from this work, researchers recommend interested school and community groups consider the following approaches for successful summer learning:

- *Commit to having a summer program by the end of December, with early planning sustained through regular meetings.*

- *Develop a teacher selection process that encourages effective, motivated teachers to work in the program.*

- *During teacher training, provide teachers with the curriculum and with opportunities to practice instructional techniques such as mock run-throughs of the lessons.*

- *Consider enrichment activities and field trips that can help build skills and background knowledge and provide students "camp-like" experiences similar to higher-income peers.*

- *Recruit students early, publicizing the goals of the program clearly to students and parents and establishing clear attendance expectations.*

- *Consider ways to maximize academic time on task in the program. (Augustine)*

Effective summer learning programs have followed diverse models for success, but they have in common a focus on continuous planning and assessment and on seizing the summer setting and culture as a means to helping students acquire and retain skills while keeping them engaged. They demonstrate the promise of summer learning, often with community partners, to help educators and young people achieve performance targets and ignite a passion for learning that can last all year.

ABOUT THE AUTHOR

Gary Huggins is chief executive officer of the National Summer Learning Association. Huggins has more than 15 years of experience in leading education and environmental policy organizations and served as executive director of the Aspen Institute's Commission on No Child Left Behind, a bipartisan effort to identify and build support for improvements in federal education policy to spur academic achievement and close achievement gaps, for nearly 5 years.

REFERENCES

Alexander, K. L., Entwisle D. R., & Olson L. S. (2007). Lasting consequences of the summer learning gap. *American Sociological Review, 72,* 167–180.

Augustine, C. H. (2012, November). *Summer learning in school districts: Emerging lessons from the field.* Brief distributed at National Summer Learning Association 2012 Summer Changes Everything conference, Pittsburgh, PA.

Bottoms, G. (2010). *Summer strategies for successful transitions from middle to high school.* Baltimore, MD: National Summer Learning Association.

Cooper, H., Nye, B., Charlton, K., Lindsay, J., & Greathouse, S. (1996). The effects of summer vacation on achievement test scores: A narrative and meta-analytic review. *Review of Educational Research, 66,* 227–268.

McCombs, J. S., Augustine, C. H., Schwartz, H. L., Bodilly, S. J., McInnis, B., Lichter, D. S., and Cross, A. B. (2011). *Making summer count: How summer programs can boost children's learning.* Retrieved from http://www.rand.org/pubs/monographs/MG1120

National Summer Learning Association (NSLA). (2012a). *2012 Excellence in summer learning: Award-winning programs work to close the achievement gap.* Baltimore, MD: National Summer Learning Association.

NSLA. (2012b). *Best practices in summer learning programs for middle and high school youth.* Retrieved from http://www.summerbestpractices.org

NSLA. (2012c). *Summer's influence on teaching and learning all year: Smarter summers and Walmart District Learning Initiative 2012 annual report.* Baltimore, MD: National Summer Learning Association.

Priscilla Little
Research and Strategy Consultant

Engaging Families in Afterschool and Summer Learning Programs: A Review of the Research

Engaging families in afterschool and summer learning is a critical component of the 21st Century Community Learning Centers initiative. Many other expanded learning opportunities and afterschool programs also place a premium on involving families. Research shows that when families are engaged, student outcomes, such as attendance, behavior, and achievement, improve. This article opens with a definition of family engagement in afterschool and then presents a research-based rationale for why family engagement is an essential component of afterschool and summer learning programs.

What Is Family Engagement in Afterschool?

Family engagement in afterschool includes activities for and with family members that are implemented on-site, where afterschool programs are actually located. It also includes additional and important activities and behaviors that happen outside of afterschool programs that influence children's development and learning within the program, such as encouraging a student's participation, helping students make informed choices about programming, discussing a child's progress with program staff, reinforcing skills from the program at home, and being an advocate for and/or leader in the program.

> Families are critical partners in the recruitment and retention efforts of afterschool and summer learning programs.

What Are the Benefits of Family Engagement?

When afterschool programs reach out to and engage families, everyone stands to benefit—students, family members, programs, communities, and even schools. Family engagement can accomplish three specific objectives:

1. **Support improved participation in afterschool programs.** Families are critical partners in the recruitment and retention efforts of afterschool and summer learning programs. They are often a program's best ambassadors, not only in encouraging their children to participate but also in reaching out to other families to help them understand the importance of participation in afterschool programming (Lauver & Little, 2005). Once students are enrolled, family engagement can also be a factor in sustaining participation.

   - *A study of youth participation in over 600 summer and afterschool programs run by New York City's Department of Youth and Community Development showed that programs with a paid or volunteer parent liaison had higher levels of youth attendance and retention, especially for high school and community-based programs. Furthermore, the intensity of communication with families—such as holding meetings, sending materials home, and having phone conversations—was also positively associated with youth attendance rates (Pearson, Russell, & Reisner, 2007; Russell, Mielke, & Reisner, 2008).*

   - *A recent study of afterschool participation among older youth in almost 200 programs across six cities found that programs that retained at least 50% of their middle- and high-school-age participants for at least 12 months appeared to use a greater variety of parent engagement techniques than programs with lower sustained participation rates (Deschenes et al., 2010).*

   - *Evaluations of Texas programs funded by the 21st Century Community Learning Centers initiative note that students who had at least one adult family member participating with them in center activities were involved in more activities than students with no family members participating. Further, the data show that once they do participate, adult family members return to participate again at a very high rate (Texas Education Agency, 2007).*

2. **Benefit afterschool participants themselves.** When afterschool programs are intentional about their family engagement strategies, then program participants tend to exhibit better outcomes.

   - *A study of 96 school-based afterschool programs supported by the After-School Corporation (TASC) identified connections between program staff and families as one of the shared features of high-performing programs. Efforts to engage families (including hiring a parent coordinator and communicating regularly with families at pick-up time) were some of the most common features among the 10 programs whose participants had the highest academic performance (Birmingham, Pechman, Russell, & Mielke, 2006).*

- *The Massachusetts After-School Research Study examined quality characteristics via observations and surveys in 78 afterschool programs across the state, including some funded by the 21st Century Community Learning Centers initiative. It found that communication with families during pick-up and drop-off time was associated with more positive youth relations with afterschool program staff and better family and community support for the program (Intercultural Center for Research in Education & National Institute on Out-of-School Time, 2005).*

- *Afterschool programs that engage families can influence student attendance and engagement in school. For example, a quasi-experimental evaluation of New York City's Chinatown YMCA 21st Century Community Learning Centers family program found that students whose families participated in the program had higher attendance rates in school than those in a comparison group (Bennett, 2004).*

3. **Positively affect family engagement with learning at school and at home.**
   Family engagement in afterschool programs can be leveraged to improve family engagement in learning in and out of school. Specifically, studies have found that family engagement in afterschool programs can lead to greater involvement in school events, increased assistance with homework, and more encouragement for reading.

   - *A 2-year quasi-experimental evaluation of the Generacion Diez (G-10) program, which provides afterschool support to Latino students and their families, found that by the end of the second year of the program, parents of children with higher attendance rates in the G-10 program reported significant increases in the quality and quantity of parent–teacher contact as well as engagement in their children's school activities (Riggs & Medina, 2005).*

Core Principles of Family Engagement

Family engagement is a *shared responsibility* in which schools and other community agencies and organizations are committed to reaching out to engage families in meaningful ways and in which families are committed to actively supporting their children's learning and development.

Family engagement is *continuous across a child's life* and entails enduring commitment even though parental roles evolve as children mature into young adulthood.

Effective family engagement cuts across and reinforces learning in the *multiple settings where children learn*—at home, in prekindergarten programs, in school, in afterschool and summer programs, in faith-based institutions, and in the community.

For more on defining family engagement, visit the Harvard Family Research Project website: http://hfrp.org/family-involvement.

- *The national evaluation of the 21st Century Community Learning Centers initiative found that participating parents also helped their children with homework more and asked their children about class more than nonparticipating families (U.S. Department of Education, 2003).*

- *Family engagement in afterschool programs can also support more positive parent–child relationships at home. A review of nonexperimental afterschool and summer program evaluations examining family involvement found that parents who volunteer with programs report feeling closer to their children (Harris & Wimer, 2004).*

> The research is clear that afterschool and summer programs, as the bridge between home and school, are well positioned to influence families' engagement in their child's education.

Research shows that meaningful family engagement is associated with improvements in key student outcomes, including attendance, behavior, and achievement. Determining whether there is a causal relationship, however, will require additional research. Is increased family focus on their child's academic performance during the school day a result of specific strategies that afterschool and summer learning programs employ, or are families of children in afterschool simply more inclined to participate in their child's education? Both are important.

Regardless, the research is clear that afterschool and summer programs, as the bridge between home and school, are well positioned to influence families' engagement in their child's education. Therefore, as more and more local, state, and federal efforts to expand learning after school and in summer emerge, it is critical that these efforts include a strong family engagement component. Indeed, the 21st Century Community Learning Centers initiative already includes annual reporting on family involvement, sending a strong signal to programs that family engagement is important. Moving forward, all afterschool and summer programs, whether supported by local, state, or other federal funding streams, should include a robust plan for implementing and monitoring family engagement as a necessary component of effective afterschool programs.

Bridging Schools and Families

The Greenwood Shalom afterschool program is located in a predominantly black and Latino neighborhood in Boston. The program provides homework support, computer instruction, arts and crafts, and literacy lessons. At the end of the day, everyone gathers for sharing and reflection. Parents are commonly seen lingering to talk with staff and report feeling comfortable and welcome. As one parent said, "Even if I have a problem at home, I can go and talk to them." (Kakli, Kreider, & Little, 2006).

ABOUT THE AUTHOR

Priscilla Little is an independent research and strategy consultant who has been working on issues related to effective afterschool and summer learning programs for over a decade. Her clients include national education research firms, state education agencies, not-for-profit agencies, and private foundations. She is currently working for the Wallace Foundation to support its afterschool system-building work, as well as with the U.S. Department of Education on a research study to investigate good and innovative practices in 21st Century Community Learning Centers programs. The views represented in this article are solely her own and do not represent those of her clients.

REFERENCES

Bennett, E. T. (2004). *Family involvement and school performance in the Chinatown YMCA 21st Century Community Learning Center* (Unpublished master's thesis). Fordham University, New York.

Birmingham, J., Pechman, E. M., Russell, C. A., & Mielke, M. (2006). *Shared features of high-performing after-school programs: A follow-up to the TASC evaluation.* New York, NY: After School Corporation.

Deschenes, S. N., Arbreton, A., Little, P. L., Herrera, C., Grossman, J. B., & Weiss, H. B. (with Lee, D.). (2010). *Engaging older youth: Program and city-level strategies to support sustained participation in out-of-school time.* Cambridge, MA: Harvard Family Research Project.

Harris, E., & Wimer, C. (2004). *Engaging with families in out-of-school time learning: Out-of-school time evaluation snapshot No. 4.* Cambridge, MA: Harvard Family Research Project.

Intercultural Center for Research in Education, & National Institute on Out-of-School Time. (2005). *Pathways to success for youth: What counts in after-school.* Boston, MA: United Way of Massachusetts Bay.

Kakli, Z., Kreider, H., & Little, P. (2006). *Focus on families: How to build and support family-centered practices in after school.* Retrieved from Harvard Family Research Project website: http://www.hfrp.org/family-involvement/publications-resources/focus-on-families!-how-to-build-and-support-family-centered-practices-in-after-school

Lauver, S., & Little, P. M. D. (2005). Recruitment and retention strategies for out-of-school time programs. *New Directions for Youth Development, 2005*(105), 71–89.

Pearson, L. M., Russell, C. A., & Reisner, E. A. (2007). *Evaluation of OST programs for youth: Patterns of youth retention in OST programs, 2005–06 to 2006–07.* Washington, DC: Policy Studies Associates.

Riggs, N. R., & Medina, C. (2005). The Generacion Diez after-school program and Latino parent involvement with schools. *Journal of Primary Prevention, 26*(6), 471–484.

Russell, C. A., Mielke, M. B., & Reisner, E. R. (2008). *Evaluation of the New York City Department of Youth and Community Development Out-of-School Time Programs for Youth initiative: Results of efforts to increase program quality and scale in year 2.* Washington, DC: Policy Studies Associates.

Texas Education Agency. (2007). *21st Century Community Learning Centers: Evaluation of projects funded during the 2004–2005 school year.* Austin, TX: Author.

U.S. Department of Education. (2003). *When schools stay open late: The national evaluation of the 21st Century Learning Centers program, first year findings.* Washington, DC: Author.

Shawn Stelow Griffin
Vice President for Education and
Children's Services, The Finance Project

Laura Martinez
Former Senior Program Associate,
The Finance Project

The Value of Partnerships in Afterschool and Summer Learning: A National Case Study of 21st Century Community Learning Centers[1]

The 21st Century Community Learning Centers initiative, funded by the United States Department of Education, supports community learning centers that provide academic enrichment opportunities during nonschool hours for children, and particularly for students who attend high-poverty and low-performing schools (U.S. Dept. of Education, 2003). While the initiative was first enacted as part of the reauthorization of the Elementary and Secondary Education Act in 1994, it remained minimally funded until 1998. Congress rapidly increased appropriations for the initiative from 1998 through 2002; and with the exception of modest increases in funding from 2007 to 2009, funding levels have been maintained at a little less than $1.2 billion since then. With the reauthorization of the Elementary and Secondary Education Act in 2001 (No Child Left Behind), the administration of 21st Century Community Learning Centers funds—as a federal discretionary program—was transferred to state education agencies.

The most recent reauthorization of this initiative incorporates the latest thinking regarding the importance of strong, diverse community partnerships to maximize the impact of federal investments, especially in expanding learning in afterschool and summers. Many state education agencies now require local 21st Century Community Learning Centers programs to collaborate with community partners in order to receive funding. A growing number of state afterschool networks are helping to advance school, community, and family partnerships to provide more learning opportunities, time, and resources.

---

1. This article is part of a series of technical assistance resources on financing and sustaining out-of-school-time and community initiatives developed by The Finance Project with support from the Charles Stewart Mott Foundation. These tools and resources are intended to assist policy makers, program developers, and community leaders in developing financing and sustainability strategies to support effective initiatives.

Currently, there are almost 11,000 21st Century Community Learning Centers programs across the nation (Profile and Performance Information Collection System, 2012).[2] Most of these programs have cultivated robust partnerships with a diverse set of community partners, including colleges and universities, youth development organizations, libraries, museums, city parks departments, faith-based organizations, schools, and many more community-based for-profit and nonprofit organizations. Partnerships have strengthened local programs by supporting afterschool and summer programs in ways that are unique and meaningful to their own community.

The Finance Project staff has worked extensively with 21st Century Community Learning Centers grantees, national stakeholder groups, and state education agencies to understand the factors that lead to the long-term sustainability of these programs. Not surprisingly, programs that are supported by strong and diverse community partnerships are more likely to sustain themselves over the long term. This article explores these partnerships more deeply in an effort to

- *illustrate how states have used the 21st Century Community Learning Centers initiative to engage a diverse set of partners to leverage and sustain local programs;*

- *highlight innovative partnership approaches in Florida, Oregon, Vermont, and Wisconsin; and*

- *identify cross-cutting themes and trends to understand the value of partnerships in leveraging the federal investment in 21st Century Community Learning Centers.*

Using Partnerships to Leverage Resources

The U.S. Department of Education's guidelines for the 21st Century Community Learning Centers initiative strongly encourage local grantees to establish partnerships with other local organizations and agencies. State afterschool networks also encourage and facilitate such partnerships, and many state education agencies formally require that 21st Century Community Learning Centers grantees partner with at least one other organization in order to qualify for state funding. For example, Florida's 2012–13 Request for Proposals requires applicants to identify current public/private partnerships that were or will be used to develop, implement, evaluate, and sustain the centers (Florida Dept. of Education, 2012). The focus on partnerships by the U.S. Department of Education, the building of statewide infrastructures by state afterschool networks, and state mandates have resulted in an unduplicated count of 44,621 21st Century Community Learning Centers partnerships across the nation in 2010—an average of 9 partnerships per local program (Afterschool Alliance, 2012).

2. According to the PPICS website (http://ppics.learningpt.org/ppicsnet/public/default.aspx), "The purpose of this system is to collect basic information about 21st CCLC programs across the United States. PPICS was created in 2003 at the commission of the US Department of Education (ED). The system was built to help ED track 21st CCLC programming following the transition from federal to state administration, which took place in 2001. Each year, PPICS is used to collect program data from some 3,000 21st CCLC grants covering close to 9,000 centers serving 1.5 million student attendees."

Types of Partnerships

Local partnerships allow each local program to leverage a variety of community resources. As reported in the national Profile and Performance Information Collection System for the 21st Century Community Learning Centers initiative (Afterschool Alliance, 2012), partnerships provide support for seven major contribution types:

- *evaluation services;*
- *fundraising;*
- *programming or activity related services;*
- *goods;*
- *volunteer staffing;*
- *paid staffing; and*
- *other contributions.*

Most partnerships provide services in more than one domain. Nearly 36% of these partners provide programming or activity-related services, followed by goods (20%) and volunteer staffing (14%). Of the 44,621 partners reported by grantees in 2010, most are community-based organizations or nonprofits (28%). The second largest partner type, at 27% of all partnerships, falls within the "other" category, which includes units of city or county government, regional/intermediate education agencies, health-based organizations, libraries, museums, parks and recreation districts, the Bureau of Indian Affairs, schools/agencies, and private schools.

Monetary Value of Partnerships

The Profile and Performance Information Collection System also asks grantees to place a monetary value on their partnerships. In 2010, grantees reported that partners contributed over $230,000,000 across the 3,450 grants they supported. Further, over the past 5 years, partners have contributed over $1 billion to support 21st Century Community Learning Centers programming. (See also the article in this book "School-Community Learning Partnerships: An Essential to Expanded Learning Success" by Priscilla Little.)

Some states, like Wisconsin, produce an annual report of the impact of their 21st Century Community Learning Centers initiative statewide. In its 2009–10 report, that state valued the donations (in-kind and monetary) of 968 partner organizations statewide at $3.4 million—a contribution of $3,512, on average, per partner (Wisconsin Dept. of Public Instruction, 2011). In addition to having a real financial value in terms of services provided, partners often contribute other highly valued resources and supports to the children and youth served by local programs. Partners can reinforce the importance of learning, provide personalized attention to struggling students, broaden children's learning experiences through sponsoring field trips and other off-site activities, and fill in critical gaps in services.

Promising State Practices

Though the vast majority of 21st Century Community Learning Centers partnerships are with community-based organizations or nonprofits, the breadth of partnerships varies among communities and states. State leaders have reported that partnerships across many domains are key to the success of programs in their states.

The types of partnerships formed and the benefits they generate for children and youth served are typically different for programs located in rural areas versus those in large localities.

In Wisconsin, where partnerships are a required grant/program component, "nontraditional" partners have proven to be very important for smaller cities and rural communities to enrich afterschool programs. These nontraditional partners include businesses and individuals that do not necessarily have an immediate connection to youth. For example, at the San Juan Diego Middle School, the 21st Century Community Learning Centers program has a partnership with a local trucking company. This company supports the afterschool program by providing older students with industry specific, skill-building supports such as a curriculum unit to teach map-reading skills using a GPS.

Vermont has also reported that the partnerships developed in their smaller localities are unique. Over one-third of the schools in Vermont have fewer than 100 students. In some cases partners for the 21st Century Community Learning Centers programs based at these schools are not organizations, but individuals. In one community, a dogsled racer works with students, while in another, an individual who is a program partner teaches students how to make baskets—both are unique activities in their community's fabric and way of life. One Vermont leader stated she feels that the many individual partners' in-kind contributions are most likely seriously underestimated by grantees when entering this data into the Profile and Performance Information Collection System. She also noted that an important component of these partnerships, especially in smaller communities, is the relationship-building that takes place, for example, at town meetings, where personal relationships and stories about the impact on individual or groups students of local 21st Community Learning Centers programs are often shared.

On a larger scale, Oregon is using VISTA volunteers at the state level to teach 21st Century Community Learning Centers program staff about different types of partnerships. VISTA volunteers have noted that program directors have many different definitions and examples of partnerships. The volunteers have worked to help program staff understand the difference between a robust partnership and a fee-for-service relationship. In Fall City, Oregon, the 21st Century Community Learning Centers program awarded a small ($4,000 per year) contract to the local arts council to fund two artists to work with students in their program twice weekly. Over time, the relationship has strengthened as both the program and the Arts Council saw value and results from the partnership. Now, while the initial contract remains, the Arts Council provides two staff members as an in-kind contribution to the program.

In Florida, partnerships are a required component of local programs. Many programs across the state have formed partnerships that capitalize on the abundance of local natural resources; for example, programs might include a focus on marine life or on caverns found within a state park. Another innovative practice in Florida includes partnerships between programs and local businesses and industries. For example, in Fort Lauderdale, the Space Explorers Program partners with the Kennedy Space Center, while the Zoo Explorers Program partners with the local zoo. As another innovative example, one high school principal formed partnerships with local businesses during the after school hours to offer jobs to the students within the context of his school's 21st Century Community Learning Centers program. State leaders are promoting this concept and exploring other ways to keep older youth actively engaged in programs in light of the many demands on youths' time in the afterschool hours.

Considerations for the Future

Over the past 10 years, millions of elementary and secondary students who have participated in 21st Century Community Learning Centers programs have benefitted in myriad ways from the wide range of partnerships available in communities across the country. State departments of education, local community organizations, schools, and state afterschool networks have played a key role in the growth of these robust partnerships. While the comprehensive national data set containing the details, types, and financial impacts of these partnerships is not publicly available on an up-to-date basis, a limited review of data sets supplied by programs, as well as data obtained from interviews with key informants, provides a foundation for understanding the landscape of partnerships and their non-monetary benefits.

The data on partnerships and state examples highlighted in this article are an important first step in maximizing 21st Century Community Learning Centers federal funding and sustaining afterschool programs in schools and communities. Many state leaders and local community, school, and afterschool stakeholders are setting clear expectations for the types and number of partnerships that grantees are expected to develop. There are several things states can do to increase and strengthen partnerships:

- *Offer meaningful incentives to the organizations that partner with 21st Century Community Learning Centers grantees and other similar afterschool and summer programs that have meaningful school-community partnerships. Incentives might include state income tax deductions for private sector partners, bonus funding to appropriate nonprofit partners, or transportation allotments for programs meeting quality standards.*

- *Provide training and technical assistance regarding best practices in partnership development and sustainability tailored for various settings (e.g., urban, towns, rural) and for various types of potential partnerships (e.g., nonprofits, small or large businesses, colleges, hospitals, city and county governmental agencies).*

- *Create statewide or local award programs for outstanding partnership efforts in 21st Century Community Learning Centers programs and similar afterschool and summer programs, perhaps working with Chambers of Commerce, United Ways, state 21st Century Community Learning Centers offices, and state afterschool networks.*

- *Provide more specific definitions regarding what constitutes a partnership versus a contractual relationship and take into account the contribution of time and other resources by individuals and organizations to provide a fuller understanding of the opportunities, challenges, and successes.*

One of the most successful aspects of the 21st Century Community Learning Centers initiative has been the focus on leveraging community partners to provide experiences that youth might not otherwise be able to access through the school day or in a school-based afterschool program that merely extends the school day. In the future, it is important that federal, state, and local leaders involved in these programs expand knowledge about how to build successful community-school-family partnerships in order to improve the quality of opportunities provided to participating students. Also it is important to improve how programs quantify the return-on-investment of these robust and varied partnerships in order to illuminate how the federal government's relatively modest investment in afterschool programs has been more than matched by the talent, supplies, volunteers, space, and general support of school-community partnerships.

In summary, clearly the inclusion of strong partnership provisions in most 21st Century Community Learning Centers has added valuable learning resources and improved the quality of the opportunities provided to students in their afterschool and summer programs.

For More Information

See http://www.financeproject.org/

Selected resources on the financing and sustainability of afterschool programs include the following:

Cutting Costs, Keeping Quality: Financing Strategies for Youth Programs in a Difficult Economy by Jennifer Holland and Shawn Stelow Griffin, The Finance Project, 2012. http://www.financeproject.org/publications/FinancingStrategiesToolkit.pdf

Making the Match: Finding Funding for After School Education and Safety Programs by Kate Sandel, Cheryl Hayes, Brittany Anuszkiewicz, Carol Cohen and Sharon Deich, The Finance Project, August 2007. http://www.financeproject.org/publications/MakingTheMatch.pdf

Forming Partnerships to Meet the Administrative Needs of Youth-Serving Organizations by Torey Silloway and Lori Connors-Tadros, The Finance Project, January 2011. http://www.financeproject.org/publications/FormingAdminPartnership.pdf

A Guide to Successful Public-Private Partnerships for Out-of-School Time and Community School Initiatives by Sharon Deich, The Finance Project, January 2001. http://www.financeproject.org/publications/ostpartnershipguide.pdf

Sustaining 21st Century Community Learning Centers: What Works for Programs and How Policymakers Can Help by Amanda Szekely and Heather Clapp Padgette, The Finance Project, September 2006. http://76.12.61.196/publications/sustaining_21cclc.pdf

ABOUT THE AUTHORS

Shawn Stelow Griffin is the vice president for education and children's services at the Finance Project (TFP), where she develops tools and resources to support the financing and sustainability of programs and initiatives across a number of social service disciplines. An expert presenter on financing and sustainability issues, Griffin manages research projects analyzing costs and financing strategies for education programs at both the school system and initiative levels. Prior to joining TFP, Griffin served as the team leader for the 21st Century Community Learning Program at the United States Department of Education and director of youth development at the Maryland State Department of Education.

Laura Martinez was a senior program associate at the Finance Project, and is currently living in Seoul, Korea. While at The Finance Project she conducted research and produced reports and tools for policy makers and other stakeholders on the financing and sustainability of out-of-school-time initiatives and other youth-related programs. Prior to joining The Finance Project, Martinez was the grants manager for LA's BEST After School Enrichment Program, a multi-million after school program in Los Angeles.

REFERENCES

Afterschool Alliance. (2012). 21st Century Community Learning Centers federal after school initiative. Retrieved from http://www.afterschoolalliance.org/policy21stcclc.cfm

Florida Department of Education. (2012). *Request for proposal (RFP) for discretionary, competitive projects. Project Year 2012–2013*. Retrieved from http://www.fldoe.org/curriculum/21century/pdf/1213RFP.pdf

Profile and Performance Information Collection System. (2012). Number of grantees and centers by state report. Retrieved from http://ppics.learningpt.org/ppics/reports/numByState.asp

U.S. Department of Education. (2003). *21st Century Community Learning Centers program description*. Retrieved from http://www2.ed.gov/programs/21stcclc/index.html

Wisconsin Department of Public Instruction. (2011). *21st Century Community Learning Centers, executive summary, 2009–2010*. Retrieved from http://dpi.wi.gov/sspw/pdf/clcexecsumm.pdf

Kristin Nafziger
Project Director, Edvance Research, Inc.

Candace M. Ferguson
21st CCLC State Coordinator, Texas
Education Agency

Texas Afterschool Centers on Education (ACE): Achieving Positive Results and Preparing Texas Students for College and the Workforce

The Texas Afterschool Centers on Education (ACE) program is one of the largest statewide afterschool programs in the country, serving over 180,000 students at nearly 1,000 sites. The ACE program is administered by the Texas Education Agency (TEA) and is funded through the 21st Century Community Learning Centers initiative of the U.S. Department of Education.

A recent evaluation of the ACE-21st Century Community Learning Centers[1] found the following when program participants were compared to nonparticipants:

- *ACE program participation for students in grades 9–10 was associated with higher scores in reading/English language arts and mathematics on the Texas Assessment of Knowledge and Skills (TAKS).*

- *ACE program participants in grades 6–12 had fewer disciplinary incidents than nonparticipating students.*

- *Participation of students in grades 4–11 was associated with fewer school-day absences.*

- *ACE participants in grades 7–11 who attended 30 days or more and participants in grades 4–5 and 7–11 attending 60 days or more had an increased likelihood of grade promotion. For high school students attending 60 days or more, there was a 97% chance of being promoted to the next grade level.*

---

1. TEA released updated evaluation results in the 4th quarter of 2012. For access to those findings please see http://www.tea. state.tx.us/index4.aspx?id=2908&menu_id=949.

When comparing high attenders (students who attended 60 days or more) and low attenders (students who attended 30–59 days) in ACE programs, participants in grades 4–12 attending 60 days or more of programming had higher levels of TAKS scores in reading/English language arts and mathematics, fewer disciplinary incidents, fewer school-day absences, and an enhanced likelihood (23–40%) of grade promotion.

The evaluation also revealed the following:

- *Program quality* matters. *Centers implementing higher-quality practices were correlated with greater reductions in disciplinary referrals and higher rates of grade promotion than programs less apt to implement these practices.*

- *Connections with other organizations and agencies within the community greatly enhance afterschool centers programming options.*

ACE Program Background

The federal funding that currently supports ACE actually began in 1994 as small, federally operated pilot program created under the reauthorized Elementary and Secondary Education Act. In the late 1990s and early 2000s, the funding for the 21st Century Community Learning Centers initiative grew strategically and significantly, such that in 2002 the initiative was transferred to the states to lead and coordinate.

> Program quality *matters.* Centers implementing higher-quality practices were correlated with greater reductions in disciplinary referrals and higher rates of grade promotion than programs less apt to implement these practices.

Texas wisely used this transfer to establish the ACE program in 2002. Since 2008, ACE has evolved significantly in the wake of a major strategic overhaul that year that was designed to revamp its quality and identity and strengthen its focus. What follows are the resulting strategies and actions that were undertaken to develop a much stronger statewide infrastructure and support system for high standards and continuous improvement of afterschool learning across the state.

Needs Assessment as a Driver of Strategic Changes and Improvements

The overall goal of the ACE program is to have all students graduate from high school prepared for college and the workforce. To achieve this goal, ACE's objectives are to improve academic performance, attendance, behavior, promotion rates, and graduation rates.

It is important to highlight here that the ACE program evaluation finding cited earlier in this article reveals that TEA is making significant progress towards achieving these five objectives. The restructuring and reform efforts described below have created the conditions for achieving success.

After establishing a common goal and set of objectives for the ACE program through the initial phase of the strategic planning effort, TEA began to restructure the program to provide program staff the tools and resources needed to develop a sustainable afterschool program. In collaboration with its program enhancement and quality assurance contractor, Edvance Research, Inc., TEA conducted a comprehensive review of program processes and procedures, as well as a needs assessment with grantee and center leaders. Based on this combined information, TEA implemented many significant changes in the program.

Through the needs assessment, TEA learned that many grantees had never been formally trained in project management, data and financial management, or human resources. TEA knew that to restructure the program, it was critical that grantees be properly trained, given the necessary resources and tools, and held accountable for managing their resources effectively and meeting performance measures. Regardless of the grant size or geographical locations, each grantee would be held to the same statewide standards, yielding a consistent set of performance expectations.

Stronger Local Programming Through More Rigorous Requirements and New Tools

As of 2008, TEA required a full-time project director for each local ACE grantee and full-time site coordinators for each center included in the grant. (Note: ACE grantees may operate multiple sites or centers.) By 2011, a family engagement specialist position was added to the list of required position for grantees. These positions are critical to the success of the local centers.

Yet, having these individuals physically present was not enough. In partnership with TEA, Edvance developed training tools and resources focused on assisting grantees in

- *meeting state and federal grant requirements,*

- *providing timely and accurate reporting to TEA,*

- *implementing appropriate fiscal controls, and*

- *conducting an external evaluation.*

To implement these tools and resources successfully, TEA worked with Edvance to develop a well-defined "blueprint" for program implementation. This blueprint was intended to help grantees and prospective grant applicants understand ACE program requirements and provide links to useful tools and information about best practices. The blueprint contains five categories of activities and program requirements:

1. Planning
2. Resourcing
3. Implementing
4. Managing
5. Enduring

To support the implementation of the blueprint, TEA created an assessment system to track the status of each grantee's compliance with federal and state requirements and research-based practices. The assessment system includes a self-assessment tool that is completed by each grantee in the fall, a desk review of the grantee's approved grant application along with annual program reports submitted to TEA, and site visits.

TEA provides regional technical assistance consultants to support all ACE grantees, including

- *conducting the annual ACE program assessment (described above) to determine needs for technical assistance based on grant requirements and research based best practices,*

- *providing ongoing technical assistance based on need, and*

- *conducting monthly data and spending analyses.*

Additionally, ACE program staff have an array of online tools available to them via a learning portal that houses webinars, podcasts, and tutorials.

Through the implementation of these new monitoring and technical assistance processes, ACE students, parents, and communities have benefited through an increased retention of project directors; improved grant spending; and on-time, accurate data reporting.

The Future of ACE

The ACE program continues to identify opportunities to assist students in achieving academic success, particularly with a newly developed statewide standardized assessment that is aligned to the state's college and career ready standards. TEA is focusing on ways to improve planning, partnerships, evaluation results, training tools, and other quality-enhancement resources—and these efforts are reaping important benefits for students. In fact, the recently released ACE evaluation results (2012) found that implementing higher-quality practices is correlated, for example, with greater reductions in disciplinary referrals and higher rates of grade promotion than programs that are less apt to implement these practices (Naftzger et al., 2012).

> Through the implementation of these new monitoring and technical assistance processes, ACE students, parents, and communities have benefited through an increased retention of project directors; improved grant spending; and on-time, accurate data reporting.

Expanding Partnerships

TEA encourages grantees and project directors to seek out potential partnerships with local organizations and businesses. The recent ACE evaluation (2012) found that connections with other organizations and agencies within the community greatly enhance afterschool centers programming options (Naftzger et al., 2012).

One recent major initiative was to increase family engagement activities within the local ACE programs. ACE partnered with Skillpoint Alliance, a nonprofit organization that creates partnerships between industry, education, and the community that support the life success of individual students while meeting employers' needs for a qualified workforce. In a demonstration project, ACE offered 10 scholarship opportunities to interested parents of afterschool students in the Bastrop area to apply and participate in Skillpoint Alliance's Gateway Health Care program to be trained as certified nurse aides. Nine family members of ACE students graduated from the 3-week program in the spring of 2012, and five graduates received jobs within 1 week of passing their state exam. This project not only engaged parents in the program but also provided them the opportunity to advance their own careers and the economic outlook for their families.

Use of Evaluation Data and Information for Continuous Improvement

As mandated by the federal statute, TEA must conduct a comprehensive evaluation of the effectiveness of its programs and activities funded by the 21st Century Community Learning Centers program. Also, individual grantees must conduct a local/independent evaluation of their programs to assess progress toward achieving TEA's goal and objectives.

The current statewide evaluation, *Statewide Assessment of 21st CCLC Programs: Innovative Strategies, Student Behaviors, & Student Success*, was awarded to the American Institutes for Research. The focus of the evaluation is twofold:

- *Assess the local ACE program operations, student participation, and student achievement outcomes.*

- *Identify and describe innovative strategies and approaches implemented by successful centers.*

Preliminary evaluation findings have guided TEA in the ongoing development of program guidelines, goals, allowable activities, and other related programmatic decisions.

In 2010, TEA enhanced the independent evaluation requirements for local ACE grantees. These evaluations guide the type and level of support provided by each regional technical assistance center, as well as assist grantees to further refine and improve their programs. While TEA reviews these evaluations on an annual basis, the technical assistant providers monitor the status of the evaluation process monthly and assist grantees with any issues that surface to ensure an annual evaluation is completed.

Tailoring Training and Resources to Meet Local Needs

The statewide and local ACE grantee evaluations also assist in identifying training needs. Based on these findings, TEA and Edvance have structured training efforts to focus on such areas as intentional programming, needs assessment, and family engagement. The delivery of these training sessions have been designed to incorporate a blended learning approach, allowing grantees, project directors, and site coordinators the opportunity to learn in face-to-face, online, and self-paced environments.

One of the ACE grantees, Taylor Independent School District, has embraced intentional programming training. Taylor's site coordinators participated in both the pilot training and a full 2-day training. Since the training, the coordinators have been meeting weekly to develop activities based on student voice and academic need. Each activity is designed around achieving a "SMART" goal (specific, measurable, achievable, relevant, and time-bound) for increasing student performance. Coordinators have engaged in discussions across sites and grade levels to develop activities that are aligned with the school day and that are both rigorous and engaging.

Texas ACE grantees are also focused on offering more STEM activities. At the 2012 federal 21st Century Community Learning Centers Summer Institute, five Texas grantees were featured as part of the STEM Showcase. Grantees from Austin, Fort Worth, Manor, Taylor, and the University of Texas at Tyler Ingenuity Center demonstrated activities related to career exploration, robotics, gaming, and integrating the arts to move from STEM to STEAM (science, technology, engineering, arts, and math). These grantees have developed partnerships with community-based programs, including local Parks and Wildlife, Girlstart, and local entrepreneur groups, to give students more hands-on opportunities to increase their knowledge of and interest in STEM careers.

Conclusion

The Afterschool Centers on Education Program—the Texas 21st Century Community Learning Centers program—has had a substantial positive impact on the student performance of hundreds of thousands of students across Texas over the past few years. Through these expanded learning opportunities, provided after school and during the summer in almost 1,000 sites across the state, TEA is making significant strides toward accomplishing its goal for all Texas students to graduate high school prepared for college and the workforce. TEA has used strategic planning, evaluation, and various other tools and strategies to strengthen and enhance the Afterschool Centers on Education Program, yielding solid and demonstrable student results.

ABOUT THE AUTHORS

Kristin Nafziger is a founding partner of Edvance Research, Inc. and serves as executive vice president for emerging practices. In this position she is responsible for identifying and keeping educators informed about new evidence-based programs and practices that show promising results. As part of her role at Edvance, Nafziger leads the technical assistance and quality assurance project for the Texas Education Agency to support the ACE program. Edvance Research is a women and minority, employee-owned firm headquartered in San Antonio, Texas, with offices in Austin, Texas (www.edvanceresearch.com).

Candace M. Ferguson is the state coordinator for the Texas 21st Century Community Learning Centers (CCLC)/Afterschool Centers on Education (ACE) Program, administered by the Texas Education Agency and funded by the 21st Century Community Learning Centers initiative administered by the U.S. Department of Education (http://www.tea.state.tx.us/index2.aspx?id=3546&menu_id=814). Ferguson has over 12 years of experience in state, local, and nonprofit sectors, a majority of which have been spent working with disadvantaged and at-risk youth. She worked as an afterschool site coordinator with the YMCA, a juvenile probation and parole officer supervising a variety of youth, and a grants monitor for the Office of the Governor's Criminal Justice Division.

REFERENCES

Naftzger, N., Manzeske, D., Nistler, M., Swanlund, A., Rapaport, A., Shields, J., . . . Sugar, S. (2012). *Texas 21st Century Community Learning Centers: Final evaluation report*. Naperville, IL: American Institutes for Research.

Susan Martz
Director, Office of Student Support Services,
New Jersey Department of Education

Improving Results and Expanding Learning: Using Research and Evaluation to Inform Practice in New Jersey 21st Century Community Learning Centers

The 21st Century Community Learning Centers program in New Jersey is offering expanded learning opportunities to thousands of students, with significant and positive results. The program aims to assist children who attend low-performing schools in high-poverty areas to attain the skills needed to meet the state's content standards (www.state.nj.us/education/21cclc).

Currently, nearly 17,000 youth are participating in these important learning opportunities in 21st Century Community Learning Centers programs at more than 122 sites across the state. The state's program goals call for a well-aligned, engaging, and individualized expansion of learning time beyond the school day that provide

- *remedial education activities to increase students' college and career readiness;*

- *a broad array of creative activities (art, music, dance, recreation, and cultural activities) that complement the school day and equalize enrichment opportunities;*

- *family literacy and other activities that assist families in becoming full partners in the education of their children; and*

- *support services that target social, emotional, and character development to deter problem behaviors.*

Since the inception of the 21st Century Community Learning Centers program, the New Jersey Department of Education (NJDE) has promoted program quality and continuous improvement by applying promising practices described in the emerging body of research on expanded learning programs and other research on teaching and learning. New Jersey's 21st Century Community Learning Centers program embeds many of the recommendations highlighted by the Institute of Education Sciences in a seminal publication, *Structuring Out-of-School Time to Improve Academic Achievement: A Practice Guide* (Beckett et al., 2009). Going beyond the federal requirements, New Jersey's program requirements have evolved to support college and career readiness and to embed the components of successful expanded learning opportunities. Of equal importance in informing programmatic decisions is state-level information provided by the state's program evaluator.

New Jersey significantly modified its program in 2010 to require many of the strategies that the NJDE had been promoting in recent years and that put into practice the latest research on expanded learning.

This redesign conveys the expectation that local programs would incorporate five major elements:

1. **Aligning the 21st Century Community Learning Centers program with school-day learning to provide more time for youth to practice skills and expand knowledge.**
   The state's 21st Century Community Learning Centers programs are expected to link their activities to the New Jersey Core Curriculum Content Standards and the Common Core State Standards. Further, they are expected to document these links with the school day through lesson plans, progress reports, and regularly scheduled meetings. Activities are designed to assist youth with the development of skills as well as content knowledge. Centers must focus on one of the following themes: science, technology, math, and engineering (STEM); civic engagement; career awareness and exploration; or visual and performing arts.

   To support the alignment with the school day, programs are expected to have regularly scheduled communication and intentional planning between school-day and center staff. Each program designates a regular school-day staff person at each school site to coordinate communication with the afterschool program to help them support school needs. Afterschool program staff participate in school meetings and committees, such as professional learning communities and school improvement teams.

   Certified teachers are required for academic remediation activities in 21st Century Community Learning Centers programs. Local programs coordinate with their affiliated schools to identify appropriate staff for the center and hire classroom teachers who demonstrate success during the school day to continue to build a positive relationship.

   21st Century Community Learning Centers programs link professional development to identified, school-based goals and learning objectives and conduct joint training for both school-day and afterschool staff on relevant topics, such as how children and youth learn and develop, how to establish appropriate learning environments, and how to deliver crosscurricular content.

2. **Developing the capacity of staff and promoting networking.** New Jersey's 21st Century Community Learning Centers programs are expected to build relationships with school-day staff through joint professional development opportunities between school-day/district and center staff. This joint professional development provides a forum for staff to learn about each other's assets while acquiring a common professional language, learning the same instructional strategies and techniques, and gaining new information about programs and approaches being implemented.

   New Jersey's programs are also participating in action research to self-evaluate and continuously improve their programs using research-based practices. This strategy provides the opportunity for job-embedded professional development through a community of practice. The strategy also promotes more intentional and frequent interaction between the evaluator and program staff to assess the effectiveness of the practices being implemented.

3. **Maximizing student engagement and attendance.** New Jersey's programs operate at least 3 hours per day, 5 days per week, during the school year and at least 4 hours per day, 4 days per week, for 4 weeks in the summer to engage youth in additional learning opportunities and reduce summer learning loss. The required theme-based programming establishes relevance and interest through cross-content integration of information and skills. It also roots experiences in the real-world and promotes multisession involvement.

   To address the challenge of enticing youth to attend regularly, local programs are required to provide transportation, offer engaging learning experiences, create a youth-centered environment, and use guided-inquiry to increase opportunities for experiential learning, problem solving, self-direction, creativity, exploration, and expression.

Aligning the 21st Century Community Learning Centers Program With the School Day and Maximizing Student Engagement

Golden Gate, Inc. has partnered with the Woodlynne School District to implement a civic engagement curriculum theme. Using lessons in American history and journal writing, students gain an appreciation of the history of the United States and connect what they have learned to the map project. The program is also designed to enhance language arts, reading, and comprehension skills and to provide a "fun" way of learning history.

Developing the Capacity of Staff and Promoting Networking

The **Foundation for Educational Administration** conducted joint professional development for Jersey City school-day and afterschool staff to increase understanding and support implementation of the Common Core State Standards in their 21st Century Community Learning Centers program. This training facilitated productive reflection and exchange on how the 21st Century Community Learning Centers program could support the school day lessons.

Student voice is critical to student engagement. To include youth intentionally in the design of learning experiences that are relevant and interesting to them, programs are expected to have a student council that meets at least bimonthly.

4. **Establishing partnerships and focusing on sustainability.** Each of New Jersey's 21st Century Community Learning Centers programs is expected to create and maintain a set of partnerships that produce tangible resources that directly benefit participants. To assist programs in meeting this expectation, the centers are required to maintain a stakeholder advisory board comprised of partners, collaborators, the evaluator, parents, a youth representative, and other interested parties that meets at least quarterly. The advisory board offers guidance in the areas of program planning, implementation, evaluation, and sustainability.

   The NJDE collaborates with NJSACC-New Jersey's Afterschool Network to provide training and technical assistance to the 21st Century Community Learning Centers programs and other potential grantees. These professional development opportunities have focused on promoting partnership building and program sustainability, among other research-based strategies that support quality afterschool programs statewide. Together NJDE and NJSACC developed the NJ Celebrates Afterschool Toolkit to help programs conduct open house events for parents, community members, and potential partners to increase awareness of the program's offerings and benefits.

5. **Promoting family engagement.** The program's advisory board includes parent representation. Also, programs are expected to provide parents with an opportunity to provide input on all facets of the program, inform parents of participants' progress, and formally invite parents to attend program events. Also, local programs are required to provide adult family members of participating students with opportunities to participate in an array of literacy activities.

Assessing Program Performance and Using Data for Continuous Quality Improvement

Using the state-level goals and objectives that are prescribed by the NJDE, local 21st Century Community Learning Centers programs establish their own performance indicators. They contract with independent evaluators to conduct local evaluations to measure progress toward the achievement of goals, objectives, and indicators. The local evaluation gauges the impact of the program on participating students and families, including student attendance, student engagement during the school day and during the afterschool program, parental involvement, and skills acquired by parents.

NJDE has contracted with American Institutes of Research to conduct a state-level evaluation of its 21st Century Community Learning Centers programs. Positive findings in the evaluation of the 2009-10 programs noted in Table 1 include the following:

- *Students who attended the center for 70 days or more during the school year performed better on state assessments in mathematics compared to similar students who did not participate in the center.*

- *Students with higher attendance in 21st Century Community Learning Centers programs showed greater improvement in teacher-reported student motivation, attentiveness, pro-social behaviors, and homework completion/ quality.*

- *Students who participated in the program for multiple years performed better on state assessments in reading and mathematics.*

....

Table 1. Positive student outcomes linked to 21st Century Community Learning Centers program participation.

Outcome Type	Predictor Used	Observed Effect Size	Significance Level
Teacher-Reported Changes (Teacher Survey)			
In terms of being attentive	Number of 21st CCLC days attended	+ .019* points (0-100 scale) per day	p < 0.1 (Significant)
In terms of behaving well	Number of 21st CCLC days attended	+ .017* points (0-100 scale) per day	p < 0.05 (Significant)
In terms of improving homework	Number of 21st CCLC days attended	+ .034* points (0-100 scale) per day	p < 0.05 (Significant)
State Assessment Changes			
Mathematics	Attending 21st CCLC at least 70 Days	+ 6.32% SD***	p < 0.01 (Significant)
Mathematics	Number of continuous years in the 21st CCLC program	+ 12.7% SD	p < 0.01 (Significant)
Reading	Number of continuous years in the 21st CCLC program	+ 10.7% SD	p < 0.01 (Significant)

* Unstandardized coefficient

** To better assess outcomes, teacher survey items were converted to Rasch scale scores. Note that the observed correlation may not be linear.

*** "SD" stands for Standard Deviation.

Naftzger, N., Vinson, D., Manzeske, D., and Gibbs, C. (2011). *New Jersey 21st Century Community Learning Centers (21st CCLC) impact report 2009–10.* Naperville, IL: American Institutes for Research.

Leading Indicator System to Make Further Advancements in Quality and Achievement

One of the goals of the statewide evaluation is to provide 21st Century Community Learning Centers grantees with feedback about their performance in the areas of program design and delivery. NJDE is therefore working with American Institutes of Research on the development of a *leading indicator* system to enhance its understanding of the impact of the New Jersey 21st Century Community Learning Centers program.

The focus of the leading indicator system is on quality implementation that has potential to *lead to* positive youth outcomes, rather than just focusing on assessing the achievement of youth outcomes *after* the program year is completed. This system innovation will continue to keep New Jersey's 21st Century Community Learning Centers programs and other interested afterschool and summer learning programs in the state moving forward.

Conclusion

The 21st Century Community Learning Centers in New Jersey are providing critical learning opportunities tied to important education goals to thousands of young people across the state. Independent evaluations of the impact of local programs show they are making a positive difference in student achievement and teacher-reported student motivation, attentiveness, pro-social behaviors, and homework completion/quality.

These improved student outcomes did not happen by accident. The NJDE, along with local school and statewide and community partners, have worked diligently on five improvement strategies. New efforts to make future advances are under way, utilizing the latest research on quality and outcome improvement.

ABOUT THE AUTHOR

Susan Martz directs the Office of Student Support Services at the New Jersey Department of Education. She has been the director for the 21st Century Community Learning Centers grant program for the past 10 years. Martz has over 30 years of experience in education as a teacher and administrator at both the state and local levels. She holds a master's degree in education from Rutgers Graduate School of Education.

REFERENCES

Beckett, M., Borman, G., Capizzano, J., Parsley, D., Ross, S., Schirm, A., & Taylor, J. (2009). *Structuring out-of-school time to improve academic achievement: A practice guide* (NCEE #2009-012). Washington, DC: National Center for Education Evaluation and Regional Assistance, Institute of Education Sciences, U.S. Department of Education. Retrieved from http://ies.ed.gov/ncee/wwc/publications/practiceguides

Naftzger, N., Vinson, D., Manzeske, D., and Gibbs, C. (2011). *New Jersey 21st Century Community Learning Centers (21st CCLC) impact report 2009–10*. Naperville, IL: American Institutes for Research.

Joseph Davis
Chief Operating Officer, Florida Afterschool Network

Lani Lingo
Director, 21st Century Community Learning Centers, Bureau of Family and Community Outreach, Florida Department of Education

Shelah Woodruff
Program Specialist, Bureau of Family and Community Outreach, Florida Department of Education

Strategies Used to Improve Florida's 21st Century Community Learning Centers

"When a 21st Century program is done right, it is often the very best thing in a child's life." This credo, oft-repeated in Florida, clearly defines the importance of the 21st Century Community Learning Centers to our nation's school children. Florida is working hard to make this belief a reality for 80,000 young people and their families in hundreds of sites across the state.

The success of 21st Century Community Learning Centers, and the afterschool and summer programs they fund, does not happen by accident across a state. They need to have three critical components:

- *Inspired programming*
- *Well-structured and diverse program offerings*
- *Results-oriented focus*

Inspired Programming

The key to the success of Florida's 21st Century Community Learning Centers is *inspired programming*. There is a major emphasis on providing students with fun, hands-on, engaged learning experiences that are tied to the regular school day. The effectiveness of Florida's programs depends on these four simple elements:

- *Fun: Students should find the experience interesting and enjoyable.*
- *Hands-on: Students should physically participate in activities.*
- *Engaged learning: Students should be mentally involved in activities.*
- *Tie-in: Connecting afterschool activities to regular school-day lessons makes activities relevant and more memorable.*

Two simple concepts have been consistently emphasized during professional development sessions with grantees:

1. "Teaching within the margins" was born out of the common frustration of school-day teachers who, *due to constraints of the school day, were rarely able to engage in the hands-on learning activities suggested in the margins of their textbooks.* By encouraging grantees to seek out teacher editions of classroom textbooks and identify these extension activities, "teaching within the margins" ties 21st Century Community Learning Centers afterschool programs to the regular day with fun activities that students enjoy. This additional exposure to information helps them learn more about the subject matter.

2. All program activities must have an academic component. Grantees are asked to design activities that intentionally relate to academic principles. If the activity is playing basketball, for example, then students are learning statistics. If students have an opportunity to work with animals, they should identify biological principles. If students build robots, they do so with the goal of solving tasks and practicing engineering concepts. The state's grantees recognize that although it takes more time to create quality, daily lesson plans in an afterschool program, in the end students embrace these meaningful experiences, thus learning more and enjoying the program more.

These community-based partners include Boys and Girls Clubs, local YMCAs, churches and faith-based coalitions, cities unaffiliated with school districts, and other organizations that have decided to become stakeholders and active participants in the academic and personal welfare of some of Florida's most needy children.

Well-Structured, Diverse Programming

Florida's 21st Century Community Learning Centers are among the most well-structured and programmatically diverse out-of-school programs for students attending Title I, school-wide program-eligible schools. Part of that structure includes minimum time requirements set by the state. Every 21st Century Community Learning Centers program in Florida must offer services for 36 weeks and a minimum of 12 hours per week. This requirement provides students with ample opportunities to engage in math, reading, and science enrichment, as well as a wide array of fine arts education, physical recreation, character building, service learning, tutoring, entrepreneurial education, and other personal enrichment activities not always available during the regular school day.

Florida's 21st Century Community Learning Centers also recognize that *communities* are at the core of successful programs. Half of the state's 21st Century Community Learning Centers programs are operated by community- or faith-based organizations that make a point of reaching out to the surrounding community to procure business partnerships, expertise in enrichment areas, and best practice recommendations. These community-based partners include Boys and Girls Clubs, local YMCAs, churches and faith-based coalitions, cities unaffiliated with school districts, and other organizations that have decided to become stakeholders and active participants in the academic and personal welfare of some of Florida's most needy children.

Results-Oriented Focus

To enhance accountability and data-driven best practices, Florida uses extensive data tracking and monitoring procedures. Florida's 21st Century Community Learning Centers program requires all subgrantees to submit monthly attendance numbers to the Florida Department of Education, and the Department plans site visits, program monitoring, and technical assistance accordingly. State leadership uses this information, as well as the requisite data collected through the federal 21st Century Community Learning Centers Profile and Performance Information Collection System (PPICS), to ensure that programs operate as intended.

Data collected through PPICS demonstrates the continuing success of Florida's programs. In the 2007–08 program year, 78% of regularly participating 21st Century Community Learning Centers students statewide either maintained or showed growth in math, and 79% maintained or showed growth in reading, as determined by report card grades. Furthermore, 75% of Florida's 21st Century Community Learning Centers students demonstrated improvement in submitting homework on time—a crucial skill needed for academic success in the regular school day (Learning Points Associates, 2009).

> Half of the state's 21st Century Community Learning Centers programs are operated by community- or faith-based organizations that make a point of reaching out to the surrounding community to procure business partnerships, expertise in enrichment areas, and best practice recommendations.

While these numbers represent the entire state, exemplary programs boast even greater achievements, especially when compared to peers from the same school who did not attend afterschool programs. For example, one program met all of its academic objectives in the 2010–11 program year when, on average, 84% of attending middle school students maintained or demonstrated improvement in math, 94% in language arts, and 85% in science. These students attend schools in which peers perform at 59% proficiency in math, 62% in reading, and 40% in science on the Florida Comprehensive Assessment Test, demonstrating the need for focused and engaged attention to academics in afterschool (Silver & Albert, 2011).

The fun, hands-on academic enrichment activities in Florida's 21st Century Community Learning Centers programs, planned and taught by certified teachers, clearly affect these scores. Moreover, studies show that students who regularly attend afterschool programs improve their regular school-day attendance and participation (Afterschool Alliance, n.d.); For example, PPICS data shows that 80% of students demonstrated an increase in class participation in the 2007–08 school year (Learning Point Associates, 2009). Because students must be present in the regular school day in order to participate in 21st Century Community Learning Centers programs, they absorb more lessons that are later reinforced after school. This additional time in the classroom—learning with peers and from a certified teacher—also positively affects student achievement and relationships.

Strategies and Expectations for a Successful Statewide Program

The state of Florida employs the following strategies and expectations to support the efforts of local school and community groups to provide inspired programming, deliver well-structured and diverse program offerings and activities, and focus on the following results:

- *Strong professional development*

- *Student investment and engagement*

- *Effective evaluation of grant objectives*

- *Partnership development and advocacy*

Strong Professional Development

Excellent afterschool programs depend largely on the talents and abilities of staff and leaders. Program leadership must employ staff who will be able to develop positive relationships with afterschool participants of all ages and grade levels. Strong professional development makes program staff aware of the impact of their decisions, the way they think about the program and participants, and how they handle challenges. Excellent professional development is based on the established needs of administrators, teachers, and other staff and should involve training in programmatic curricula, student safety, and youth development principles.

> Strong professional development makes program staff aware of the impact of their decisions, the way they think about the program and participants, and how they handle challenges.

In addition, all of Florida's subgrantees are required to send at least three representatives to the annual Florida Afterschool Conference. During this weeklong event, project directors, site coordinators, and teachers are given opportunities to visit a 21st Century Community Learning Centers site, attend professional development sessions, learn more about state requirements and procedures, and present best practices and ideas at roundtables hosted by program staff.

Student Investment and Engagement

While individuals who are committed to and engaged with the program are essential for its success, without effective student investment, some programs become just another drop-in afterschool care service. Evidence suggests a correlation between frequent attendance in structured afterschool programs and positive outcomes in and out of school (Afterschool Alliance, n.d.). Based on 21st Century Community Learning Centers program surveys, students who participate in structured, engaging afterschool programs attend school more regularly and improve behavior and academic achievement (Learning Point Associates, 2009). Providing free, exceptional opportunities to improve academic achievement undoubtedly encourages parents to send their children to 21st Century Community Learning Centers programs. However, the best way to ensure student investment is to provide fun, hands-on, high-interest activities taught by concerned, informed, and engaging adults who are passionate about the success of their students.

Effective Evaluation of Grant Objectives

A strong evaluation plan helps ensure that 21st Century Community Learning Centers programs make continuous progress towards achieving proposed objectives for participating students and parents. Program evaluation plans should be built from well-developed program objectives, should carefully select performance indicators and outcome measures, and should focus on maximizing student academic progress and personal development. Afterschool programs should not only use the evaluation tools to collect data and measure the effectiveness of the program, but focus on evaluation as a tool of self-improvement. In Florida, programs are required to assess progress toward grant objectives twice a year. They must also demonstrate programmatic changes based on the results of such evaluations. Therefore, formative assessments are used to improve current program activities and strategies, while summative assessments inform the construction of continuation applications and help tailor next year's program.

> Program evaluation plans should be built from well-developed program objectives, should carefully select performance indicators and outcome measures, and should focus on maximizing student academic progress and personal development.

A Winning Formula for Engaging Students and Improving Lives

What would it be like to go around the world in 60 days? Students attending Midway Safe Harbor find out by using their math skills to calculate costs and exchange rates and then by researching the culture of each of the countries. This is Midway's formula: an hour of academics and an hour of enrichment centered on the same theme. And in 2010–11, the majority—68% of regular program participants or more—either improved or maintained their grades in reading and math.

Midway Safe Harbor, in partnership with the Boys & Girls Club of Central Florida, brings a community struggling with high poverty and crime together to provide safe, enriching learning opportunities for kids. The program, located in Sanford, Florida, transforms school lessons into highly engaging activities, making sure that the students are not only getting the academic knowledge the school district says they need but are also getting the kinds of learning opportunities they themselves want. For example, programs available to younger students focus on improving literacy while older students have access to credit retrieval courses, helping them graduate on time.

Partnership Development and Advocacy

As more attention is focused on the needs of youth development, community leaders, policymakers, and practitioners are finding ways to increase support for more afterschool programs of a higher caliber. Florida's 21st Century Community Learning Centers work closely with statewide advocacy organizations like the Florida Afterschool Network and the Florida After School Alliance to develop afterschool quality standards, promote and provide professional development for afterschool staff, and advocate on behalf of afterschool students.

The Florida Afterschool Conference is just one example of the need for and potential impact of community partners on a statewide level. The convention is a joint venture organized by the Florida After School Alliance and 21st Century Community Learning Centers state leadership and is sponsored by afterschool advocates throughout Florida, including the Florida After School Alliance, the Florida Afterschool Network, the Florida Alliance of the Boys & Girls Clubs, and county-based afterschool advocacy organizations.

These relationships—coupled with the other strategies and practices outlined in this report—have helped to make sure that 20% of Florida's children attend afterschool programs. While this rate is impressive, especially considering the national rate is estimated at 15%, the Afterschool Alliance (2011) notes that "state leaders can do much more to ensure that Florida's youth have the benefit of access to quality afterschool offerings as demand continues to grow in the state."

Conclusion

Afterschool time can be a valuable tool in augmenting the education of our nation's children. Inspired by a commitment to fun, hands-on, engaged learning; enabled by multiple community partnerships; and driven by results-oriented accountability, Florida's 21st Century Community Learning Centers programs continue to thrive and enrich the lives of more than 80,000 children and families throughout the state. Florida's next step—and perhaps the next step for 21st Century Community Learning Centers nationwide—must be to encourage state and national leaders to see the excellent practice and promise of expanded learning and afterschool programs, to advocate for afterschool opportunities, and to help ensure that more children can receive the high quality out-of-school programming already practiced at Florida's sites.

ABOUT THE AUTHORS

Joseph Davis is an expanded learning advocate serving as the chief operating officer for the Florida Afterschool Network. Previously, Joe served as chief of the Bureau of Family and Community Outreach at the Florida Department of Education. As bureau chief, he oversaw the Department's 21st Century Community Learning Centers afterschool program, as well as dropout prevention, parent involvement, safe schools, and faith- and community-based initiatives.

Lani Lingo has been the director of the 21st Century Community Learning Centers program at the Florida Department of Education, Bureau of Family and Community Outreach, since 2006. During her tenure as state director, Ms. Lingo has championed the inclusion of STEM and now STEAM (science, technology, engineering, art, and math) initiatives, the integration of academic subjects, and project- or problem-based learning in afterschool programs.

Shelah Woodruff is a program specialist with the Florida Department of Education, Bureau of Family and Community Outreach. Her primary responsibility is facilitating Florida's 21st Century Community Learning Centers programs at the state level.

REFERENCES

Afterschool Alliance. (n.d.). 21st Century Community Learning Centers federal afterschool initiative. Retrieved from http://www.afterschoolalliance.org/policy21stcclc.cfm

Afterschool Alliance. (2011). Afterschool progress report and consumer guide: Florida: How Florida is helping to keep the lights on after school. Retrieved from http://www.afterschoolalliance.org/Progress-Reports.cfm?state_abbr=FL&level=1

Learning Point Associates. (2009). *21st Century Community Learning Centers (21st CCLC) analytic support for evaluation and program monitoring: Florida 21st CCLC 2008 annual performance report*. Retrieved from Profile and Performance Information Collection System website: http://ppics.learningpt.org/ppics/reports/2008APRPDFS/FL.PDF

Silver, S. E. & Albert, R. J. (2011). *21st Century Community Learning Centers administered by Coordinated Child Care of Pinellas, Inc: Summative evaluation report of the school-based program, year 2*. Retrieved from http://florida21stcclc.com/reports/summative.php

Mark H. Emery
Administrator, Office of After-School Programs,
Fairfax County (VA) Public Schools

Patricia McGrath
Region 4 Operations Manager, Fairfax County (VA)
Neighborhood and Community Services

Working Together: How a County Government and a School District Joined to Provide All Middle Schools Engaging, Safe, and Effective Afterschool Learning Opportunities

In Fairfax County, Virginia, the Fairfax County Public Schools (FCPS) and the Fairfax County government (FC) have taken the initiative to establish and fund afterschool opportunities for middle school students. This investment and partnership expanded a 2-day afterschool program in some schools to a 5-day program in all 26 FCPS middle schools. Now in its 6th year, the program has generated improvements in academics, behavior, relationships, and school and community connectedness, with an average weekly attendance of over 19,000 students.

Demonstrated Need

The middle school afterschool program was introduced in 2001 when the Fairfax Partnership for Youth (FPY), a local public-private partnership serving as an intermediary, helped establish a mini-grant process to fund afterschool activities. Seed money was provided by the Fairfax County Board of Supervisors, and local school-community coalitions provided matching funds and programming support.

That same year, the results of a countywide youth survey indicated that 57% of respondents spent time at a friend's house without an adult present, 34% spent time at least once a week when no parents were present, and 50% hung out at a mall or in a parking lot three or more times a month. Respondents reported lower-than-average neighborhood attachment and connectedness toward school (Development Research and Programs, 2001).

In response to these survey results, the Fairfax County-Falls Church Community Services Board established a partnership with FCPS and FPY. Using funds from a 3-year Virginia State Incentive Grant, the board adapted selected evidence-based prevention programs to an afterschool environment and provided training for staff. At the same time, FPY received two capacity-building grants from the Governor's Office for Substance Abuse Prevention and formed the Fairfax County After-School Network to increase community awareness of and support for expanded afterschool opportunities.

By spring 2004, all the middle schools were receiving mini-grants to sponsor afterschool activities at least 2 days a week. These activities were a mix of primarily academic support and enrichment and prevention-based programming. Average weekly attendance was about 3,000 students.

During this period, Fairfax County experienced a marked increase in youth gang activity. With more than 100 gangs operating in the county, middle school youth were increasingly recruited to join gangs, with disengaged, immigrant youth most at risk. The documented lack of adult-supervised activities for middle school youth was apparent, and at nearly every Gang Prevention Task Force Forum held throughout the county, the number one prevention initiative discussed was the need to expand middle school afterschool programs.

In fall 2004, the school board invested nearly $1 million in afterschool programs and formed an Office of After-School Programs (OASP). A year later, the Fairfax County Board of Supervisors earmarked over $3 million to implement a 3-year expansion of afterschool programming to 5 days a week in all 26 middle schools. A school-county collaborative partnership was developed between OASP and the Department of Community and Recreational Services—now Neighborhood and Community Services (NCS)—to implement this initiative; the time frame for full implementation was one year.

Coordination Is Key

Since the end of the 2006–07 school year, all middle schools have had a comprehensive, 5-day afterschool program in place with a full-time afterschool program specialist on site. The afterschool specialist plans, develops, and implements afterschool activities and schedules all community use of the school buildings and grounds. The specialist is a 12-month school employee and is part of the school's administrative team. This structure facilitates a strong link between afterschool and in-school activities and programs—one of the keys to the success of this initiative.

Afterschool programs cannot meet the needs of students, schools, families, and communities, nor are positive outcomes achievable, unless program leaders are strategic and intentional in both design and implementation. Fairfax program leaders took that approach very early in the process by utilizing a theory of change guided by an extensive logic model. Starting with the unique school-county partnership that drove this initiative, the logic model itself summarizes the key elements of the program, articulates outcomes, determines how those outcomes can be measured, and makes the links between the program elements and desired outcomes.

Each middle school develops and implements its own budget and program based on a planning process in which (a) needs are initially identified, (b) specific programs and activities are selected to address those needs, (c) outcomes are aligned to the goals, and (d) performance measures are established for assessment. As the needs of each school are different, the goals, program activities, and outcomes also differ. Each afterschool program must address the four key strategies that stem from the logic model: academic support and enrichment; social skills and youth development; physical, health, and recreation support; and family and community involvement. Each afterschool activity is linked to one of these strategies and, in turn, is aligned with one or more of the school division's student achievement goals: academics, essential life skills, and responsibility to the community, thereby linking all activities to the school day.

The 2011–12 school year marks the 6th year of the 5-day afterschool program, which runs from regular dismissal times until as late as 6:00 p.m. in 26 middle schools. An additional middle school provides a 3-day afterschool program. FCPS provides late bus transportation 3 days per week, and there is parent pick up all 5 days. The program is free and open to all middle school students.

> Counselors, classroom teachers, and afterschool staff work collaboratively to identify students who may be struggling academically or socially.

The FCPS-FC afterschool program helps students meet local and state academic standards and offers students a broad array of enrichment activities. Each middle school has outreach efforts in place to recruit underserved and underrepresented students into academic enrichment activities. Counselors, classroom teachers, and afterschool staff work collaboratively to identify students who may be struggling academically or socially and then recruit and encourage those students to participate in academic support programs and other activities.

FCPS-FC has received a 21st Century Community Learning Centers grant that supports two middle schools. Local resources support the afterschool program at these schools, and the 21st Century Community Learning Centers funds support a summer school initiative. Additionally, a number of ethnically diverse community partners provide student and parent support and a parent literacy program at these schools. With the exception of the summer program and community partnership base, there is almost no difference between the afterschool activities at the 21st Century Community Learning Centers sites and the other middle schools.

This prevention-based afterschool initiative was implemented with a fully integrated evaluation model and outcomes measures. Program outcomes are examined through multiple measures: planned and unplanned site observations; quarterly progress reports that include process measures, as well as correlations between dosage in afterschool and changes in grades, absenteeism, and discipline referrals; student, teacher, staff, and parent surveys; and academic and behavioral data. Correlations among these multiple measures are investigated to obtain a more complete picture of the impact of the program.

Major Outcomes

What have been some of the key outcomes and benefits of the FCPS-FC Middle School After-School Program?

- **Increased academic performance.** *Between the 2005–06 and 2010–11 school years, there was a 54% reduction in the percent of Ds and Fs in core subjects—English, math, science, and social studies (Fairfax County Public Schools[FCPS], 2011b). Of those students who received one or more Fs in a core subject, 72% attended less than 30 days of afterschool (FCPS, 2011c).*
- **Increased classroom participation.** *79% of classroom teachers agree or strongly agree that classroom participation of afterschool participants has improved (FCPS, 2010).*
- **Improved homework completion rates.** *72 percent of classroom teachers agree or strongly agree that homework completion rates of afterschool participants have improved (FCPS, 2010).*
- **Improved student behavior.** *73 percent of classroom teachers agree or strongly agree that the classroom behavior of afterschool participants has improved (FCPS, 2010). Of those students who received a behavior infraction, 73 percent attended less than 30 days of afterschool (FCPS, 2011c).*
- **Better peer relations, emotional adjustment.** *83 percent of parents agree or strongly agree that their child seems happier or less-stressed since attending afterschool (FCPS, 2011a).*
- **Better attitudes towards school.** *84 percent of parents agree or strongly agree that their child has a better attitude towards school (FCPS, 2011a).*
- **Reduced gang crime.** *There has been a 32 percent drop in youth gang activity between 2006 and 2008 as afterschool attendance doubled (Fairfax County Coordinating Council on Gang Prevention, 2007).*

Conclusion

Much of the success of this initiative can be attributed to the strong collaborative partnership between school, school district, and county government staff charged with developing and implementing this effort. Other strategies that have been integral to its success include

- *conducting youth surveys and needs assessments,*
- *having a structural base and action plan in place and ready to go when resources became available,*
- *designating site directors as full-time staff and part of the school's administrative team,*
- *linking local school and community needs to afterschool activities and outcomes,*
- *having teachers and administrators who saw the needs within their school that could be met by afterschool,*
- *incorporating afterschool as an integral part of the school day without replicating the school day,*

- *leveraging existing financial commitments and personnel,*
- *having the support and leadership of school principals, and*
- *being accountable.*

The afterschool program is a key element in the efforts of the school division and the county to improve academic performance, develop healthy and successful youth, and combat gangs. The program is not intended to be regarded simply as child care or as a mere extension of the school day. On the contrary, it provides each participating youth with greater opportunities to form relationships with caring adults; to contribute to the community; to acquire new skills in a supportive environment; to be safe and secure; to form healthy relationships with peers; and to develop the attitudes, skills, and knowledge to thrive in the workplaces and communities of the 21st century.

ABOUT THE AUTHORS

Mark H. Emery is administrator of the Office of After-School Programs, Fairfax County Public Schools, where he oversees the development and implementation of afterschool programs in 27 middle schools. He is chair of the Virginia Partnership on Out-of-School Time and a board member of the Fairfax Partnership for Youth and the Fairfax County Boys' and Girls' Club. Emery formerly served as director of extended learning and development for the Council of Chief State School Officers and chair of the Fairfax County School Board. He is retired from the Naval Research Laboratory and holds a Ph.D. in Physics from the University of Iowa.

Patricia McGrath is the Region 4 Operations Manager for Neighborhood and Community Services in Fairfax County, Virginia. She was the division supervisor for teens, as well as branch manager for middle school afterschool programs for the Fairfax County Department of Neighborhood and Community Services. McGrath has over 20 years of experience in prevention program development and evaluation.

REFERENCES

Development Research and Programs, Inc. (2001). *Communities That Care: Fairfax County survey of youth risks and assets.* Retrieved from Fairfax County, Virginia, website: http://www.fairfaxcounty.gov/demogrph/pdf/youth2001.pdf

Fairfax County Coordinating Council on Gang Prevention. (2007). *Fairfax County gang prevention 2005–2006 status report.* Retrieved from www.fairfaxcounty.gov/gangprevention/gangpreventionreport_092407.pdf

Fairfax County Public Schools. (2010). [After-school program teacher survey]. Unpublished raw data.

Fairfax County Public Schools. (2011a). [After-school program parent survey]. Unpublished raw data.

Fairfax County Public Schools. (2011b). [Enrollment and marks, 2005–06 through 2010–11]. Unpublished Education Decision Support Library data.

Fairfax County Public Schools. (2011c). [Student Information System reports]. Unpublished raw data.

Lauren Stevenson
Principal, Junction Box Consulting

Cristy Johnston Limón
Executive Director, Destiny Arts Center, Oakland, CA

Tilly Reclosado
Assistant Instructor, Destiny Arts Center, and Student,
San Francisco State University

Community-Based Afterschool and Summer Arts Education Programs: Positive Impact on Youth and Community Development

Community-based arts education programs can have a significant and positive impact on participating youth—*and* on overall community development. Typically delivered after school, over the weekend, and during the summer, such programs should be regarded by community, state, and federal leaders as an effective tool for responding to 21st century educational and civic challenges.

Like other forms of out-of-school-time programming, the value of community-based youth arts programs is often assessed against measures used to gauge school success— for example, participants' test scores, school attendance, graduation rates, or progress in mathematics and literacy development. These measures are important, and research finds a positive relationship between participation in afterschool and summer community arts programs and these types of outcomes (Heath, Soep, & Roach, 1998).

In this article, however, we focus on the impact of community-based arts programs on youth development and community development—two other key areas of outcomes highlighted in research and best practice in community arts. We do this for two reasons. First, we believe that these impacts often mediate or help to explain some of the impacts seen on school-related indicators—that is, that positive development and an opportunity to have a meaningful impact in one's community are key to engagement and success in school, life, and work. Second, youth and community development are important domains of impact in their own right and are essential for addressing civic challenges of the 21st century—a century in which communities are increasingly diverse and in which educational, racial, and socio-economic inequality persist.

For this article, we weave together evidence from research—in particular, the body of studies in the new arts education research clearinghouse, ArtsEdSearch (www.artsedsearch.org)—with evidence from best practice at the Destiny Arts Center in Oakland, California (Destiny). The latter, we present from the perspective of Destiny's executive director (Cristy Johnston Limón), one of its youth leaders (Tilly Reclosado), and a researcher who conducted a study at the organization (Lauren Stevenson). Destiny provides dance, theater, and martial arts instruction to youth ages 3–18, intentionally serving some of the most chronically underserved young people in Oakland, as well as middle-income and affluent families seeking exposure to culturally and socio-economically plural communities. Young people come to Destiny's center in North Oakland for classes after school, on weekends, and during the summer, and Destiny sends instructors to teach in afterschool programs in over 45 public schools in the East Bay.

Young people come to Destiny's center in North Oakland for classes after school, on weekends, and during the summer, and Destiny sends instructors to teach in afterschool programs in over 45 public schools in the East Bay.

Youth Development

Describing Destiny's impact from her perspective as a youth participant, Tilly Reclosado says, "At Destiny I got to work with choreographers, write a script, learn lines and act, all whilst building a family in a safe community outside of my home. Destiny taught me to be more aware—of myself, of the people and world around me, and of all things artistic. Creating and performing a show enlightened me on the significance of hard work, planning ahead, and thinking on my feet." Reclosado's words echo the research on community youth arts programs, which finds that such programs are not only effective

Qualities of Community Youth Arts Programs That Promote Positive Youth Development

- **Youth-centered.** Effective community youth arts programs respect young people as artists and support them in cultivating their own artistic voice.

- **Knowledge-centered.** In community arts programs, young people develop knowledge in an art form and knowledge about themselves, their communities, and ideas they wish to express in their artwork.

- **Assessment-centered.** The arts involve cycles of planning, practice, and performance and opportunities to make learning visible.

- **Community-centered.** Effective arts programs forge a sense of community among participants that facilitates the risk-taking and self-expression required in artistic endeavors.

at fostering young people's artistic development but also their cognitive, social, and personal growth. The arts learning environment that these programs offer embodies the qualities that youth development scholars (McLaughlin, 2000; Eccles & Gootman, 2002) find are key for effective youth development programs (Stevenson & Deasy, 2005). They are, following the phrasing of youth development expert Milbrey McLaughlin (2000) and cognitive scientists at the National Academy of Sciences (Bransford, Brown, & Cockings, 1999), youth-centered, knowledge-centered, assessment-centered, and community-centered.

Research has identified a range of youth development outcomes associated with participation in community youth arts programs. These include skills and capacities prized in the Common Core and by leaders wishing to prepare students for life and work in the 21st century, including persistence, leadership, and collaboration (Weinstein, 2010, Kang Song & Gammel, 2011), creative thinking (Heath & Roach, 1999, Hui & Lau, 2006); problem solving (Rostan, 2010); agency (Stevenson, 2011), motivation (Catterall & Chapleau, 1999; Rostan, 2010), and empathy (Catterall & Chapleau, 1999).

Not surprisingly, given the centrality of self-discovery and self-expression to artistic practice, research also finds that community youth arts programs help young people develop self-confidence, self-efficacy, and self-awareness (Heath & Roach, 1999; Stevenson, 2011); and the ability to self-regulate and express emotions (Ross, 2000; Stevenson, 2011). Reclosado underscores the importance of this set of outcomes in her experience at Destiny. "The act of transforming myself into a character," she says of her training in theater in particular, "made me much more aware of myself and the emotions I feel. I find that I analyze the way I feel and try to find out why I feel that way. I feel more in control of myself when I can understand what I am feeling and the reasons behind it."

> Research finds that the positive development that young people experience in community arts programs is related to success in other areas of their lives.

Due to the collaborative nature of the artistic practice at Destiny, as participating youth become more capable of self-awareness and self-expression, they also become more visible to and more aware of one another and forge connections across lines of social difference that divide them in their schools and neighborhoods (Stevenson, 2011).

Importantly, research finds that the positive development that young people experience in community arts programs is related to success in other areas of their lives. Youth who participate in such programs, for example, are less likely than their peers to engage in delinquent and violent behavior (Respress & Lufti, 2006) or exhibit behavioral and emotional problems (Wright et al., 2006), and they are more likely to participate in school leadership and have better attendance and higher academic achievement (Heath, Soep, & Roach, 1998).

Community Development

In research at Destiny, Stevenson (2011) found that participating young people extended Destiny's impact to their surrounding community in two ways. First, having experienced personal growth by learning about themselves, one another, and social issues addressed in their performances, Destiny youth "walked differently in the world" (Stevenson, 2011, p. 126). They related to the world with more awareness, openness, confidence, and understanding, and in doing so, had positive effects on their families, schools, and communities. Second, she found that Destiny youth had impact through their performances, which sparked audience members to think differently about their own lives, learn something that would change the way they treat other people, want to take action to make their community a better place, and learn something about people of a different racial and/or ethnic background from their own. In these ways, Stevenson found that Destiny's impact "scales radially" (Stevenson, 2011, p. 130)—participating young people create waves of positive impact that ripple outward into their surrounding communities.

As the executive director at Destiny, Cristy Johnston Limón intentionally leverages young people's involvement in Destiny programs to engage their families and facilitate community development in Oakland. "By engaging young people in meaningful ways," she says, "youth arts organizations enjoy a powerful entry point to serve entire families and their communities." Destiny provides opportunities for parents and family members to work together on performances, projects, and fundraisers.

> Destiny provides opportunities for parents and family members to work together on performances, projects, and fundraisers.

Similar to what youth experience at Destiny, Johnston-Limon finds that parents forge new relationships; address issues of class, race, privilege, and social change; learn about themselves and others; and ultimately alter the way they interact with individuals who are different. In this way, Destiny provides an avenue for residents concerned about young people's health and well-being to reinvent their community in line with the values of interconnectedness, social responsibility, and care. As cities like Oakland struggle to rebuild once vibrant and bustling neighborhoods and commercial hubs, cultural organizations like Destiny can help address disinvestment, build audiences, and become mechanisms for rebuilding a sense of place and connection.

Research supports the idea that youth arts organizations can be effective resources for community development. Studies find, for example, that participation in the arts in the teen years relates to greater community involvement, volunteerism, and political participation in adulthood (Catterall, Chapleau, & Iwanaga, 2009; Heath & Roach, 1999). Studies also find that a high percentage of young people who engage in the arts commit to their local community as adults, contributing to its economic and civic growth and participating in and patronizing the arts (Heath & Roach, 1999; Rabkin & Hedberg, 2011).

Providing in-school and afterschool enrichment programs in 45 public schools in the California East Bay—some supported by funding from the 21st Century Community Learning Centers initiative—Destiny also helps schools strengthen their connection with the communities they serve. Instructors bring to the school programs the community-centered culture in which they are steeped at Destiny. At the end of each semester, Destiny also hosts a community event bringing together students from the different school programs. These events provide an opportunity for students to become visible in their communities and to develop a sense of connection across neighborhoods and schools.

Recommendations for Policymakers

Local and state policymakers should regard community-based youth arts programs as a key tool for responding to 21st century educational and civic challenges. We offer the following recommendations to support such programs and ensure their sustainability and accessibility to large numbers of community youth.

- *Local policymakers can work with state legislators to create and market incentives for artists to live and work in blighted neighborhoods (for example, live/work zoning, tax breaks, special-use districts, and enterprise zones) and strengthen blight ordinances that incentivize the creative use of commercial spaces.*

- *By working with local and regional arts commissions and councils, municipal governments can fund and create programs that foster partnerships between arts organizations, schools, and artists. Such programs can engage youth arts organizations in creating and exhibiting art that then engages the broader community in reusing and revitalizing underutilized urban spaces, including, for example, placing art in vacant storefronts, participating in mural design programs, and supporting other public art projects and events.*

- *Municipalities should invest in the creation of cultural spaces and youth arts organizations as resources for positive youth development and as community "hubs" where youth and their families can contribute to creating thriving communities and serve as meeting places for creative and cultural exchange (e.g., Hub San Francisco, Hub Berkeley[1]).*

- *Community leaders should leverage the effective community engagement and youth development strategies that youth arts organizations employ to address issues of public safety and gang and gun violence. Youth arts organizations can serve socio-economically diverse populations, offer a variety of entry points that attract broad audiences providing opportunities to create cross-cultural and intergenerational links, and help break down barriers that create tensions that ultimately lead to violence.*

---

1. For more information, see http://bayarea.the-hub.net.

- *State legislators have an opportunity to bolster funding for arts enrichment programs during the school day and in afterschool and summer learning programs that effectively partner with local arts and youth development organizations that specialize in creative engagement. In Santa Fe, New Mexico, for example, legislators established a set-aside for arts funding in the schools. Similar state and federal initiatives provide critical funding to ensure the next generation has the skill set necessary to thrive in the creative economy and modern workforce.*

For More Information

ArtsEdSearch (www.artsedsearch.org) is the nation's one-stop shop for research and policy related to arts education. The national Arts Education Partnership developed ArtsEdSearch as a resource for policymakers and education leaders to better understand and articulate the role that arts education can play in preparing students to succeed in the changing contexts of the 21st century. ArtsEdSearch currently includes summaries of close to 200 research studies, syntheses of the major findings of these studies, and implications of the collected research for educational policy.

Websites

Destiny Arts Center: www.destinyarts.org
Arts Education Partnership: www.aep-arts.org
ArtsEdSearch: www.artsedsearch.org

ABOUT THE AUTHORS

Lauren Stevenson is the principal at Junction Box Consulting, where she specializes in research, policy, and program development connecting arts, education, and youth engagement. The former senior associate for research at the national Arts Education Partnership, Stevenson has been a leader in arts and education for over 15 years and is the co-author of two books on the arts and educational change. She holds a PhD in education administration and policy analysis from Stanford University.

Cristy Johnston Limón is the executive director of Destiny Arts Center in Oakland, California. The founding director of a San Francisco community development organization, she piloted San Francisco's Neighborhood Marketplace Initiative, leveraging public policy and funding to create working partnerships between schools, civic organizations, churches, businesses, and property owners to revitalize blighted commercial districts by engaging local artists, residents, and youth. She is formerly a state legislative aide and served on the board of San Francisco's Japanese Community Youth Council. A native of San Francisco of Guatemalan parents, an early music and dance education in her urban community sparked a lifelong interest in civic engagement, community development, youth, and the arts.

Tilly Reclosado grew up in Oakland, and started taking classes at Destiny Arts when she was 5 years old. She has attended several Bay Area public and charter schools and became an active member (dancer, writer, actor, and performer) of the Destiny Arts Youth Performance Company in high school. From student to teacher, Reclosado now serves as an assistant instructor in hip-hop classes at Destiny's main site. She is also now attending San Francisco State University.

REFERENCES

Catterall, J. S., Chapleau, R., & Iwanaga, J. (1999). Involvement in the arts and human development. In E. B. Fiske (Ed.), *Champions of change: The impact of the arts on learning* (pp. 1–18). Washington, DC: Arts Education Partnership.

Eccles, J., & Gootman, J. A. (Eds.). (2002). *Community programs to promote youth development.* Washington, DC: National Academy Press.

Heath, S. B., Soep, E., & Roach A. (1998). Living the arts through language-learning: A report on community-based youth organizations. *American for the Arts Monographs, 2*(7), 1–20.

Heath, S. B., & Roach, A. (1999). Imaginative actuality: Learning in the arts during nonschool hours. In E. Fisk (Ed.), *Champions of change: The impact of the arts on learning* (pp. 19–34). Washington, DC: Arts Education Partnership and President's Committee on the Arts and the Humanities.

Kang Song, Y. I., & Gammel, J. A. (2011). Ecological mural as community reconnection. *International Journal of Art & Design Education, 30*, 266–278.

McLaughlin, M. W. (2000). *Community counts: How youth organizations matter for youth development.* Washington, DC: Public Education Network.

Rabkin, N., & and Hedberg, E. (2011). Arts education in America: What the declines mean for arts participation (Research Report #52). Washington, DC: National Endowment for the Arts.

Respress, T., & Lutfi, G. (2006). Whole brain learning: The fine arts with students at risk. *Reclaiming Children & Youth, 15*(1), 24–31.

Ross, J. (2000, April). *Art and community: Creating knowledge through service in dance.* Paper presented at the meeting of the American Educational Research Association, New Orleans, LA.

Rostan, S. M. (2010). Studio learning: Motivation, competence, and the development of young art students' talent and creativity. *Creativity Research Journal, 22*, 261–271.

Stevenson, L., & Deasy, R. J. (2005). *Third space: When learning matters.* Washington, DC: Arts Education Partnership.

Stevenson, L. M. (2011). *Creating destiny: Youth, arts and social change* (Unpublished doctoral dissertation). Stanford University, Stanford, CA.

Weinstein, S. (2010). "A unified poet alliance": The personal and social outcomes of youth spoken word poetry programming. *International Journal of Education & the Arts, 11*(2).

Wright, R., John, L., Alaggia, R., & Sheel, J. (2006) Community-based arts program for youth in low-income communities: A multi-method evaluation. *Child and Adolescent Social Work Journal, 23*, 635–652.

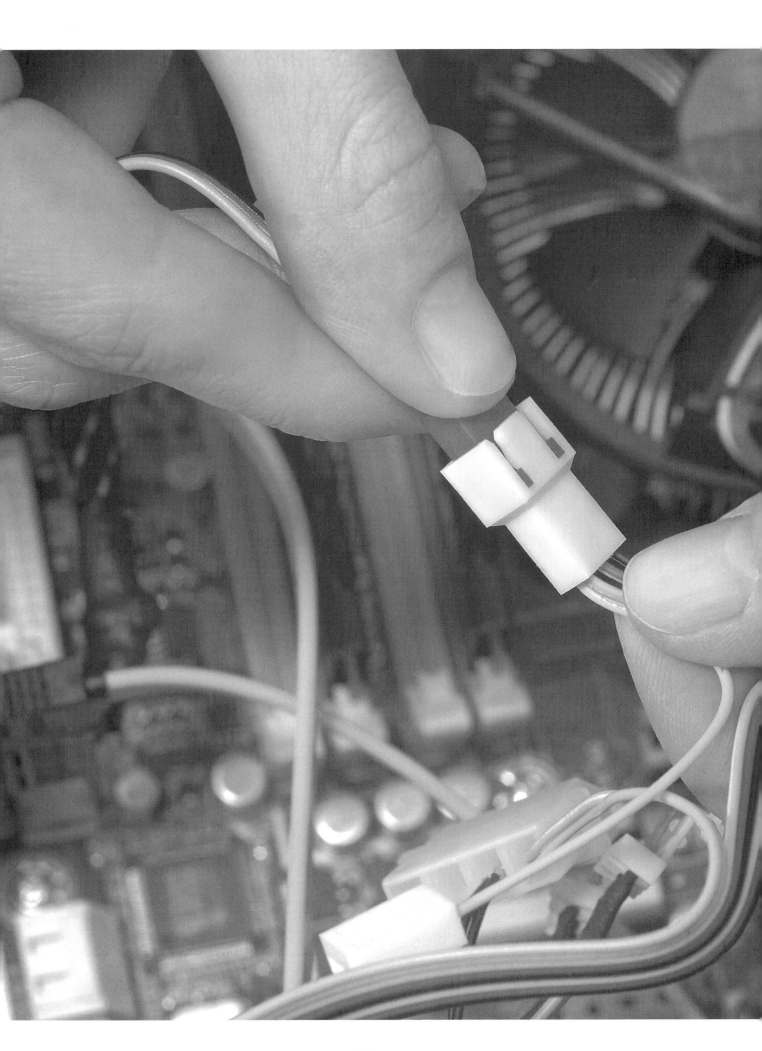

The Power of Community-School Partnerships in Expanding Learning

4

Gail Connelly
Executive Director, N
Elementary School F

Paul G. Young
Former Executive Di
Association and Adj

More Than Just Another "To-Do" on the List: The Benefits of Strong School, Principal, and Afterschool/ Community Relationships

The research is clear: *Principals matter* in the outcomes of their schools (Young, 2009). Next to having a great teacher in the classroom, strong principal leadership is the second most important factor in improving student outcomes. Moreover, research shows that high quality afterschool and summer learning programs also play an important role in helping students achieve academically, socially, emotionally, and physically (Vollmer, 2010). Therefore, it seems logical to suppose that collaboration between principals and afterschool and summer learning leaders would occur quite naturally; however, they often do not do so, despite knowing that they should.

While sharing the leadership responsibility for the success of children and youth in school, after school, and during the summertime poses many challenges, there are increasing examples of how to make this collaboration not only work well, but yield very positive results. The benefits of strong principal and afterschool/community relationships are numerous and should not be regarded as just creating more tasks or work to handle. Overcoming these challenges requires a paradigm shift about the distinctive, yet complementary purposes of school, afterschool, and summer learning. This paradigm shift incorporates rethinking and redefining staff roles and responsibilities; community engagement; and how, when, and where children and youth learn and flourish.

That is why the boards of directors of the National Association of Elementary School Principals (NAESP) and the National Afterschool Association (NAA) joined together in 2009 to challenge our members to "build a new day for learning," aimed at achieving innovative reform within schools and through quality afterschool and summer learning programs. This does not mean just adding more responsibility to the jobs of principals and afterschool leaders. Rather, it means pursuing a clear path to achieving operatively designed learning and developmental goals for students based on enriched and experiential learning. When principals and afterschool leaders share leadership responsibilities, they can create seamless connections between school and afterschool and between school and summer learning programs resulting in higher levels of achievement, a well-rounded education, and fulfillment for all children and youth. Further, they can engage and involve parents and families across the continuum, from school to afterschool and then to their homes, leading to greater satisfaction with and support for public schools.

> When principals and afterschool leaders share leadership responsibilities, they can create seamless connections between school and afterschool and between school and summer learning programs, resulting in higher levels of achievement, a well-rounded education, and fulfillment for all children and youth.

NAESP's *Leading Afterschool Learning Communities* (2006) emphasizes the importance of strong school/afterschool partnerships in the context of laying out a set of research-based standards for what principals should know and be able to do to ensure highly effective afterschool and summer learning programs and initiatives. High-quality afterschool and summer learning programs offer a unique opportunity to provide students with enrichment and support to augment and reinforce the learning and cognitive growth that is achieved during the school day and year. Such programs incorporate an expansive vision of learning and a strong commitment to collaborate with schools to manage resources.

Setting standards for "bridging" school, afterschool, and summer learning for the benefit of students is an important start, but it takes a significant commitment of resources to achieve the desired results. Federally funded programs for afterschool and summer programs offer a real opportunity for principals and afterschool and summer leaders from the community to come together to provide academic enrichment opportunities during nonschool hours for children, particularly for students who attend high-poverty and low-performing schools. As a result, many outstanding practices and initiatives have emerged in communities across the nation in terms of rethinking the time and place of the learning day to improve student achievement. It is clear that strong partnerships focused on creating a shared vision, collaborative planning, and fostering a common culture emphasizing high achievement are keys to successful school/afterschool partnerships.

What follows is a set of key insights, principles, and practices for partnership and collaboration that will reinforce the efforts of schools, afterschool, and summer learning programs to enhance learning and achievement.

Relationship building is the cornerstone to achieving positive school/afterschool outcomes for children and youth.

Across the nation there are scores of model programs featuring successful partnerships between principals and afterschool and summer learning program directors. These programs provide students with positive and safe environments, empower learning and academic success, and encourage an ongoing collaboration among peers, adults, and the greater community that puts the needs of the students first.

Scott Langham, principal of Bay Minette Elementary School in Baldwin County, Alabama, works collaboratively with Cherry Penn, president of the Alabama Community Education Association, who is also the After School Childcare Program supervisor and 21st Century Community Learning Centers grants program manager for Baldwin County. "The Project Tiger Paws has provided a quality afterschool program and plays a vital role in providing opportunities for our students to realize learning can be fun," Langham said in an article for the Press-Register Community News last year. "The 21st Century Community Learning Centers program provides outstanding enrichment activities for the students at Bay Minette Elementary School, which encourages the students to think of themselves as capable learners" (Press Register, 2010).

Shared vision, planning, and culture are essential to effective school/afterschool/summer learning efforts.

Increasingly, principals and afterschool leaders are being expected to do more with less. Some principals may think of afterschool as an additional task they must manage; more realistically, afterschool affords solutions to their many challenges in meeting the learning, social, and emotional needs of students. When principals and afterschool directors provide a common vision, encourage collaborative planning, and foster a professional culture of mutual support for effective program implementation across all institutional settings, they help every student have a better chance for success.

IS 318 middle school in Brooklyn, New York, makes afterschool part of the school culture, a key factor in their success as a school. Principal Fortunato Rubino, Assistant Principal John Galvin, and afterschool leaders work with teachers and community-based organizations to offer students academic help as well as up to 40 different enrichment activities, including ceramics, art, band, guitar, fitness, homework help, reading and math programs, photography, cheerleading, volleyball, basketball, yoga, academic contests, computer arts, theater/drama, chorus, orchestra, bicycling, cross-country, football, soccer, baseball, track, wrestling, softball, field hockey, martial arts, debate, yearbook, newspaper, student government, technology, and more (Jacobs, 2011).

Effective planning solidifies school/afterschool/summer learning collaboration.

Effective planning is essential for the success of school, afterschool, and summer learning initiatives. It must involve the principal and the afterschool and/or summer learning program site leaders and cannot be delegated to others. Each must know how and be able to connect and form a strong professional relationship and foster similar relationships among their respective professional staffs. Increasingly, for example, principals are instituting collaborative intervention-planning practices that involve their staffs and afterschool personnel in data analysis and the development of coordinated team approaches to helping students achieve.

School/community partnerships improve academics, attendance, and more for students at Holmes Junior High School in Cedar Falls, Iowa. Principal David Welter credits their afterschool program ECHOES (Every Child Has the Opportunity to Excel and Succeed), which offers a wide variety of programs and builds many positive adult-child relationships. According to Welter, the data that has been collected since their program was initiated in the 2002–03 school year show that collaboration between the Cedar Falls Community School District and the Cedar Falls community, along with innovative and engaging learning opportunities tied to academics and a caring and energetic staff, has produced positive results for their students. Tracking of students involved in the ECHOES program showed significant improvement in attendance, fewer behavioral referrals, and better grades (Welter, 2010).

Effective afterschool and summer learning programs expand learning opportunities.

They do not replicate classroom lessons. Principals and afterschool leaders should meet briefly each week to coordinate their communications and plan the alignment of learning activities with the strong caution that afterschool and summer learning programs and activities not lead to a replication of what happens during regular school hours or the regular school year and thus simply become "more school" after school.

> Planning must involve the principal and the afterschool and/or summer learning program site leaders and cannot be delegated to others.

Rather, both principals and afterschool leaders should want afterschool and summer learning to be the time and place in which young learners are free to explore, develop, and be enriched in a variety of differently structured activities and environments. Many successful programs are designed to offer activities, experiences, and relationships that promote students' social and emotional development, often reducing the risk of delinquent behavior and further enhancing their academic performance and motivation to continue to learn. For some learners, the standard school day or school year does not allow adequate time to learn what is necessary for success in the modern workforce and world. High quality afterschool and summer learning programs provide more time and opportunity for those who need it most, taking into account and accommodating the different ways students learn.

Dayton's Bluff Elementary was once one of the worst performing schools in Saint Paul, Minnesota. The school has deliberately worked over the past 10 years to collaborate across sectors, improve professional development, provide innovative approaches to learning, and truly let research drive decision making. The Achievement Plus program has been critical to the success of Dayton's Bluff. Established as a partnership between Saint Paul Public Schools and the Amherst H. Wilder Foundation, Achievement Plus works to improve student achievement in Saint Paul's urban schools, while also creating an urban education model and demonstration site. With the help of Achievement Plus, Principal Andrew Collins and the teachers have been able to collaborate across sectors—bringing together teachers, parents, and community leaders—to improve student engagement and parental involvement, develop afterschool opportunities, and provide students with a wide range of opportunities that foster safe and supportive learning environments. From a recreational center attached to the school to programs that offer health care services and information on housing and literacy, Dayton's Bluff offers students and their families increased opportunities for success ("St. Paul Elementary School," 2010).

Conclusion

NAESP and NAA will continue to encourage acceptance of the value of strong school/afterschool/ summer learning program partnerships. Our organizations also see 21st Century Community Learning Centers as a real opportunity to build and "test drive" these partnerships, so current proposals to water down or eliminate the partnership requirements and afterschool provisions in the program guidelines make little sense. We therefore see the need to expand the federal appropriations for afterschool programs rather than cut them back; moreover, we should avoid loading up these initiatives with extraneous requirements that can undermine their original and fundamental purposes. At the same time, we will support key initiatives that improve and strengthen best practices in the field, including

- *pre-service training for principals that defines, details, and showcases evidence-based practices of effective, high quality afterschool programming;*

- *joint leadership training for principals and afterschool leaders;*

- *development of learning communities where school/afterschool/community representatives share the school as the hub of activities; and*

- *investments in school and afterschool training opportunities and staff professional development so that children and youth in both settings will be served by qualified personnel.*

For some learners, the standard school day or school year does not allow adequate time to learn what is necessary for success in the modern workforce and world. High quality afterschool and summer learning programs provide more time and opportunity for those who need it most, taking into account and accommodating the different ways students learn.

Student learning is no longer the sole province of schools. Therefore, it is imperative that principals and afterschool program site leaders, along with their faculty and staff colleagues, strive to build strong ties of mutual support for enriching the experiences of children and youth in schools and afterschool and summer learning programs in every learning community throughout our nation. As the nation's economy improves, we also welcome state and local efforts to develop policies and make financial investments that invite and encourage expanded learning opportunities after school and during the summertime through strong school-community partnerships.

ABOUT THE AUTHORS

Gail Connelly is the executive director of the National Association of Elementary School Principals (NAESP) and president of the NAESP Foundation, located in Alexandria, Virginia. NAESP leads advocacy and support efforts on behalf of its 23,000-member network of elementary and middle school principals. Connelly's 35-year career in education and association management ranges from early childhood to adulthood with specialized knowledge of K–8 educational administration.

Paul G. Young has served in leadership roles with the National Association of Elementary School Principals (president, 2002–03), and the National AfterSchool Association (president & CEO, 2010–12). In addition, his experience as a principal and an afterschool program director has provided him special, practical insights into the needs of principals and afterschool professionals as they work to create expanded learning opportunities for children and youth. He is passionate about helping principals and afterschool professionals align school and afterschool and equipping young educators with the principles needed to become outstanding leaders and contributors to the profession.

REFERENCES

Jacobs, T. (2011). I.S. 318 Eugenio Maria De Hostos. Retrieved from Insideschools website: http://insideschools.org/middle/browse/school/643

National Association of Elementary School Principals. (2006). *Leading after-school learning communities: What principals should know and be able to do*. Alexandria, VA: Author.

National Association of Elementary School Principals. (2010). *Collaborating to build a new day for learning: A toolkit for principals, afterschool, and community leaders*. Alexandria, VA: Author.

Press-Register Staff. (2010, March 5). Principal and after-school program director recognized by Alabama Community Education Association [Blog post]. *Mobile Press-Register*. Retrieved from http://www.makeitstick.org/content/st-paul-elementary-school-makes-learning-stick

St. Paul elementary school makes learning stick [Blog post]. (2010, July 23). Retrieved from http://www.makeitstick.org/content/st-paul-elementary-school-makes-learning-stick

Vollmer, J. (2010). *Schools cannot do it alone*. Fairfield, IA: Enlightenment Press.

Welter, D. (2010, August 6). Iowa school/community partnerships improve academics, attendance, and more! [Blog post]. Retrieved from http://www.makeitstick.org/content/iowa-school-community-partnerships-improve-academics-attendance-and-more

Young, P. (2009). *Principal matters: 101 tips for creating collaborative relationships between after-school programs and school leaders*. New Albany, OH: School-Age NOTES.

Jodi Grant
Executive Director, Afterschool Alliance

Joan Higginbotham
Director of Community Relations, Lowe's

Reinaldo Llano
Director of Community Relations,
Bright House Networks

Lisa Lucheta
Principal and Owner, Torani

Business Leaders: Expanding Afterschool and Summer Learning Opportunities Can Make a Bottom Line Difference

For a number of years, business leaders have voiced concern over the future workforce, citing that many young people entering the workforce are ill equipped. Leaders say students need stronger social, teamwork, and critical thinking skills, as well as more opportunities to learn and explore in a hands-on setting.

Jodi Grant, executive director of the Afterschool Alliance, sat down with several business leaders who serve on the Afterschool Alliance Board of Directors to gain a better understanding of their perspectives, and to discuss how afterschool programs can help.

• •

A new study is issued every couple weeks that raises alarm over our future workforce. Often cited is the need for stronger communication, teamwork, leadership and critical thinking skills, as well as more science, technology, engineering, and math students. What is the most important skill set tomorrow's workforce needs, and are we doing enough to develop those skills?

Reinaldo Llano: I've seen the reports, and they ring true. One of the reasons our company, Bright House Networks, and the cable industry more broadly, are so supportive of afterschool programs is that we know they can help our workforce pipeline. We need employees with a broad range of skills, from excellent social and communications skills for customer service and sales to highly skilled technicians who can continually develop as new products are introduced to the market.

Joan Higginbotham: Academics are paramount; but they are not sufficient without social, communication, and critical thinking skills.

We are in a different place than my parents were; the workplace is highly technical. Employees need to think about what is happening and make real-time decisions that require a lot of thought. The ability to get along in a team setting is also essential for success.

Lisa Lucheta: From a purely business perspective, the skills required of our future workforce are different from those of even the recent past. In this highly technical, connected world, critical problem solving, collaboration, and innovative thinking will be key skills. Afterschool programs are essential in delivering content that support development of these skills.

Higginbotham: Afterschool helps in all of these arenas. Not only do students get academic enrichment, they build social skills in group settings, thus, self-confidence and self-esteem, which are critical to self-development.

What is so special about the kinds of experiences afterschool programs provide?

Lucheta: Opportunities for creative development and self-expression have been minimized or eliminated in the regular school day for many children. Afterschool programs place a priority on creative youth development. They play a critical role in sparking interest in learning for kids, helping to keep kids in school and on a path to graduation.

In an afterschool program, kids might work together to build a community garden or develop a music video; in doing so, they must lead, negotiate, plan, and communicate. And all the while they are learning, being expressive, and creating something of value.

Llano: Afterschool programs are great at exposing students to career paths. Kids have the chance to develop informal, friendly relationships with experts and professionals and really get their hands around a subject matter. An engineer may help them build robots, or a visiting artist may design a mural with them.

Afterschool programs incorporate incredible hands-on projects that make intimidating subjects like science and technology exciting and appealing. We desperately need more young people to engage in these subjects, and to pursue tech careers.

Higginbotham: Afterschool programs provide exposure. For a lot of youth, that is all they need. . . . You can't do something if you don't know it exists.

This is particularly true in underserved communities. These kids might not have the same opportunities as other kids. An internship in an office, or a visit to a real science lab, may be their first experience of a professional setting. It can provide a whole new view of the world and unlock their own potential.

We must ensure these children have exposure to the experiences that quality afterschool programs offer. It can provide the impetus for kids to strive to do something with their lives.

· ·

From a business standpoint, what will be the impact on our nation if we don't ensure all kids have access to these kinds of experiences?

Higginbotham: If we don't start taking the need to develop these skills seriously, we'll have to import a skilled workforce. The quality of education has declined, and many of our students in the U.S. are not competing on the same level with their peers across the ocean.

We are missing an enormous opportunity to cultivate this generation of students, and that concerns me on several levels. From a business standpoint, who is going to run our future businesses? From a personal standpoint, how are our young people going to fend for themselves as adults in an ever-increasing competitive global market?

· ·

You sound pretty passionate about this. Why is this issue important to you?

Higginbotham: I had the sort of experience we're talking about as a kid, in a program called Inroads, and it had a tremendous impact on me and my career.

I was good with math and science, but I did not know what to do with my skills until I took part in Inroads. The program showed me what I could do with math and science in the real world . . . and led me to pursue a career in engineering and then to become an astronaut.

Llano: My whole life is shaped by my afterschool experience. I was at a critical point in high school. I had really disconnected from school, had stopped going to class and started to fail, when a counselor suggested I take part in an afterschool program.

In the program, we received college and career counseling and went on college field trips. More importantly, someone inspired me to do my best. Our rapport with the afterschool staff was different than any I had ever had with an adult or educator.

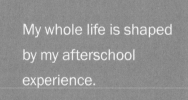

My whole life is shaped by my afterschool experience.

I will never forget visiting the family of one of the afterschool staffers. It was my first visit to a community outside of my experience. She had gone to Wellesley and her family lived in an upscale neighborhood in Massachusetts. They were my first Latino role models; they gave me something to strive to become. I thought, "I want a house like this, a neighborhood like this."

She also sacrificed to run our afterschool program. She could have worked anywhere, making much more money. That put a personal onus on us to be the best we could be; we felt accountable to her and ourselves.

It was the afterschool program that connected me back into school, inspired me to get involved, to meet people and make friends.

Lucheta: I've seen the "spark" that afterschool programs can ignite firsthand, through our work with local programs. From "teaching" science and art classes at our local Northern San Mateo County Boys and Girls Club to sponsoring an 8-week art class in a San Francisco Beacon program to interacting with our nationwide afterschool label contest winners, it is clear to me that the engagement, potential for learning and social interaction present in these programs provide tremendous opportunities for these children to be more successful in school and in their lives.

....

Lisa, tell us more about Torani's work to support afterschool programs. Why have you made afterschool programs a focus of your charitable work?

Lucheta: For Torani, being in business is more than just doing business. It's about the positive impact we make in our communities. It's also about adding creativity to people's lives.

Since 1925, Torani has made ingredients that go into flavorful and creative beverages worldwide. Our flavoring syrups, sauces, and other beverage products are synonymous with creativity and invention. Our interest in creative expression led us to focus our activities on youth in our communities and their access to creative expression.

For the last 9 years, Torani has conducted our "Art for Kids" label contest in afterschool programs nationwide. The afterschool students' winning artwork is displayed around the world on bottles of our Torani syrup. Torani donates 5% of the sales of these syrups to the Afterschool Alliance.

It's very gratifying for us to know we are promoting the artistic talents of children through our contest and, that through this program, we are making a financial contribution to quality afterschool programs.

....

What has been the impact on your business?

Lucheta: We have begun to incorporate our community efforts around afterschool into our work with our value chain partners. One example of this was Torani's "Our Café Gives Back" program in Seattle. We engaged our café partners in the area by creating Torani beverages whose sales would benefit the local afterschool program of their choice. It was a good way for our customers to engage their customers in an effort that would directly benefit their community.

The Art for Kids program has also been wonderful in nurturing employee morale and the collaborative team approach that is part of our culture at Torani. Our entire team votes on the artwork to be selected for the labels each year in April. Team members are delighted to present awards to the winning students, bring them Torani syrup with their own labels, and host an Italian soda and pizza party for their programs. It helps us all to be closely aligned with our vision and values, to benefit from each others' thinking, and to spur growth and innovation. The program resonates with our team members.

Reinaldo, Bright House Networks has also created a company-wide afterschool initiative, supporting efforts to expand programs nationally and donating more than $1 million to local afterschool programs. What led Bright House Networks to invest in afterschool?

Llano: We have our customers to thank for guiding us toward investing in afterschool. In 2005, we conducted consumer research to better understand the issues our customers cared about and where they thought we could best make an impact. Our customers told us loud and clear that afterschool programs were important to them, and they felt Bright House Networks could help.

We have a relationship with our customers; they allow us in their homes to provide cable service. Our afterschool investments allow us to give back and get involved in our communities in a personal way.

We provide financial support to key organizations in our service areas, such as Boys & Girls Clubs, Police Athletic Leagues, YMCAs, and smaller afterschool providers. We also offer free high speed Internet for computer labs, video services, and equipment that give kids access to technology and information. Nationally we are a champion for the Afterschool Alliance and their phenomenal work to expand and improve afterschool programs to the millions of young people and their families who really need and want them.

The unique nature of afterschool programs—the variety of partnerships and partners, the quality of programming, the creativity and flexibility of the space—makes it a really great fit for us to put our resources to use for the community.

What has been the impact on your business?

Llano: People have a more positive view of our company since we began investing in afterschool programs. We have great stories to tell about the impact we are making— and even better, we have made meaningful connections in the communities we serve. We have seen kids' lives changing.

Supporting afterschool programs has helped differentiate us in a positive way to our customers.

Do any of you have any final words of advice or recommendations to offer?

Lucheta: Our collective passion for and commitment to high quality afterschool experiences is evident. Business leaders, whether they are heads of large corporations in the nation's biggest cities or they run small businesses anywhere in this great nation, should weigh in to ensure that quality afterschool programs are well supported and are available and accessible to all children in every community across America. It is in the business interest to strengthen the 21st Century Community Learning Centers to make sure they include school-community partnerships and engaged learning that broadens our young people's skills. We need to do more to support and build local afterschool and summer learning partnerships in neighborhoods that don't have them, but need them. It's nothing short of a national imperative in order to ensure that America remains competitive and maintains its leadership in our global economy.

ABOUT THE PARTICIPANTS

Jodi Grant has served since 2005 as executive director of the Afterschool Alliance, a nonprofit public awareness and advocacy organization working to ensure that all children and youth have access to quality, affordable afterschool programs. Previously, she served as director of Work and Family Programs with the National Partnership for Women and Families. Grant has also worked on Capitol Hill in various Senate staff positions.

Joan Higginbotham is director of community relations for Lowe's, Inc. An engineer and a former NASA astronaut, she flew aboard Space Shuttle Discovery mission STS-116 as a mission specialist. Higginbotham is the third African American woman to go into space. She has a bachelor's degree in electrical engineering from Southern Illinois University and two master's degrees—one in management and one in space systems—from Florida Institute of Technology. She has earned many varied awards, from the Commendation of Merit for Service to the Department of Defense to the Presidential Sports Award in bicycling and weight training. She joined the board of the Afterschool Alliance in 2010.

Reinaldo Llano is director of community relations for Bright House Networks, the nation's 6th largest owner and operator of cable systems, serving 2.4 million customers. He is responsible for a multi-million dollar charitable giving and community outreach program. Llano has served on the Afterschool Alliance board since 2007 and is actively engaged in a number of other community and youth-serving organizations. He is a proud graduate of afterschool programs, which he credits with helping him stay in school and launch a successful career.

Lisa Lucheta is principal and owner of Torani, a company that produces flavoring syrups, sauces, and blended drink bases. Started in 1925 by her grandparents Rinaldo and Ezilda Torani, the company currently engages over 100 employees. Torani products are made in South San Francisco, California, and are distributed in more than 40 countries. Vice-chair of the Afterschool Alliance board, Lucheta has served on the organization's board since 2007.

Reuben Jacobson
Senior Associate for Research and Strategy,
Coalition for Community Schools at the Institute
for Educational Leadership

Martin J. Blank
President, Institute for Educational Leadership
and Director, Coalition for Community Schools

The Afterschool and Community School Connection: Expanding Learning Opportunities and Partnerships

When community and school leaders in Tulsa, Oklahoma, faced the challenge of providing meaningful instruction, youth development, and recreational opportunities for students during the summer, they turned to their existing community school partners for help. Over 40 partners provided summer learning experiences for about 400 children, just as they do during the regular school year, both after school and during the school day. Without a culture of partnerships, children would not have these rich opportunities available for learning and development.

Tulsa is one example of an increasing number of communities across around the country that are using the community school strategy and its reliance on partnerships to provide expanded learning opportunities—before, after, and during traditional school hours, as well as on weekends and during summers.

Just as community schools typically orchestrate local partnerships in order to provide afterschool programs, comprehensive afterschool programs that have strong community partners—such as those funded with 21st Century Community Learning Centers initiative monies—can more easily be broadened and deepened to become community schools. For example, the Lincoln Community Learning Centers Initiative was built with 21st Century Community Learning Centers funds, and Chicago has used these funds in a similar way in many schools. The funding stream provided by this key federal initiative has, in fact, been a vital resource for the afterschool component of community schools across the nation.

Partnerships are essential in the current economic climate. Funding from states, cities, and districts for summer and afterschool opportunities has been drastically reduced, and fewer students are receiving afterschool academic reinforcement and enrichment, as well as summer supports that are essential in improving student outcomes (Fleming, 2011; Benning & Athavaley, 2009). With budgets under continued threat and challenging economic prospects, schools must build deep and intentional relationships with community partners to expand learning opportunities. In addition, these circumstances make it even more important to maintain strong support for the 21st Century Community Learning Centers initiative and to encourage greater use of federal Title I monies for community schools and for expanded learning opportunities after school and during the summers.

The Community School Strategy

What are community schools, and how do they work? A community school is a place and a set of partnerships connecting school, family, and community. Community schools reach families and community residents by extending learning after school, over weekends, and during the summertime and by making the school open to the entire neighborhood.

In many ways, a community school is like a smartphone. With a smartphone, you can select any "app" and receive the services you need. At a community school—as a "smartschool"—key stakeholders, including students, parents, educators, community members, and partners, all work together to determine what "apps," or what opportunities and supports, students, family members, and residents need. They identify partners who can provide those opportunities, and then integrate partner assets and expertise into the core work of the school, helping to enrich the curriculum, construct deep and motivating student learning experiences during and beyond the school day, and create the right conditions for teaching and learning.

What sort of opportunities do community schools typically offer? The answer varies based on local need and resources, though most typically offer a combination of the following:

- *Early childhood opportunities*
- *Engaged learning in the classroom*
- *Expanded learning opportunities, including afterschool and summers*
- *Family engagement*

- *Health and social supports*

- *Youth development*

- *College and career assistance*

- *Community engagement*

Like a smartphone, community schools also have an operating system that makes all the "apps" work in a synchronized manner. A school-site leadership team, often comprised of a supportive principal, teachers, students, parents, support staff, community partners, and others, is responsible for creating a shared vision, identifying desired results, and helping to align and integrate the work of partners with the school. Additionally, a community school coordinator—ideally full time—is an essential ingredient of successful efforts. The coordinator works hand-in-hand with the principal, and is responsible for building relationships with school staff and community partners, engaging the community, and coordinating an efficient delivery of supports to students, both inside and outside of the classroom.

Community schools function and are sustained most effectively when they are part of a system of community schools that spans grade levels, school buildings, and school districts and are embedded in the culture of the school district and the community. These scaled-up systems typically have a community leadership group, as well as an intermediary organizational partner that connects school-site work to communitywide decision making. Community-level strategies can have significant benefits for scaled-up expanded learning efforts.

In Tulsa (www.tacsi.org), where there are 22 community schools and a community leadership group that includes two superintendents and community leaders, it was natural for leaders who wanted to create enriching summer opportunities to reach out to community partners. They asked partners such as the American Red Cross, Boy Scouts, the Tulsa City-County Library, the Tulsa Health Department, and others, who were already organized at the community level and were already working in community schools, to step up and fill in the summer gap—and they did. Community school coordinators, primarily funded through Title I, are essential to getting partners organized to support students.

In Multnomah County (Portland), Oregon, multiple community partnerships align expanded learning opportunities for afterschool, weekends, and summers with the core mission of the school system to support student learning. There are 68 Schools Uniting Neighborhoods (SUN) community schools (http://web.multco.us/sun/sun-community-schools) in the county. At the systems level, the SUN Coordinating Council brings together representatives from each of six participating school districts, the county, the Portland mayor's office, and business and community partners to drive the SUN initiative. The lead partner at each SUN school signs a collaboration agreement that establishes the results and strategies they will use to achieve results. The agreement, which is reviewed annually, states that "All SUN CS (community schools) services are to be linked with the school day and are planned and delivered in close collaboration with the school principal and staff." A recent study found that students in SUN schools have higher attendance and earned more credits towards graduation than their matched peers.

The community school strategy supports rural communities in identifying expanded learning opportunities, as well. The Bangor Area School District in rural Pennsylvania has 3,347 students, 35% of whom were eligible for free and reduced lunch in 2010–an increase of 12 percentage points over 4 years. Bangor's schools are part of the United Way of Greater Lehigh Valley's Community Partners for Student Success (COMPASS), a regional community school initiative. The initiative leverages 21st Century Community Learning Center dollars, as well as community-based assets. Bangor's community schools partner with local banks, community colleges, faith-based institutions, local government, and others, to support expanded learning activities. According to Jill Pereira, the director of COMPASS, "The community school strategy has helped Bangor engage local partners such as the business community differently. They are more than funding partners as they support apprenticeships, weekend and summer learning experiences, service projects, and more."

> The importance of parent engagement to a child's academic success is widely acknowledged . . . Parents also are decision makers who are part of the process of identifying programs and activities for students.

The importance of parent engagement to a child's academic success is widely acknowledged, and community schools offer multiple pathways to engage parents. In a community school, parents often participate in adult-focused activities in the school building, such as ESL or GED classes, family literacy programs, and computer training. These activities are often provided in conjunction with afterschool, evening, and weekend programs and in collaboration with community partners. Community schools also involve parents through family nights; intensive parent outreach, including home visits; and parent leadership programs.

Parents also are decision makers who are part of the process of identifying programs and activities for students. In Cincinnati (http://clcinstitute.org/), parents at Ethel M. Taylor Academy participate in the school's Local School Decision Making Committee (LSDMC), which makes decisions about which partners to bring into the school to support student learning. For example, the LSDMC assessed afterschool providers and made the decision to offer tennis lessons. This choice strengthened the neighborhood by bringing activity to an under-utilized community tennis court while also teaching students about math principles in an engaging manner.

Many other places use a partnership strategy to expand learning opportunities in their community schools as well. In New York City, the Children's Aid Society (http://nationalcenterforcommunityschools.childrensaidsociety.org) serves as the lead partner agency for 22 community schools. Funded in part by 21st Century Community Learning Centers and Title I funds, they provide enriching afterschool activities such as dance, music, cooking classes, leadership development, and college readiness activities to support student learning.

Partnerships support college and career goals as well. In Philadelphia, the Netter Center for Community Partnerships at the University of Pennsylvania (http://www.upenn.edu/ccp/index.php) provides enriching and engaging opportunities to students at nearby Sayre High School. Teachers extol the benefits of having a partner with expertise and resources to support classroom instruction through activities such as hands-on labs and small group projects led by Penn students. Participating students are developing college and career readiness skills in the health field through expanded learning opportunities that include clinical practice, outreach to the community, community health development projects, health careers education, and professional skills development.

Beyond their direct impact on students and their families, community schools offer another crucial advantage to school and community leaders: community schools generate public support for public education. Community schools and comprehensive afterschool programs with community partners are often strongly connected.

By mobilizing the assets and expertise of community partners to offer enriched and expanded learning opportunities for students after school and over weekends and summers and to address nonschool factors influencing achievement, community schools give everyone a role and a responsibility in the education of our young people. From a community-schools perspective, a range of stakeholders across various sectors of the community—business, higher education, nonprofit, government, faith-based and neighborhood groups—must contribute to the education of our children. Our nation will only achieve its education goals by engaging the entire community in deep and purposeful partnerships with the host of organizations in our communities that have a stake in the success of our young people.

> Beyond their direct impact on students and their families, community schools offer another crucial advantage to school and community leaders: community schools generate public support for public education.

Recommendations

A community's decision to expand learning opportunities and partnerships after school and during the summer can be a catalyst for developing a community school. Conversely, community schools are a natural venue to expand learning and partnerships for students and families beyond the typical school day and year. Both necessitate adopting effective strategies for engaging in an open and positive dialogue with school and community entities, mobilizing all the assets in a community, aligning efforts with the school's improvement plan, and affirming a commitment to enriching and engaging opportunities that motivate students to learn and expand their experiences so that they can be successful.

We offer the following recommendations for schools, school districts, and partners in order to strengthen learning opportunities after school and over the summer using community school partnerships.

- **Maximize the funding, partnership, and family engagement elements of the 21st Century Community Learning Centers initiative to develop and deliver comprehensive afterschool and summer learning programs.** *If appropriate, sustain these efforts by building them "up and out" to be community schools.*

- **Encourage greater use of the federal Title I monies, including supplemental educational services (SES) monies, both for expanding learning opportunities after school and during summers and for initiating and sustaining community schools.**

- **Apply the community school strategy to enhance and sustain expanding learning opportunity efforts.** *Successful community schools around the country have incorporated afterschool and summer learning and expanded learning partners as a central part of their work.*

- **Incentivize partnerships that support expanding learning afterschool and over summers.** *More places are seeing that expanded learning opportunities are most effective when supported and sustained by multiple partnerships. Funders should require or incentivize community school partnerships as part of their application process.*

- **Leverage funding through the community school strategy.** *Community schools are able to leverage funding from partners; city, state, and federal government; philanthropies; and other sources. By diversifying their funding, community schools ensure continued support of expanded learning opportunities and other activities.*

For More Information

Learn More

Visit a community school. The best way to see the myriad of activity taking place before, during, and after the school day is to visit one of the many community schools around the country.

Read More

Community-Based Learning: Engaging Students for Success and Citizenship (http://www.communityschools.org/assets/1/AssetManager/CBL_Book_1_27_06.pdf)

www.communityschools.org

Expanding the learning day: An essential component of the community schools strategy in *New Directions for Youth Development*, Fall 2011.

Scaling Up School and Community Partnerships: The Community Schools Strategy (www.communityschools.org/scalingup) guides schools, districts, and partners through the stages of starting and scaling up a community school strategy.

Financing Community Schools: Leveraging Resources to Support Student Success (http://www.communityschools.org/resources/capacity_building__finance.aspx)

ABOUT THE AUTHORS

Reuben Jacobson is the senior associate for research and strategy for the Coalition for Community Schools at the Institute for Educational Leadership. Previously, Reuben worked at the American Institutes for Research (AIR) and spent two tremendously challenging and wonderful years teaching fifth and sixth grade students in D.C. Public Schools as a D.C. Teaching Fellow. Reuben has a master's degree in education policy from the George Washington University and a master of arts in teaching degree from American University.

Martin J. Blank is the president of the Institute for Educational Leadership and the director of the Coalition for Community Schools. A VISTA volunteer in the 1960s, Marty has extensive experience developing school and community partnership and was co-author of the seminal report *Together We Can: Crafting a Profamily System of Education and Human Services*.

REFERENCES

Benning, T., & Athavaley, A. (2009, June 25). The summer of their discontent. *The Wall Street Journal*. Retrieved from http://online.wsj.com/article/SB1000142405297020462190457424777292809 5730.html

Fleming, N. (2011, June 2). Summer budget crunch: Call for cuts or creativity? [Blog post]. Retrieved from http://blogs.edweek.org/edweek/beyond_schools/2011/06/a_few_weeks_ago_i. html?qs=summer

Elaine M. Johannes
Associate Professor and Extension Specialist –
Youth Development, School of Family Studies
and Human Services, Kansas State University

Cathy Mullins
Assistant to the Provost/Grants Officer,
Shawnee State University

Marcia J. Dvorak
Director, Kansas Enrichment Network,
University of Kansas

Bringing Universities Into the Mix: New Opportunities for Enhancing Afterschool and Summer Learning Programs

We can be wise only together.

- Margaret J. Wheatley

The Potential of Partnerships for Creating New Opportunities

Combining the efforts of afterschool providers and institutions of higher education creates a wealth of opportunities for children and communities:

- *Padgette, Deich, and Russell (2010) suggest that postsecondary institutions can help with data collection, research, and program evaluation; provide facilities and staff training; identify quality curricula and link programs to statewide standards; and provide mentors and volunteers.*

- *America's Promise notes that postsecondary institutions can serve as catalysts, conveners, providers, partners, innovators, and civic generators (America's Promise, 2004, p. 14).*

- *Lawson (2010) outlines a partnership model that specifies a variety of supports that can be provided by universities to community partners, including*

  - service learning programs and internships for undergraduate and graduate students that place them in community-based settings;

  - joint grant development and other revenue-generating programs and services;

- initiatives designed to provide training, technical assistance, and capacity-building supports; and

- a centralized office with stable, visible, and talented leaders who provide a single point of contact and a firm basis for ongoing communication and partnership management.

Tapping and utilizing these resources allows afterschool programs to benefit from a rich exchange of knowledge and experiences.

There are many examples of powerful afterschool-higher education collaboration in urban areas and medium to large cities. Schools and community groups based in smaller towns and rural communities, however, often do not regard public colleges and universities—which might be 50 or 100 miles away—as a resource for starting up, expanding, or improving afterschool and summer learning programs or for assisting them with their 21st Century Community Learning Centers. Likewise, many colleges and universities also may not see the potential for an afterschool partnership with schools and community groups in small towns and rural areas.

These partnerships are worth exploring, however, because they combine both like-minded and unlike-minded individuals and organizations into creative alliances that can achieve powerful results. While such partnerships require time; commitment; and systematic, intentional, results-focused efforts, they can also eliminate inefficient institutional siloing, unnecessary competition, and contentious thinking. This potential can be explained this way: "[L]arge-scale social change comes from better cross-sector coordination rather than from the isolated intervention of individual organizations" (Kania & Kramer, 2011, p. 38).

Bringing New Experiences to Students in Hutchinson, Kansas

Botany. Nursing. Physical therapy. Computer design. These classes are not typical for young people, but thanks to a partnership with the Hutchinson Community College, middle school students are able to see what these educational and career paths are like.

Nickerson School District, South Hutchinson, Kansas, is home to the Leadership Enrichment and Academic Learning Academy, which works with 369 children in grades K–12 to improve behavior and engagement in learning through community partnerships, notably with local universities. Inside the classroom, college aides are among the program instructors that help students form aspirations for their futures and prepare for higher education. Outside the classroom, middle school and high school students take part in awareness learning days at Hutchinson Community College, where they have the opportunity to explore new fields of study in a hands-on environment and university setting. At the culmination of eighth grade, students take a trip to Kansas State University where they tour the campus and meet with students serving as program ambassadors. In high school, students work closely with Hutchinson Community College and Sterling College on their performing arts programs, where they produce single act plays. The students are involved in every aspect of the show, including script writing, acting, designing lighting and sound systems, and set building.

The following real-life examples tell the story and show the potential of university-afterschool partnerships that could be created in every state, especially states with large numbers of rural or low-income communities.

....

Shawnee State University

Shawnee State University (SSU) is the lead institution of the Ohio South Consortium that manages the 21st Century Community Learning Centers programs established as "After School Malls" in 39 school-based sites across seven school districts in Appalachian Ohio. The area is made up of small, rural towns with high unemployment, high poverty, and low educational attainment. The university is an open-access institution with a mission to serve communities, including providing afterschool services.

The Ohio South Consortium reflects a robust school-university collaboration. Participating school districts interview and hire 21st Century Community Learning Centers site coordinators, who meet regularly to share ideas and resources and assist the consortium director in planning professional development. The university writes the grants, manages research, houses administrative staff, serves as fiscal agent, and schedules evaluation visits. University facilities house afterschool events. Faculty and student clubs provide learning experiences and connect programs to resources.

SSU also offers a summer enrichment day camp for students in the region. Students from 21st Century Community Learning Centers sites receive scholarships to attend and are provided transportation.

Bloom Vernon Elementary School

Bloom Vernon is one of SSU's long-time 21st Century Community Learning Centers partners. Assistant Principal Sandy Smith notes, "The university's involvement is a huge plus. Shawnee provides accountability, administrative and technical support, and has helped our district and others in the county build relationships that extend beyond the afterschool programs." The school district credits afterschool programming for generating life-changing differences for many attendees.

The Ohio South Consortium and SSU have provided the operational framework for southern Ohio's 21st Century Community Learning Centers program for 12 years. The collaboration works well because of well-established relationships between the university and the community, starting with their collaboration in 1992 to expand Tech Prep programming to area high school students. Largely a commuter campus, SSU has a familiar feel to local residents. Even if funding levels change for the 21st Century Community Learning Centers programs, SSU will doubtless remain an active partner in providing a safe learning environment to students enrolled in afterschool and summer programs.

....

Kansas State University

Though there is some measure of funding available to support 21st Century Community Learning Centers in rural areas, resources are often inadequate, resulting in an uneven patchwork of afterschool programs with varying standards and limited scopes. The good news is that opportunities to address these challenges exist through partnerships with land grant universities located in each state and territory of the United States.

Through its extension educator network, Kansas State University, the oldest land grant university in the nation, has successfully built and sustained partnerships for rural afterschool. The university has established partnerships with an array of local afterschool programs, from small town stand-alones to large, centrally administered 21st Century Community Learning Centers afterschool programs. Additionally, Kansas State supports 4-H afterschool clubs on three military installations.

Given the variety of operational challenges that 21st Century Community Learning Centers grantees in rural areas may face, partnering with land grant universities provides many types of support to help programs overcome those challenges. Such partnerships can provide university students with opportunities for student teaching and conducting research studies and concomitantly can provide afterschool and summer programs with additional staff and evaluation services. While these are typical examples of community partnerships for most major universities, regardless of their mission or location, there are additional important extension/outreach roles especially for land grant universities:

- *conducting needs assessments to establish afterschool programs;*
- *training for program leaders in evidence-based practice, positive youth development, and learning theory;*
- *identifying quality curriculum (e.g., science, healthy living, citizenship) that can be appropriately tailored for delivery in rural areas;*
- *bringing resources to the community through grant writing and marketing;*
- *cooperating with programs that address the needs of families; and*
- *providing research-based information for public policy changes (Ferrari, Linville, & Valentine, 2003).*

Council Grove, Kansas

Council Grove (population 2,182) is one rural community that has partnered successfully with Kansas State University to host a 21st Century Community Learning Centers program. Council Grove wanted to broaden its afterschool offerings to address the community's high child obesity rate and lack of formal venues for physical activity for children and youth. With an understanding of the university's mission, leadership in Council Grove and Unified School District 417 worked with university faculty to acquire federal funding for a 5-year research and extension project, the "Power Up Club" for elementary students in an afterschool setting. Focusing on healthy living and physical activity, the club was led by Council Grove high school students who had been trained in an evidence-based health curriculum by Kansas State faculty. In addition to training, university faculty provided evaluation support and documentation of the program's impact on youth. The success of the program motivated Council Grove high school students to expand "Power Up Clubs" into summer healthy-activity day camps, and the program has become a model for rural afterschool programs across the state (Children, Youth and Families Education and Research Network, n.d.).

This successful partnership between a major university and a small town would have not been possible without an understanding of the land grant university's mission—teaching, research, and outreach—and a respect for the capacity of town and afterschool leaders. It is this sort of mutual understanding that will serve afterschool programs well as they seek to partner with their state's land grant universities.

Kansas Enrichment Network

The Kansas Enrichment Network serves as an intermediary to afterschool providers across the state. Seeking "collective impact," the network collaborates with afterschool programs, universities, and a host of other community-based organizations. The University of Kansas manages the fiscal responsibilities, freeing the network to establish partnerships that strengthen services to 21st Century Community Learning Centers grantees and other afterschool providers.

Recently, the Kansas Enrichment Network facilitated an outreach effort by Kansas State and Cornell University to provide training in positive youth development to afterschool providers. Dropout prevention events were enhanced through Wichita State University's assistance. A statewide infrastructure around science, technology, engineering, and math (STEM) has been created for stakeholders in Kansas who seek to increase STEM opportunities for youth. Outreach to afterschool program providers across the state, including those in rural and low-income communities, was strengthened through collaborations with the University of Kansas, Fort Hays State, Johnson County Community College, Kansas City Kansas Community College, and intermingling partnerships through Kansas State. Collectively, these higher education partners are bringing valuable stakeholders, resources, rigor, and relevancy to the table.

Faculty members on the network's advisory board heighten benefits. Presentations and discussions afford members increased understanding of youth and brain development and promising practices. Credibility soars as afterschool research is sprinkled into conversation.

Recommendations

- **Schools should seek out institutions of higher learning.** *If you are involved in a local afterschool program or a local or state afterschool network, seek out help and support from your local colleges, especially land grant institutions or public colleges in rural areas because they often have a mission to improve educational and youth development opportunities and to strengthen communities and schools. For a land grant university, this connection is typically managed through its extension services, employing both university and community-based educators.*

- **Colleges and universities should seek out afterschool partnerships.** *If you are professionally affiliated with a university, especially a land grant institution or a public college in a rural part of a state, seek outreach opportunities by considering partnerships with 21st Century Community Learning Centers sites and other afterschool programs because they help fulfill that aspect of your mission.*

- **Partnerships require a full commitment.** *When you create partnerships, you should build in the time and commitment to ensure that they are strong and sustainable. Relationships must be built and nurtured before partnerships are realized. This requires time and dedication from all stakeholders. Commitment flourishes when partnerships complement each other's strengths and support each other's weaknesses to the desired purpose. Partners should foster open communication and celebrate success.*

- **Partnerships should blend rigor and relevancy.** *All stakeholders seek quality opportunities for children and youth to prepare them for success in school and life. Universities foster rigorous research, innovative ideas, and knowledge of promising practices. They can contribute to partnerships by unpacking research to make it relevant and practical for program implementation.*

- **Success depends on mutual understanding and mutual respect.** *Partners should work to foster understanding across community sectors. They should learn about each other, develop mutual respect, and commit to the common purpose.*

ABOUT THE AUTHORS

Elaine M. Johannes is associate professor and an extension specialist in the School of Family Studies and Human Services at Kansas State University. She is also the co-director of Kansas Operation Military Kids (OMK) and co-principal investigator of the seven-state Community Program to Prevention Childhood Obesity, funded by USDA/AFRI. Johannes has directed two, 5-year USDA grants in the prevention of youth-related problem behaviors (e.g., substance abuse, teen pregnancy, school dropout, delinquency, and violence) through effective afterschool programming in Kansas.

Cathy Mullins is the academic grants officer and assistant to the provost at Shawnee State University. Since 2000, she has successfully authored several 21st Century Community Learning Center grants for southern Ohio school districts, as well as served in a consultant capacity for other organizations' submissions. Mullins holds an MBA and BS in Communications from Ohio University.

Marcia J. Dvorak, statewide network lead of the Kansas Enrichment Network, has worked in the youth development field for 5 years. Previously, she was a teacher, director of gifted education, and elementary principal in Illinois. Dvorak holds a PhD in curriculum and teaching from the University of Kansas, a master's degree in educational administration from Western Illinois University, and a bachelor's degree in elementary education from Quincy University.

REFERENCES

America's Promise—The Alliance for Youth. (2004). *Connecting communities with colleges and universities: Strategies to strengthen local promise efforts through higher education involvement.* Retrieved from http://www.compact.org/wp-content/uploads/resources/downloads/APEU04.pdf

Children, Youth and Families Education and Research Network. (n.d.). Local CYFAR program spotlight: Power Up Club, Morris County, Kansas. Retrieved from http://www1.cyfernet.org/cyfar/02-08-KS-Power.html

Ferrari, T., Linville, I., & Valentine, N. (2003, April 21). 4-H afterschool rationale, program delivery models, and theoretical base: A reference for extension professionals. Retrieved from Florida 4-H Youth Development website: http://florida4h.org/afterschool/doc/FerrariPaper.doc

Kania, J., & Kramer, M. (2011, Winter). Collective impact. *Stanford Social Innovation Review.* Retrieved from http://www.ssireview.org/images/articles/2011_WI_Feature_Kania.pdf

Lawson, H. (2010). An appreciation and a selective enhancement of the developing model for university-assisted community schools. *Universities and Community Schools*, 8, 5–20.

Padgette, H., Deich, S., & Russell, L. (2010). *Strengthening partnerships and building public will for out-of-school time programs.* Retrieved from National League of Cities website: http://www.nlc.org/find-city-solutions/iyef/afterschool/afterschool-tools--resources

Val Marmillion
President and Founder, Marmillion + Company

Gene Rose
Executive Vice President, Marmillion + Company

With contributions from the Children's Museum of Indianapolis, Birmingham Civil Rights Institute, Missouri Botanical Garden, and Children's Museum of Pittsburgh

Museums as 21st Century Partners: Empowering Extraordinary "iGeneration" Learning Through Afterschool and Intergenerational Family Learning Programs

Research indicates that informal learning institutions, such as museums, zoos, and aquariums, contribute to nurturing the development of children and families through experiential educational offerings. Indeed, participation in purposeful youth museum programs can greatly enhance and foster family learning. Falk and Dierking (2010) note that 95% of a child's time learning science does not happen in school and that there are many informal learning opportunities for parents to provide their children with a sense of how the world works around them. Thus, what happens outside of school profoundly influences learning. In fact, as much as 33% of the variance in student achievement can be attributed to differences between children whose parents read to them, encourage them to go to college, and take them to the library and cultural events and children whose parents do not provide those supports (Goodwin, 2011).

As research by Weiss, Little, Bouffard, Deschenes, and Malone (2009) found, "Forty years of steadily accumulating research shows that out-of-school or 'complementary learning' opportunities are major predictors of children's development, learning and educational achievement." Even more troubling is that "economically and otherwise disadvantaged children are less likely than their more-advantaged peers to have access to these opportunities" (p. 2).

Learning in the 21st century requires students of the "iGeneration" to develop a set of skills needed to succeed in the workforce and to become productive citizens in our society (Rosen, 2011). These skills cannot be developed in isolation; they depend on the social learning experiences offered in institutions like museums. Through a variety of strategies, including partnering with afterschool and summer learning programs and 21st Century Community Learning Centers, these institutions are modeling the kind of learning that will help parents support and encourage more independent thinking in their children and cultivate their lifelong interest in the world around them.

Extraordinary Family Learning Destination Consortium

A national consortium of 16 large and geographically dispersed museums, zoos, botanical gardens, and historic sites—with a combined market area of over 80 million people—has formed to improve their offerings, services, and outreach to students and schools. The Extraordinary Family Learning Destination Consortium provides the gateway to a "must see and do" collection of exceptional family learning experiences. It seeks to build the capacity of its member organizations to transform the lives of children and families while better serving the communities in which the organizations are located.

The consortium includes

- *Abraham Lincoln Presidential Library and Museum (http://www.alplm.org)*

- *Atlanta History Center (http://www.atlantahistorycenter.com/)*

- *American Folk Art Museum (http://www.folkartmuseum.org/)*

- *Birmingham Civil Rights Institute (http://www.bcri.org)*

- *Children's Museum of Indianapolis (http://www.childrensmuseum.org)*

- *Children's Museum of Pittsburgh (http://www.pittsburghkids.org)*

- *Colonial Williamsburg (http://www.history.org)*

- *Denver Botanic Gardens (http://www.botanicgardens.org/)*

- *George Washington's Mount Vernon Estate, Museum & Gardens (http://www.mountvernon.org/)*

- *Heard Museum (http://www.heard.org)*

- *Kentucky Horse Park (http://kyhorsepark.com/)*

- *National Mississippi River Museum & Aquarium (http://www.mississippirivermuseum.com/)*

- *National Railroad Museum (http://www.nationalrrmuseum.org/en-us/default.aspx)*

- *Please Touch Museum (http://www.pleasetouchmuseum.org/)*

- *San Diego Zoo (http://www.sandiegozoo.org)*

- *Tennessee Aquarium (http://www.tennis.org/Home.aspx)*

> The Extraordinary Family Learning Destination Consortium provides the gateway to a "must see and do" collection of exceptional family learning experiences.

Collectively, the organizations in the consortium constitute a rich resource for afterschool and summer learning programs and 21st Century Community Learning Centers throughout America. They also provide powerful examples of partnerships with afterschool and summer learning programs for other museums, zoos, and historic sites across the nation.

Exemplary Programs

The following are four specific examples that are working particularly well that involve consortium members:

The Children's Museum of Indianapolis – Starpoint Summer Camp and Museum Apprentice Program (MAP).
Each year, more than one million people visit the 11 exhibit galleries in the Children's Museum of Indianapolis, featuring the arts, science, and the humanities. The museum has adopted intergenerational family learning as its signature educational theory. The interactions among family members, spurred by a visit to the museum, result in a greater sense of family connectedness (Wood & Wolf, 2008); moreover, such positive experiences also strengthen the connection of families to museums (Wood & Wolf, 2010).

Two exemplary programs for community and neighborhood youth at the museum were developed to serve children in the summer and after school. One is the 6-week StarPoint summer camp program, which targets approximately 120 underrepresented youth ages 6 - 12 each summer. The camp is structured around exhibit themes and incorporates elements of the arts and humanities, science and technology, and social awareness. The overall goal of StarPoint is to motivate children to become self-directed learners.

Youth participants in MAP acquire or strengthen skills for 21st century learners. For instance, James has been a part of MAP since age 13 and now volunteers in the museum's biotechnology lab on a regular basis.

"I have learned leadership skills and how to work on a team with people with different ways of thinking," he says.

Two of his favorite activities include producing the MAP Music Festival as part of the "Rock Stars, Cars, and Guitars" exhibit and participating in the Lego League as part of the "Lego Castle Adventure" exhibit.

Researchers at Johns Hopkins University documented that access to summer learning opportunities can have a significant effect on the academic future of low-income youth. "More than half of the achievement gap between lower- and higher-income youth can be explained by unequal access to summer learning opportunities. As a result, low-income youth are less likely to graduate from high school or enter college" (Alexander, Entwisle, & Olson, 2007). The StarPoint program helps to bridge this gap. Many StarPoint youth return annually, and several of their parents were once participants in the camp.

A second, more in-depth experience, the Museum Apprentice Program (MAP), is offered each year to approximately 30 youth, ages 13–18. These students come from varied socio-economic backgrounds and represent urban and suburban public schools, private schools, and home-schooled students. The museum's staff is a natural fit for afterschool and summer programs; they can facilitate learning for these youth by providing access to content and technology for research, arranging field trips and site visits, connecting youth with guest experts, and serving as mentors.

• •

Birmingham Civil Rights Institute – Parents Plus Program

The Birmingham Cultural Alliance Partnership (BCAP) consists of a partnership with all of the museums in the city of Birmingham, including the Jazz Hall of Fame, Birmingham Museum of Art, McWane Science Center, Southern Museum of Flight, Birmingham Botanical Gardens, the Vulvan Park and Museum, and the Birmingham Civil Rights Institute. In adherence to the requirements for funding through the 21st Century Community Learning Centers initiative, the BCAP is primarily reaching low-income students who are on the free or reduced lunch program. One of the key features of the partnership is its Parents Plus program that produces parenting workshops focused on addressing children's behavioral issues, relieving stress, and establishing more discipline at home.

> One of the key features of the partnership is its Parents Plus program that produces parenting workshops focused on addressing children's behavioral issues, relieving stress, and establishing more discipline at home.

The efforts of the Birmingham Civil Rights Institute (BCRI) provide a powerful example of connecting affiliated institutions with schools to support student learning. BCRI helps students make cultural connections in the community by spending 2 weeks at each museum. The Institute's permanent and multimedia exhibitions provide a self-directed journey through Birmingham's contributions to the civil rights movement and human rights struggles. With a grant from the 21st Century Community Learning Centers initiative, in a partnership with local schools, more than 200 students take part each year in on-site programs at the school and field trips to each of the museums.

On-site tutoring by museum staff at schools is focused on improving reading and math scores. In addition, the staff provides support for cultural enrichment, physical fitness, and nutrition education activities, as well as youth mentoring programs focused on teaching conflict resolution, leadership, and confidence. Students also learn about volunteering and giving back to the community through civic education and service learning.

Missouri Botanical Garden – Community Science Investigators Project

As one of the top three botanical gardens in the world, the Missouri Botanical Garden (MOBOT) includes a 79-acre urban oasis that is a National Historic Landmark. It also serves as a center for science, conservation, education, and horticultural display, and as such, it includes sophisticated grounds and family programs. One program focuses on biodiversity and sustainability and encourages underserved children to explore nature in their local communities and in their own backyard.

Through a partnership with local schools, and with support from a 21st Century Community Learning Center grant, the institution delivers programming from 4:00 to 6:00 p.m. every day for elementary and high school students within the St. Louis Public Schools. High school students provide co-teaching and mentoring for elementary students.

The afterschool program provides an intentional, rigorous connection to what students are learning during the school day in math, science, the arts, and other subjects and helps them understand the interrelationships among these subjects. In addition, instructors establish expectations for engagement that will inspire student curiosity. By holding family science nights as part of these programs, MOBOT engages families as part of their year-round programming. Parents are encouraged to ask questions and learn as a family unit so they understand how to model the kind of interaction they can have with their children on their own.

Jamiya, age 10, who comes from a single parent home with five other siblings, has shown improvement in her social skills, test scores, and overall grades as a result of her participation in the afterschool program. Prior to entering, she was very quiet and withdrawn, but she now socializes with the other students and shows strong leaderships skills as a blossoming cheerleader and dancer. Without the afterschool program she would not have access to additional academic tutoring, girl scouting, cheerleading, tennis, golf, photography, storytelling workshops, cooking, and African dance through the Harambee Institute.

Children's Museum of Pittsburgh – Youthalive Afterschool Program

The Children's Museum of Pittsburgh has delighted children and families for 28 years through its "Play With Real Stuff" philosophy that asserts that hands-on, interactive learning experiences in which children create and experiment with tangible materials are essential to a child's development.

The museum's YouthAlive Afterschool program partners with nearby middle schools and hosts an afterschool program for sixth and eighth graders. Local artists work with students in a variety of activities that combine the arts and the sciences, such as printmaking, silk screening, pottery, stained glass art, sewing, soldering, and woodworking. The museum's goal is to encourage students to think differently about the learning that takes place in their classroom. Exploration, discovery, and inquiry skills are emphasized throughout the program.

The YouthAlive program is focused on African American and inner-city students. The museum offers a tiered program in which students can get paid if they continue with YouthAlive after ninth grade, or they can receive credit for volunteer hours by participating in a VolunTeens program.

As part of the program, the museum holds an open studio night and dinner for parents of participating children and provides tickets to cultural events in the area to encourage parent-child interaction in informal settings throughout the community. In addition, the museum partners with the University of Pittsburgh Center for Learning to research the life skills that students are learning in out-of-school environments and to study the rich learning that occurs when parents and children are interacting in informal exhibit settings.

Conclusion

The projects and activities described above exemplify the collaborative work produced by museums that ultimately engages youth and their families in afterschool and lifelong learning experiences. Yet, there is more work to be done to address the inequities that exist among populations with regard to access to high quality, informal learning experiences. Developing more museum partnerships with afterschool and summer learning programs in schools and community organizations is one way to overcome this gap.

Overall, there is great potential for the consortium to leverage the major investments made in afterschool and summer programs by the 21st Century Community Learning Centers initiative, the C.S. Mott Foundation, and others to broaden access to high quality, informal learning opportunities in the community and in afterschool and summer learning programs. These programs answer the call of 21st century learning by providing children with opportunities to develop new talents, accomplish larger goals, and build a repertoire of lifelong learning skills for the future.

ABOUT THE AUTHORS

Val Marmillion is a strategic communications specialist and president and founder of Marmillion + Company, a firm that during the last 20 years has provided services to numerous local and national organizations, associations, and businesses.

Gene Rose, a former journalist and government communicator, serves as the firm's executive vice president. The Children's Museum of Indianapolis, the Birmingham Civil Rights Institute, Missouri Botanical Garden and the Children's Museum of Pittsburgh contributed information for this article, on behalf of the Extraordinary Family Learning Destination Consortium. The consortium promotes intergenerational learning experiences at the nation's most prestigious family institutions.

REFERENCES

Alexander, K., Entwisle, D., & Olson, L. (2007). Lasting consequences of the summer learning gap. *American Sociological Review, 72,* 167–180.

Falk, J. H., & Dierking, L. D. (2010). The 95 percent solution. *American Scientist, 98,* 486–492.

Goodwin, B. (2011). *Simply better: Doing what matters most to change the odds for student success.* Denver, CO: McRel.

Rosen, L. D. (2011). Teaching the iGeneration. *Educational Leadership, 68,* 10–15.

Weis, B., Little, P., Bouffard, S., Deschenes, S., & Malone, H. (2009). *The federal role in out-of-school learning: After-school, summer learning, and family involvement as critical learning supports.* Retrieved from Harvard Family Research Project website: http://www.hfrp.org/content/download/3312/97076/file/CL- FederalRoleInOutOfSchoolLearning.pdf

Wood, E., & Wolf, B. (2008). Between the lines of engagement in museums. *Journal of Museum Education, 33*(2), 121–130.

Wood, E., & Wolf, B. (2010). When parents stand back is family learning still possible? *Museums and Social Issues, 5*(1), 35–50.

Dennie Palmer Wolf
Principal Researcher, WolfBrown

Leaf Palaces and Illustration Worlds, or Why the Arts Belong in Out-of-School-Time and Afterschool Programs

As I worked on this article, Hurricane Sandy blew through New York. In my part of Brooklyn, school children had a full week of "out-of-school" time. In those long days I saw cardboard-box houses, gory detailing on Halloween costumes and ghostly front porches, Lego empires and Minecraft worlds, and leaf palaces in playgrounds. It has been a kind of natural experiment—and testament to the very human urge to create, make, and imagine.

> Educating imaginative students will require in- and out-of-school opportunities, the rigor of classroom explorations, and the informal investigations that out-of-school time can nurture.

So it is sobering to think about what has happened to the opportunities to create during the school day. Since accountability for student achievement in math and reading has climbed, and budgets for public education have shrunk, time in the school day for what many people deem "noncore" courses like art, music, and even science, has been shaved. We can—and should —protest this loss. First, federal education laws actually include the arts in the definition of "core subjects." Second, as a nation, we can't afford not to turn that very human urge to create into educated imaginations. At the same time, these constraints should also spur us to seize the opportunities of out-of-school time and in afterschool and summer learning programs. Educating imaginative students will require in- and out-of-school opportunities, the rigor of classroom explorations, and the informal investigations that out-of-school time can nurture.

Think about it this way: Expanded learning opportunities in afterschool and summer programs may provide a setting particularly suited to arts learning. Educators can do more with these ungraded, uninterrupted blocks of time:

- **Offer longer stretches of learning.** *In the school day, time is frequently carved up in 40–50 minute segments. This is hardly enough time to set up, paint, and clean up—or compose—or rehearse.*

- **Introduce children to all kinds of teachers.** *In engaging afterschool and summer learning programs, arts specialists can teach new types of classes, classroom teachers can show off their arts skills, teaching artists can be instructors, and community volunteers can share their skills.[1]*

- **Permit cross-age grouping.** *With no age- and grade-based structures, young people can work across ages and experience levels in ways that permit mentoring, modeling, and apprenticeships.*

- **Foster cross-disciplinary projects.** *Without the subject-matter strictures and structures of the school day, a theater project can be equal parts local history, interviewing skills, and theater production.*

- **Be porous.** *Well-designed afterschool and summer programs, because of their flexibility, allow for more travel and excursions. This could be a quick trip to collect leaves for a printing project, time in the school auditorium to watch the high school step team perform, or a more structured outing to a museum that includes learning to use public transit.*

- **Send the 24/7 message.** *When arts learning extends into out-of-school time, it communicates the message that the arts are not just a "class" but an avocation —even a way of being. A child can carry a sketchbook anywhere; (s)he can write lyrics on the bus.*

A Case in Point: Providence ¡*CityArts*! for Youth

Located in Providence, Rhode Island, ¡*CityArts*! is a community arts organization that has been providing free professional arts education to local young people ages 8–14 since 1992. Acknowledging the need for arts learning out of—as well as in—school, ¡*CityArts*! has joined forces with the Providence Afterschool Alliance (www.mypasa.org), a citywide effort to create "after zones," areas of the city served by a common campus where young adolescents can engage in an elective set of courses that range from athletics to arts. At one participating middle school, Roger Williams, ¡*CityArts*! supports classroom teachers in integrating the arts, partners with arts specialists, and teaches free-standing arts classes in out-of-school time both on campus and at its own studios.

Arts and Evidence-Based Practices

The staff at ¡*CityArts*! think long and hard about designing and implementing the courses that they teach in extended learning time, drawing on a range of evidence-based practices. Just a few examples illustrate how much more than "make and take" these 10-week courses are:

---

1. For two examples of this in action see www.bigthought.org/BigThought/SubNavPages/ThrivingMinds and www.citizenschools.org.

- *Each course is an exploration of major arts skills and techniques folded into a major project where students apply those capacities (Burnaford, Aprill, & Weiss, 2009). For instance in the course Illustration World, 11- to 14-year-olds explore a variety of 2D media, from paint to pastels to pen and ink, and learn the art of bookmaking. They also learn how to create characters and worlds to tell a story, creating books of their own. In the course Community Mural, 8- to 10-year-olds conceive, plan, and paint a giant mural for a community health clinic and plan for its opening.*

- *Each course develops life skills, like communication: ¡CityArts! teaching artists make time for discussion and reflection, interviewing and presenting in ways that build young people's language skills—a particularly important part of learning in a neighborhood where as many as one in three families speaks a language other than English. These are exactly the kinds of oral language outcomes that are featured as an integral part of the English language arts standards in the Common Core.[2] For example, in a current course on heritage, students and teaching artist Victoria Ray have vigorous talks about what makes someone who they are—bringing in everything from accent to dress to what foods they like. At the end of the course, they exhibit and explain their work.*

- *Each course recognizes that family engagement can significantly amplify learning. At the end of every session, youth plan a "Teach Back" session where they become the instructors, make a lesson plan, and invite whomever they want. In that session, they teach the lesson to their guests. Families get an evening out, they experience of the pleasure of being a learner, and they get a deeper understanding of their children's talents and interests. In a neighborhood where many families struggle economically, these events are also a chance to celebrate families' hopes and aspirations for their children.*

The presence of these strong and evidence-based practices is beginning to have a clear impact on Roger Williams students' learning and behavior. As of the 2011–12 school year:

- *chronic absenteeism has dropped from 42% to 29%,*

- *discipline referrals have decreased by 10%: and*

- *since 2009, the percentage of students scoring proficient or above on state tests of student achievement has risen by at least 10 percentage points (from 31% to 41% in reading; from 19% to 32% in writing) (Wolf, Farbman, & Sherlock, in press).*

Developing Human Capital

¡CityArts! staff knows that these positive outcomes only occur with high-quality teaching and learning. As a result, the organization invests heavily in building the human capital it takes to do this work well.

Sustaining experienced teachers and teaching artists. The organization created a position for a director of education, who has the explicit assignment of building a culture of learning and reflection for adults as well as young people. In this position, Adrienne Gagnon observes every class and talks with each instructor about it design and implementation. At the end of each course, Gagnon holds a focus group for young people in which they talk with

2. See www.corestandards.org/assets/CCSSI_ELA%20Standards.pdf.

her—without their teacher—about what they wanted to do, what they learned, and what they think could be better. Building on this knowledge, Gagnon designs regular workshops in which teachers explore the needs and questions identified through those observations. This year, for example, the teaching artists are looking at how they can support student collaboration, having seen how much support young people need in this area and how individualized many of their course projects were. Every Thursday night, the studios are open after the last class so that teaching artists can stay on to do their own work in a collegial atmosphere. The organization makes a similar investment with their partner teachers at Roger Williams. In August, before school started, ¡CityArts! brought researcher Eileen Landay from the ArtsLiteracy Project to talk about her new book, *A Reason to Read: Linking Literacy and the Arts*. The second half of the day they spent in the studios working on arts-integration projects that could fuel English language arts learning throughout the year.

Expanded day teaching artist project: Building the next generation. Executive Director Barbara Wong knows, however, that she also has to build the skills of the next generation of teachers and teaching artists. Three years ago she and her staff wrote and won a 3-year AmeriCorps grant to fund the Expanded Day Teaching Artist Project (EDTAP). This project supports five full-time (1,700 hours/year) and 21 part-time (300 hours/year) members working as teaching artists in the two middle schools that are partnering with ¡CityArts!. Team members apply and are selected for a combination of their arts skills and commitment to service in the public schools. Once they are accepted, team members receive an extraordinary level of professional development throughout the year that they serve with EDTAP:

- *They teach side-by-side with skilled arts specialists during the school day, learning many of the important strategies for being effective teachers in an urban middle school that is striving to improve.*

- *In the afterschool hours they work in a the well-run PASA program, staffed with a skilled site coordinator, where they are able to observe and learn how other arts and youth development organizations design and deliver programs.*

- *In addition, every Friday, team members have an entire day devoted to their professional growth. In the mornings they meet together to go over the triumphs and challenges of the past week, discuss major issues, and attend meetings and events relevant to their practice. (For example, they recently went to hear Milton Chen from the George Lucas Foundation and Edutopia speak.) In the afternoons, they curate and post student work, write individual blogs about student learning, and plan for their courses.*

The Need for Policy Supports and Funding to Provide Access to Quality Afterschool and Summer Learning Infused With the Arts

Giving all children the chance to grow up imaginative means that we have to keep a variety of art disciplines within the regular school day and year. At the same time, those hours will, for the foreseeable future, be limited. So there is an equally important need for accessible, quality afterschool and summer learning that features the arts and other forms of creative work. This demands, however, that communities make exactly the kinds of commitments that Providence has:

1. funded options for expanded learning days with teaching artists who work both in

the school day and in well-run afterschool programs and include time for elective and sequential arts learning for all children;

2. municipal and state funding for free and affordable high quality afterschool programs;

3. eligibility for experienced local cultural organizations to be partners and providers; and

4. continued federal funding for public service options, like Americorps, which make it possible for talented individuals to be supported and trained while they offer their time and energy.

Without such commitments, access to high quality imaginative activity could become a luxury good open to only those children whose families can locate and afford fee-based extended learning opportunities. Without those commitments, children growing up in the contemporary United States, particularly those who live in poor neighborhoods, will experience an imagination divide perfectly aligned to the income divide their families struggle with.

For this reason, we should take our commitment to growing up imaginative even further. While most afterschool and summer learning programs already embrace—and some vigorously advocate for—the notion that out-of-school learning programs should be more than additional hours of homework and tutoring, the federal 21st Century Community Learning Centers initiative should strengthen this program requirement so that it is universally accepted and applied. Afterschool and summer learning programs must *enrich* and *extend* learning, including the arts. Similarly, arts and cultural groups must continue to be eligible providers.

Continuing professional development must be built into those same programs. In fact, we need Artistcorps—a national program offering an affordable way to train a new generation of skilled and experienced teaching artists coupled to a set of public service opportunities for any adults who want to do the work of passing on imagination.

Those leaf palaces towering in Brooklyn playgrounds? Those illustration worlds coming to life in Providence—one day they might be buildings, bilingual children's books for the next generation of young readers, or novels that delight and console—but only with universal opportunities to play, make, and invent.

The author wishes to thank Barbara Wong, Adrienne Gagnon, and Victoria Ray from Providence ¡*CityArts*! for Youth for their assistance in preparing this article.

ABOUT THE AUTHOR

Dennie Palmer Wolf is a researcher and writer who has long argued for the role of the arts in development and education. Her current work focuses on the research, policies, and initiatives that would guarantee all children the opportunity to develop their creative capital. For current colleagues, projects, and writing see www.wolfbrown.org.

REFERENCES

Burnaford, G. E., Aprill, A., & Weiss, C. (2009). *Renaissance in the classroom: Arts integration and meaningful learning*. New York, NY: Routledge.

Wolf, D., Farbman, D., & Sherlock, D. (In press). *Advancing arts education through an expanded school day: Lessons from five schools*. Boston, MA: National Center for Time and Learning

Barbara K. Stripling
Assistant Professor of Practice, Syracuse University

School and Public Libraries: Enriching Student Learning and Empowering Student Voices Through Expanded Learning Opportunities

I Am

by Brother Poet

I speak therefore I think,

I think therefore I am,

Being of existence, I am a voice,

A voice in this world that should be heard,

Outspoken yet underspoken,

I have much to say, but nothing to say at all.

- *Reading for Their Life* by Alfred W. Tatum (2009)

Our society may have no greater obligation than to ensure that every young person develops the academic, social, and personal attitudes and capacities that will lead to a fulfilling and successful life. Youth follow a journey first to discover and then to develop their own talents, interests, preferences, and personal voice. For some, the path to developing their unique capacities and establishing their distinctive identities and voices is paved with multiple opportunities to read, explore, experience, and pursue interests during the out-of-school-time hours. For others, their voices are stifled by limited access to books, trips, learning experiences, and technology. This lack of access can have dire consequences, leaving our youth with restricted voices and "nothing to say at all."

The lack of access is most pervasive for our young people during out-of-school-time hours. The Carnegie Council on Adolescent Development (1992) reported that young people have an average minimum of 1,900 hours of time out of school every year that can be filled by activities of their choice. Libraries, both public and school, have an important role in empowering student learning and voices through expanded learning opportunities after school and during the summer.

....

What does the research say about libraries and expanded learning time?

A major goal of libraries has always been literacy for all people (Lyman, 1977). The impact of participation in library programs and services during afterschool, weekends, and summers is significant. Instead of spending their summer with no books to read, disadvantaged youth who have access to libraries have increased access to books; research has shown that youth who have greater access to books read more (Krashen, 2004). The more that young people read, the better they read (Krashen, 2009). A research study in California found that the number of hours that the school library was open was significantly related to test scores at the elementary, middle, and high school levels (Achterman, 2008). A Massachusetts study found that students at the elementary, middle, and high school levels who have access to afterschool hours in their school library exhibit higher achievement on the state test (Baughman, 2000). In Missouri, research determined that summer reading participation was significantly correlated with achievement on the state test (Quantitative Resources, 2008).

Expanded learning literacy experiences are particularly important in providing equitable opportunities for learning and reading for disadvantaged youth to prevent the summer slide when, on average, students lose up to one month of instruction, and disadvantaged students lose even more (Cooper et al., 1996). A research brief published by the New York State Library summarizes the critical importance of libraries' providing rich reading experiences for disadvantaged youth after school and during the summer: "Differences in out-of-school access to books, positive reading practices, and connections with institutions supportive of self-discovery and reading, account for much of the disparity in student academic success" (Balsen & Moore, 2011, p. 2). Two-thirds of the reading achievement gap for ninth graders can be traced to "unequal access to summer learning opportunities" (Balsen & Moore, 2011, p. 1).

Afterschool, weekend, and summer programming in libraries has positive impacts on communities as well as young people. Many public and school libraries engage the parents in their children's literacy development through family literacy or parent education programs, including providing parent guides, modeling read-alouds and lapsits[1], helping parents with their own literacy needs, and guiding them in the selection of books for their children (Dowd, 1997; Cerny, 2000; Kupetz, 1993). Libraries can build their community focus by promoting public discussions (Weibel, 1992), using cooperative and creative play to foster the sharing of cultural practices (Neuman, 1994), and supporting parents who speak a language other than English at home or who have low literacy levels (Celano & Newman, 2001).

---

1. Lapsits are expressive reading and conversation with a child nestled in a lap.

A powerful draw for youth to participate in expanded learning time activities at the library is access to technology. Research has found that higher income children benefit more from access to technology than lower-income children because lower income children are less likely to have strong parental guidance in modeling the use of the computer and, therefore, often resort to simply playing games (Forum for Youth Investment, 2005). The guiding support of a librarian enables all young people to have successful technological experiences.

....

What can we learn from examples of library expanded learning time programming?

Some libraries maintain expanded learning programming independently, such as the LEAP afterschool program of the Free Library of Philadelphia that is designed to serve low-income youth from 6 to 18 years of age. This is a full-bodied program that includes homework help, access to technology, cultural and educational programming, and even career development activities (Forum for Youth Investment, 2005). The Enoch Pratt Free Library in Baltimore has designed a youth program of community service in which students are trained to work as interns in library branches and learn to conduct library programs for children and youth (Forum for Youth Investment, 2005). Other libraries (both public and school) provide expanded learning programming to youth through partnerships with various community agencies and afterschool and summer programs.

The Phoenix Public Library's Teen Central program, for example, partners with a number of city agencies and businesses to provide social support (e.g., a teen hotline) and training in film editing and financial literacy (Forum for Youth Investment, 2005). The After School Matters (ASM) program in Chicago is the result of a partnership among the City of Chicago, the Chicago Public Schools, the Chicago Park District, and the Chicago Public Library. In 2005, this program operated in more than one-fourth of the city's high schools, offering paid apprenticeships, career exposure, arts, educational enrichment, and a drop-in center (Forum for Youth Investment, 2005). The J. Lewis Crozer Public Library in Chester, Pennsylvania, partners with the 21st Century Community Learning Centers afterschool and summer programs at Chester Community Charter School to sponsor activities throughout the year designed to foster a love of books in children and families (http://www.chestercommunitycharter. org/21st-century-community-learning-centers-21st-cclc-program).

A third approach that libraries have taken to provide expanded learning opportunities is to focus on outreach, especially to the teen community. The Tucson-Pima Public Library has created Teen Centers, offering technology training and career development opportunities, and giving young people the chance to advise the library and provide community service (Forum for Youth Investment, 2005). In New York City, the three public library systems and school libraries have partnered to create a joint summer reading program that includes booklists and activities for all age levels and outreach through an interactive summer reading website (Barber & Wallace, 2006).

What recommendations will help public and school libraries design successful expanded learning time programs and services and work more effectively with afterschool and summer programs?

Based on the research and examples of expanded learning time programs in and with school and public libraries, a number of recommendations can be made to enhance the success of such programs.

Engage the entire community. Encourage a communitywide expectation that afterschool, weekend, and summer programs will work collaboratively with school and public libraries to offer children and youth an engaging set of library-related learning opportunities.

Form the programs around a youth-development vision. Programs should be designed around the principles of youth development rather than the deficit model. Youth development principles include providing youth with choices, ensuring that they have opportunities to develop and express their own voice, strengthening their self-confidence by ensuring that they have successful experiences, providing opportunities for relationship building and socializing with friends, and focusing on learning.

Commit to funding, staff, and resources. Successful programs are integrated into the regular operation of the library, with a strong commitment to providing dedicated staff, resources, and ongoing funding. Appropriate books, technology, and other resources are important, but most important to participating youth are caring and energetic adults who provide guidance, support, and training and create a safe and welcoming environment.

Develop partnerships among school and public libraries, community agencies, and schools that operate afterschool and summer programs, and businesses. Expanded learning time programs are most successful when they are developed and operated through partnerships because the various entities involved bring different areas of expertise and broader community support. Partnerships with community agencies, especially those operating or coordinating afterschool and summer programs, as well as local businesses, enable school and public libraries to design programs to serve the whole family and to customize aspects to fit the needs and interests of their local community. Programs that reach out to teens as well as younger children often include the teens themselves as partners in operating the program. As a result, teens develop important leadership and collaboration skills.

Foster innovative thinking that builds on the strengths of all partners. In order to take advantage of the unique strengths of each agency involved in planning afterschool and summertime library opportunities, library and community leaders need to open the lines of communication and creative thinking. Several strategies may help communities establish "innovation zones" where all ideas are welcomed and partnerships are built: Form advisory committees that bring together leaders in school and public libraries, afterschool programs, and community agencies to form plans and design programs; conduct focus groups and town halls to solicit creative ideas from diverse constituencies; provide mechanisms for community organizations to describe and offer their unique programs and expertise; and maintain an active outreach program to solicit new ideas and feedback from potential partners and contributors.

Provide meaningful activities in structured and welcoming environments. Teenagers enjoy opportunities that are both meaningful and enjoyable and expose them to potential careers, internships, and service to the library or in the community. Afterschool and summer learning programs should therefore be composed of multifaceted, enriching experiences involving reading and sharing, technology, education, the arts, imaginative problem solving, and creativity. By collaborating with youth-serving organizations that offer afterschool, weekend, and summer programs (for example, those that feature the arts, literacy, STEM, or sports and recreation), public and school libraries can add substantive and enriching activities, new expertise, and key resources to the mix for youth.

Advocate and plan for sustained support. In order to sustain support for expanded learning time programs and services, libraries must implement active advocacy efforts, reaching out to the youth they would like to serve, families in the community, community agencies and partners, local businesses, and government officials with messages about the importance of this programming for the community and the successes that youth have experienced through afterschool, weekend, and summer programs. As part of their partnership, school and public libraries and community-based organizations that offer afterschool and summer programming should align their services, build on each other's strengths, and promote each other. Library leaders should encourage foundations, local, state and federal officials to expand funding and support to library, school, afterschool and summer collaboration to expand offerings and the number of young people served.

Conclusion

Public and school libraries can, indeed, play an important role in providing environments and opportunities for young people to develop their strengths, pursue their interests, and express their own voices. Programs offered by libraries after school and during the summer can help struggling and disadvantaged young people catch up, keep up, and get ahead by giving them rich and meaningful learning experiences during those many hours when they are not in school. Partnerships among all agencies serving youth and their families—public libraries, school libraries, afterschool and summer programs, and schools—build an ecosystem of caring and enrichment that supports high levels of engagement and achievement for our youth.

For More Information

For additional examples of the types of expanded learning programs available to youth through school and public libraries, see the following websites:

Learning Opportunities, Careers

Chicago Public Library -www.chipublib.org/forteens/teenspoptopics/jobscareers.php

Grand Island (NE) Senior High - http://www.theindependent.com/news/local/after-school-program-gives-students-time-for-homework-and-other/article_2e08f9b3-6c63-5809-b661-6c3723432643.html

Makerspaces in Libraries

http://www.forbes.com/sites/tjmccue/2011/11/15/
first-public-library-to-create-a-maker-space/

http://spotlight.macfound.org/blog/entry/Maker-Spaces-in-Libraries/

http://theunquietlibrarian.wordpress.com/2012/06/28/
makerspaces-participatory-learning-and-libraries/

The Arts

Denver Public Library: http://kids.denverlibrary.org/fun/afterschool.html

ASAP Theatre Works: http://www.phillyasap.org/Drama.aspx

Science

LEAP into Science: http://www.fi.edu/leap/#how

SciDentity: http://scidentity.umd.edu/

ABOUT THE AUTHOR

Barbara K. Stripling has had a 35-year career as a school librarian and library administrator. Formerly director of library services for the New York City schools, Stripling is now assistant professor of practice in the School of Information Studies at Syracuse University. Stripling is president-elect of the American Library Association. She will serve her term as president in 2013-14.

REFERENCES

Achterman, D. I. (2008). *Haves, halves, and have-nots: Schools libraries and student achievement in California* (Doctoral dissertation, University of North Texas). Retrieved from http://digital.library.unt.edu/ark:/67531/metadc9800/m1/1/high_res_d/dissertation.pdf

Balsen, K., & Moore, D. (2011). *The importance of summer reading: Public library summer reading programs and learning* (Research Brief No. 1). Retrieved from http://www.nysl.nysed.gov/libdev/summer/research.htm

Barber, P., & Wallace, L. (2006). Libraries can serve as key out-of-school time players. *American Libraries, 37*(11), 39.

Baughman, J. (2000, October). *School libraries and MCAS scores: Making the connection.* Symposium conducted at Simmons College, Boston. Retrieved from http://web.simmons.edu/~baughman/mcas-school-libraries/Baughman%20Paper.pdf

Carnegie Council on Adolescent Development. (1992). *A matter of time: Risk and opportunity in the non-school hours.* Retrieved from http://carnegie.org/fileadmin/Media/Publications/A_matter_of_time.pdf

Celano, D., & Newman, S. B. (2001). *The role of public libraries in children's literacy development.* Harrisburg, PA: Pennsylvania Department of Education Office of Commonwealth Libraries.

REFERENCES (CONTINUED)

Cerny, R. (2000). Family literacy programs: Joint projects of the programs and services departments. *Journal of Youth Services in Libraries, 13*(2), 27–29.

Cooper, J. M., Nye, B. A., Charlton, K., Lindsay, J., & Greathouse, S. (1996). The effects of summer vacation on achievement test scores: A narrative and meta-analytic review. *Journal of Educational Research, 66,* 227–268.

Dowd, F. S. (1997). Evaluating the impact of public library storytime programs upon the emergent literacy of preschoolers. *Public Libraries, 36*(6), 346–358.

Forum for Youth Investment. (2005). *When school is out, museums, parks and libraries are in* (Out-of-School Time Policy Commentary #9). Retrieved from http://www.forumfyi.org/files/OSTPC9.pdf

Hartman, M. L. (2011). Out of school and in the library: Connecting with resources in the out of school time (OST) field. *YALS 9*(4), 10–12.

Krashen, S. (2004). *The power of reading: Insights from the research* (2nd ed.). Portsmouth, NH: Heinemann.

Krashen, S. (2009). Anything but reading. *Knowledge Quest, 37*(5), 19–25.

Kupetz, B. N. (1993). A shared responsibility: Nurturing literacy in the very young. *School Library Journal, 39*(7), 28.

Lyman, H. H. (1977). *Literacy and the nation's libraries*. Chicago, IL: American Library Association.

Missouri Department of Elementary and Secondary Education, Missouri State Library. (2008). *Show me connection: How school library media center services affect student achievement.* Retrieved from http://dese.mo.gov/divimprove/lmc/documents/plainenglish.pdf

Neuman, S. B., & Roskos, K. (1994). Bridging home and school with a culturally responsive approach. *Childhood Education, 70*(4). Retrieved from http://www.freepatentsonline.com/article/Childhood-Education/15443839.html

Tatum, A. W. (2009). *Reading for their life: (Re)building the textual lineages of African American adolescent males*. Portsmouth, NH: Heinemann.

Weibel, M. C. (1992). *The library as literacy classroom: A program for teaching*. Chicago, IL: American Library Association.

Barry Ford
Director of Public Affairs and Advocacy,
United States Tennis Association

Tennis in Afterschool and Summer Programs: A Winning New Model to Expand Fitness and Learning

The expanded learning community is uniquely positioned to provide opportunities for children and youth to be physically active in safe, accessible spaces.

The introduction of quality physical activity and sports programming in afterschool and summer programs is a critical strategy in the fight to reverse the crisis of childhood obesity in this country (Robert Wood Johnson Foundation, 2011). The crisis has garnered growing attention in recent years. Nearly one-third of American children and adolescents, age 2–19, are either overweight or obese; moreover, since 1980, the rates of childhood obesity have tripled (CDC, 2012). In fact, the Robert Woods Johnson Foundation (n.d.) warns that if this trend is not reversed "we are in danger of raising the first generation of American children who may live sicker and die younger than the generation that preceded them."

The primary causes of childhood obesity are well understood (Levi, Segal, St. Larent, & Kohn, 2011). In simplest terms, children and youth consume more calories than they burn off through physical activity or growth. The expanded learning community (which includes schools, nonprofits, state networks, local funders, and local intermediaries) is uniquely positioned to provide opportunities for children and youth to be physically active in safe, accessible spaces, while acquiring the knowledge and skills to live active and healthy lives at healthy weights.

In addition to its key role in reversing childhood obesity, a CDC study (2010) found that quality and consistent physical activity —at least 60 minutes a day—has many other health benefits and is positively associated with improved academic performance, increased concentration and attention in class, and improved classroom behavior. The study recommended that education leaders incorporate sports programming and physical activity into afterschool programming as a way of supporting the academic mission of schools (CDC, 2010).

This article describes how changes in the game of tennis and the vision and energy of local nonprofits, schools systems, and state-level leaders can democratize the opportunity to be physically active during out-of-school time and can have a positive effect on expanding learning after school and during the summer. Other types of physical activities might also offer such opportunities if we think creatively about imbuing expanding learning time programs with physical activities aimed at educating the whole child and reinforcing learning in creative, active ways.

Tennis as Intervention

Over the last few years, the United States Tennis Association (USTA) has worked with grassroots leaders, tennis providers, afterschool programs, schools, school districts, and private and commercial clubs that serve substantial youth populations to pilot and then fully implement the most substantial change to the game of tennis in a generation. In January 2012, the USTA changed the rules of tennis to scale the sport appropriately for children and launched an initiative, 10 and Under Tennis, to encourage them to take up the sport. Now, children between the ages of 6 and 10 years old play on courts sized appropriately for them. They use tennis balls that are larger, move slower through the air, and bounce at an ideal height. Children now also use newly designed racquets that are a more appropriate size and weight for their age. What these changes have meant for the afterschool world is that now tennis can be played in almost any recreational setting without the need for traditional courts, and it can be introduced by caring adults who have no formal tennis background.

The examples that follow illustrate how afterschool and summer programs have integrated tennis programming with a resulting positive impact on both participants and providers.

Georgia

In the spring of 2009, the Georgia Afterschool Investment Council (GAIC), the state afterschool network lead in Georgia, partnered with the USTA and a select number of Georgia-based National Junior Tennis and Learning Chapters to launch the Georgia Afterschool Tennis and Education program. The Georgia Afterschool Tennis and Education program, or GATE, is a tennis, fitness, and learning program that primarily serves economically disadvantaged youth living in Atlanta, Savannah, and Augusta. The GATE program, created to increase physical activity and fitness in Georgia's youth, exposes youth to new mentor relationships and enhances existing afterschool programs that serve young people in the hours after the school day ends and during the summer months. The GATE program strives to accomplish this by providing a tennis component, usually offered two to three times a week, to afterschool and summer learning programs that serve children in targeted neighborhoods.

After being launched in 2010, the GATE program grew in 2011 by 15%, serving 36 sites and over 1,400 young people, ages 6–12. These sites included elementary schools, middle schools, Boys and Girls Clubs, YMCAs, city and county recreation facilities, a public housing unit, several 21st Century Community Learning Centers, and Department of Health and Human Services Temporary Assistance for Needy Families (TANF) grantees. The GATE program sites provide a minimum of 6–8 weeks of programming in the fall and spring, during which participants are likely to be exposed to tennis 2–3 hours a week.

....

New Jersey

The National Junior Tennis & Learning of Trenton (NJTLT) is a nonprofit, community-based organization dedicated to improving the lives of young people from varied socio-economic and cultural backgrounds through tennis and education programming. It serves annually 2,500 young people annually. NJTLT created the Academic Creative Engagement curriculum in response to requests from its school partners. NJTLT was aided in this venture by financial support from local sponsors, as well as funding from the federal 21st Century Community Learning Centers initiative as a New Jersey sub-grantee. The Academic Creative Engagement curriculum is a free afterschool educational and fitness program that supports classroom instruction by using an academic curriculum connected to the sport of tennis, 21st century skills, and the new Common Core State Standards. The curriculum provides key developmental assets to participating children, gives them access to safe and healthy educational opportunities, and encourages parents to participate in their child's learning.

NJTLT typically implements the Academic Creative Engagement curriculum in an afterschool setting by having approximately 30 students per session participate 2–3 days a week for a 6–8 week session. NJTLT offers three such sessions for youth throughout the school year (fall, winter, and spring) and then offers a summer session that uses a more intensive programming model. On each Academic Creative Engagement program day, the students are divided into two groups. For the first 45 minutes, one group of students learns about tennis and exercise with a tennis professional while the other group participates in academic enrichment activities focusing on math, literacy, and nutrition. After 45 minutes, the groups rotate their focus for the remaining 45 minutes.

Online assessment surveys are used to measure program outcomes. In addition, report card grades and student reflections are included in the evaluation process.

> The Academic Creative Engagement curriculum is a free afterschool educational and fitness program that supports classroom instruction by using an academic curriculum connected to the sport of tennis, 21st century skills, and the new Common Core State Standards.

Virginia

For the last 2 years, the USTA has partnered with Newport News Public Schools and the Newport News 21st Century Community Learning Centers programs to bring the 10 and Under Tennis program to local schools and the broader community. With the enthusiastic support of the USTA and its Virginia state affiliate, USTA Virginia, over 300 of the school district's third graders who participate in 21st Century Community Learning Centers programs have been given the opportunity to engage in tennis programming through 10 and Under Tennis. The school system has connected math and reading activities to its tennis programming to give participants a complete experience, exercising both the body and the mind. The system also plans to link the tennis program to students' school-based physical fitness program as a way of fostering greater health and wellness.

After students have completed the 10 and Under program, they are encouraged to participate in the tennis programs sponsored by Newport News Department of Parks, Recreation, and Tourism, as well as those sponsored by other local clubs and wellness centers. City leaders hope that the tennis component of its 21st Century Community Learning Centers programming will result in having young people not only develop an attachment to and proficiency in the sport of tennis but also in having them develop the confidence, character, and resilience to succeed in and graduate from high school.

Recommendations

The following recommendations are offered to guide key local stakeholder groups in planning and implementing a successful sports or physical activity program (whether tennis or another activity) as part of high quality afterschool and summer programming:

....

Afterschool and Summer Learning Providers

- *The successful integration of physical activity into an afterschool program requires that a provider be fully committed to facilitating this type of program enhancement, requiring resources in terms of time, space, and talent.*

- *Afterschool providers should develop partnerships with individuals and organizations that have deep expertise in the sport to make the overall effort successful.*

- *The afterschool or summer learning leader should design the physical activity or sports activity not only to expand fitness time and opportunities, but also to reinforce other learning goals of the program, including developing and enhancing skills that are important to students' success during the school day (for example, reinforcing the importance of academic success, responsibility, teamwork, and persistence).*

- *Providers must make any physical activity component of their programs engaging and interesting for the young people involved. They should choose activities that will enable youth participants to experience early success and competence.*

- *Afterschool state networks and intermediaries should assist in quality programming and expansion by*
    - making sure there is adequate program dosage and intensity provided for participants;
    - having a streamlined monitoring and evaluation process;
    - involving city-level elected officials; and
    - assigning dedicated staff for administration of program effort; and helping secure national, regional, and local funding sources.

Sports Organizations or Physical Activity Groups

- *Groups should understand their core competencies and have those be the focus of any collaboration. They should not stray from what they know and do well.*

- *Groups should look for partnerships that allow them to add value without straying from their mission. Yet, it is very important to reinforce the particular learning goals of the afterschool or summer partner programs, as well as other goals including responsibility, attendance, and teamwork.*

- *Groups should be ready to commit to a multiyear relationship (3 years or more) so that they are able to demonstrate the efficacy of their program or sport.*

- *In addition to supporting and enhancing the services of an afterschool provider, groups should also work to increase the capacity of those providers so that they can successfully implement the sports or physical activity program independently over time.*

Conclusion

The health and the quality of life that our children will enjoy are threatened by cultural trends that inhibit the development of healthy habits. Schools undervalue and greatly limit physical education and physical activity during the school day. Too many communities in this country have limited access to healthy and nutritious foods. Finally, too many young people spend too many hours in front of electronic screens instead of engaging in active play.

Communities throughout the country can begin to reverse the effects of these trends by harnessing the energy and resources of local and state networks of afterschool and summer learning providers and making more intentional use of those hours that young people are not in school. In addition to keeping young people active, partnerships between out-of-school-time providers and tennis and other fitness organizations—can also broaden young peoples' skill sets and opportunities—a winning combination. We do not have to settle for a future in which our children live shorter and sicker lives than we have lived.

For More Information

www.usta.com/Youth-Tennis/National-Junior-Tennis-Learning/NJTL

www.usta.com/About-USTA/thebigserve/afterschool-adoptaschool

www.usta.com/About-USTA/thebigserve/resources

www.afterschoolga.org

ABOUT THE AUTHOR

Barry Ford is the director of public affairs and advocacy for the United States Tennis Association and has been a member of the USTA national staff since 2006. He leads the association's efforts to build and deepen its relationships with public sector policy makers at every level of government and to expand the availability of quality, tennis-themed, out-of-school- time programs throughout the country. Ford is a board member of the Afterschool Alliance and served as vice president for external relations at the After-School Corporation (TASC). He brings 26 years of professional experience as a government official, lawyer, nonprofit executive, and political candidate to this work. Ford holds an AB degree from Harvard College and a JD from Harvard Law School.

REFERENCES

Centers for Disease Control and Prevention. (2010). *The association between school based physical activity, including physical education, and academic performance.* Retrieved from http://www.cdc.gov/healthyyouth/health_and_academics/pdf/pa-pe_paper.pdf

Centers for Disease Control and Prevention. (2012). Data and statistics: Obesity rates among all children in the United States. Retrieved from http://www.cdc.gov/obesity/data/childhood.html

Levi, J., Segal, L. M., St. Larent, R., & Kohn, D. (2011). *F as in fat: How obesity threatens America's future.* Retrieved from http://www.healthyamericans.org/assets/files/TFAH2011FasInFat10.pdf

Robert Wood Johnson Foundation. (n.d.). The challenge. Retrieved September 1, 2012, from http://www.rwjf.org/childhoodobesity/challenge.jsp

Randy Neve
Program Manager, Marshfield Clinic and Network
Lead, Wisconsin Afterschool Network

Gladys Bartelt
Educational Consultant, Marshfield Clinic

The Mutual Benefits of Health Care and Afterschool Collaboration

Research identifies quality education as a key determinant of good health. Moreover, recent research from the expanded learning field has documented the significant potential that afterschool programs have for improving students' health and academic success. An investment in infrastructure that supports strong collaboration between afterschool and health care can enhance the potential of afterschool programs to address many of the compelling academic and health needs faced by children.

Many children who participate in afterschool programs face serious risk factors such as poverty and poor school performance (Wisconsin Department of Public Instruction, 2011). These young people can benefit most from a well-designed collaboration between health care providers and afterschool programs. The case study presented in this article illustrates the point.

Background: Health and Education Connections

Being overweight or clinically obese are both largely the result of physical inactivity and poor diet. These conditions can increase the risk for diabetes, high blood pressure, high cholesterol, asthma, arthritis, and poor health status (U.S. Department of Health and Human Services, 2008). Only 38% of students in grades 9–12 are meeting the current Centers for Disease Control (CDC) recommendation of 60 minutes of physical activity on most days of each week (CDC, 2011).

One reason for the low rate of physical activity is the rapid increase in recreational use of media such as TV, movies, computers, video games, and music. While the American Academy of Pediatrics (2010) recommends children have less than 2 hours of screen time/day, a 2010 national study reported that 8–18 year-olds devoted an average of

7.5 hours/day to such sedentary behaviors. This is more than 53 hours/week and does not include time spent using the computer for school or talking/texting on a cell phone (Kaiser Family Foundation, 2010). Research shows that high levels of media use are also associated with obesity, attention difficulties, and sleep and eating disorders (Kaiser Family Foundation, 2004).

Research has also established a strong correlation between health and education. An individual's education level has been found to be a determinant of his/her health, regardless of the type of health outcome scholars studied, including the likelihood to develop diseases, the likelihood to survive diseases, and self-reports of health status (Cutler & Llera-Mooney, 2006).

New research has shown evidence of the important role that afterschool programs can play in supporting positive educational and health outcomes. Studies indicate that children involved in afterschool programs are significantly less likely to be obese at follow-up than nonparticipants (Mahoney, Lord, & Carryl, 2005). Teens who do not participate in afterschool programs are nearly three times more likely to skip classes, three times more likely to use marijuana or others drugs, and are more likely to drink, smoke, and engage in sexual activity. Studies show children who take part in afterschool programs attend school more regularly and have higher aspirations for finishing school and going to college. They are half as likely to drop out of high school and 30% less likely to participate in criminal activities, saving an estimated $2.50 in crime-related costs for every $1 invested in afterschool programs (Afterschool Alliance, 2008).

A Case Study: How One of Wisconsin's Largest Health Care Providers Is Connecting Health Care and Afterschool

Marshfield Clinic is the largest private group medical practice in Wisconsin and one of the largest in the United States. The clinic is involved in local, regional, and statewide initiatives to advance the quality of afterschool programs that serve thousands of Wisconsin children and youth each day. The Clinic's Center for Community Outreach provides user-friendly tools, learning events, technical assistance, action plan strategies, and other resources to help afterschool programs focus on evidence-based strategies to improve child and youth outcomes associated with academic success, healthy active living, and personal and social development.

Marshfield Clinic as a local resource and an afterschool learning lab. For the past 22 years the Marshfield Clinic has operated a comprehensive afterschool program known as Youth Net. Youth Net is open 5 days a week throughout the year with a focus on academic success, healthy active living, and personal and social development. Annually, Youth Net serves over 350 Marshfield-area children and youth ages 8–18, with a daily attendance average of 155. Over 70% of these students qualify for free-and-reduced lunch, and 43% receive special education services. Children are referred to the program due to poor school performance, behavioral issues, and family conflict. The following are core program components:

Homework Club. Homework Club is a program for youth in grades 2 through 6. AmeriCorps members, mentors, and other staff provide academic assistance and support. Math, reading, and computer labs are available each day. Incentive programs encourage regular participation. Consistent attendance at Homework Club has been shown to boost the academic and behavior performance of participating youth (Marshfield Clinic, 2011). Due to strong ties with area schools, what is learned at school is reinforced in the afterschool setting.

Healthy, active, living. Physical activity and nutrition education are an intentional part of the daily programming. Physical fitness activities and nutrition education are available daily in collaboration with the Marshfield Area YMCA and Marshfield Parks & Recreation Department. Healthy snacks are provided daily.

Teens United. Teens United is a program for youth in grades 7 through 12. Academic assistance is provided to all participants. Educational, recreational, and vocational activities are provided to facilitate personal and social development and improve health and academic outcomes.

Summer program. A day-long summer program is offered 5 days a week with an emphasis on education and health and wellness. Collaborating with the School District of Marshfield and University of Wisconsin-Marshfield/Wood County, Youth Net staff teach School District of Marshfield summer school classes with a specific outreach to Youth Net participants. Transportation and a lunch program are provided to all participating youth. An afternoon summer program focusing on literacy, health, and recreation rounds out the summer program.

Family nights. Family nights occur monthly and provide an opportunity for families to socialize with each other and Youth Net staff around a meal and participate in educational and fun activities.

Marshfield Clinic's AmeriCorps Afterschool Initiative as a regional resource for better afterschool linkages with health. In 2012, 24 Marshfield Clinic Afterschool AmeriCorps members were placed in afterschool programs, providing 40,800 hours of direct service. Some of the most successful programs were located in small, rural communities that would otherwise not be able to offer afterschool services nor connect better learning supports with better health activities. Furthermore, Marshfield Clinic worked closely with the State Department of Public Instruction to make this valuable resource available to their 21st Community Learning Center sites in Marshfield Clinic's service region.

> Some of the most successful programs were located in small, rural communities that would otherwise not be able to offer afterschool services nor connect better learning supports with better health activities.

Members worked directly with children and youth by implementing Marshfield Clinic's Youth Net program's case management system. In addition, members provided direct service to local public schools, further strengthening the ties between afterschool and day school and between education and health activities.

Marshfield Clinic as a state-level resource: Wisconsin Afterschool Network. Since October 2008, Marshfield Clinic has provided leadership and been the fiscal sponsor for the Wisconsin Afterschool Network (WAN). Wisconsin is one of 41 states that receive funding from the Charles Stewart Mott Foundation to provide statewide leadership for afterschool programs. Marshfield Clinic is the only health care provider in America serving as the host for a statewide afterschool network. However, health care providers in other states could be a strong force for afterschool, too.

In the previous 3 years, the Wisconsin Afterschool Network (WAN) has experienced an expansion of authentic partnerships, braiding and blending policy development efforts between individuals and organizations that historically have not reached consensus on afterschool issues.

WAN's role in facilitating this interaction has served to revitalize network participation. Current efforts have been launched to create a comprehensive statewide system for professional development for afterschool programs that is available and accessible to all Wisconsin providers.

A carefully designed enrollment process for afterschool programs has the potential (with parental approval) for programs to communicate directly with a child's primary care provider to design preventive services to meet the identified needs of enrolled youth.

Marshfield Clinic's Case Management System: Linking Data for Afterschool Improvement and Health Services

A carefully designed enrollment process for afterschool programs has the potential (with parental approval) for programs to communicate directly with a child's primary care provider to design preventive services to meet the identified needs of enrolled youth, for example, early and periodic screening, well-child visits, immunizations, behavioral health appointments/treatment plan compliance, dental screening and sealants, and asthma case management).

Marshfield's case management process has incorporated results of seminal research by the Harvard Family Research Project, including key elements found to be necessary for afterschool programs to achieve the quality needed for positive outcomes.

The case management system is a five-step process:

1. A formal enrollment interview, conducted with both the child and parents/guardian, starts the process of assessing the needs of the child, supports establishing preliminary goals and objectives, facilitates establishment of rapport, provides an opportunity to answer questions and obtain signatures on release-of-information forms.

2. Once a child is enrolled, teachers are contacted to assist in assessing needs regarding academic success, personal/social development, and healthy active living. Working as a team, day school and afterschool staff tailor intentional and sequential programming to meet individual needs.

3. A case management team convenes to review information collected through the enrollment interview and teacher contact.

4. The team develops a case management plan for each enrolled child.

5. Case management plans are reviewed throughout the year to determine progress and to be adjusted as needed to increase the potential for successful outcomes.

Recommendations for Afterschool and Health Care Collaboration

What follows are several key recommendations for both health care providers and afterschool providers.

Health care providers can offer the following:

- *Case management/health improvement plans for youth enrolled in afterschool programs. If thoughtfully designed, the registration/intake forms for the afterschool program can serve as a gateway for communication between afterschool and the health care provider (with parent permission).*

- *Services designed to meet the identified needs of enrolled youth (e.g., early and periodic screening, well-child visits, immunizations, behavioral health appointments/treatment plan compliance, dental screening and sealants, asthma case management)*

- *Oversight and advice to help leverage the full scope of local community resources*

- *Support and advice to state and local afterschool networks*

Afterschool and health care can collaborate to achieve the following:

- *Address the prevention needs of youth in ways that transcend the capacity of traditional schools, afterschool programs and health care providers*

- *Support schools and afterschool programs by identifying and addressing health and health-related problems that may interfere with the ability to learn*

- *Support working families by allowing parents to stay at work while the education and routine health care needs of their children are met*

- *Work to contain costs by reducing the number of hospital and emergency room visits*

- *Strengthen the connection between key community stakeholders and key leaders from health care, education, business, governmental systems, and other community sectors*

- *Work to meet the strategic goals of health providers' (immunization rates, well child check-ups, etc.) Support children in the development of positive health habits that they will carry across the lifespan*

- *Develop meaningful relationships with qualified staff, which can have a positive influence on the health and behavior of children and their families*

Conclusion

While on the surface it appears unusual to have health care providers and afterschool programs working together over a region and state, the mutual benefits are positive and significant for both entities. Since so many children and youth attend afterschool programs each day, these programs are natural venues for health care providers to reach large numbers of children with relative ease, especially as the country moves more assertively into health care reform. Working together, these unlikely partners can have a very positive impact on education, youth development and health outcomes.

ABOUT THE AUTHOR

Randy Neve, network lead for the Wisconsin Afterschool Network (WAN), provides support, oversight, and leadership for all WAN teams/committees as they work toward development of statewide school-age partnerships, policies, and systems of quality. Over the past 15 years as Afterschool Program Manager for Marshfield Clinic, Neve has acquired significant experience in the design, development, and delivery of comprehensive, research-based afterschool programming. He has successfully served as the WAN Network Lead for the past 3 years.

Gladys Bartelt, education specialist, serves as a consultant for WAN's professional development system, the development of afterschool health services, and pilot programs through Marshfield Clinic AmeriCorps. Bartelt has over 30 years of experience working in all areas of education. She is particularly skilled in the development of individualized case management techniques for at-risk youth enrolled in afterschool programs.

REFERENCES

Afterschool Alliance. (2008). *Afterschool programs: Making a difference in America's communities by improving academic achievement, keeping kids safe and helping working families.* Retrieved from http://www.afterschoolalliance.org/documents/outcomes_0208.pdf

American Academy of Pediatrics. (2010). Media education [Policy statement]. Retrieved from http://pediatrics.aappublications.org/content/126/5/1012.full

Centers for Disease Control. (2011). Physical activity facts. Retrieved from http://www.cdc.gov/healthyyouth/physicalactivity/facts.htm

Cutler, D. M., & Lleras-Mooney, A. (2006). *Education and health: Evaluating theories and evidence* (National Poverty Center Working Paper #06-19). Retrieved from http://www.npc.umich.edu/publications/workingpaper06/paper19/working-paper06-19.pdf

Harvard Family Research Project. (2006). *Yale study of children's after-school time.* Retrieved from http://www.hfrp.org/out-of-school-time/ost-database-bibliography/database/yale-study-of-children-s-after-school-time

Kaiser Family Foundation. (2010). *Generation M2: Media in the lives of 8- to 18-year-olds.* Retrieved from http://www.kff.org/entmedia/entmedia012010nr.cfm

Kaiser Family Foundation. (2004). *The role of media in childhood obesity* [Issue Brief]. Retrieved from http://www.kff.org/entmedia/upload/the-role-of-media-in-childhood-obesity.pdf

Mahoney, J. L., Lord, H., & Carryl, E. (2005). Afterschool program participation and the development of child obesity and peer acceptance. *Applied Developmental Science, 9,* 202–215. Retrieved from www.leaonline.com/doi/abs/10.1207/s1532480xads0904_3

Marshfield Clinic. (2011). *Marshfield Clinic Youth Net program 2010–2011* [Fact sheet]. Marshfield, WI: Author.

U.S. Department of Health and Human Services. (2008). 2008 physical activity guidelines for Americans. Retrieved from http://www.health.gov/paguidelines/guidelines/default.aspx

Wisconsin Department of Public Instruction. (2011). *21st Century Community Learning Centers: Executive summary, 2010–2011.* Retrieved from http://dpi.wisconsin.gov/sspw/pdf/clcexecsumm10_11.pdf

Afterschool and Summer Programs as Catalysts for Engaging Families

5

Arnold F. Fege
Former Director of Public Engagement and Advocacy, Public Education Network

Anne Foster
Executive Director, Parents for Public Schools

Building Powerful Partnerships With Parents and Communities: Integrating 21st Century Community Learning Centers With Education Change and Reform

What if parents and the community came *first* in education reform? The current test score accountability movement—birthed by the *Nation at Risk* report, followed by the Goals 2000: Educate America Act, reinforced by the No Child Left Behind law, and reaffirmed by the Race to the Top reforms—has relegated parents and community to a low priority in policy, low priority in practice, and low priority in partnership.

There is one program, however, that should serve as a signature element of the next version of the Elementary and Secondary Education Act (ESEA): 21st Century Community Learning Centers. It is one of the few programs at the federal level that requires a deep partnership between the school, community, and parents as a condition for funding.

Even as ESEA is being considered for reauthorization, both the Obama administration and Congress continue to resist robust support for parent involvement, community engagement, coordination of services, and partnership building, relegating them to the back burner as strategies for increasing achievement or reforming schools. In an over 800-page ESEA proposal passed by the Health, Education, Labor, and Pensions Committee in October 2011, community partnerships and parent engagement are mentioned, sadly, as mere afterthoughts but are never required or considered as priority elements of reform. Yet, at the same time, public opinion polls conducted by Gallup, and other research conducted over more than 40 years, find that involving parents or engaging families in their children's education and schools is one of the highest priorities for improving American education (Bushaw & Lopez, 2011; Public Impact, 2007).

While a national debate rages about how to "fix" America's schools and improve public education, many public schools and their communities have already realized that there is no silver bullet. Yet, one thing is crystal clear in the swirl of evolving and often conflicting reform efforts: Failing to engage parents and the community dramatically lowers the prospect of increasing the number of students going to college or being prepared for a 21st century career.

> Failing to engage parents and the community dramatically lowers the prospect of increasing the number of students going to college or being prepared for a 21st century career.

The research over the years is both extensive and conclusive regarding the importance of parents and community engagement related to increased student learning (Sanders, 2006). It was the 2009 research that came out of the Chicago Consortium, led by Dr. Tony Bryk, however, that should have been a wake-up call to policy makers to move parent and community partnerships from rhetoric to reality, making these partnerships a core element of change essential to increased student achievement (Bryk, Sebring, Allensworth, Luppescu, & Easton, 2009).[1] In short, research reveals that *good things happen when the public is involved*—citizens feel ownership, share responsibility and accountability for results, and support sustaining change, no matter how many principals or superintendents come and go.

The wheel does not have to be reinvented, however. Established in 1994, the 21st Century Community Learning Centers program has spawned almost 11,000 centers nationwide. As part of their core purpose and function, these centers bridge school-based learning with its natural counterpart, *community-based learning*, through partnerships with parents, United Ways, 4-H groups, libraries, YMCAs, Boys and Girls Clubs, higher education, nonprofits, museums, educators, parks and recreation departments, municipalities, businesses, and other community organizations. These partnerships not only advance learning and use time wisely before and after school and during the summers, they also help build strong public schools and community demand for sustaining change. Drawing on the strengths brought by partner organizations, each center includes a range of services tailored to the needs of each school community. Services provided by centers typically include several of the following: health care, tutoring, afterschool programs, English as a second language classes, parent training, college-access services, and math and reading classes.

Given both the significant need for and interest in these services in communities across the country, wouldn't it be a remarkable achievement if, in the reauthorization of the ESEA and in subsequent appropriations measures, 21st Century Community Learning Centers were to be expanded to support more school-community partnerships, from the current nearly 11,000 to possibly as many as 20,000 to 30,000?

---

1. Bryk's most recent research gives evidence from Chicago on how the organization of schools and community context influences the capacity to enhance student engagement and advance student learning.

Cincinnati provides a good case example of why this would make a lot of sense. Deciding a number of years ago that there was a pressing need to reconnect the public with its public schools, the community developed community learning centers in 31 of the district's 43 low-income schools. Each of the programs focused on academic enrichment opportunities for students, and the first nine centers in Cincinnati were funded with federal grants in 2004.

Both the Cincinnati chapter of Parents for Public Schools (PPS) and the Cincinnati STRIVE Partnership, a local affiliate of the national Public Education Network (PEN), came together, along with dozens of other community-based organizations in Cincinnati, to support the leadership, implementation, evaluation, accountability, and sustainability of each of the centers. PPS and STRIVE were natural partners to strengthen public education in the community by mobilizing, engaging, and training parents through partnership connections–and notably, they were provided the incentives to do so by the federal 21st Century Community Learning Centers initiative.

> The 21st Century Community Learning Centers are intended to bridge school and community and to build the resources, supports, and community buy-in that are essential to making expanded school time successful.

As Cincinnati's community learning centers continue to grow, they will need to be able to measure their impact. Aware of the importance of demonstrating accountability to the community through the use of quantifiable metrics, the local centers have developed a Learning Partner Dashboard through funding provided by the school district, Microsoft, Proctor & Gamble, and the STRIVE Partnership. The dashboard provides individualized student academic and developmental data to the school resource coordinators.

The dashboard uploads student data from the school system database, and then program coordinators add data about the services that each student currently receives. The coordinators then match students with the additional services they need based on an analysis of gaps between student performance and behavior on the one hand and received services on the other. If a student fails the state math tests, for example, the student is flagged in the system, and the coordinator matches the student with a math tutor. If a student has trouble getting to school on time, a match is made with a social worker to support to the family.

The 21st Century Community Learning Centers initiative should not be confused with the recent push for extended school time, although the two are not mutually exclusive. The 21st Century Community Learning Centers are intended to bridge school and community and to build the resources, supports, and community buy-in that are essential to making expanded school time successful. Depending on the community, the initiative provides vitally important opportunities to students and their families, such as:

- *tutoring*
- *college access*
- *mentoring*
- *internships*
- *health and wellness*
- *parenting classes*
- *community engagement*
- *hands-on, creative learning in areas such as STEM, the arts, and sports*

Efforts to extend time in school should therefore complement the 21st Century Community Learning Centers initiative in order to ensure wise and creative use of time and partnerships. Unfortunately, many plans for extending time in school often focus only on adding small increments of time— for example, 30 to 60 minutes a day. The school day still ends well before parents come home from work, which means that many children in those schools still need care and support after school, and of course, during the summertime. If a school or community wants, therefore, to extend the school day or year, decision makers should work with families to make sure the additional time is actually more engaging, interesting, active and relevant than the typical school day. In addition, programs like the 21st Century Community Learning Centers and similar efforts (e.g., community schools) should not be destroyed in the process. That would be a huge net loss, not a net gain. Indeed, we know that schools alone—without the academic supports, enrichment, and personalization provided by 21st Century Community Learning Centers programs and other afterschool and summer learning programs—will not lead us to 21st century achievement.

> Indeed we know that schools alone— without the academic supports, enrichment, and personalization provided by 21st Century Community Learning Centers programs and other afterschool and summer learning programs—will not lead us to 21st century achievement.

Crystal Hoffman is a parent and a parent leader/volunteer at her children's school, Pleasant Ridge Montessori in Cincinnati. She talks about how the school's 21st Century Community Learning Centers resource coordinator brings together partners from the community to support academic success and to make the school more open and accessible to the community. She notes that:

- *local businesses volunteer in the school,*
- *a GED program is available for families,*
- *the gymnasium is used for a table tennis club several nights a week,*
- *there is an afterschool program that offers motivating experiences for students, and*
- *the program offers both homework tutoring and enrichment activities and reaches out to the student and family's unique learning and support needs.*

The work of 21st Century Community Learning Centers was recently validated by an independent study that concluded that these programs do, indeed, contribute to increased achievement for the PreK through eighth grade low-income students whom they serve (Brown, 2011). Schools that reach out to parents and the community and that integrate community supports into the school day show increases in student learning. Moreover, parents feel more satisfied, and the public is assured that their efforts are making a meaningful contribution to their students and their community (Brown, 2011). For PEN and PPS, as national organizations with community-based affiliates, the study reinforces the value of deep collaboration with their local members in support of reform efforts.

Massachusetts Secretary of Education Paul Reville and Teachers College/Columbia University Professor Jeffery Henig sum it up when they say: "When thinking about their own families, parents take it as a given that nonschool factors—good health, good food, emotional well-being, safety, stability, enrichment activities, positive peer influences, parental encouragement, and guidance—affect whether their children will thrive" (Henig & Reville, 2011). With their richly diverse afterschool and summer learning program offerings, their school-community partnerships, and their emphasis on family engagement, 21st Century Community Learning Centers should be significantly expanded, not have their funding diverted for other purposes. As the economy starts to recover, school districts, local governments, states, and the federal government should be investing in this collaborative, cost-effective approach to improving education and strengthening communities and schools. 21st Century Community Learning Centers are not just good policy; indeed, they are good common sense as well.

Cleveland Afterschool Program Opens Doors for Parents

Spread across eight sites in Cleveland, Open Doors Academy (ODA) believes that "it takes a community to raise a child" and provides a multitude of ways for parents to be involved. This includes participating in project-based learning and team building among students, attending family events with their children, and volunteering on field trips and/or a variety of educational workshops that teach parents how to recognize their child's learning style.

This unique program begins in the sixth grade and has a 7-year curriculum plan for participating students. ODA serves 300 middle school and high school students that live in high-risk environments. For those students who completed all 3 years of the middle school program, 100% of them went on to graduate from high school.

Parents are viewed as critical partners and are required to contribute at least 16 service hours every year to their child's programming. Through activities such as calling parents when their children are excelling, ODA is successfully working to create a positive, supportive atmosphere for students and their parents. This positive reinforcement led to 98% of parents completing the service requirements in 2011.

ABOUT THE AUTHORS

Arnold F. Fege was the director of public engagement and advocacy for the former Public Education Network. A former public school teacher, principal, curriculum director, and assistant superintendent, he has over 30 years of federal legislative and policy experience covering issues of community engagement and parent involvement. Fege serves as a board member of Parents for Public Schools.

Anne Foster is the national executive director of Parents for Public Schools. She served for 9 years as a member of the Richardson (TX) Independent School District Board, including 7 as president of the board. Foster founded Realtors Supporting Richardson Schools to bring the real estate community into active support for public schools, and she also served as the first executive director of Raise Your Hand Texas (RYHT), a public education advocacy organization.

REFERENCES

Brown, J. (2011, November 19). Study confirms value of CPS' learning centers. *Cincinnati Enquirer*. Retrieved from http://clcinstitute.org/wp-content/uploads/2011/12/Study-confirms-value-of-cps-from-enquirer.pdf

Bryk, A. S., Sebring, P. B., Allensworth, E., Luppescu, S., & Easton, J. Q. (2009). *Organizing schools for improvement: Lessons from Chicago*. Chicago, IL: University of Chicago Press.

Bushaw, W. J., & Lopez, S. J. (2011). Betting on teachers: The 43rd annual Phi Delta Kappa/Gallup poll of the public's attitudes toward the public schools. *Phi Delta Kappan*. 93(1), 8–26.

Henig, J. R., & Reville, S. P. (2011). Outside-in school reform [Commentary]. *Education Week 30*(20), 23, 28.

Public Impact. (2007). School turnarounds: *A review of the cross-sector evidence on dramatic organizational improvement*. Lincoln, IL: Center on Innovation & Improvement.

Sanders, M. G. (2006). *Building school-community partnerships: Collaboration for student success*. Thousand Oaks, CA: Corwin Press.

Delia Pompa
Senior Vice President of Programs,
National Council of La Raza

Family Involvement as a Critical Element of Quality Expanded Learning Opportunities

Take the time to bond with families. To some we are like a second parent, and we are seen as a partner as we watch their children grow. The parents want you to feel what they feel and what they've been through and take the time with them.

- Chicago Afterschool Provider

The relationship between providers, parents, and youth should be circular—communication should flow openly.

- Chicago Afterschool Parent

They (staff) do keep me involved, but you know what? I put myself out there . . . you (staff) need anything, call me up.

- Washington DC Afterschool Parent

Quality expanded learning opportunities after school and during summers not only build youth's academic and social skills, they provide the opportunity for them to contribute to their communities' development. Particularly for Latino students, who are often some of the most vulnerable and underserved in the educational system, these programs can be their connection to a variety of sources of support in their academic and developmental growth. The core of successful programs is a close connection to their families and communities.

These fundamental lessons have emerged over the last 5 years, as the National Council of La Raza (NCLR) has strengthened its efforts to build the capacity of its network of affiliated schools and community-based organizations to provide quality expanded learning opportunities programs for Latino students. During this period, it has become increasingly clear that certain strategies and practices make the most positive difference.

The following best practices, based on a review of the literature and the experiences of NCLR practitioners in the field, can and should be applied across expanded learning programs working with vulnerable populations:

- **Communication and trust between parents and program staff should be consistent.** *Maintaining regular communication and accurately conveying program goals to parents and families can be challenging; however, providers should make it a priority to understand the values and needs of the families served. An NCLR provider in the Rio Grande Valley uses home visits, for example, as an effective way to develop and maintain relationships with families and to learn first-hand what is important to them and their children's education and development.*

- **Wrap-around services accessed through a school or a community-based organization can offer invaluable opportunities for engagement for any program.** *Approximately 70% of NCLR affiliates offer wrap-around services, including counseling, snacks and meals, fitness and nutrition education programs, and classes for parents. Parents in these programs especially appreciate the opportunity to support their child's learning by participating in many of these activities. The higher a family's engagement with an organization, the more trust that is built and the higher the possibility for their sustained participation in programs.*

- **Programs should operate as a bridge between parents and schools.** *Parents who lack information about the education system, or whose level of engagement is otherwise limited during regular school hours, often rely on afterschool and summer learning programs to learn about their child's progress. Afterschool and summer programs can provide parents the tools and resources to become active advocates for their child's education. One NCLR affiliate in Los Angeles ensures parents have a voice in the program by circulating a survey that asks parents to list the core values they want their kids to be taught during the life skills portion of the afterschool program. The selected values are then featured in weekly programming. Another NCLR affiliate program involves parents through a Consejo de Padres (parent council) that helps reach out to other parents to get them involved as volunteers and in planning special events.*

- **Programming can be enhanced through community partners.** *Expanded learning programs represent a critical opportunity for youth, particularly underserved youth, to gain competitive skills, such as global literacy and problem solving, and to develop their creativity and capacity to innovate* *through additional academic supports and enrichment activities. Community partners can enhance the effectiveness and reach of an afterschool program's activities. An NCLR-affiliate school in Houston seamlessly integrates community art and music resources by working with a local nonprofit organization that offers a mariachi afterschool club, providing not only music instruction but access to musical instruments. Close collaboration with families and community groups makes it more likely that the participating students will receive the full range of learning opportunities they need to be successful, and they'll get them in a positive, engaging environment.*

- **Active family involvement can help parents understand a program's value and provide critical support for their child's attendance and engagement.** *Some afterschool and summer programs have poor attendance because the programming may not be engaging or interesting to youth. Programs may also be poorly subscribed because parents have little knowledge or involvement in these programs, so they do not understand the value of the programs and do not encourage or expect their children to attend. The Big Thought afterschool and summer programs in Dallas, for example, have high attendance rates, especially among hard-to-reach, low-income Latino students. Program leaders assertively reach out to families through a variety of community- and faith-based organizations to encourage their children to participate and attend regularly. The powerful combination of Big Thought's highly engaging programming, which integrates the arts through all subjects, and its extensive family and community outreach efforts has resulted in a nearly 90% attendance rate for its programs.*

> Afterschool and summer programs can provide parents the tools and resources to become active advocates for their child's education.

In a time of severe constraints on public financing and deep budget cutbacks, it is very important to examine the key elements that maximize program impact for students and their families. Families and community partners are invaluable in ensuring that the components of effective programming for students are in place in afterschool and summer programs. They help elevate the program's value and raise awareness about

Wausau, Wisconsin

In Wausau, Wisconsin, the school district's summer program was poorly attended by youth from some student subgroups, including struggling, low-income white students, as well as Hmong and Latino students, who needed additional learning support the most. The summer learning coordinator and principals of the participating schools turned this situation around by communicating directly with the families and by working through community intermediaries to explain both the specific types of assistance that students would receive to help them catch up and keep up and also the wide selection of fun, broadening experiences that students could choose.

the necessary resources to implement it effectively. Everybody wins!

For More Information

Additional resources for effectively engaging families in afterschool and summer programs can be found at the following websites:

- The National Council of La Raza (NCLR) has published *Core Qualities for Successful Expanded Learning Time Programs*, which builds on existing research and assessment tools to address the unique needs of community organizations and schools serving Latino students and their families. http://www.nclr.org/index.php/issues_and_programs/education/programs/extended_learning_time_programs/

- With a grant from the New York Times Foundation, TASC has developed a guidebook for parent engagement, *Increasing Family and Parent Engagement in After-School,* which outlines 15 examples of how site coordinators and staff are successfully engaging parents at their after-school program. It also contains sample materials that program sites can use to improve parent involvement. http://www.tascorp.org/content/document/detail/1455/

- Child Trends has published a research-to-results brief, *Building, Engaging, and Supporting Family and Parental Involvement in Out-of-School Time Programs,* that discusses elements of family involvement and why it matters for out-of-school-time programs. The brief also examines some of the issues that programs face when attempting to engage parents, and it offers suggestions for how programs and staff can encourage family and parental involvement. http://www.childtrends.org/Files/Child_Trends-2007_06_19_RB_ParentEngage.pdf

ABOUT THE AUTHOR

Delia Pompa is senior vice president for programs at the National Council of La Raza. Throughout her career, Pompa has focused on creating new responses to the needs of Hispanic families and children within leading local, state, and federal agencies and national and international organizations. As an educator, Pompa has been especially instrumental in helping academic institutions understand and respond to the needs of underserved children and their teachers. She is the former director of the Office of Bilingual Education and Minority Languages Affairs in the U.S. Department of Education and the former executive director of the National Association for Bilingual Education.

REFERENCES

Afterschool Alliance. (2008). *Afterschool: Supporting family involvement* (Issue Brief 32). Retrieved from http://www.afterschoolalliance.org/issue_briefs/issue_parent_involvement_32.pdf

Durlak, J. A., & Weissberg, R. P. (2010). *The impact of after-school programs that promote personal and social skills*. Retrieved from http://casel.org/publications/the-impact-of-after-school-programs-that-promote-personal-and-social-skills/

Montes, M., & Campisteguy, M. (2008). *Latino family engagement in after-school programs*. Retrieved from http://www.nclr.org/index.php/publications/latino_family_engagement_in_after- school_programs/

Montes, M. (2009). *Latino youth in expanded learning time programs*. Retrieved from http://www.nclr.org/index.php/publications/latino_ youth_in_expanded_learning_time_programs/

Weiss, H., & Lopez, M. E. (2009). Redefining family engagement in education. *Family Involvement Network of Educators (FINE) Newsletter, 1*(2). Retrieved from http://www.hfrp.org/family-involvement/publications-resources/redefining-family-engagement- in-education

Priscilla Little
Research and Strategy Consultant

Evidence-Based Strategies for Supporting and Enhancing Family Engagement

Family engagement should be a vital component of any strategy to expand learning opportunities for children and youth after school and during the summertime—whether at the organizational, community, state, or national level. Under current federal guidelines for the 21st Century Community Learning Centers initiative, "family engagement" takes the form of activities to support parental involvement and family literacy. All centers are required to track and report the number of family members who participate as part of the annual Profile and Performance Information Collection System (PPICS). Consistently those data indicate that the majority of centers do, indeed, provide these important activities for families.

> [21st Century Learning Centers] are supporting some of the most economically needy families in the country.

In 2010 alone, 9,139 centers (approximately 85% of all centers funded) served over 250,000 family members; the average adult attendance at adult activities was almost 28 family members. Further, data indicate that of the centers funded in 2010, over 60% served students eligible for free and reduced lunch, indicating that these centers are supporting some of the most economically needy families in the country. Summary data from the past 5 years of reporting indicate that the centers have cumulatively served over one million family members, with the average adult attendance per center rising each year.[1]

---

1. The data presented here are part of an unpublished data set archived at the 21st Century Community Learning Centers Profile and Performance Information Collection System (PPICS).

Figure 1. 21st Century Community Learning Centers adult family member participation, 2006–2010.

APR Year	School Year Only	Summer Only	Both	Total	N Centers	Avg. Adult Attendance per Center
2006	148,193	14,680	40,170	203,043	9,353	21.7
2007	165,960	12,537	34,249	211,192	8,987	23.5
2008	183,560	12,429	30,554	223,042	9,053	24.6
2009	173,791	14,031	27,199	213,552	8,704	24.5
2010	201,410	13,796	40,936	253,404	9,139	27.7
5-Year Total Parents Served				1,104,233		

Despite impressive numbers of families served, however, many 21st Century Community Learning Centers and other afterschool and summer programs struggle with more fully engaging families. This article presents six research-derived strategies that afterschool programs can and do use to engage families. A set of additional resources for educators and program managers is also included, along with examples drawn from several programs that have experienced noteworthy success in engaging families.

What can afterschool and summer learning programs including 21st Century Community Learning Centers do to support and improve family engagement? The following are six research-based strategies that 21st Century Community Learning Centers and other similar programs can use to improve their family engagement efforts (Bouffard, Westmoreland, O'Carroll & Little, 2011; Little, 2011).

1. **Have adequate and welcoming space to engage families.** Helping families feel welcome is an important first step on the road to building trusting relationships with families. 21st Century Community Learning Centers and other similar afterschool and summer programs can help families feel welcome by establishing a "family corner" in which family members can find resources about the program and services in the community. They can also make sure the signage at the center is welcoming and accessible in the languages spoken by the families served.

2. **Establish policies and procedures to promote family engagement.** To ensure that family engagement is a priority, afterschool and summer programs should include a section on family engagement in their operations manuals, laying out their strategies for engaging families; they should also consider including family engagement as part of their program quality standards. At minimum, this should include conducting at least one family open house per year. Many programs also have created a Family Handbook that helps family members understand the goals and purposes of the center.

3. **Communicate and build trusting relationships.** Frequent and positive communication with family members is critical to effective family engagement. This means treating family

> Frequent and positive communication with family members is critical to effective family engagement.

members with respect; asking them about their own lives and interests, as well as those of the students in the program; and ensuring that interactions with family members are not solely in response to negative student behaviors or performance. Some programs use a communications log to monitor the frequency and nature of communications with family members.

4. **Be intentional about staff hiring and training to promote effective staff-family interactions.** At the heart of quality afterschool programs are the staff who run them. Core components of effective staff-family interactions include hiring staff who reflect the demographics of the families served and who are trained in respect for cultural differences, including an examination of their own biases. Once hired, it is important to provide ongoing training and support to ensure that family engagement is part of a staff member's daily duties. In addition to external training, programs can set aside a time at staff meetings to reflect on and improve their family engagement strategies.

5. **Connect families to each other, to the program staff, to schools, and to other community institutions.** Afterschool and summer programs can play a vital role in facilitating connections, both within the program to other families and outside the program to schools and other community institutions. This role is emerging as particularly important for 21st Century Community Learning Centers, which have the opportunity to support a more holistic approach to education—one that requires afterschool programs, schools, and families to partner to provide expanded opportunities for learning throughout a longer learning day and across the entire calendar year.

Find Out What Families Think and Need

New Settlement's afterschool program at CES 64 in the Bronx decided that parent focus groups would be a good way to elicit information and initiate a strong platform for parent decision making in the afterschool program. To attract participants, flyers in Spanish and English were posted around the school and community. When the response was minimal, the site coordinator realized that this was not reaching her families. Since many parents had a history of feeling unwelcome, she had to take a different approach. She began direct outreach with a few parents, who in turn, gave her the names of others who may want to participate. She spoke to them individually, explaining the mission of her program and the need for parental input. In the end, 15 parents signed on to participate in the focus group sessions (The After School Corporation, 2006).

Case Management to Support Families' Basic Needs

The 21st Century Community Learning Centers funds a Boys and Girls Club in Buffalo, New York, that recognizes the critical role it can play in helping its participants attend the program and school healthy and ready to learn by supporting families' basic needs. It has created a full-time, salaried staff position at each clubhouse to help families deal with social issues, providing triage, case management, and referral services. It has also leveraged other resources to build an on-site kitchen that provides free meals and snacks to the program participants as well as deliberately cooks a surplus of meals and offers them to caretakers in "to go" boxes when they come to pick up their children (Manhattan Strategy Group, 2011).

6. **Help support families and their basic needs.** Support for families and their basic needs runs the gamut from providing access to community resources to hosting forums and discussion nights to address topics of concern to families to providing training on leadership and advocacy. At minimum, afterschool programs need to help families overcome logistical challenges, such as transportation, that may affect their children's participation. Many programs have community school partnerships. These partnerships can be enhanced in order to provide families with information about community resources to address particular social service needs.

While each of these strategies can serve to engage families, some research indicates that it is the constellation of many strategies that may best support participants. In a recent study of engaging older youth in afterschool, summer, and other out-of-school-time programs researchers found that programs for older youth that were successful in retaining at least 50% of the participants for 12 months or more utilized, on average, eight different family engagement strategies (Deschenes et al., 2010).

Also from the research we know that engaging families is a win-win for programs, families, and afterschool and summer learning program participants. Moving forward, as the 21st Century Community Learning Centers initiative and other efforts to expand learning beyond the school day continue to grow, it is imperative that the spotlight on family engagement, so evident in the 21st Century Community Learning Centers initiative, continues to shine throughout the expanded learning movement.

For More Information

Family Engagement in Afterschool Programs Resources

Several research-based toolkits and resources have been developed to help educators both in schools and in afterschool programs work more effectively with families.

- **Family Engagement in After School Inventory**
  Developed for 21st Century Community Learning Centers in Texas, this research-based inventory can be used as a self-assessment tool to help programs gauge their current and future capacities to engage families. http://www.texasace21.org/content/prime-blueprint-texas-ace, (see Appendix 11)

- **Focus on Families: How to Build and Support Family-Centered Practices in After School**
  A joint publication of United Way of Massachusetts Bay, Harvard Family Research Project, and BOSTNet, this resource provides four overarching strategies that programs can implement to engage families. http://www.hfrp.org/family-involvement/publications-resources/focus-on-families!-how-to-build-and-support-family-centered-practices-in-after-school

- **BOSTNet Engaging Families in Out-of-School Time Tool Kit**
  The Engaging Families Toolkit is aimed at afterschool programs and provides templates for assessing family engagement practices, developing an action plan, and designing a family engagement program. bostnet.org/matriarch/documents/EngagingFamiliesToolkit.pdf

- **Increasing Family and Parent Engagement in After-School**
  In this document TASC provides a guide for engaging parents in afterschool programs. TASC explains the importance of engaging families, offers advice and materials for effective outreach to parents, and highlights examples of successful family engagement methods.
  http://www.tascorp.org/files/1455_file_parent_engagement_03082006.pdf
- **Beyond the Bake Sale: The Essential Guide to Family-School Partnerships**
  This comprehensive family engagement resource examines, among other things, how to know whether a school or afterschool program is really open to partnerships and how to develop trusting relationships with families.
  www.thenewpress.com/bakesale

ABOUT THE AUTHOR

Priscilla Little is an independent research and strategy consultant who has been working on issues related to effective afterschool and summer learning programs for over a decade. Her clients include national education research firms, state education agencies, not-for-profit agencies, and private foundations. She is currently working for The Wallace Foundation to support its afterschool system-building work, and with the U.S. Department of Education on a research study to investigate good and innovative practices in 21st Century Community Learning Centers programs. The views represented in this article are solely her own and do not represent those of her clients.

REFERENCES

After School Corporation. (2006). *Increasing parent and family engagement after school.* Retrieved from http://www.tascorp.org/content/document/detail/1455/

Bouffard, S., Westmoreland, H., O'Carroll, K., & Little, P. (2011). Engaging families in out-of-school time programs. In H. Kreider & H. Westmoreland (Eds.), *Promising practices for engaging families in out-of-school time* (pp. 3–19). Charlotte, NC: Information Age.

Deschenes, S. N., Arbreton, A., Little, P. L., Herrera, C., Grossman, J. B., & Weiss, H. B. (with Lee, D.). (2010). *Engaging older youth: Program and city-level strategies to support sustained participation in out-of-school time.* Cambridge, MA: Harvard Family Research Project.

Little, P. (2011). *Family engagement needs inventory.* San Antonio, TX: Edvance Research.

Manhattan Strategy Group. (2011). *High school promising practices project for the 21st Century Community Learning Centers Program: Final report, addendum 2.* Washington, DC: US Department of Education.

Loras Osterhaus
Afterschool Director, Clinton Community Schools
Clinton, Iowa

Effective Strategies for Engaging Parents: Real-Life Experiences That Make a Difference

As almost all school- or community-based educators will admit, one of the biggest challenges they face is that of engaging parents or other adult caregivers meaningfully and consistently in their children's learning. Despite this challenge, educators deeply desire that parents become more involved in their children's education, as research clearly shows that there is a strong positive relationship between a student's success in school and the level of engagement by his or her parents with the school (Epstein, Clark, Salinas, & Sanders, 1997; Henderson & Mapp, 2002; Van Voorhis, 2001).

While it is important to have parents and other adult caregivers actively engaged in their children's education—not only in what is offered in school but also in afterschool and summer programs—what may work in one community or school to engage parents may not necessarily work in another setting. School and afterschool leaders must identify the barriers within their particular communities that prevent parents from being more active in their children's education. Is there a language barrier? Are there transportation issues? Do outside commitments and responsibilities, such as working more than one job to make ends meet, affect the amount of time available for parents to be involved? Are there negative attitudes toward the school system? Do families only hear from the school when their child is in trouble or having difficulty?

> School and afterschool leaders must identify the barriers within their particular communities that prevent parents from being more active in their children's education.

To address these and other challenges, Henderson and Mapp (2002) suggest the following action steps to establish effective family engagement programs:

- *Recognize that all parents, regardless of income, education level, or cultural background, want to be involved in their children's education and want their children to do well in school.*
- *Link family and community engagement efforts to student learning.*
- *Create initiatives that will support families to guide their children's learning from preschool through high school.*
- *Develop the capacity of school staff to work with families.*
- *Focus efforts to engage families on developing trusting and respectful relationships.*
- *Embrace a philosophy of partnership and be willing to share power with families. Make sure that parents and school staff understand that the responsibility for children's educational development is a collaborative enterprise.*

The 21st Century Community Learning Centers are based on improving student learning by more extensively engaging the community and families with schools and expanding opportunities after school. Clinton, Iowa, is one example of communities across the nation that takes seriously the potential of combining these purposes to enhance and improve student success.

Family Engagement in Clinton, Iowa

The Student Adventures Afterschool program in Clinton was established in 2003 with support from a 21st Century Community Learning Centers grant. Prior to receiving the grant, Clinton Community Schools had already established strong community partnerships, which laid a solid foundation to launch the new afterschool initiative and to build upon in it future years.

Clinton's Student Adventures Afterschool program currently serves students at six sites, four at the elementary level and two in middle schools. The program employs a combination of three strategies to help families become more engaged in its afterschool programs: partnerships, volunteerism, and regular and frequent communication.

....

Partnerships

Clinton's afterschool and summer programs are very fortunate to have developed supportive partnerships with a set of community-based organizations that are also committed to encouraging and promoting family engagement in a child's educational experience. These partnerships are founded on the premise that afterschool and summer program providers will be much more successful in engaging families by collaborating with community partners that already enjoy positive relationships with students and families.

One such example is a partnership with the local YWCA, which has developed a "Family Get Fit" program. The primary objective of this program is to have families "get fit" together through a set of fitness and nutrition activities facilitated by the local YWCA. Families who are involved with this program will have four opportunities to meet with a YWCA staff person as their motivational coach to help them through the program. All families involved will also listen to fitness and nutrition experts. Families have the chance to earn a free membership to the YWCA and to participate in four family fun events during the course of the program.

The afterschool program in Clinton also works with the local substance abuse council in conjunction with its "Eat With Me" campaign to promote wellness and family meal time together. The afterschool program advertises the campaign as part of the afterschool registration process; additionally, afterschool program staff participate on the committee that oversees this program.

An additional partner that has supported family engagement is Mighty Books, Jr., which provides family literacy activities. This program allows parents to access a website from home and spend quality time with their child, reading at their own convenience. The afterschool program tracks the use of the website, and to date, the initiative has received a positive response from parents.

Volunteerism

The Clinton afterschool and summer programs offer the parents of participating children the opportunity to play an active role by asking them to volunteer to assist with some of the academic enrichment activities, especially field trips. To date, this strategy has met with moderate success largely due to the demands on many parents who must work multiple jobs to make ends meet in the current economy; however, the afterschool and summer programs are committed to giving parents this opportunity to see firsthand what their child is learning so that they can be an active participant in the learning process.

These programs offer a variety of academic enrichment activities on a weekly basis for students and their families. As part of their regular responsibilities, program staff members regularly communicate with parents regarding upcoming activities to encourage their involvement. Enrichment activities offered to families include, for example, trips to a local "family" museum, science and environmental activities through the county conservation office, and safety activities through the local sheriff's department. The primary emphasis is to give parents the opportunity to be involved in their child's educational growth outside of the regular school-day classroom and to see some of the enriching things their child is learning. For the parents who have volunteered, this has been a great way to see school in a more positive light.

Communication

One of the most important aspects of the Clinton programs is communication, both internally and externally. Program staff regard communication as a major responsibility, to assure both that parents of children in the programs know the value of afterschool and that the community is informed of program activities and successes on a regular basis to help promote the benefits of the afterschool and summer programs.

One staple of the afterschool programs for the past 7 years is the annual Lights On Afterschool event in the fall. Not only is this event well attended by families who have children in the afterschool program, but also by the community as a whole, drawing close to 1,000 people every year. This event not only helps bring awareness of the value of afterschool programs to the community, but it also gives families the opportunity to spend quality time together by sharing a meal and other fun activities.

The Clinton program also utilizes monthly newsletters at each site to highlight success stories, upcoming events, and opportunities to volunteer. For example, the newsletter is regularly used to promote "Family Nights." During the Family Nights, families first enjoy a meal together, and then program staff update parents on afterschool issues. Additionally, one of the program's community partners regularly provides a family activity and explains what it offers students in the program. Parents also have the opportunity to share their thoughts or concerns with staff in order to give them a voice in the program.

The primary emphasis is to give parents the opportunity to be involved in their child's educational growth outside of the regular school-day classroom and to see some of the enriching things their child is learning.

The Clinton afterschool and summer programs have found that, collectively, three engagement strategies have worked well for all program stakeholders: community partnerships, volunteerism, and regular and frequent communication with parents and adult caregivers. The 21st Century Community Learning Centers have as core principles expanding learning opportunities after school and during the summer and engaging community organizations and families. This powerful combination of essential elements reinforces Clinton's program strategies for helping more students succeed in these challenging times.

Conclusion

The Clinton programs are firmly committed to continue using these three strategies, but program staff also realize that they will need to fine tune and explore additional strategies so as not to become stale. The program has just begun, for example, to explore a "Parent University" program as a component of the Family Nights events. Staff have identified three possible courses: "A Father's Owner's Manual," "Developing Family Traditions," and "How Do We Know What Children Need?" Implementing this concept will integrate all three engagement strategies: partnerships (community partners will help present identified topics), volunteerism (parents will help implement and deliver the program), and communication (parents will have access to a wealth of new information).

All such efforts, both present and future, are directed towards helping parents see school in a more positive light, leading to more involvement in their child's education and to a greater capacity to support their child's success in school and life.

ABOUT THE AUTHOR

Loras Osterhaus is afterschool director for the Clinton Community Schools in Clinton, Iowa. A graduate of the University of Iowa, he has served as a professional educator for 17 years, including the past 10 in the afterschool field. In 2008 he was named one of 18 national "Afterschool Ambassadors" by the Afterschool Alliance in Washington, DC.

REFERENCES

Epstein, J. L., Clark, L., Salinas, K. C., & Sanders, M. G. (1997). *Scaling up school-family-community connections in Baltimore: Effects on student achievement and attendance.* Paper presented at the annual meeting of the American Education Research Association, Chicago, IL.

Henderson, A. T., & Mapp, K. L. (2002). *A new wave of evidence: The impact of school, family, and community connections on student achievement.* Austin, TX: National Center for Family and Community Connections with Schools.

Van Voorhis, F. (2001). Interactive science homework: An experiment in home and school connection. *NAASP Bulletin,* 85(627), 20–32. Retrieved from http://www.sagepub.com/kgrantstudy/articles/10/van%20Voorhis.pdf

Anne T. Henderson
Senior Consultant for Community Organizing and
Engagement, Annenberg Institute for School Reform

Carol Sills Strickland
Independent Consultant

Engaging Families in Afterschool and Summer Learning Programs for Middle School Youth

For over 30 years, research evidence has been growing that engaging families in children's learning has a powerful, positive, and lasting impact on students' academic outcomes and life prospects (Henderson & Mapp, 2002; Jeynes, 2005). Most of this research has been done in schools, but there is ample reason to consider applying what has been learned to programs that provide expanded learning opportunities to children and youth after school hours and during the summertime.

Research and Background

Consider the important new study *Organizing Schools for Improvement: Lessons from Chicago* (Bryk, Sebring, Allensworth, Luppescu, & Easton, 2010). This study identifies "close ties with families and the community" as one of five "essential ingredients" that characterize schools that have improved significantly compared to schools that have stagnated or declined. The others are strong leadership, high professional capacity, instructional guidance, and a student-centered learning climate.

In schools that have turned around, teachers are familiar with students' cultures and backgrounds. They spend time in the community, invite parents to observe in classrooms, try to understand parents' concerns, and embrace parents as partners. Parents respond by becoming involved in school activities and addressing teachers' concerns about their children's schoolwork.

Not only can community-based programs benefit from incorporating these same elements, but in turn, they can help schools develop closer ties with families and surrounding community. Afterschool programs make it a priority to create a welcoming environment in which parents can feel comfortable engaging in their children's education (Strickland & Jean, 2005). When community organizations work inside schools, they can create a gateway for parents to become more involved in their children's learning.

Conversely, community organizations that operate such programs can provide an opening to the neighborhood for teachers. For example, a local program could sponsor a "community walk" for school and program staff to tour neighborhoods and identify local assets. Family members and local residents can serve as tour guides.

A key difference between high- and low-achieving students is how they spend their out-of-school time. Afterschool and summer programs often cultivate links with community partners and school programs, such as AVID and Gear-Up, to expand resources available to students and their families. Through these connections, families can have access to a variety of academic and extracurricular activities, such as tutoring, martial arts, music, drama, and dance, as well as education classes for parents. These opportunities allow and encourage adolescents to explore the larger world with guidance from their families (Henderson, Mapp, Johnson, & Davies, 2007).

> When community organizations work inside schools, they can create a gateway for parents to become more involved in their children's learning.

In a study of 21st Century Community Learning Centers, Strickland and Jean (2005) reported on promising practices that promote family participation in children's learning. The six programs in the study—half of which served middle school students—employed a variety of strategies to engage parents. In all sites visited, children generally responded positively to their parents' presence. Parents of students in the middle grades noticed improved behavior, attitudes, and communication at home, as well as greater attention to schoolwork, all of which they attributed to their children's participation in the program.

Corwin Middle School 21st Century Community Learning Centers Program in Pueblo, Colorado

The afterschool program at Corwin Middle School maintained both informal and structured communication with students' families. Whether face-to-face exchanges at pick-up time, or through monthly newsletters the site coordinator published with student help, families were made aware of what was happening with their students (Strickland & Jean, 2005).

Families liked the way parent-teacher conferences were coordinated with the afterschool program's family night. During the Family Night/Conference, teachers were in the gym during the afternoon and early evening, and a simple dinner was available. Parents said they could easily find and talk with teachers, then make follow-up appointments if needed. Because several teachers worked in the afterschool program, parents were familiar with them, which also helped create a welcoming feeling for families.

A key to the program's success was hiring "community advocates" to focus on families whose children were struggling in school. The advocates built relationships and offered assistance without "meddling" in families' lives. In home visits, the advocates listened to what parents wanted then connected families to resources and made referrals to counseling. The advocates also built rapport with students and teachers and helped "work things out" to avoid suspension. When the program began in 2000, attendance at parent-teacher conferences averaged about 23%. During the second year, parent participation shot up to 90% and remained at that level.

While the Corwin afterschool program ceased operating at the end of the 2008 funding cycle, the program's foundational commitment to family engagement continues to exert major influence to the present day. Corwin has been restructured as a magnet school that requires 18 hours of volunteering per family each year, thus ensuring that parents are significantly involved. The former director of the 21st Century Community Learning Centers program at Corwin Middle School is now in charge of the Upward Bound program at Pueblo Community College. She has cultivated significant parent participation in that program, which serves some of the same families whose children attended the afterschool program at Corwin Middle School. Corwin's legacy of strong family engagement endures!

Elmont Memorial Junior-Senior High School in Nassau County, New York

Communication with parents is an integral part of Elmont's before-school and afterschool support programs for 600 seventh- and eighth-grade students. Parents and teachers collaboratively design academic intervention plans that give personalized support for class work and the New York State Assessments. Teachers follow up by tailoring instruction to meet students' needs. The program is staffed entirely by teachers from the school, allowing close alignment with what's being taught in the classroom (National Education Association, 2011).

Almost 100% of the students enrolled at Elmont are children of color, and many are from immigrant families and single-parent households. The school had, however, a 94% graduation rate in 2011, exceeding the state standard of 80%. Over 90% of its graduates attend college. In 2006, when the program began, only 31% of Elmont students earned an advanced Regents diploma. In 2010, it rose to 49% (New York State Education Department, 2011).

··

Salomé Ureña de Henríquez Campus in Manhattan

Salomé Ureña de Henríquez is a community school developed by the New York City Department of Education and the Children's Aid Society, a local nonprofit organization. The campus serves a low-income Latino population and includes three middle schools and a high school. A full-time parent coordinator arranges for adult education (including ESL, GED, computer, financial literacy, and citizenship classes), as well as parent support groups, clubs, and advisory councils.

Through leadership training, parents learn to advocate for themselves and their children. They go to City Hall to promote afterschool and school-based health centers, launch letter-writing campaigns for immigrant rights and youth summer work opportunities, and do community organizing for housing rights. In addition, they learn how to navigate the education system, how to make the best use of parent-teacher conferences, and what to do to get a child admitted to college.

A recent evaluation of afterschool programs at six Children's Aid Society middle schools shows that students made significantly greater gains in math, reading, and positive behaviors than students who did not participate in these afterschool programs. Finally, the evaluation noted that the Children's Aid Society's community school model contributed to a positive school climate and enhanced support structure not usually found in stand-alone afterschool programs (Krenichyn, Clark, & Benitez, 2007).

What Do Families Want?

A study in four U.S. cities asked African American parents about what they want in afterschool programs (Robinson & Fenwick, 2007). For participating parents, "afterschool programs are more than a place for homework, a snack, and basketball," they offer hope for improving their children's life chances. In the parents' opinion, the following features are what make a high quality program:

- **Commitment to learning:** *Achievement, motivation, homework completion, school engagement, reading for pleasure, and math competence*
- **Constructive use of time:** *Participation in creative and fun activities*
- **Support:** *Personal attention, positive family communication, a caring environment, and positive adult relationships*
- **Social competence:** *Interpersonal and cultural competence, decision making, and conflict resolution*
- **Boundaries and expectations:** *High expectations and adult role models*
- **Positive identity:** *Self-esteem, personal power, and a positive view of the future*

Effective Strategies

Middle school students experience significant and often difficult transitions. Providing young people with expanded learning opportunities afterschool and summers, while simultaneously engaging families in those programs and in the regular school day, creates a "win" for everyone involved. These programs, including those supported through the 21st Community Century Learning Centers initiative, should take advantage of their less formal settings and frequent connections to community partners to reach out to families. By linking families more closely to afterschool and summer learning programs, as well as to schools and other supportive community institutions and organizations, they can improve student success. Below are several strategies that merit attention and inclusion:

> By linking families more closely to afterschool and summer learning programs, as well as to schools and other supportive community institutions and organizations, they can improve student success.

Focus school-family-program partnerships on improving student outcomes.
Link the content of afterschool classes and tutoring to the school curriculum, and use student achievement data to hone in on skills that need strengthening. Be sure to deliver the actual programming in hands-on, interesting, and engaging ways because doing more of the same is unlikely to boost student achievement. Helping families stay current with their students' progress keeps information flowing full circle. Families are much more likely to understand, accept, and accommodate suggestions if educators and staff of community partner organizations work together in afterschool or summer settings to explain data and provide recommendations.

Communicate frequently with families about their child's progress and about ways they can address their child's unique learning interests and needs.
Adolescents will profit by personal attention from adults, including their parents, in afterschool and summer programs. Adults in these programs should meet regularly with parents before and after school hours to discuss student progress, share information, and confer on strategies to support learning. Programs should involve parents, as well as use classroom teachers, staff of youth development organizations, and well-organized volunteers from cultural and scientific professional associations and other community groups, to increase the amount of personal attention accorded to youth to help more of them succeed.

Collaborate with parents to develop individualized intervention plans for students.
Classroom teachers, community teachers, and youth development staff in the afterschool and summer programs should use meetings with parents to provide recommendations of specific academic support programs for students at risk of falling behind. Teachers and program staff subsequently should develop instructional strategies based on feedback from parents and should incorporate those strategies

in the expanded learning settings and during the regular school day. These planning sessions are also useful venues for identifying student and family interests (for example, music, sports, fitness, robotics competitions, technology, languages) that expanded learning programs can then include in their offerings, weaving in needed basic skills and social and emotional development.

Build relationships and a sense of community with families.
School-community partnerships can employ "community advocates" who develop rapport with families whose children are at risk of failure or dropping out of school. Advocates can help bring about positive changes in their children through sharing both good and bad news and helping them to understand their children and communicate with them better. This rapport can, in turn, be used to develop more relevant and engaging afterschool, evening, weekend, and summer programming and opportunities for families (for example, sessions on the requirements for attending and succeeding in college, joint family-student art or math nights, and cooking and family gardening classes).

Provide a safe space for families and school staff to connect.
Comprehensive afterschool programs, including 21st Century Community Learning Centers—along with their community partners—should turn their schools into hubs of community life. They could, for example, create a "family room" on campus that provides a welcoming space for parents and other caregivers to attend workshops. The room can be staffed by a parent coordinator or a community resident whose children graduated from the school. Community partners can sponsor community-building events, such as an annual heritage or neighborhood celebration, that bring hundreds of families and other community members to the school.

Build parents' capacity to participate in multiple ways.
Expanded learning programs, including 21st Century Community Learning Centers programs, can develop and help coordinate parent leadership institutes. (See for example the Parent Leadership Institute offered by the Children's Aid Society in New York City.) This type of leadership training can advance parents' capacity to contribute to the life of their children's schools (Epstein et al., 2009). In a yearlong institute, for example, parents could learn many ways to foster their own and their children's education, support their families financially, develop social capital, and advocate for high quality schools for their own and other people's children. Leadership development can also include showing parents how to secure more expanded learning opportunities for their children and how to identify community partners needed to improve the afterschool and summer programs that their children attend.

Both research and practice make clear that neither schools nor afterschool programs will succeed in improving student outcomes without engaging families. *If families are out of the loop, there is no loop,* and the focused energy that is needed to make and sustain gains will dissipate. Fortunately, there is much good information on how to do this effectively if we will just make use of it.

For More Information

Family-School-Community Partnerships 2.0, a new report from the National Education Association, offers many examples of wrap-around and community education programs that collaborate with families to support student achievement. For a free copy of the report, go to www.neapriorityschools.org/family-school-community-partnerships.

Afterschool Programs as an Oasis of Hope for Black Parents in Four Cities is a 2007 report from the Black Alliance for Educational Options (BAEO) that includes detailed information about family engagement in afterschool programs. It is available online at www.baeo.org/files/mottSummary.pdf.

Focus on Families! How to Build and Support Family-Centered Practices in After School is a 2006 report from the Harvard Family Research Project that profiles programs that engage families and offers information about strategies and approaches. To download a free copy, go to www.hfrp.org/out-of-school-time/publications-resources/focus-on-families!-how-to-build-and-support-family-centered-practices-in-after-school.

The Harvard Family Research Project website has an entire section on out-of-school time, with several publications, evaluations, and recorded webinars available for free download. See www.hfrp.org/out-of-school-time and www.hfrp.org/complementary-learning.

The Coalition for Community Schools has published a number of reports and studies on the benefits of community schools for students and families. The most recent is *Community Schools Research Brief, 2009.* To download a free copy, go to www.communityschools.org/assets/1/AssetManager/CCS%20Research%20Report2009.pdf.

The Children's Aid Society's National Center for Community Schools recently published a user-friendly manual entitled *Building Community Schools: A Guide for Action.* To download a free copy, go to www.nationalcenterforcommunityschools.org.

ABOUT THE AUTHORS

Anne T. Henderson, a senior consultant to the Community Organizing and Engagement Program at the Annenberg Institute for School Reform, is co-author (with Karen L. Mapp, Vivian Johnson, and Don Davies) of *Beyond the Bake Sale: The Essential Guide to Family-School Partnerships* (New Press, 2007) and many other reader-friendly publications on the impact of family engagement on student achievement.

Carol Sills Strickland is an educational researcher who focuses on youth development in afterschool and summer programs, parent/family participation in education, program evaluation and planning, and youth engagement in education. Based in Washington, DC, she works as an independent consultant with national and local nonprofit organizations.

REFERENCES

Bryk, A. S., Sebring, P. B., Allensworth, E., Luppescu, S., & Easton, J. Q. (2010). *Organizing schools for improvement: Lessons from Chicago*. Chicago, IL: University of Chicago Press.

Epstein, J. L., Sanders, M. G., Simon, B. S., Salinas, K. C., Jansorn, N. R., Van Voorhis, F. L. (2009). *School, family, and community partnerships: Your handbook for action*. Thousand Oaks, CA: Corwin Press.

Henderson, A., & Mapp, K. L. (2002). *A new wave of evidence: The impact of school, family and community connections on student achievement*. Austin, TX: Southwest Educational Development Lab.

Henderson, A., Mapp, K. L., Johnson, V., & Davies, D. (2007). *Beyond the bake sale: The essential guide to family-school partnerships*. New York, NY: New Press.

Jeynes, W. H. (2005, December). *Parental involvement and student achievement: A meta-analysis* (Research Digest). Retrieved from Harvard Family Research Project website:http://www.gse.harvard.edu/hfrp/projects/fine/resources/digest/meta.html

Krenichyn, K., Clark, H., & Benitez, L. (2007). *Children's Aid Society 21st Century Community Learning Centers after-school programs at six middle schools: Final report of a three-year evaluation: 2004–2007*. New York, NY: The Children's Aid Society.

National Education Association. (2011). *Family-school-community partnerships 2.0: Collaborative strategies to advance student learning*. Washington, DC: Author.

New York State Education Department. (2011). *The New York state school report card: Accountability and overview report 2009–10: Elmont Memorial High School*. Retrieved from https://reportcards.nysed.gov/files/2009-10/AOR-2010-280252070002.pdf

Robinson, G., & Fenwick, L. (2007). *Afterschool programs as an oasis of hope for black parents in four cities*. Washington, DC: Black Alliance for Educational Options.

Strickland, C., & Jean, I. (2005, April). *Promising practices that promote family participation in afterschool programs: Another link to positive educational outcomes*. Paper presented at the Annual Meeting of the American Educational Research Association, Montreal, Canada.

Paula E. Egelson
Director of Research, Southern Regional
Education Board

Family Involvement in Expanded Learning Programs for High School Students

Research, common sense, and practical experience all make it crystal clear: *Family involvement is critical for student academic success.* Consider the following research findings:

- *Low parent interest in a child's schooling is associated with substandard student achievement (Steinberg, 1996).*

- *Bogenschneider (1997) studied 8,000 high school students in nine high schools in Wisconsin and California and found that when parents were involved in their teen's schooling, students reported higher grades in school. Parental involvement showed consistently positive results, regardless of the education level of the parent.*

- *Parents play a critically important role in their children's academic achievement and social-emotional development (Comer, 1980; Eccles & Harold, 1996).*

- *Various parenting, volunteering, and home learning activities positively influence student grades, number of course credits completed, attendance, behavior, and school preparedness, regardless of student background and past achievement (Simon, 2001).*

Family involvement is also critical to student success in expanded learning programs offered after school, on weekends, and during the summer. Moreover, many such programs offer literacy and other educational activities for the entire family, and these programs are, therefore, of particular importance to students who attend high-poverty and low-performing schools. According to Ellen Gannett, director of the National Institute on Out-of-School Time, afterschool and summer learning programs "integrate the best of teaching and learning and engage youth in active, positive youth development and enrichment opportunities that will inspire them to become academically successful, good citizens, physically and emotionally healthy, artistic, social, problem solvers, and lifelong learners" (Gannett, 2012). In fact, 21st Century Community Learning Centers, the federally funded expanded learning programs, have been shown to improve student grades and test scores, lower dropout rates, and generate a sense of competence among students (Hoover-Dempsey et al., 2005).

Elements of Family Involvement

Most expanded learning programs include a family involvement component. At the most basic level, programs typically incorporate a system of communication with families, a plan for family involvement, and an inviting program environment for families. High quality programs, however, also include many or all of the following components:

- *They establish a parent/community advisory committee that meets regularly.*
- *They distribute a family handbook that can include such items as family support activities, a calendar of events and guidance in helping children in school.*
- *They offer educational experiences for families and share community resources with families.*
- *They collect informal and formal feedback from families and community partners to determine program strengths and weaknesses.*

Expanded learning opportunities at the secondary level for students can include, but are not limited to, work-based experiences, use of innovative technology, preparation for college and careers, community service, and/or personalized school plans. In the remainder of this article, we will explore the involvement of families in expanded learning programs for secondary students and offer recommendations in developing this component.

Effective Strategies for Family Involvement in Secondary-Level Expanded Learning Opportunity Programs

A variety of family involvement strategies are available for parents of high school students participating in expanded learning programs.

Homework/tutoring contracts. One such strategy is a *homework/tutoring contract* for families, parents, and guardians, such as the one developed by the Center for Afterschool Education at Foundations (Weisburd, 2007). This model flexibly addresses whether the parent wants the student to do homework during the afterschool program, how the student works best, and when the student needs assistance.

College application assistance. Another effective strategy for involving families in expanded learning programs is to hold information sessions for parents and students to discuss the college application process. During these sessions, staff can also provide parents with information about financial aid (Peterson & Fix, 2007). Family tours of local colleges are also a helpful activity in the college preparation process.

Alternative schools. For academically challenged students, Big Picture Learning offers a promising approach. Established in 1995, this organization (http://www. bigpicture.org/) operates an alternative school model for unsuccessful students in 60 sites across the country. As part of the model, students create a personalized educational plan with their parents. Technology and community resources are important components of the program, and students take advantage of learning opportunities before and after school, at home, and within the community (Alliance for Excellent Education, 2011).

Examples of Successful Secondary Expanded Learning Programs

Among the many expanded learning programs designed for high school students, the following program examples are noteworthy for both their reach and their documented successes with older youth.

Results show that participants missed fewer days of school, failed fewer courses, and had higher graduation rates and lower dropout rates than their high school counterparts.

After School Matters. Successful secondary expanded learning programs often focus on careers and/or college preparation. After School Matters (ASM) is a nonprofit organization that offers Chicago teenagers high quality, out-of-school time opportunities in the arts, science, sports, technology, and communications at no charge (www.afterschoolmatters.org). Its project-based programs introduce teenagers to careers in education and help them develop job skills. The program provides regular updates about student progress to parents, as well as offering community updates and regular e-newsletters. Results show that participants missed fewer days of school, failed fewer courses, and had higher graduation rates and lower dropout rates than their high school counterparts.

Breakthrough Collaborative. Another example of a successful expanded learning opportunities program for youth is the Breakthrough Collaborative (www.breakthroughcollaborative.org). It has locations both domestically and internationally. Breakthrough Collaborative launches motivated middle school students on the path to college and prepares secondary students for careers in education. In 33 years, Breakthrough has assisted 20,000 students in preparing for college. This program is focused on preparing high-achieving middle-school students who are primarily of color and from low-income families to enter and succeed in college-preparatory high school programs. Breakthrough Collaborative also recruits and trains outstanding high school and college students to become teachers and to teach other students about careers in education. This program offers services to students and their families that include academic enrichment, one-on-one tutoring, and secondary and college preparation. For the Breakthrough Collaborative, family support is paramount in ensuring student success. Parents attend parent/teacher conferences, student orientation, and family reunions. Eighty-five percent of Breakthrough "teachers" show a strong interest in teaching following a summer internship.

Young Audiences Arts for Learning. This national not-for-profit arts-education organization recently celebrated its 60th anniversary (www. youngaudiences.org). The organization is located in over 20 states. It includes in-school, afterschool, and family programs and allows young people to work with professional artists to learn, create, and take part in the arts. There are family nights that include arts appreciation, productions, and presentations. Over the years a correlation has been shown between student participation in Young Audiences and improvements in their academic performance and standardized test scores, increases in student attendance, and decreases in dropout rates.

> . . . a critical starting point is to make family involvement activities relevant for family members. These activities should have a targeted educational focus and be fun.

A growing number of state afterschool networks are working to expand the connection between afterschool and summer programs and participation in careers and postsecondary education. Increasing family engagement is often an important part of the set of strategies discussed. Along those lines, in June 2012, a successful statewide forum on college and career readiness in Indiana was co-hosted by the Indiana Afterschool Network in partnership with the Commission for Higher Education/ Learn More Indiana, American Graduate Initiative, Indiana Department of Education, and the Expanded Learning and Afterschool Project (Indiana Afterschool Network, 2012).

Recommendations for School and Community Groups

As community or school groups implement family involvement activities in expanded learning programs provided to high school students, the following recommendations will help make the planning and development process easier:

1. Sometimes the parents that need—and may even want—to be deeply involved the most in the success of their high school students, may themselves not have graduated from high school and/or may not have "good memories" of high school. Therefore, a critical starting point is to make family involvement activities relevant for family members. These activities should have a targeted educational focus and be fun. Afterschool, weekend, and summer programs can offer parents a more comfortable, flexible setting in which to engage with their young people and become involved in their education. Creating a program that reflects the desires of the families and the students themselves can lead to offering programming that better matches their interests and needs, helps with program improvements, and increases attendance and parental investment.

2. Afterschool, weekend, and summer programs for secondary students are positive avenues to learn about and experience career and college possibilities. These important learning opportunities for students can be made more meaningful if they include engaging activities to help family members learn about those options, including about how to pay for future postsecondary education.

3. Often afterschool, weekend, and summer programs for secondary students have a variety of school-college-workforce-family partnerships. So it is worth analyzing which of the partner organizations have particularly strong connections to families and then take advantage of those linkages to create the family involvement options. The majority of parents want to be involved in their young people's current and future education, but many face barriers that prevent them from doing so. Many regular school-day programs do not have the resources or the time to reach out to families who are interested but may be reluctant to participate. It is important to take time to identify what resources already exist in the community and enlist their help.

4. Parents, school personnel, and community partners are all stretched for time and resources. Programs should be sure to eliminate duplication and maximize resources when developing the family involvement activities. Does a neighboring community group, 2- or 4-year college, workforce preparation program, or high school have a similar program? They should collaborate and share resources. Aligning the family component to educational goals is a must. Paramount goals are helping more students graduate from high school and preparing students for college and careers. Parents also enjoy activities, however, that offer a chance to socialize and discuss concerns with other parents and staff. So afterschool, weekend, and summer programs can also be an important forum for identifying and providing resources and services that strengthen families as well as connect them more directly to the educational goals.

For More Information

The following publications are examples that offer suggestions for strengthening family engagement in expanded learning programs:

Ferguson, C., Jordan, C., & Baldwin, M. (2010). *Working systematically in action: Engaging family and community.* Austin, TX: SEDL.

Henderson, A. (2007). *Beyond the bake sale: The essential guide to family/school partnerships.* New York, NY: New Press.

ABOUT THE AUTHOR

Paula E. Egelson, a native of the Midwest who has worked extensively in the South, has worked as a community organizer, a classroom teacher, a director of school improvement, and a policy analyst. She currently works as the director of research for the Southern Regional Education Board in Atlanta.

REFERENCES

Alliance for Excellent Education. (2011, August). *Expanded learning opportunities: A more comprehensive approach to preparing high school students for college and a career* (Issue Brief). Retrieved from http://www.all4ed.org/files/ExpandedLearningOpps.pdf

Bogenschneider, K. (1997). Parental involvement in adolescent schooling: A proximal process with transcontextual validity. *Journal of Marriage and the Family, 59,* 718–733.

Comer, J. P. (1980). *School power: Implications of an intervention project.* New York, NY: Free Press.

Eccles, J. S., & Harold, R. D. (1996). Family involvement in children's and adolescents' schooling. In A. Booth & J. Dunn (Eds.), *Family-School Links* (pp. 3–34). Mahwah, NJ: Lawrence Erlbaum.

Gannett, E. (2012, Spring/Summer). Expanded learning: Opportunities for partnerships with a new twist and a new name [Commentary]. *Research and Action 33*(2), 6–7. Retrieved from http://www.wcwonline.org/Research-Action-Report-Spring/Summer-2012/commentary-expanded-learning-opportunities-for-partnerships-with-a-new-twist-and-a-new-name

Goerge, R., Cusick, G. R., Wasserman, M., & Gladdin, R. M. (2007, January). *After-school program and academic impact: A study of Chicago's after school matters* (Issue Brief No. 112). Chicago, IL: Chapin Hall Center for Children at the University of Chicago.

Hoover-Dempsey, K. V., Walker, J. M. T., Sandler, H. M., Whetsel, D., Green, C. L., Wilkins, A. S., & Closson, K. (2005). Why do parents become involved? Research findings and implications. *The Elementary School Journal, 106*(2), 105–130.

Indiana Afterschool Network. (2012). College and career readiness forum: KnowHow2Go through afterschool. Retrieved from http://www.indianaafterschool.org/CollegeCareerReadinessForum.shtml

Peterson, T. K., & Fix, S. (Eds.). (2007). *Afterschool advantage: Powerful new learning opportunities.* Mooresville, NJ: Foundations, Inc.

Simon, B. S (2001). Family involvement in high school: Predictors and effects. *NASSP Bulletin, 85*(627), 8–19.

Steinberg, L. (1996). *Beyond the classroom: Why school reform has failed and what parents need to do.* New York, NY: Simon & Schuster.

U.S. Department of Education, Office of Elementary and Secondary Education, Academic Improvement and Teacher Quality Programs, 21st Century Learning Centers. (2011). *Family involvement brief.* Retrieved from http://y4y.ed.gov/Content/Resources/FI_Research_Brief_09212011.pdf

Weisburd, C., (2007). *Academic content afterschool style.* Mooresville, NJ: Center for Afterschool Education at Foundations, Inc.

A Growing Nationwide Infrastructure for Quality, Expansion, and Partnerships

6

Terry K. Peterson
Senior Fellow, College of Charleston

Steve Fowler
Partner, FowlerHoffman, LLC

Terri Ferinde Dunham
Partner, Collaborative Communications Group

Creating the Recent Force Field: A Growing Infrastructure for Quality Afterschool and Summer Learning Opportunities

Over the past 15 years, an increasingly vital and complex infrastructure has helped fuel and sustain the afterschool and summer learning movements. With the aid of both formal and informal intermediaries, this evolving infrastructure works to improve quality and increase access in order to help more young people catch up, keep up, and get ahead in engaging, safe, and supervised settings. This infrastructure has helped more than two million young people participate in afterschool and summer learning opportunities over the past 10 years.

No one agency, organization, or group is responsible at the community, state, or national level for the hours from 3:00–6:00 p.m. on weekdays or in the summer, while most parents are working. Despite the increase in availability of afterschool and summer programs, 15 million children still go home alone with no adult supervision during these hours. Many schools, educators, families, and community- and faith-based organizations seek to fill these gaps with positive developmental experiences and expanded learning opportunities, but too often these programs can be disconnected, underfunded, and underutilized in many communities.

To meet these challenges, this growing infrastructure for expanded learning, both after the school day ends and during the summertime, provides the supports and resources that would be impossible for any single program or organization to create. Public funding has been critical, fueled by the growth in federal funding for the 21st Century Community Learning Centers initiative since 1997 and in some cases by growth in state funding, such as California's After School Education and Safety program. Notably, quality systems have grown exponentially with the development and the adoption of quality standards now established in more than 34 states. The articles in this section of *Expanding Minds and Opportunities* focus in detail on some of the elements of this essential infrastructure.

Below we summarize some of the recent dynamics of this unique infrastructure by looking at five critical components of the current afterschool "force field." This sometimes invisible but veritable force field of organizations, policies, funding, networks, and research creates opportunities and removes barriers to expanded learning opportunities for millions of young people in rural and suburban communities, as well as small towns and large urban areas nationwide.

Afterschool Force Field

....

FORCE #1: Federally funded 21st Century Community Learning Centers program

Broad bipartisan support contributed to the creation of the 21st Century Community Learning Centers initiative as part of the Elementary and Secondary Education Act (ESEA) of 1994. This bipartisanship has extended across the years in securing the reauthorization of the initiative in Title IV, Part B of the ESEA, as amended in 2002, and also in generating substantial increases in federal appropriations for the initiative from 1997 to 2012.

The consistency and growth of the program—from $1 million in 1997 to more than $1 billion 15 years later—has been a major catalyst for the field. Local 21st Century Community Learning Centers programs serve as models of best practice, help define quality, provide professional development, and focus on academic outcomes, thus compelling all kinds of afterschool programs to be more intentional in their design and approach. The shift of responsibility for awarding 21st Century Community Learning Center grants in 2002 from the federal to the state level led to state education agencies assigning staff and even creating divisions with responsibility for administering the program and supporting quality afterschool in their state. These entities not only manage grant competitions and monitor programs but also support the development of program indicators and sponsor conferences and trainings that deepen understanding of effective afterschool programming.

Community-school partnerships are required for successful 21st Century Community Learning Centers programs. Along with family engagement, these collaborations are unique features of the type of innovative learning opportunities that 21st Century Community Learning Centers created as compared to most other federally or state-funded programs.

A number of national, regional, state, and local foundations have contributed to the development of quality programming and support networks for these community learning centers. From the beginning, the C. S. Mott Foundation has been a critical ally in this growth and the nationwide infrastructure it represents.

As of May 2012, there were 4,619 21st Century Community Learning Centers local grantees funding afterschool and summer programs for almost 1.7 million children and youth in 11,068 school-based and community-based centers across the country (Afterschool Alliance, 2012). The program is so popular and competitive that only one out of three local requests for funding is awarded. Over the last 10 years, $4 billion in local grant requests had to be denied because of the lack of adequate federal funding and intense competition (O'Donnell & Ford, 2013).

Many state departments of education, along with other state and community partners, are aggressively working to improve the quality and results of expanded learning programs, while at the same time keeping the programming relevant and attuned to the needs of today's students. Several articles in the Infrastructure section of *Expanding Minds and Opportunities* present, in-depth, the strategies states are taking to keep afterschool and summer 21st Century Community Learning Centers programs constantly improving and addressing contemporary issues.

Several states have moved to expand learning beyond the traditional school day and year through positive new working relationships among classroom teachers and community-based practitioners, or "second-shift" educators. The biggest such state initiative, both in terms of the number of programs affected as well as the scale of investment, is in California where several thousand schools with community partners are helping expand education and enrichment opportunities to tens of thousands of struggling and low-income students. In many ways, the California program is working in parallel and in concert with the 21st Century Community Learning Centers initiative. This is an important approach from which other states could learn to make large-scale policy improvements in expanded learning.

. . . .

FORCE #2: *Statewide afterschool networks: Coalitions for policy, funding, and quality*

Weaving the voices of many into one collective and strategic policy agenda is a fundamental element of the force field that is provided by statewide afterschool networks. Now in 41 states, these networks are designed to create sustainable structures of statewide, regional, and local partnerships, particularly school-community partnerships, focused on supporting policy development at all levels.

These statewide entities of grassroots and grasstops leaders—from the governors' office and legislature to business, education, and community leaders—are driving the movement and leveraging a vast array of resources into expanded learning programs. With modest but consistent investment from the C. S. Mott Foundation and other national, state, and local funders, the networks do "a lot with a little" by focusing relentlessly on a common agenda to expand program availability and ensure quality learning experiences.

Over the past 12 years these networks grew from a simple idea to a powerful force now emerging in all 50 states.

FORCE #3: Citywide systems: Coordinating data, dollars, and development

With the statewide afterschool networks force at the state level, a complementary force is rising from cities and communities to link out-of-school-time players and stakeholders. At the local level, intermediaries connect public and private funders with providers, serving as the nucleus and guiding coordinator within a community's multifaceted network of government, schools, nonprofit organizations, and expanded learning programs. The Wallace Foundation has played a pivotal role in seeding intermediaries in a number of cities.

Some of the most influential leaders in the country are mayors and local municipal leaders who understand deeply that young people need more opportunities to succeed. They are taking the charge of advancing learning by coordinating the work of municipal agencies, including parks and recreation departments, human services offices, museum and library systems, arts organizations, housing authorities, and other public service entities. Equally impressive, local leaders from United Ways, faith communities, and community-based organizations are stepping up to develop systems of support—realizing the value of collaboration rather than operating in isolation.

The depth of this element of the afterschool infrastructure is apparent in the work of the National League of Cities Institute for Youth, Education and Families (YEF Institute). Here, a national membership organization is supporting summits and online learning communities with mayors, council members, and other municipal leaders and their staffs to inform local officials about the education, public safety, and economic development benefits of afterschool. It is providing new tools to improve local programs, from Connecticut and Texas to Minnesota and North Carolina to Washington State and Tennessee.

FORCE #4: Established body of research and evidence

Now we know: quality afterschool and summer learning opportunities work. We know that quality expanded learning programs are associated with increased academic performance, increased attendance in school, significant improvements in behavior and social and emotional development, and greater opportunities for hands-on learning in important areas that are not typically available during the traditional school day. Throughout *Expanding Minds and Opportunities* are numerous examples that define and demonstrate engaged and enriched learning.

Other sections of the *Expanding Minds and Opportunities* compendium detail the research, including the strong, comprehensive meta-analysis by Joseph Durlak (Loyola University Chicago) and Roger Weissberg (University of Illinois at Chicago) and the longitudinal work by Deborah Vandell (University of California-Irvine) and the Harvard Family Research Project. The recent significant growth and depth of the research and best practice base is a very positive force.

Just 15 years ago, tools and materials were limited to a few quality sources such as the National Institute on Out-of-School Time (NIOST) and organizations in the community education field. Now there are thousands of tools and resources available. The Harvard Family Research Project (HFRP)'s Out-of-School Time (OST) Program Research and Evaluation Database (www.hfrp.org/out-of-school-time/ost-database-bibliography), led by Heather Weiss, is a compilation of profiles written by HFRP of research studies and evaluations of OST programs and initiatives. The National Network of Statewide Afterschool Networks (www.statewideafterschoolnetworks.net/) has more than 500 resources to support systems-building. The Finance Project's Out of School Time Information Resource Center (www.financeproject.org/index.cfm?page=25) shares resources that help leaders address financing and sustainability issues for out-of-school-time programs. The National Summer Learning Association maintains a summer learning library and produces extensive research briefs (www.summerlearning.org/?page=library), and the Afterschool Alliance presents hundreds of research summaries and issue briefs, including a summary of studies documenting afterschool outcomes (www.afterschoolalliance.org/research.cfm).

New continuous improvement tools and reports, some highlighted in this Infrastructure section of *Expanding Minds and Opportunities*, provide an unequivocal force supporting and propelling quality expanded learning opportunities across the country.

FORCE #5: *Building the movement: The Afterschool Alliance*

Finally, there is a growing interconnection of many diverse groups, including educational and youth development institutions and community, cultural, and scientific organizations, working to expand and enrich learning in engaging and broadening ways. Not too long ago these schools and community and faith-based organizations were largely disconnected.

The Afterschool Alliance, formed in 1999, is connecting diverse and important players from the local, state, and national levels in the expanded learning space to come together for the common purpose of building public will to strengthen the infrastructure for expanded learning. At the federal level, the Afterschool Alliance is a leading voice for children, youth, families, and communities, dedicated to raising awareness of the importance of afterschool programs and advocating for more afterschool investments.

Each October, the Afterschool Alliance annually hosts Lights On! Afterschool—an essential grassroots education and advocacy effort. In 2012, more than one million people gathered at more than 9,000 sites across the country and at U.S. military bases worldwide to participate in an unparalled rally for afterschool programs.

The Afterschool Alliance produces and disseminates a vast array of fact sheets, issue briefs, research, and polling information that have come to be highly regarded. Its report *America After 3PM* (2009), the nation's most in-depth study of how America's children spend their afternoons, finds that 15 million young people—more than a quarter of our nation's children—are alone and unsupervised after school.

Conclusion

The force field for expanded learning opportunities is comprised of more individuals and institutions than can be named in one article. Notable forces that have contributed mightily to the force field include the National AfterSchool Association, which connects afterschool professionals; Foundations, Inc., which provides high quality professional development; the Coalition for Community Schools, which helps build up and out afterschool programs into community schools and community learning centers; and the Coalition for Building After-School Systems, which builds citywide afterschool systems. The new Expanded Learning and Afterschool Project shares cutting-edge best practices. The American Institutes for Research's Profile and Performance Information Collection System (PPICS) is designed to inform and improve the 21st Century Community Learning Centers across the United States.

> Education, community, and state leaders, as well as foundations and national organizations, can and should now capitalize on this infrastructure to advance cutting edge learning and youth development.

The evidence of the force field is also seen in emerging special interest groups, such as the American Educational Research Association OST Special Interest Group (SIG), and the Grantmakers for Education's Out of School Time Funders Network. Successful afterschool programs have also benefited greatly from the leadership and resources of independent community and faith-based programs; many local, regional and national foundations; and affiliates of major, nationwide organizations such as the Ys, 4-H, Boys and Girls Clubs, and Communities in Schools. Additionally, statewide and regional conferences and the nation's regional education labs have contributed significantly to the identification and spread of best practices.

The articles in *Expanding Minds and Opportunities* demonstrate the recent breadth, depth, and growth of the infrastructure supporting quality expanded learning opportunities in afterschool and summers. Education, community, and state leaders, as well as foundations and national organizations, can and should now capitalize on this infrastructure to advance cutting edge learning and youth development.

ABOUT THE AUTHORS

Terry K. Peterson is called "the King of Afterschool" by former United States Secretary of Education Richard W. Riley. Terry has a long and successful history of helping local, state, and national organizations develop strategies and partnerships for comprehensive education reform and expanded learning opportunities. He has worked internationally in Argentina, Mongolia, Brazil, Northern Ireland, China, and South Korea. He currently is Senior Fellow and Director of the Afterschool and Community Learning Network at the College of Charleston.

Steve Fowler of FowlerHoffman LLC—consultants on communications strategies for system and policy change—contributes to several initiatives on expanded learning opportunities for children and youth in afterschool and summer programs. He is currently also serving as an advisor to SRI International's project on the role of social networks in disseminating science content in California's afterschool system. His hands-on experience as a state senator in Nebraska taught him how policy making and budgeting really work.

Terri Ferinde Dunham has managed the National Network of Statewide Afterschool Networks for 10 years, building an infrastructure for network development. As a partner at Collaborative Communications Group, she works with foundations, nonprofits, government agencies, and communities to reimagine when, where, and how children and adults learn. Currently, she also leads the Expanded Learning and Afterschool project, working to promote afterschool and summer learning programs as sustainable affordable approaches for expanding learning. Previously, she held outreach and communications positions for 10 years at the United States Department of Education under Republican and Democratic administrations.

REFERENCES

Afterschool Alliance. (2009). *America after 3PM*. Retrieved from http://www.afterschoolalliance.org/AA3_Full_Report.pdf

Afterschool Alliance. (2012). 21st Century Community Learning Centers: Providing afterschool and summer learning supports to communities nationwide. Retrieved from http://www.afterschoolalliance.org/21st%20CCLC%20Fact%20Sheet_5_3_12_FINAL.pdf

O'Donnell, P., & Ford, J. (2013). The continuing demand for 21st Century Community Learning Centers across America: More than four billion dollars of unmet need. In T. Peterson (Ed.)., *Expanding Minds and Opportunities: Leveraging the Power of Afterschool and Summer Learning for Student Success*. Washington, DC: Collaborative Communications Group.

An-Me Chung
Former Program Officer, C.S. Mott Foundation

Gwynn Hughes
Program Officer, C.S. Mott Foundation

Terri Ferinde Dunham
Partner, Collaborative Communications Group

Making Partnerships Work for Policies That Expand Learning Opportunities: Statewide Afterschool Networks

Statewide afterschool networks are defining new ways of collaborating and shaping policies and practices for afterschool and expanded learning opportunities across the country. From Rhode Island to California, this national network of statewide afterschool networks has successfully sustained an afterschool movement dedicated to ensuring that all students have access to engaging and effective programming. "There is no doubt that these systems and infrastructures are based on the ideas that individuals and institutions can work toward a common goal and that long-term partnerships can make a difference," notes Heather Weiss, founder and director of the Harvard Family Research Project.

Now in 41 states, with expectations of growing to more, the statewide afterschool networks—through the support of the C.S. Mott Foundation and other funders—are focused on actively engaging and educating key decision makers in support of effective school and community-based afterschool programs, particularly in underserved communities.

Designing a New Way for Collaboration

Since 2002, the C.S. Mott Foundation has provided competitive funding to coalitions of key stakeholders in states committed to furthering afterschool and expanded learning policies and practices. The initiative was built on the public-private partnership started in 1998 between the U.S. Department of Education (ED) and the C.S. Mott Foundation to support the 21st Century Community Learning Centers grant program. The public dollars directly support the programs, while the Mott Foundation funds activities better suited to philanthropy than government, such as providing technical assistance, generating public will, identifying promising practices, supporting research and evaluation, and developing options for public policy.

Statewide Afterschool Networks

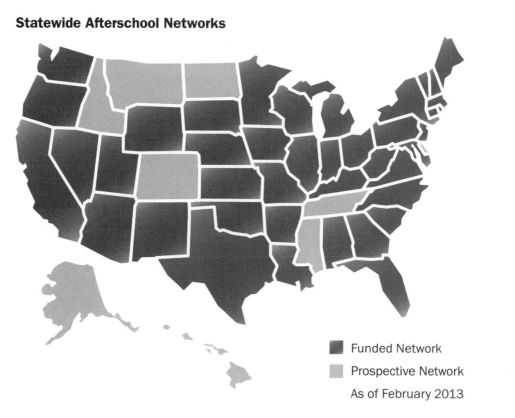

■ Funded Network

▨ Prospective Network

As of February 2013

After the federal program grew from $40 million in 1998 to $1 billion in 2002, administration of the initiative devolved primarily to the states. The C. S. Mott Foundation adopted a strategy to build a national expanded learning infrastructure that would connect grassroots and grasstops institutions and organizations and that would offer competitive funding to one statewide entity in each state. The design was to provide the "glue funding" to form networks that require a partnership between the state department of education and influential organizations and key stakeholders in a state. The mission was to build a wider, deeper, and stronger afterschool movement that would weather a distressed economic climate, changes in political leadership, and other challenges to comprehensive education programs.

The overarching goal was to build coalitions of diverse organizations working together to leverage public and private funding and partnerships in pursuit of good policies and practices. "No one 'owns' the field of afterschool. Networks must organize one voice, one message, and agree upon policy that helps all," explains Janelle Cousino, vice president at FowlerHoffman and a technical assistance provider to the networks. Networks function through a common vision, collective action, and shared responsibility and establish themselves as the "go to" source for research, examples of good practices, and expertise on afterschool and expanded learning opportunities.

Impact of the Statewide Afterschool Networks

Few other educational initiatives have the 10-year track record of the statewide afterschool networks. These networks have been key to advancing policy initiatives such as students' ability to earn academic credit for learning that takes place outside of school hours, promoting school-community partnerships, and securing and sustaining resources despite difficult economic times. These networks are also cultivating multiple leverage points to expand learning opportunities, including aligning afterschool and summer learning with policy agendas in education, child care, health and wellness, juvenile justice, nutrition, and others. Impact is assessed across a spectrum of results, from policy wins to diffusing threats to cutting afterschool funding to assisting municipal leaders in supporting quality afterschool programming. Even with limited resources and capacity, networks are high-impact investments.

An internal evaluation report from the Harvard Family Research Project (HFRP) (2010) concluded, "networks have made real strides toward building statewide infrastructure and policy support for afterschool programs, and have done so against a backdrop of change and uncertainty" (p. 51).

For more than a decade networks have ascribed to three common goals and report on their activities against those goals:

1. **Create sustainable partnership structures for policy development.** Networks understand that partnerships of influential individuals, agencies, and organizations are essential in showing policymakers and others that the support and need for afterschool programs is widespread and real. "Creating networks that are widely representative means continually working to bring new voices to the table while keeping all members of the network engaged," remarked Kacy Conley, network lead for the Pennsylvania Statewide Afterschool/Youth Development Network.

   Engaging the right stakeholders helps make the network agenda fit the needs of the state and makes it more likely that policy developments align with the network goals. Impact is measured in small and large ways:

   The Positive Youth Development Grant Program Act was passed by the Arkansas legislature in 2011 and signed into law. It builds off of the 2008 recommendations of the Governor's Task Force on Best Practices for After-School and Summer Programs by establishing a structure for a system of state-funded afterschool and summer programs.

   In Illinois, the After-school Youth Development Program Act, SB 3543, was signed into law in July 2010 and creates a framework for coordinating and strengthening afterschool services in the state.

Statewide Afterschool Network Goals

2002–present

1. Create a sustainable structure of statewide, regional, and local partnerships, particularly school-community partnerships, focused on supporting policy development at all levels.

2. Support the development and growth of statewide policies that will secure the resources necessary to secure and sustain new and existing school-based and school-linked afterschool programs.

3. Support statewide systems to ensure programs are of high quality.

In Rhode Island, the General Assembly passed H5967, which created a Joint Legislative Taskforce on Summer Learning. The taskforce also explored several high quality summer programs for all grade levels and made recommendations on ways to improve access to summer learning in the state. The taskforce reported its findings and recommendations in a report to the General Assembly in May 2010 and helped to develop the framework for funding that was included in the state FY2013 budget to pilot this work.

2. **Support statewide policies to secure funding.** Expanded learning opportunities are funded by an array of public and private dollars from multiple levels of government and under many agency banners—from human services to childcare to juvenile justice to education. Yet if bringing together the varied pieces and players in the afterschool picture is a challenge, many network leads say that educating policymakers on the need for more funding in an era of record budget deficits is the most pressing challenge today.

    Lean state budgets have led many networks to adopt a more comprehensive approach to funding and expanding learning opportunities. Although difficult, new funding is possible. Examples include the following:

    Connecticut successfully advocated for the creation of a new $5 million annual grant program for afterschool programming (now $4.5 million).

    The Massachusetts state legislature created a statewide commission to examine the state's afterschool programs and recommend improvements. The commission's report helped build support for a more than 150% increase in funding for state programs, from $2 million to $5.5 million.

    The Washington legislature passed the 2007–2009 biennial budget with $3 million allocated specifically for afterschool grants, marking the first time that the budget ever included dedicated state funds to support afterschool programs.

    Shaping policy to make afterschool and summer learning an "allowable" use of existing or new funding also advances the work significantly. For instance, in Oregon, the state passed a law in which $260 million in "school improvement funds" can be used for a variety of programs that raise student achievement, including afterschool programs.

3. **Support systems to ensure quality.** The quality design and delivery of afterschool and summer programs is a top priority of every afterschool network. Networks spearhead tough conversations about quality, bring the right stakeholders to the table, and facilitate consensus on standards and creating quality systems. "Quality is the most important conversation we can have," said Katie Magrane, lead of the Massachusetts Afterschool Partnership (MAP). "We can all agree that afterschool and out-of-school-time programs should be providing youth with hands-on experiential activities that complement in-school learning, support social-emotional development, and have an intentional focus on student outcomes."

More than 34 states[1] now have quality standards for afterschool and summer programs and most were developed (directly or indirectly) by the networks. The standards development process itself is an engagement process, with networks counting upwards of 70 organizational partners engaged and hundreds of program staff and families involved.

Networks have also created self-assessment tools, common indicators for youth outcomes, and quality improvement systems. Widely adapted by other states, the New York network recently revised the Program Quality Self-Assessment (QSA) Tool. This tool is mandated by the New York State Education Department for all 21st Century Community Learning Centers in the state, the Office of Children and Family Services for programs receiving After School Advantage funds, and by New York City's Department of Community and Youth Development for programs receiving funds for out-of-school-time programs.

> Networks have also created self-assessment tools, common indicators for youth outcomes, and quality improvement systems.

Additionally, networks play a key role in professional development of afterschool professionals, providing conferences, workshops, webinars, academies, and other supports for frontline afterschool staff and directors. "We work to broker professional development opportunities," said Jamie Knowles-Griffiths, network lead for the North Carolina Center for Afterschool Programs (NC CAP). "We work with school districts, colleges and others to involve afterschool professionals." Laveta Wills-Hale, lead for the Arkansas Out of School Network, added, "Networks bring people together to define quality. We're working to ensure expanded learning opportunities are supported, sustained, and aligned with education systems."

Unencumbered Supports: Afterschool Technical Assistance Collaborative (ATAC)

Nearly every day a network will contact a member of the Afterschool Technical Assistance Collaborative (ATAC) seeking advice on issues small and large, from how to engage key stakeholders to how to refine a governance structure for the network to how to pursue a policy agenda like awarding credit to students based on mastery of content and skills as opposed to seat time. The easy accessibility of ATAC to the networks and the "just in time" technical assistance has been critical to the health, longevity, and sustainability of the networks. "I turn to our national partners at ATAC to get the pulse of national discussions and work that's being done by other networks across the country. This helps us adapt to broader issues and utilize what's working elsewhere to benefit Iowa," explained Michelle Rich, network lead of the Iowa Afterschool Alliance.

---

1. Several states are currently developing quality standards.

Before the first cohort of statewide networks was selected, ATAC was formed as a team of national organizations and leaders funded by the C.S. Mott Foundation to support the networks. ATAC includes the Afterschool Alliance, American Institutes for Research, Council of Chief State School Officers (CCSSO), the Finance Project, National Conference of State Legislatures, National Governors Association, and National League of Cities, with assistance from Terry Peterson of the College of Charleston Foundation, FowlerHoffman, Mainspring Consulting, and Collaborative Communications Group.

By modeling partnerships needed to influence policy at the national level, ATAC supports the networks directly through its expertise, advice, and potential collaborations with initiatives such as STEM, early childhood, or digital media and learning. "We often say that our role is to facilitate and 'set the table' providing the space and time for collaborating on network challenges and opportunities," remarked Victoria Wegener, a partner at Mindspring Consulting, a key technical assistance provider to the networks. With the support of ATAC, the ability to network and share experiences and strategies with one another both in-person and virtually through national meetings, monthly calls and webinars, and an online community has been crucial to the success of networks. In addition, individual ATAC organizations work on projects to educate their members on how afterschool advances policy priorities, like the CCSSO Innovation Lab Network or the National League of Cities Institute for Youth, Education and Families support to mayoral summits across the country.

The Future

For more young people to succeed educationally and in life, a strong education system that includes both school and expanded learning opportunities throughout the year is vital. "It is imperative that we focus a spotlight on the ways kids learn, the opportunities they need to succeed academically, and how we might shape a system that encourages more of them to stay in school, graduate, and go on to become productive contributors to society," articulates William S. White, president and CEO of the C.S. Mott Foundation. A system that scaffolds multiple approaches, demands innovation, reinforces learning in and out of school, and provides students with a diverse array of school and community-based educators is a giant step in the right direction.

Although there is not yet a silver bullet for fixing public education, afterschool programs are a "silver lining," and the statewide afterschool networks need to maintain their important role in re-imagining how, when, and where students learn.

The opportunities afforded by being a part of a vibrant national network allow each statewide afterschool network to stay abreast of the latest innovations, people, resources, issues, and windows of opportunity and prepare for thoughtful and strategic action over the long haul. A 21st century learning system that ensures all young people have the opportunity to succeed in school and work, and contribute to society, depends on the diligence, organization, and passion of the networks and their ability to constantly evolve and embrace challenge.

ABOUT THE AUTHORS

An-Me Chung served as a program officer at the C.S. Mott Foundation from 2000–2010 where she focused grantmaking on building systems to support young people with optimal opportunities for learning and enrichment beyond the traditional classroom. She currently serves as associate director of education for U.S. Programs at the John D. and Catherine T. MacArthur Foundation. In this role, she focuses on grants relating to public education and the implications for education of young people's use of digital media. Previous jobs include associate director at the National Institute on Out-of-School Time at the Center for Research on Women, Wellesley College. There, she worked with the Corporation for National and Community Service and the U.S. Department of Education and directed the Save the Children Out-of-School Time Rural Initiative. Chung holds a BS from Washington University in St. Louis, a PhD from Yale University, and completed a post-doctorate fellowship at Columbia University.

Gwynn Hughes is a program officer at the C. S. Mott Foundation where she manages the Learning Beyond the Classroom portfolio, seeking to provide optimum opportunities for academic support and enrichment for young people to learn and develop in school, summer, and afterschool. Formerly, Hughes was executive director of the Massachusetts Afterschool Partnership (MAP)—the Massachusetts statewide afterschool network— where she led a statewide coalition to improve afterschool programs, including the establishment of a legislative commission on afterschool and out-of-school time and the identification of new state funding for afterschool programs. Hughes holds a bachelor's degree from Wellesley College, a juris doctorate degree from Northeastern University and a master's degree in music from the University of Virginia.

Terri Ferinde Dunham manages the National Network of Statewide Afterschool Networks and creates opportunities for the networks to connect and share learning. As a partner at Collaborative Communications Group, she works with foundations, nonprofits, government agencies, and communities to reimagine when, where, and how children and adults learn. Currently, she also leads the Expanded Learning and Afterschool project funded by the C. S. Mott Foundation. Previously, she served for 10 years at the U.S. Department of Education where she produced a live, interactive television program featuring school and community leaders.

Tom Torlakson
California State Superintendent of Public Instruction

Jennifer Peck
Executive Director, Partnership for
Children and Youth

Taking Expanded Learning to Scale: California's Road to Success

California has an exciting story to tell. Since 2007, roughly 4,500 schools in our state have been able to offer afterschool (and in some cases summer learning) programs to thousands of students in high-poverty communities thanks to California voters' support of Proposition 49[1] and to the federal investment in the 21st Century Community Learning Centers program. We are striving for every one of these programs to be filled with engaging, hands-on, relevant, and exciting learning opportunities that support mastery, expand horizons, and draw on the talents of both school and community educators.

Presently, our afterschool field in California is in a great deal of transition, as we seek to take our work to the next level. Since we began investing state and federal resources in afterschool programs in the late 1990s, a great deal has changed in our state; and the needs of children, families, and schools have intensified in a variety of ways. In addition, we have learned a considerable amount about what it takes to provide high quality afterschool experiences to students that lead to better outcomes for children, families, and schools.

Because of these factors and more, we have become intensely focused on making sure that our investments in afterschool programs—nearly $700 million per year in California when state and federal funding are combined—are having the greatest possible impacts on student learning and success. We are changing the way we do business by transforming our approach from one that for too long operated on a parallel

---

1. In 2002, California voters approved Proposition 49, which constitutionally mandated increased state grant funds that leverage community resources for before and afterschool programs in public elementary and middle schools to provide tutoring, homework assistance, and educational enrichment. See *California Education Code (EC)* 8482.

track to the regular school day to one that involves schools and partners working side by side to expand learning beyond the school day and school year.

It is well known that dollars do not always equal results. California leaders have been keenly aware that we need to become a state recognized for the quality of our out-of-school-time investments and not just for being the state spending the most money on these important programs.

To address this, in 2006 we—as policy maker and advocate working together—developed critical implementing legislation before over $400 million in new funding went out across the state.[2] This legislation focused grants on the lowest-income communities, increased grant sizes, and improved the accountability system to look at a range of academic and other student success measures beyond just test scores. An expansion of this scale presented many challenges, but these new policies put us on a very promising path.

Over the years, we have joined many others in our state in intensive efforts to identify how to best support programs to achieve the maximum level of impact on student learning and success. We have chosen to focus on a few critical strategies that we believe will leverage the best results and outcomes from California's sizable investment in expanded learning, including making state policy more targeted, flexible, and responsive to local needs; prioritizing summer learning; encouraging school-day educators and community partners to work as a team in every aspect of program operation; and institutionalizing a definition of high quality expanded learning opportunities to ensure programs focus on what works.

Specifically, here are some of the things we have been able to accomplish together as a statewide team focusing on these goals:

Examining how the state invests its dollars in improving program quality and impact. To this end we have

- *created a new division at the California Department of Education solely focused on out-of-school-time investments and brought in smart new leadership from the field to lead this division;*

- *implemented a strategic planning process that includes both department staff and field representatives and is developing improvements to our statewide and regional systems of program support; and*

- *begun to re-examine our laws governing state and federal afterschool funding to identify where we can simplify and streamline processes, provide more flexibility to local programs, and ensure accountability structures that are appropriately matched to program goals.*

> California leaders have been keenly aware that we need to become a state recognized for the quality of our out-of-school-time investments and not just for being the state spending the most money on these important programs.

2. Prior to the passage of Proposition 49, California allocated $120 million annually to the After School Learning and Safe Neighborhoods Partnerships Program. Proposition 49 expanded this existing program to $550 million annually, and renamed the program the "After School Education and Safety Program."

Tackling the huge gap in summer learning opportunities for students in California.
Together we are

- *raising awareness about the devastating effects of summer learning loss with policy makers, educators, and the public;*

- *making existing funding for summer learning programs more flexible and effective at the local level through legislation; and*

- *adopting a new approach to high quality summer learning programs that moves us away from the old remedial summer school model and moves us toward programs that integrate learning with enrichment, nutrition and outdoor experiences, and the fun—and effective—summer learning experiences that all children deserve.*

Institutionalizing the "expanded learning" frame as the way we do business.
To this end, we are

- *creating a definition of high quality expanded learning that can inform policies that impact out-of-school-time programs, as well as school improvement funding and other resources that contribute to an expanded learning day and year;*

- *considering the range of approaches to expanding learning time a community might implement, including afterschool and summer, community schools, and linked learning at the secondary level;*

- *identifying key factors to success of any expanded learning approach, such as partnerships between schools and community organizations, and implementing practices that effectively engage students as well as their families;*

- *developing and creating effective messaging to key stakeholders of what we already know through experience and research—that when done well, afterschool, summer, and other forms of expanded learning programs can absolutely support student learning; and*

- *engaging principals and superintendents as our partners and champions in communicating the value of expanded learning opportunities.*

As we embark on this exciting transformation, we are going in with our eyes wide open. We know that the expanded learning terminology, and the policy implications that go with it, has been the subject of a challenging debate at the federal level and around the country. We know that some in the afterschool world feel justifiably nervous about funds being diverted to only adding minutes or hours to the school day, without really doing anything differently. And we also know that those fears could be realized if strong policies and practices are not in place reflecting both what we know about how kids learn most effectively and the components that must be in place to effectively utilize additional learning time.

We believe that local communities need to decide which approach(es) makes the most sense for their student population. We also believe that embracing the expanded learning frame will allow us to build much-needed bridges between community-based program providers and the schools they serve and give us an opportunity to talk about how all partners—schools, community organizations, and families—can contribute to student learning and success.

Many programs in California have already proven just that. With a relatively small amount of money, these programs provide a different type of academic content that is standards aligned but project based, offer homework help, serve nutritious snacks, teach children (and their parents) about healthy eating, offer physical activity that has regrettably all but disappeared from the school day, and increase student engagement in school.

> With a relatively small amount of money, these programs provide a different type of academic content that is standards aligned but project based, and increase student engagement in school.

For example, in a 20-year UCLA longitudinal study, researchers found that elementary school students who participated for 3 or more years in LA's BEST afterschool program were about 20% less likely to drop out of school than similar students who did not attend LA's BEST (Huang et al., 2005; LA's BEST, 2006). A 2011 UCLA study confirmed the lasting impact of high quality afterschool programs showing that students who participated in LA's BEST in their elementary school years demonstrated gains in math, science, and history GPAs as well as standardized test scores in 8th grade (UCLA National Center for Research on Evaluations, Standards, and Student Testing, 2011).

Participants in 86 Oakland Unified School District afterschool programs—virtually all of which are state- or federally funded—increased their school-day attendance by 35,343 days in 2010–11, earning the district close to $1 million in additional revenue (Public Profit, 2011).

Blair High School in Pasadena, a 21st Century Community Learning Centers grantee, increased its on-time graduation rate by 28% over 4 years, which school leaders in large part attribute to academic supports such as embedding tutoring into sports and enrichment activities and credit recovery programs provided by the BlairLEARNS program (Blair International Baccalaureate High School, 2007).

The operative factor in these successes is "high quality." We in California know very well from our experiences in scaling up that helping programs provide meaningful and impactful learning experiences for children that support school success is no simple task. We have learned that many expanded learning programs are not as effective at improving student outcomes when they work in isolation from schools. We have learned that it can be challenging to get busy, pressured educators to find the time and will to collaborate in a meaningful way with community partners. We have learned that when schools and partners develop a shared vision for student success, pool their human and financial resources, and fully take advantage of the resources our state provides for expanding learning time, kids do better.

Here in California, in addition to getting our own house in order around operating a strong system of training and professional development for afterschool staff, we know that we also have to support schools and districts in their capacity to take advantage of expanded learning partnerships and promote the idea that facilitating student learning is a joint endeavor between all parties. This takes more than talk—this takes creative collaboration.

For example, here at the California Department of Education and in the field, we are discussing concrete ways that California's 4,500 expanded learning programs can support schools in the task of implementing the Common Core Standards. We are piloting efforts to bring more hands-on science education to students through afterschool and summer learning programs. We are dedicating half of our 21st Century Community Learning Centers funding to high schools and using that resource to boost college and career readiness.

> We are piloting efforts to bring more hands-on science education to students through afterschool and summer learning programs. We are dedicating half of our 21st Century Community Learning Centers funding to high schools and using that resource to boost college and career readiness.

Conclusion

We are very proud of what we have collectively accomplished in our state. We have made serious investments in expanded learning programs, and we are serious about making these investments as effective as possible. We recognize we are constantly learning about what works best, and we have much more to do in order to ensure that all students receive a strong, well-rounded education. We believe the only way to move closer to that goal is through partnerships—between policy makers and stakeholders; between school districts and community partners; within and across all kinds of public agencies; and between students, parents, and their schools. It is only through genuine partnerships that we can truly expand high quality learning opportunities for all students.

ABOUT THE AUTHORS

Tom Torlakson was elected in 2010 to a 4-year term as California's State Superintendent of Public Instruction. He has served as a classroom teacher and coach and as a member of the Antioch Council, Contra Costa County Board of Supervisors and the California State Senate and State Assembly. In 1998, Torlakson authored legislation leading to the development of the largest system of afterschool programs in the nation. In 2006, he authored the bill that led to the 300% expansion in these programs so that they now reach 4,000 schools around the state. Born in San Francisco, Torlakson earned the Vietnam Service Medal while serving in the U.S. Merchant Marine. He earned a BA in history, a life secondary teaching credential, and an MA in education from the University of California, Berkeley.

Jennifer Peck was a founding staff member of the Partnership for Children and Youth in 2001 and has served as its executive director since 2003. In late 2010, Jennifer was appointed senior policy advisor and transition team director for Tom Torlakson, the newly elected State Superintendent of Public Instruction. Prior to joining the Partnership, Jennifer spent 8 years as an appointee of President Bill Clinton at the U.S. Department of Education, where she supported implementation of numerous initiatives including student loan reform, School-to-Work, and 21st Century Community Learning Centers.

REFERENCES

Blair International Baccalaureate High School. (2007). *2006–2007 BlairLEARNS High School Program data points*. Pasadena, CA: Author.

Huang, D., Kim, K. S., Marshall, A., & Pérez, P. (2005). *Keeping kids in school: An LA's BEST example*. Los Angeles, CA: National Center for Research on Evaluation, Standards and Student Testing Retrieved from http://www.lasbest.org/download/keeping-kids-in-school

LA's BEST After School Enrichment Program. (2006). *Annual report 2005–2006. Caught up in the act . . . of success*. Retrieved from http://www.lasbest.org/download/2005-2006-annual-report

Public Profit. (2011). *Oakland out-of-school time programs findings report* [Executive Summary]. Retrieved from http://www.ousd.k12.ca.us/cms/lib07/CA01001176/Centricity/Domain/79/Oakland_OST_Findings_Report_Executive_Summary_10.17.11.pdf

UCLA National Center for Research on Evaluations, Standards, and Student Testing (CRESST). (2011). Supporting student success in middle schools: Examining the relationship between elementary afterschool program participation and subsequent middle school attainments [Executive Summary]. Retrieved from http://www.lasbest.org/download/executive-summary

Christopher Coleman
Mayor, St. Paul, MN

Karl Dean
Mayor, Nashville, TN

James Mitchell, Jr.
City Council Member, Charlotte, NC

Betsy Price
Mayor, Fort Worth, TX

Ronnie Steine
Councilman- At-Large, Nashville, TN

Municipal Leadership Is Essential: Quality Afterschool Opportunities Strengthen Cities and Our Youth

Times have changed. In order for the United States and our cities to remain the beacons of hope they have been for the world, it is our responsibility to help our young people develop the skills and talents to find gainful employment and to attract businesses to our cities. Leaders across organizations and institutions, along with parents, have to work together toward the common goal of supporting our youth; no one should presume to take on this goal alone. There are too many social and economic challenges that affect outcomes for young people today that unfortunately make it so easy for many youth to take the wrong turn. As mayors and councilmembers, we have come to learn that in order to ensure that our young people get and stay on the right track, we have to get involved early and create opportunities throughout our communities to help them thrive. *Their success* is the success of our cities. Conversely, the unfortunate reality is that *their failure* is also our failure.

As mayors and councilmembers, we have come to learn that in order to ensure that our young people get and stay on the right track, we have to get involved early and create opportunities throughout our communities to help them thrive.

It is common knowledge that children spend 80% of their waking hours outside of school. While we agree that more can and should be done to educate our cities' youngest residents during the school day (and that cities have an important role to play in supporting educational efforts), most mayors do not control their school systems. We are in a unique position, though, to use our mayoral and council "bully pulpit" and leadership to enhance the options that children and youth have during that other 80% of time by creating high quality expanded learning opportunities in the afterschool hours, on weekends, and during summers.

Growing Municipal Support

Over the years, there has been a growing interest from municipal leaders in supporting afterschool efforts, as the National League of Cities documented in a recent report highlighting our four cities and 23 others (Spooner, 2011). Why? Because our charge as mayors and councilmembers is to keep our cities safe, spur economic growth, ensure a high quality of life, and provide access and opportunity for all. This is not always easy to do given the difficulties many of our communities face. Fortunately, there are many ways that afterschool and expanded learning opportunities can help city officials confront many pressing local challenges such as public safety, school attendance and truancy, low academic achievement and graduation rates, college and career preparation, civic engagement, hunger and obesity, and risky behaviors such as substance abuse and teen pregnancy. Our efforts to address these challenges are aligned with and supported by a strategy of providing resources and building partnerships to support afterschool programs.

City governments are essential partners with school districts and nonprofit organizations in supporting local youth. Many municipalities already provide a complement of opportunities to their young people via their parks and recreation departments, police athletic leagues, libraries, and museums. Often though, we have seen that communities take a siloed approach, with each program or department trying to solve challenges on its own rather than taking a more integrated approach in which partnerships with other city agencies, schools, and an array of nonprofit afterschool programs can have even greater impact. A powerful way to unite these programs is to include them as part of a citywide system of public, private, and community-based afterschool and expanded learning opportunities. Working together, community leaders can

- *improve the quality of programs,*
- *target programs and investments to youth most in need,*
- *provide joint training to providers from different organizations, and*
- *work collectively to increase participation rates.*

Citywide System Approach

Over the past decade, municipal leadership—and in particular, strong leadership by the mayor—has been a powerful catalyst for progress in the development of citywide systems of afterschool programming. As mayors and councilmembers, we have made afterschool a priority in our cities and have called upon our agency heads to work with school leaders and other youth-serving, community-based organizations to create, strengthen, or expand afterschool learning opportunities. Taking on such an effort is too heavy a burden for any one agency or organization alone; but working together as a group of passionate and committed leaders in a city, we are accomplishing amazing things for our youth.

Time and time again, we have seen how a high quality afterschool program can change a young person's life and how such programs can have a positive ripple effect on families and neighborhoods. Our desire is to substantially increase the number of young people across our cities who have access to and participate in a quality programs. We know that the more often a child comes to a program and the longer he or she stays engaged, the greater impact it will have on that child's life. Trying to scale up is not easy; it requires an intentional plan with focused goals and action steps developed with a number of key community and school partners.

Mayors and other city leaders are in a great position to begin these important conversations and to bring key partners to the table. These leaders may include school superintendents and other district officials, school board members, chiefs of police and other law enforcement officials, United Way executives, leaders of large and small nonprofit organizations, college and university representatives, chambers of commerce and the local business community, the philanthropic community, faith-based organizations, parents, and youth themselves. The mayor's and councilmembers' commitment to an issue can often inspire unlikely organizations to engage in a collective plan or communitywide system to support young people that can have more power and impact than individual efforts.

The key elements that make up such a system are committed leadership from multiple stakeholders, a coordinating entity to manage all of the moving parts, strong and reliable data, a focus on quality, thoughtful efforts to increase participation, and careful multiyear planning (Wallace Foundation, 2008). The purpose of using a comprehensive approach is to determine the programs we have in our community, their locations, the nature and level of demand from youth and their families, and the neighborhoods that lack afterschool opportunities. Then, we can target resources to ensure that young people have adequate and appropriate access to quality programs.

> The key elements that make up such a system are committed leadership from multiple stakeholders, a coordinating entity to manage all of the moving parts, strong and reliable data, a focus on quality, thoughtful efforts to increase participation, and careful multiyear planning.

We are also developing standards to ensure all programs in our communities are of high quality and that providers and parents know what a quality program looks like. Additionally, we are coordinating professional training for program providers to help them support the developmental needs of young people. Perhaps most importantly, our cities are developing data management systems that track student participation in afterschool programs and give us information about their school attendance and behavior so that program staff can intervene and help where needed. This new ability to measure the impact of afterschool programs helps us ensure that our resources are well spent and allows us to communicate the importance of continued investment to our constituents.

City Investments to Support Afterschool Are Worth It

Over the past decade the growth of federal funding provided through the U.S. Department of Education's 21st Century Community Learning Centers initiative has helped cities across the country increase program slots and partner with schools and community-based organizations to develop comprehensive programming. While this has been an invaluable source of support for programs, the federal grants are time limited, and the resources are never enough to meet the demand. To augment these dollars, resources provided by cities, parents, nonprofits, and local philanthropies have made a big difference in meeting local demand for afterschool programs. We have to "put our money where our mouth is" if we hope for others to join us with their own resources as well.

Despite the extreme pressures on municipal budgets in these last several years, many of us have worked hard either to realign municipal funding, invest new dollars from city general funds, or at least hold the line to protect afterschool budgets. For example, in a flat budget environment, Nashville Mayor Karl Dean proposed one new initiative in his 2009 budget: resources for the Nashville After Zone Alliance (NAZA) to implement a coordinated afterschool network that partners with a wide variety of neighborhood organizations to bring academic and enrichment opportunities to middle school youth. "There is tremendous need for afterschool programs for our middle school students— only 10% of our 21,000 middle schoolers participate in a structured afterschool program," Dean said at the time. "What we have learned over the last several months is that, in addition to need, there is tremendous interest from our students to be a part of these programs when they're offered. My goal is for NAZA to sustain the expansion and existence of neighborhood-based programs for the long-term."

In response, the Nashville Metro Council appropriated $400,000 for the city's first Afterzone, then included an additional $600,000 to launch the second in January 2011. The FY12 $800,000 allocation seeded a third Zone, launched September 2012, with a fourth Zone on track for the 2013–14 school year. Mayor Dean appointed a director of afterschool initiatives in his office to manage the planning, implementation, and evaluation of the AfterZone rollout. Ronnie Steine, councilman-at-large, has been a long standing champion of afterschool in Nashville. He said, "In an environment of limited resources, one has to prioritize, and our city leadership understands we cannot back up for our young people. This means we have to support and nurture our youth when not in school so they can succeed in school."

Leaders in Charlotte, North Carolina, have also focused on the needs of middle school students and, in particular, have recognized that afterschool programs could be a deterrent to juvenile crime. Over a decade ago, councilmembers and school board leaders made a joint commitment to invest city and school dollars to launch three new middle school afterschool programs. Councilmember James E. Mitchell has had a steadfast commitment and passion for youth and has fought to keep funding alive for these programs, despite budget battles. Mitchell shared, "I am very proud of the Charlotte City Council's commitment to afterschool programs and to the success of our youth. The city now funds six different providers for a total of $2.4 million dollars from our Community Development Block Grant (CDBG) allocation." The city's former police chief also served as a critical champion for afterschool, underscoring the connection to keeping youth safe, and current Mayor Anthony Foxx has committed his support to afterschool and young people.

Resources to support afterschool can come from many different places. Since 2001, the city of Fort Worth has dedicated more than $1.4 million annually to support afterschool programming in four school districts through partial proceeds from a one-half cent sales tax dedicated to a crime control and prevention district. Some of the tax revenue is used for afterschool programs because city leaders made a clear case that having afterschool programs is part of an overall crime prevention strategy. City partnerships with school districts can encourage additional commitments. Fort Worth Independent School District agreed to the joint creation of "Fort Worth After School," using general operating funds to match $1.1 million of the city's commitment and employing staff to oversee the 84 school-based programs. Federal 21st Century Community Learning Centers grants add $4 million to afterschool programs. The city's willingness to use voter-supported tax levies has resulted in a large pool of sustainable and flexible funding that puts the city in a strong position to lead afterschool system-building efforts. "We simply must invest in the future of our city, and that starts with giving every child the opportunity and tools they need to be successful in the classroom, and ultimately, in life," said Fort Worth Mayor Betsy Price. "We in Fort Worth are very proud of the bond between the city and the Fort Worth ISD to provide local children fun, healthy, productive and education-based alternatives to staying home alone. Now, thanks to our new Wallace Foundation grant, we're very excited about the chance to take our afterschool system to a whole new level."

> Fort Worth's willingness to use voter-supported tax levies has resulted in a large pool of sustainable and flexible funding that puts the city in a strong position to lead afterschool system-building efforts.

Aligning and making better use of existing resources in an era of tight budgets is another strategy. In-kind investments can sometimes be as important as financial resources. Creating joint-use agreements for city and school buildings, as well as shared maintenance of facilities, vehicles, parks, and athletic fields can open up more and better afterschool and summer opportunities. Sometimes the greatest need may be to identify a staff person to kick off a citywide effort and begin bringing multiple cross-sector partners to the table. No matter how much we galvanize other leaders across our community to invest time, resources, space, technology, training, and equipment, we cannot overlook how valuable the contribution of a passionate and knowledgeable staff person can be to lead a citywide system building effort.

For instance, in 2006, Saint Paul, Minnesota, Mayor Christopher Coleman formed the Second Shift Commission, a broad stakeholder group representing the city of Saint Paul, the Saint Paul Public Schools, and large and small community-based organizations, to figure out how to increase access to effective afterschool learning opportunities while creating a bridge to in-school learning. Mayor Coleman appointed his staff to lead the commission's work. Their recommendations led to a new city-school-community partnership called Sprockets—a coordinating entity, structured as a citywide out-of-school-time network. Both the Sprockets director and data system project lead are is housed in the city's parks and recreation department and three staff are "on loan" from the YWCA of St. Paul and the Center for Democracy and Citizenship at Augsburg College. The team focuses on improving quality, building a citywide data system, piloting shared learning programs between teachers and youth workers, and advancing a framework of youth success as learners, contributors, and navigators. In addition, Sprockets works with four neighborhood network teams of youth serving organizations that link youth development opportunities and services at the neighborhood level. Together, the Sprockets team is bringing the community's resources to bear on a comprehensive, citywide initiative. "Sprockets has quickly built a powerful set of tools and connections to youth-serving organizations to improve their programs and help youth develop essential life skills, confidence and experience," said Mayor Christopher B. Coleman, "This is exactly what I hoped would happen when I created the citizen commission several years ago. Sprockets is one of the keys to my vision of all youth succeeding in school and life."

What City Leaders Can Do

One of the most essential actions that municipal leaders can take to drive change is simply to convene key stakeholders to discuss the afterschool needs in the community. It may seem like an easy step, but it is an important one. Mayoral and councilmember champions can lead the charge and demonstrate the importance of the issue and identify the roles each partner can play towards a solution. Often the most challenging thing is getting the right folks to the table; once they are there, city leaders can lead the group in making a "to-do list" for each stakeholder.

A second useful step is to map the distribution of afterschool opportunities that exist across the community. Providing clear, visual evidence of the lack of accessible programs in certain neighborhoods can build public and political will for afterschool investments. Without the ability to present these data, local leaders often believe that their communities may have ample program options, when the reality may be that there is seriously inadequate or unequal distribution of programs across neighborhoods. Though a mapping process may take time to complete, this is a relatively easy "win" and can help generate a deeper understanding of the local afterschool landscape and help communicate needs more clearly to key community leaders.

Taking a citywide approach often fuels further progress and drives more strategic discussions about next steps. Early analyses of community resources and needs frequently reveal troubling gaps and spark efforts among key stakeholders to fill them. It is hard to say "no" or to turn away from a map that glaringly shows high crime or poverty in a neighborhood clearly lacking afterschool opportunities—and, in fact, it would not be right or politically savvy to do so. When we saw our community's needs, we knew we had to do something about it . . . and we have.

It's All Connected

Supporting afterschool programming is part of our education improvement strategy, economic development strategy, neighborhood development strategy, and crime prevention strategy. In short, it's all connected. When young people are engaged in positive activities, there are numerous positive outcomes. It is the job of municipal officials to make those connections. Ultimately, it is our job to support our children and youth as our communities' future. If you are a municipal official, we invite you to join us in expanding and improving afterschool opportunities in your own communities. If you are a community organization leader, a parent, or a school leader, we urge you to ask your mayor and councilmembers to bring your community together to plan how to make afterschool a collaborative priority for the community.

ABOUT THE AUTHORS

Saint Paul Mayor **Chris Coleman** has advocated for education, public safety, and economic development in his 6 years as mayor and for 6 years before that as a city councilmember. Prior to becoming an elected official, he spent 8 years as a county public defender and prosecutor and also worked in nonprofit finance. A champion of education, Mayor Coleman launched Sprockets, a citywide out-of-school-time network that developed the first data system of its kind in the state. His leadership in transportation led to the Central Corridor, the largest transit project in Minnesota history. He is currently 1st vice president of the National League of Cities.

Mayor **Karl Dean** is in his second term as Nashville's mayor. He has made education and youth, public safety and economic development his major priorities. Under his leadership, Nashville has dramatically lowered its truancy rate and increased its graduation rates. In 2011–2012, he served as co-chair of the National League of Cities Council on Youth, Education and Families.

James E. Mitchell, Jr., is a native of Charlotte, NC, where he has served on the Charlotte City Council since 1999 as the District 2 representative and as a vocal champion for afterschool and other youth opportunities. Mitchell is the immediate past president of the National League of Cities.

Mayor **Betsy Price** was elected mayor of Fort Worth June 18, 2011. Since then, she's been actively engaging the city's young people, working to create jobs, fighting for fiscal accountability and open government, building a citywide health and fitness initiative, and being a cheerleader for local public schools. A successful business owner for 17 years, Mayor Price began her career in public service as Tarrant County Tax Assessor in 2000 and quickly used her business experience to make her department one of the most efficient in Texas, saving taxpayers millions of dollars.

Councilman-at-Large **Ronnie Steine** is a 17-year veteran of Nashville's Metro Council. In 2011–2012, he served as co-chair of the National League of Cities Council on Youth, Education and Families and currently serves on the Forum for Youth Investment's Ready By 21 National Leadership Council. He received the Afterschool Alliance's State Champion Award for Tennessee in 2010.

REFERENCES

Spooner, B. S. (2011). *Municipal leadership for afterschool: Citywide approaches spreading across the country*. Washington, DC: National League of Cities. Retrieved from http://www.nlc.org/find-city-solutions/institute-for-youth-education-and-families/afterschool/municipal-leadership-for-afterschool-citywide-approaches-spreading-across-the-country

Wallace Foundation. (2008). *A place to grow and learn: A citywide approach to building and sustaining out-of-school time learning opportunities*, Retrieved from http://www.wallacefoundation.org/knowledge-center/after-school/key-research/Pages/Sustaining-Out-of-School-Time-Learning-Opportunities.aspx

Nicole Yohalem
Senior Director, Forum for Youth Investment

Robert C. Granger
President, William T. Grant Foundation

Improving the Quality and Impact of Afterschool and Summer Programs: Lessons Learned and Future Directions

The afterschool field has made important progress in the past 15 years, particularly since the federal 21st Century Community Learning Centers Program rapidly expanded starting in 1998. Increased federal, state, and local support demonstrates that taxpayers and policy makers want safe and engaging activities for young people while parents work. As a result, afterschool options have grown rapidly, with programs adding spaces and expanding to new sites. At the same time, funders and practitioners have created infrastructure—namely state and local intermediary organizations—to advocate for the field and support its expansion.

The evidence that afterschool programs can deliver on multiple goals—academic, social, and behavioral—is much stronger than it was 15 years ago. However to produce positive effects, programs must be effectively designed and delivered. As afterschool and summer learning programs have made a greater claim on public resources—and the economy has tightened—they are experiencing increased pressure to justify support. The prevailing view seems to be that if these and other social programs are going to draw significant funding, they need to be able to produce positive results consistently. Similar accountability pressures have occurred in other sectors such as preschool, K–12 education, and mentoring. One result of this pressure is increased attention to program quality within the field; and as we discuss later, a great deal that has been learned in that regard is now being incorporated into afterschool and summer program design and delivery.

Some of the pressure on afterschool has come from K–12 education, which is itself being pushed to improve achievement and attainment. As interest grows within the education community about how afterschool and summer programs can play a role in "expanded learning" efforts, challenging questions related to mission persist for providers. What should be the focus of afterschool programs? Is developing "21st century skills" such as personal responsibility, teamwork, and persistence paramount, or should programs be concerned with a narrower set of academic outcomes? Should programs be operated by schools, community organizations, or both? Should services be delivered in school buildings or elsewhere in the community?

Although research does not provide clear answers to these questions, in part due to variation in local needs, goals, and program design, it does affirm the increased focus within the field on defining and improving program quality. As noted above, programs can have positive effects on academic, social, and behavioral outcomes, but not all programs that set out to achieve such effects do so, and we know that quality varies both within and across sites. Understanding why this is so has become an important priority. Are varying results due to program content? Program processes and structure? Characteristics of the organization implementing the program (for example, how well that organization is run or its rates of staff turnover)? Features of the surrounding community (for example, youth being able to safely get to the program regularly)?

While much more needs to be learned, especially about how organizational and community factors affect afterschool program effectiveness, current research does confirm a consensus among practitioners—that program processes, content, and structure matter. Focusing on these features has some important advantages. In contrast to community- or family-level factors, program-level features are under the control of practitioners, and thus afterschool supervisors and line staff consider them a "fair" focus for accountability. Significant progress has been made on identifying these features of program effectiveness, designing valid and reliable ways to measure them, and helping program leaders and staff assess and improve them. The remainder of this article reviews this progress and discusses our recommendations for advancing the afterschool field.

Developments in the Field

An evolving evidence base. As noted above, evidence that afterschool programs can deliver on multiple goals—academic, social, and behavioral—is much stronger than it was 15 years ago. Reviews conducted by Patricia Lauer and colleagues (2006) and Joe Durlak and Roger Weissberg (2010) were particularly useful in synthesizing the results from a large number of program evaluations. Durlak and Weissberg's review had a major influence on the field. They found, on average, programs had a positive effect on a range of academic and other important outcomes. They also began to shed light on why. They reviewed 68 evaluations of afterschool programs focused on improving personal and social skills, such as reducing risky behavior. The results drew attention to the importance of specific program features (for example, implementing active and sequential activities focused on explicit goals) in producing positive effects. Lauer and her colleagues reviewed 35 evaluations of academically focused afterschool and summer programs for low-income children. They, too, found positive news on academic measures, although they were not able to identify particular program or contextual features that predicted the positive effects beyond participation itself.

Positive effects in both reviews were driven by a subset of the programs in the sample (roughly one-third), and the evaluations included in both reviews were of relatively small programs. Among the few large-scale programs that have been rigorously evaluated, their effects are limited (Granger, 2011), and we still lack a clear understanding of why this is so. There is increasing interest in this question, however, and efforts are underway in the field to address this.

Increased understanding of high quality practice and how to measure it. Research shows that interactions among young people and adults during program activities are positively related to how well youth function and their developmental outcomes. Practitioners tend to see this as more than a useful correlation and believe that staff-youth interactions are the active ingredients that distinguish programs that make a difference from those that do not (Yohalem & Wilson-Ahlstrom, 2009). Research has not yet proven this, but it is beginning to make the case that adult/youth interactions cause youth outcomes to change. Historically, though, monitoring and accountability have focused on structural features such as staff qualifications and staff-student ratios that do not seem to predict effectiveness, at least in the K–12 research literature (Mashburn et al., 2008).

Durlak and Weissberg's analyses illuminated the importance of specific program features that might productively shape staff-youth interactions, and they did so at a time when the afterschool field was ready to listen. In 2002, the National Research Council (Eccles & Gootman, 2002) identified eight features of positive developmental settings. Since then, consensus has been building about what constitutes high quality practice in afterschool settings and how to measure it. The NRC report, along with research by Reed Larson, Deborah Vandell, Durlak and Weissberg, and others contributed to this growing consensus. By 2006, the Youth Program Quality Assessment (Youth PQA), developed by Charles Smith and colleagues at the HighScope Educational Research Foundation, was one of several observational tools designed to measure program quality being refined and used in the field to advance both research and practice.

Systemic efforts to improve quality. As measures of program quality matured, practitioners leading afterschool organizations and systems, who were eager to use research-based tools to improve their programs, began incorporating them into their staff development efforts. Increasingly, continuous quality improvement systems that include observational assessments, improvement planning, and targeted training and coaching are being implemented and enhanced at the local and state levels.

In addition, there is now limited, but promising evidence that such strategies can improve afterschool program quality. This echoes recent positive results (Allen, Pianta, Gregory, Mikami, & Lunl, 2011) in K–12 education about the impact of coaching-based professional development built around a validated tool for assessing teacher-student interactions. A rigorous evaluation of the Youth Program Quality Intervention—designed to improve practices measured by the Youth PQA—resulted in improved instruction and higher levels of staff retention in a wide range of afterschool sites (Smith et al., 2012). Designed to be responsive to the specific conditions of the afterschool field (for example, high turnover, limited training, part-time staff), the Youth Program Quality Intervention is a "low-stakes" model. Site managers are accountable for implementing continuous improvement practices rather than attaining specific thresholds of performance.

This model is now being adapted and used by more than 80 networks of afterschool and summer programs across the country, including nine state education agencies using it to support implementation of the 21st Century Community Learning Centers initiative in their states. In Michigan, for example, observational assessments of all 21st Century Community Learning Centers grantees are conducted annually using the Youth PQA, and corresponding professional development offerings are available to all grantees. A network of regional coaches provides training, coaching, and technical assistance to a subset of grantees that either refer themselves or are referred by the Michigan Department of Education (MDE). Coaches work with those sites to implement improvement plans and maintain online service logs that are accessible to MDE. Coaches are in regular communication with MDE so that quality and compliance issues can be identified and addressed quickly. Several states, including Arkansas and Vermont, have developed an integrated quality improvement system based on the Youth Program Quality Intervention that supports both 21st Century Community Learning Centers and TANF-funded school-age child care programs.

Recommendations for Advancing the Field

In order to get more afterschool and summer programs consistently producing robust, positive effects for children and youth, efforts to advance research and practice should build on the progress we have described.

- **Research.** *Instruments designed to measure program quality could benefit from revisions to make them more clear and specific. Researchers also need to produce better, scalable measures of youth behaviors and dispositions that contribute to school success, such as work habits, persistence, and engagement in learning, and others that push beyond the academic domain. More studies that assess how quality improvement approaches affect program practices are also needed (in general, results about the effectiveness of staff development programs in K–12 are mixed [Yoon et al., 2007]). Additionally, studies that confirm the belief that when staff practices improve, youth outcomes also improve would constitute a critical milestone for the field. Less likely to advance our understanding of how to improve quality are more impact evaluations of small programs. We know such evaluations can be an important gateway to gaining funding support. We already know, however, that such programs can work, but many need to do better—some much better—and the field is now headed down a fruitful path of better understanding how to define, support, and sustain high quality.*

- **Practice.** *Practitioners need more validated, cost-effective approaches for continuously improving practice. One promising approach is for practitioners to partner with researchers to develop and test different improvement approaches. Such partnerships allow for the integration of research-based tools and knowledge with local circumstances and expertise, and the current press for evidence-based practice across the human services fields could help sustain such collaborations.*

Partnerships should pioneer and test different approaches, including new assessment strategies and intentional variations in the duration and delivery of coaching and training. Rapid but disciplined research and development processes that advance practice and accrue reliable information about how to improve program quality are needed. This will require developing and institutionalizing new ways of working collaboratively across practice and research; promising strategies are being refined in health care and increasingly tested in education and human services to do just that (Bryk, Gomez, & Grunow, 2010). State afterschool networks can work with state education agencies and their research and evaluation partners to test and refine promising strategies within 21st Century Community Learning Centers-funded and TANF-funded school-age child care programs. Municipal afterschool systems can do the same at the local level, and national intermediaries can spread the word about promising practices.

● **Policy and funding.** *Afterschool and summer learning programs and systems are not able to bear the full cost of this important work of improving quality on their own. Public systems should allocate professional development and monitoring resources toward continuous improvement approaches; and foundations that support programs, infrastructure, and research should seize the opportunity to subsidize the development of tools and strategies designed to support continuous improvement.*

The afterschool and summer learning field is ripe for a focused wave of research and development that does not involve dramatic changes but rather capitalizes on the significant progress made over the past 15 years. Afterschool and summer learning programs can have positive effects on a range of important outcomes, and thus they have earned the right to be included in discussions about advancing young people's learning and development. Future investments in education and youth development should recognize afterschool and summer as important opportunities to advance student success, and more fully capitalize on growing capacity at the state and local levels to expand and improve programs.

ABOUT THE AUTHORS

Nicole Yohalem has led work related to afterschool at the Forum for You[cut off]
for the past 11 years. Prior to that she worked at the intersection of youth [cut off]
practice and research at Michigan State University Extension and the HighS[cut off]
Educational Research Foundation.

Robert C. Granger is president of the William T. Grant Foundation. From 2003 to 201[cut off]
the foundation focused a significant portion of its grant making on improving the
quality of afterschool programs.

REFERENCES

Allen, J. P., Pianta, R. C., Gregory, A., Mikami, A. Y., & Lun J. (2011). An interaction-based approach to enhancing secondary school instruction and student achievement. *Science, 333,* 1034–1037.

Bryk A. S., Gomez L. M., & Grunow A. (2010). *Getting ideas into action: Building networked improvement communities in education.* Stanford, CA: Carnegie Foundation for the Advancement of Teaching.

Durlak, J., Weissberg, R. P., & Pachan, M. (2010). A meta-analysis of after-school programs that seek to promote personal and social skills in children and adolescents. *American Journal of Community Psychology, 45,* 294–309.

Eccles, J., & Gootman, J. (Eds.). (2002). *Community programs to promote youth development.* Washington, DC: National Academy Press.

Granger, R. (2011). Our work on the quality of after-school programs: 2003–2011. *William T. Grant Foundation Annual Report.* New York, NY: William T. Grant Foundation.

Larson, R. W., Rickman, A. N., Gibbons, C. M., & Walker, K. C. (2009). Practitioner expertise: Creating quality within the daily tumble of events in youth settings. In N. Yohalem, R. Granger, & K. Pittman (Eds.), *New Directions for Youth Development* (No. 121, pp.71–88). San Francisco, CA: Jossey-Bass.

Lauer, P. A., Akiba, M., Wilkerson, S. B., Apthorp, H. S., Snow, D., & Martin-Glenn, M. L. (2006). Out-of-school time programs: A meta-analysis of effects for at-risk students. *Review of Educational Research, 76,* 275–313.

Mashburn, A. J., Pianta, R. C., Hamre, B. K., Downer, J. T., Barbarin, O. A., Bryant, D., . . . Howes, C. (2008). Measures of classroom quality in prekindergarten and children's development of academic, language, and social skills. *Child Development, 79,* 732–749.

Smith, C., Akiva, T., Sugar, S. A., Lo, Y. J., Frank, K. A., Peck, S. C., . . . Devaney, T. (2012). *Continuous quality improvement in after-school settings: Impact findings from the Youth Program Quality Intervention study.* Washington, DC: Forum for Youth Investment.

Vandell, D. L., Shernoff, D. J., Pierce, K. M., Bolt, D. M., Dadisman, K., & Brown, B. B. (2005). Activities, engagement, and emotion in after-school programs (and elsewhere). *New Directions for Youth Development,* (105), 121–129.

Yohalem, N. & Wilson-Ahlstrom, A. (2009). *Measuring youth program quality: A guide to assessment tools* (2nd ed.). Washington, DC: Forum for Youth Investment.

Yoon, K., Duncan, T., Lee, S., Scarloss, B., & Shapley, K. (2007). *Reviewing the evidence on how teacher professional development affects student achievement.* Washington, DC: Institute of Education Sciences, National Center for Education Evaluation and Regional Assistance, Regional Educational Laboratory Southwest.

Denise Huang
Project Director/Senior Researcher, National Center for Research on Evaluation, Standards, and Student Testing, University of California, Los Angeles

Using Research to Continuously Improve Afterschool Programs: Helping Students to Become 21st Century Lifelong Learners

... high quality afterschool and summer learning programs, when effectively aligned with learning opportunities provided during the school day and year, can provide an ideal setting to support successful youth development.

The challenges of the 21st century—the explosion of knowledge, the rapid advances in technology, the globalization of the economy, and the need for a creative, adaptable workforce— have profound implications for education. They have put a premium on students' ability to learn continuously, apply their knowledge to new situations, and solve complex problems.

A New Day for Learning (Time, Learning, and Afterschool Task Force, 2007) emphasized that children learn *all day*, not just during normal school hours. To meet the many challenges of the 21st century, the report urged schools and their associated afterschool and summer learning programs to develop comprehensive, integrated learning approaches that value the distinct experiences provided for children by diverse community stakeholders and at different times of the day and year.

Simultaneously, researchers and policymakers are increasing an emphasis on the inclusion of youth development principles within afterschool and summer learning program settings (Birmingham, Pechman, Russell, & Mielke, 2005; Durlak, Weissberg, & Pachan, 2010). They believe that these programs have the potential to provide students with opportunities to develop the skills, knowledge, resiliency, and self-esteem that will help them succeed in 21st century society (Little, Wimer, & Weiss, 2008; Pittman, 2003).

They also believe that high quality afterschool and summer learning programs, when effectively aligned with learning opportunities provided during the school day and year, can provide an ideal setting to support successful youth development.

This article will lay out a set of research-based principles and practices for developing, implementing, and maintaining high-quality afterschool and summer learning programs that can create productive citizens and lifelong learners of the 21st century.

Indicators of Program Quality

In 2003, prominent afterschool practitioners, political supporters, and research experts gathered at a national Afterschool Summit in Washington and identified five general performance indicators of successful afterschool programs. Such programs promote students'

- **academic achievement** *by fostering enthusiasm for learning;*

- **social attitudes and behaviors** *by emphasizing better school attendance and willingness to take personal responsibility and by providing them with leadership experiences;*

- **skill-building** *by providing activities that are outside of their comfort zones ;*

- **health (physical, mental, emotional)** *by ensuring students' safety and building resiliency ; and*

- **sense of community** *by encouraging family involvement and structuring opportunities for civic engagement (U.S. Department of Education, 2003).*

These indicators of effective afterschool and summer learning programs can be framed under three broad domains: program structure, program implementation, and program content. Table 1 identifies the core indicators of quality under each domain.

••

Table 1. Quality indicators for afterschool programs.

Program Structure	Program Content	Program Implementation
Goals clearly defined	Connects with school learning	Strong leadership
Program structures aligned with goals	Has a youth development approach	Quality staff
Program mission and vision designed to motivate staff	Relates to 21st century	Clear communication and support to all stakeholders
	Engages students	Positive relationships*
		Built in assessment and continuous improvement loop

*According to the National Partnership of Quality Afterschool Learning Study (Huang, 2010), this is found to be the common core element among quality programs.

Program structure. Afterschool and summer learning programs can powerfully communicate their program goals through clear mission and vision statements. Such statements can also motivate program staff and guide program functioning. A "theory of change" should be clearly specified to spell out what the program wants to achieve (goals and detailed objectives), then link program objectives and student outcomes to indicators of program effectiveness and quality (Anderson, 2004). These strategic procedures require intentional alignment of program activities to each program goal; alignment of goals for learning during the school day, after school, and during the summertime; and alignment of activities that promote students' interests and meet students' specific needs.

Program content. With the program structure secured, afterschool and summer learning leaders must then ensure that students have sufficient access to efficient learning tools, relevant content, and staff who are skilled in instructional content. New 21st-century curricula, including global awareness, financial and civic literacy, and creativity and the arts, can be incorporated within the framework of the new Common Core State Standards. It is also equally important for students to practice "how-to-learn skills," including (1) communication skills, (2) thinking and problem-solving skills, and (3) interpersonal and self-directional skills.

To motivate students to focus, "learning must effectively connect to students' questions, concerns, and personal experiences, thereby capturing their intrinsic motivation and making the value of what they learn readily apparent to them" (Learning First Alliance, 2001, p. 4). Afterschool and summer learning programs should therefore feature a variety of high quality activities and provide academic content through real world examples, applications, and experiences, both inside and outside of school (American Youth Policy Forum, 2006; C. S. Mott Foundation Committee on After-School Research and Practice, 2005; Westmoreland & Little, 2006).

> Effective program implementation starts with strong, knowledgeable leaders who can create a positive organizational climate.

Moreover, when instructional content, staff, and resources reinforce students' positive self-perceptions, there will be a resulting increase in positive social behaviors and academic achievement, along with fewer behavioral problems (Durlak et al., 2010).

Program implementation. Effective program implementation starts with strong, knowledgeable leaders who can create a positive organizational climate. These leaders hire quality staff and keep them updated with relevant knowledge and skills. They also create open communication among afterschool, summer learning, day school, parent, and community stakeholders. This relationship-building among adult stakeholders is critical to program success.

Moreover, the one key element that consistently stands out in research on high quality afterschool and summer learning programs is the positive relationship between staff and students. This relationship is a key determinant of student engagement in school and often leads to increased student motivation, higher academic competence, and increased valuing of school (Herrera, Grossman, Kauh, Feldman, & McMaken, 2007).

Benefits of Positive Staff-Student Relationships

Afterschool and summer learning programs have a number of distinct advantages over schools that can foster deeper staff-student relationships. In particular, with fewer curricular demands, more time is available in afterschool and summer settings for students and staff to form positive relationships. Furthermore, afterschool and summer learning programs provide students with access to an expanded network of adults and mentors in the community (Rhodes, 2004).

A study of the LA's BEST program reveals some of the key benefits of these deeper relationships with caring adults (Huang et al., 2007). Students perceived their relationships with LA's BEST staff as encouraging, positive, and supportive. In turn, students perceived themselves as behaving well, working hard, and feeling good about the experience of learning in school and at LA's BEST. Students who held positive relationships with afterschool staff were more likely to be actively engaged in the program and, in turn, were more engaged in their school during the day. Similarly, students who felt supported and encouraged by staff were more likely to place a higher value on education and have greater aspirations for their futures.

> ...students who felt supported and encouraged by staff were more likely to place a higher value on education and have greater aspirations for their futures.

Bridging School, Afterschool, Summer Learning, and Communities to Improve Student Impact

According to the Northwest Regional Educational Laboratory (2003), "After school programs need a strong connection to the learning objectives of the school day in order to increase student achievement." This continuity of learning between the school and afterschool and summer learning programs is supported theoretically in the work of Noam, Biancarosa, and Dechausay (2002). They posit that the "bridging" of school and afterschool helps to promote more meaningful academic learning. They find that congruity of environments, including congruity of learning goals and teaching styles, is associated with increased academic performance in literacy and other academic areas. They recommend that program staff communicate with day school teachers about homework and other student needs.

Since family and neighborhood factors are also strong forces in the students' lives, this "connectedness" can be further expanded into students' families and neighborhood communities through family events, internships, and community services. This would help students develop civic awareness, a stronger sense of belonging, and the characteristics of good citizenship. The Harlem Children's Zone project exemplifies the success of such practices (Dobbie & Fryer, 2011).

Being a Role Model for Learning and Improving

Finally, to promote lifelong learning for students, afterschool and summer learning programs can demonstrate that adults are willing to learn and improve as well. Effective programs employ a continuous monitoring system to determine whether they are meeting their program goals and to continuously fine-tune program implementation.

Such evaluations are simple and easy to administer. They generally involve gathering data from students, parents, teachers, school administrators, staff, and volunteers (or a sample thereof); measuring instructional and implementation adherence to program goals; providing feedback to all stakeholders for program improvement; and identifying the needs for additional implementation procedures or resources, such as increased collaboration, staff, or materials. Figure 1 illustrates the continuous nature of program monitoring and evaluation procedures.

....

Figure 1. Model of the data-based decision-making process.

Summary Recommendations for Policies and Sustainability

The following recommendations will help policymakers and afterschool and summer learning program leaders build and sustain high quality programs.

● **Recruit quality staff and reduce staff turnover.** *Although it seems obvious, recruiting and retaining high-quality staff is essential to afterschool and summer learning program success. In addition to providing equitable salaries, benefits, and career advancement opportunities, policymakers and afterschool program leaders should establish a recognition program to acknowledge the contributions of afterschool staff. Appropriate esteem titles may further help afterschool staff fulfill their intrinsic goals.*

- **Build bridges between school, afterschool, and summer learning programs.**
  Programs should include in their goals a specific objective to increase collaboration between school-day learning and afterschool and summer learning experiences. Shared professional development between classroom teachers and expanded learning staff may offer opportunities for collaboration. School-day, afterschool, and summer learning staff may use such opportunities to align curricula, enhance student engagement, develop common standards for student discipline, and use school data to support curricular decision making. This increased alignment and curricular collaboration, however, should not result by default in the dilution or elimination of hands-on learning and other student engagement, youth development, and relationship-building strategies that are also needed to make afterschool and summer learning programs effective and well attended.

- **Provide appropriate content, tools, and training.** *To combat the "digital divide" that separates children from low-income families and their more privileged peers, and to prepare students with a broad range of 21st century skills, appropriate technology and equipment need to be available at the program sites. New 21st century content, including global awareness as well as financial and civic literacy, also needs to be presented. Meanwhile, staff also need up-to-date training on the delivery of such curricula and the use of the new technologies so that they can fully support students in developing their 21st century skills.*

- **Establish networking systems.** *The neighborhood community plays a vital role in supporting students' positive development. Afterschool and summer learning programs should be encouraged to recruit and incorporate families, community members, and local services into their programs.*

Conclusion

A nationwide survey of afterschool program staff explored the reasons that they worked in this field. The single most frequent staff response was their desire to make a difference in the students' lives. Because they perceived themselves as having the ability to make a difference, staff felt a high sense of efficacy, demonstrated high expectations for students, and encouraged their students to succeed (Huang, Cho, Mostafavi, & Nam, 2008).

For students coming from disadvantaged environments, having a relationship with adults possessing these personal and professional characteristics is particularly powerful. Not only do staff have the potential to assist students with personal issues, but they also have the power to encourage and instill educational values and high aspirations. The establishment of a strong bond between students and staff directly influences student engagement in afterschool and summer learning programs and also serves as a powerful predictor of student engagement in school. With appropriate administrative and instructional content support, this unique relationship may also serve as the ideal venue for staff to mentor students in developing their 21st century skills.

When afterschool and summer learning programs provide the context for students to experience these supportive relationships, include engaging up-to-date content, complement and align with but not replicate the school day, and link to families and community, students begin to believe in their own efforts and develop the lifelong learning skills needed to be productive, global citizens of the 21st century.

For More Information

- The Partnership for 21st Century Skills (http://www.p21.org/)

- National Center for Quality Afterschool (http://www.sedl.org/afterschool/toolkits/)

- The Forum for Youth Investment (http://www.forumfyi.org/)

ABOUT THE AUTHOR

Denise Huang is a project director and senior researcher at the National Center for Research on Evaluation, Standards, and Student Testing at UCLA. She leads a research team conducting multiple research and evaluations on after school programs nationwide. Her recent work includes evaluations of afterschool programs and investigations of the effect of motivation, attribution, and effort towards academic achievement. Huang is also the co-principal investigator for the California Statewide Afterschool Evaluation Project.

REFERENCES

American Youth Policy Forum. (2006). *Helping youth succeed through out-of-school time programs.* Washington, DC: Author.

Anderson, A. A. (2004). *Theory of change as a tool for strategic planning: A report on early experiences.* Washington, DC: The Aspen Institute.

Birmingham, J., Pechman, E. M., Russell, C. A., & Mielke, M. (2005). *Shared features of high performing afterschool programs: A follow-up to the TASC evaluation.* Retrieved from http://www.sedl.org/

C. S. Mott Foundation Committee on After-School Research and Practice. (2005). *Moving towards success: Framework for after-school programs.* Washington, DC: Collaborative Communications Group.

Dobbie, W., & Fryer, R. G. (2011). Are high-quality schools enough to increase achievement among the poor? Evidence from the Harlem Children's Zone. *American Economic Journal: Applied Economics, 3*(3), 158–187.

Durlak, J. A., Weissberg, R. P., & Pachan, M. (2010). A meta-analysis of afterschool programs that seek to promote personal and social skills in children and adolescents. *American Journal of Community Psychology, 45*(3–4), 294–309.

Herrera, C., Grossman, J. B., Kauh, T. J., Feldman, A. F., & McMaken, J. (2007). *Making a difference in schools: The Big Brothers Big Sisters school-based mentoring impact study*. New York, NY: Public/Private Ventures.

Huang, D., Cho, J., Mostafavi, S., & Nam, H. (2008). *What works? Common practices in high functioning afterschool programs across the nation in math, reading, science, arts, technology, and homework—a study by the national partnership* (CRESST Report 768). Retrieved from University of California, Los Angeles, National Center for Research on Evaluation, Standards, and Student Testing website: http://www.cse.ucla.edu/products/reports/R768.pdf

Huang, D., Coordt, A., La Torre, D., Leon, S., Miyoshi, J., Pérez, P., & Peterson, P. (2007). *The afterschool hours: Examining the relationship between afterschool staff-based social capital and student engagement in LA's BEST*. Los Angeles, CA: UCLA Center for the Study of Evaluation.

Learning First Alliance. (2001). *Every child learning: Safe and supportive schools*. Baltimore, MD: Association for Supervision and Curriculum Development.

Little, P. M. D., Wimer, C., & Weiss, H. B. (2008, February). After school programs in the 21st century: Their potential and what it takes to achieve it. *Issues and Opportunities in Out-of-School Time Evaluation*, 10. Cambridge, MA: Harvard Family Research Project.

Noam, G. G., Biancarosa, G., & Dechausay, N. (2002). *Learning to bridge—bridging to learn: A model and action plan to increase engagement between schools and after school programs in Boston*. Boston, MA: Boston's After-School for All Partnership.

Northwest Regional Educational Laboratory. (2003). *Evaluating supplemental educational service providers: Issues and challenges*. Portland, OR: Author.

Pittman, K. (2003). 21st century skills and indicators. *Youth Today, 12*(7), 51.

Rhodes, J. E. (2004). The critical ingredient: Caring youth-staff relationships in after-school settings. *New Directions for Youth Development, 101*, 145–161.

Time, Learning, and Afterschool Task Force. (2007). *A new day for learning: A report from the Time, Learning, and Afterschool Task Force*. Retrieved from http://www.edutopia.org/pdfs/ANewDayforLearning.pdf

U.S. Department of Education. (2003). *After School Summit summary report*. Retrieved from Partnership for After School Education website: http://www.pasesetter.org/reframe/documents/summit.pdf

Westmoreland, H., & Little, P. M. D. (2006). *Exploring quality standards for middle school after school programs: What we know and what we need to know: A summit report*. Cambridge, MA: Harvard Family Research Project.

Patricia O'Donnell
Grant Writer/Researcher, School
of Education, Health, and Human
Performance, College of Charleston

Joseph R. Ford
Graduate Student, College of Charleston

The Continuing Demand for 21st Century Community Learning Centers Across America: More Than Four Billion Dollars Of Unmet Need

The *America After 3PM* study determined that of the 14.3 million children in self-care after school, nearly 4 million of them would like to participate in an afterschool program if one were available to them in their community (Afterschool Alliance, 2003). In a more recent study, it was determined that the number of students in self-care rose from 14.3 million in 2003 to 15.1 million in 2009, despite greater availability of afterschool care (Afterschool Alliance, 2009). This disparity prompted a study to determine to what extent the largest nationwide funding source for local afterschool and summer learning programs in, or linked to, schools is meeting the demand for requests.

This potential funding source is the federal 21st Century Community Learning Centers initiative. The 21st Century Community Learning Centers initiative, funded by the United States Department of Education, supports community learning centers that provide academic enrichment opportunities during nonschool hours for children, particularly students who attend high-poverty and low-performing schools (U.S. Department of Education, n.d.).

Although it is a federally financed program, state departments of education manage the actual competition for funding in their states. Awards are made to local schools or community groups (working with local schools) interested in offering educational, youth development, and family programming afterschool and during summers. Interestingly, the 21st Century Community Learning Centers initiative is the largest federally funded education effort that fosters both community-school partnerships and family involvement.

Because this is such a large and diverse country with many different, and often competing, education interests in the various states and localities, there is a strong need to assess over time the extent of the demand for afterschool and summer learning opportunities funded by 21st Century Community Learning Centers. So the purpose of this study was to assess the extent to which state competitions for 21st Century Community Learning Centers were able to meet local requests for funding over the past 9 years. Of particular interest were both the percentage of grant requests that were funded and the total dollar amount of requests funded over these years.

Methodology

In order to determine the number of grant applications and recipients for the 21st Century Community Learning Centers program, the online database from the U.S. Department of Education's Profile and Performance Information Collection System (PPICS) was searched. Queries were conducted by competition, by state, from 2002 to 2010 by year for each year listed below. Therefore, the data reported here are as accurate as the data held by the PPICS. These queries were conducted October–November, 2011.

> Because this is such a large and diverse country with many different, and often competing, education interests in the various states and localities, there is a strong need to assess over time the extent of the demand for afterschool and summer learning opportunities funded by 21st Century Community Learning Centers.

Results

- **Between 2002 and 2010, only about one in three applicants for 21st Century Community Learning Centers was awarded funding (See Table 1 and Figure 1).** *During this time period 19,638 grant requests were received by 21st Century, of which 7,034 were funded (35.82%).*

- **Between 2002 and 2010, nearly $4.3 billion of total requests for 21st Century Community Learning Center programming were not funded (see Table 2 and Figure 2).** *During that same time period, over $6.5 billion was requested from 21st Century funding, of which nearly $2.3 billion (34.85%) was received.*

Figure 1 displays the total number of awards requested and received each year between 2002 and 2010. Figure 2 displays the total amount of money requested and received during the same time period.

Table 1. 21st Century grant number of applications and awards, 2002–2010.[1]

Year	Applicants	Awards	Percent Awarded
2002	474	140	29.54%
2003	2,836	775	27.33%
2004	3,498	1,389	39.71%
2005	1,397	464	33.21%
2006	1,293	328	25.37%
2007	2,379	895	37.62%
2008	2,510	1,063	42.35%
2009	3,095	1,234	39.87%
2010	2,156	746	34.60%
TOTAL	19,638	7,034	35.82%

Table 2. 21st Century grant application dollar amount requested versus received, 2002–2010.[2]

Year	Money Requested	Money Granted	Percent Granted
2002	$149,577,283	$33,879,393	22.65%
2003	$902,930,300	$238,297,883	26.39%
2004	$1,267,895,855	$480,515,709	37.90%
2005	$391,072,195	$97,937,098	25.04%
2006	$405,828,894	$84,254,758	20.76%
2007	$815,515,985	$298,568,650	36.61%
2008	$994,112,531	$454,767,845	45.75%
2009	$1,100,341,496	$392,087,341	35.63%
2010	$553,286,565	$213,230,061	38.54%
TOTAL	$6,580,561,103	$2,293,538,738	34.85%

1. The data presented here are part of the Profile and Performance Information Collection System (PPICS) http://ppics. learningpt.org/ppicsnet/public/default.aspx. According to the PPICS website, "The purpose of this system is to collect basic information about 21st CCLC programs across the United States. PPICS was created in 2003 at the commission of the US Department of Education (ED). The system was built to help ED track 21st CCLC programming following the transition from federal to state administration, which took place in 2001. Each year, PPICS is used to collect program data from some 3,000 21st CCLC grants covering close to 9,000 centers serving 1.5 million student attendees."

2. Ibid.

Figure 1. 21st Century grant total number of grants and unfunded requests, 2002–2010

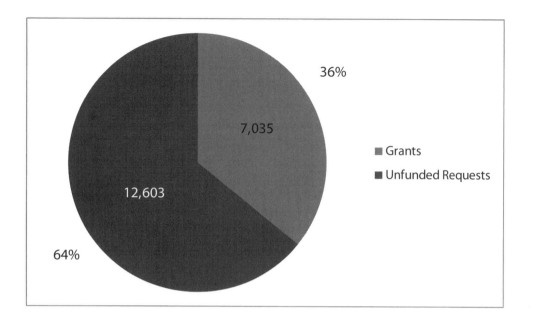

Figure 2. 21st Century grant total amount requested and received, 2002–2010

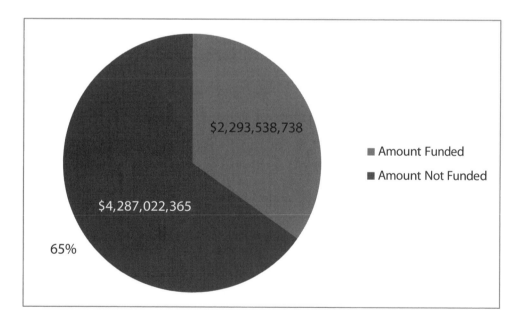

Conclusion

Looking across the states over 9 recent years, it is clear that the interest and demand has been high and remains steady for 21st Century Community Learning Centers.

On average, only about one in three grant applications receive funding. From 2002 to 2010, there were over $4 billion dollars of unfunded 21st Century Community Learning Center applications across America.

This high demand and percentage of unfunded applications should not be surprising when compared to the two national surveys conducted during this same time period, which showed a high interest by families for more quality afterschool programs across America.

Given the continuing high interest and demand for 21st Century Community Learning Centers, it would make sense to find ways to increase significantly the support and resources for school-community partnerships that expand learning after school and during the summer across America.

ABOUT THE AUTHORS

Patricia O'Donnell received her PhD in sociology from the University of Notre Dame with specialty in both criminology and research methods. She is currently a grant writer/researcher for the School of Education, Health, and Human Performance at the College of Charleston and teaches research methods to graduate students in teacher education.

Joseph R. Ford is a graduate student pursuing a master of arts in teaching with a focus on choral music education. He is a graduate of the College of Charleston with a BA in applied music.

REFERENCES

Afterschool Alliance. (2009). *America after 3PM: Key findings*. Retrieved from http://www.afterschoolalliance.org/documents/AA3PM_Key_Findings_2009.pdf

Afterschool Alliance. (2003). *America after 3PM: A household survey on afterschool in America* [Executive summary]. Retrieved from http://www.afterschoolalliance.org/press_archives/america_3pm/Executive_Summary.pdf

U.S. Department of Education. (n.d.). 21st Century Community Learning Centers: Program description. Retrieved November 20, 2012, from http://www2.ed.gov/programs/21stcclc/index.html

Allison Anfinson
Former Results Measurement Director,
21st Century Community Learning Centers,
Minnesota Department of Education

Sheila Oehrlein
Safe & Healthy Learners Team,
Minnesota Department of Education

Quality Improvement and Successes for 21st Century Community Learning Centers in Minnesota

During the 2010–11 school year, in 98 centers throughout Minnesota, 21,000 youth—many of whom were struggling in school or at risk—had opportunities to catch up, keep up, and get ahead through 21st Century Community Learning Centers.

While all 21st Century Community Learning Centers provide activities designed to address the academic needs of the students they serve, they also attend to the physical, social, and emotional needs of participants. As research has shown, youth programs designed to support social and emotional development can have a positive impact on academic performance and improved behavior (Durlak & Weissberg, 2007).

The Minnesota Department of Education has administered the 21st Century Community Learning Centers initiative since 2002 with federal funds authorized under Title IV, Part B, of the Elementary and Secondary Education Act of 2001. Across the state, 21st Century Community Learning Centers use school-community partnerships to offer afterschool, before-school, and summer learning opportunities for students attending high-poverty, low-performing schools.

For those working on 21st Century Community Learning Centers and other similar expanded learning initiatives in Minnesota, a collective focus on three elements—quality improvement, innovation, and results—is deemed essential to success. This article will discuss the state's efforts and progress associated with each of these core elements.

Promoting Quality and Innovation

A network of strategic partners, including the Minnesota Department of Education (MDE) and the University of Minnesota's Extension Center for Youth Development, provides technical assistance, training, and coaching to 21st Century Community Learning Centers grantees as they assess their programs and implement quality improvement plans.

By prioritizing a comprehensive program model, in combination with an integrated quality assessment and improvement plan, MDE pushes applicants to create youth-centered environments designed to meet the unique needs of the youth in their community.

Starting in 2006, MDE has engaged in a partnership with the Extension Center for Youth Development to offer a technical assistance program called Quality Matters. Over the course of a year, participants in Quality Matters receive training, resource materials, and hands-on support to create and sustain environments that are positive places for young people to learn and develop.

In addition to participation in training and technical assistance, all 21st Century Community Learning Centers grantees are required to include a line item in their annual budget to support ongoing quality assessment and improvement efforts. Grantees must also provide a summary of the results of their quality assessments, as well as a summary of their quality improvement plans on their annual reports to MDE. These requirements ensure that quality assessment and improvement are fully integrated in all programs.

MDE promotes innovation by setting high expectations for 21st Century Community Learning Centers grantees. This begins with the grant application. All applicants must describe how their proposed program will meet the academic, physical, social, and emotional needs of participants. By prioritizing a comprehensive program model, in combination with an integrated quality assessment and improvement plan, MDE pushes applicants to create youth-centered environments designed to meet the unique needs of the youth in their community.

Another way MDE promotes innovation is by setting high expectations for grantees to retain program participants. According to research, young people have larger gains across multiple outcomes if they are able to participate frequently and over a sustained period of time (Little, Wimer, & Weiss, 2007). Grantees are challenged to develop interesting, engaging learning opportunities that will attract and retain participants. MDE and its partners provide training and technical assistance to grantees to infuse best practices that support retention, including school-community partnerships, family engagement (Little et al., 2007) and leadership opportunities for young people (Deschenes et al., 2010).

Innovative, Effective 21st Century Community Learning Centers

Division of Indian Work, American Indian Math Project, Minneapolis

The American Indian Math Project (AIMP) is a program run by the Division of Indian Work in partnership with Anishinabe Academy, a public magnet school in South Minneapolis focused on Native American culture and language. Each component of the program is designed to help participants become productive adults by supporting their academic, social, and family connections. To achieve this, AIMP applies a comprehensive, case-management approach to the program with three key components: tutoring 4 days a week, family nights providing academic enrichment at least once a month, and recreational activities at least twice a month.

The program has been highly successful. In 2010–11, 64% of participants improved their math grades, and all of the fifth-grade participants were either approaching or achieving the math standards. Of the sixth through eighth graders served, 40% had end-of-year grades of a C or higher. Additionally, teacher survey data submitted for the same year to the U.S. Department of Education's 21st Century Community Learning Centers Profile and Performance Information Collection System showed that over half of the students made improvements in academic performance (63%), turned in homework on time (62%), completed their homework to the teachers' satisfaction (58%), and behaved well in class (52%) (American Indian Math Project, 2011).

Beacons Program, Minneapolis

Minneapolis is one of six cities participating in the national Beacons Network, turning schools into youth centers during the afterschool and summer hours. Each year, Beacons serves over 2,500 young people and their families at eight centers in the city. Each center works to increase academic achievement, school connectedness, the capacity for productive adulthood, and opportunities for youth leadership and community engagement by offering a wide variety of programs including service learning, leadership training, character and social skills development, arts and cultural enrichment, sports and recreation, mentoring, and tutoring.

The Minneapolis Beacons program has had a positive impact on the academic performance of its participants. Youth who participated more than 90 days were twice as likely as nonparticipants to be proficient in reading, based on the Minnesota Comprehensive Assessment results (Minneapolis Beacons Network, 2011). Over 70% of regular attendees had improved academic performance or participation in class (72%), according to teacher survey data submitted to the U.S. Department of Education's 21st Century Community Learning Centers Profile and Performance Information Collection System for 2010–11.

Encore, Columbia Heights Public Schools, Colonial Heights

Columbia Heights is a suburban Minneapolis community with a rapidly changing population. Columbia Heights Public Schools has used its 21st Century Community Learning Centers, called ENCORE, to help meet the needs of a growing body of students with limited English proficiency. The ENCORE program provides a unique mix of activities focused on the arts, as well as science, technology, engineering, and math (STEM). ENCORE participants have shown significant gains, both academically and socially. During the 2010–11 school year, 82% of students reported that they learned new things and 67% of students stated that the program helped them do better in school (ENCORE, 2011). Students reported that the program helped them feel good about themselves (89%), get along with others (75%), imagine life as a grownup (68%), talk to others when upset (64%), and make healthy choices (62%). Academically, students also had great gains. The majority of participants scored at or above grade level in reading (65%) and math (70%). Students who attended 30 days or more had the best performance, with 80% at grade level or higher in reading, 90% at grade level or higher in math, and 73% at grade level or higher in both subjects. English language learners were the mostly likely to show improvement and had the greatest gains in comparison to other students (ENCORE, 2011).

McGregor Public Schools, McGregor

Since 2002, McGregor Public Schools, a small rural school district in central Minnesota, has been home to a high quality afterschool program that has integrated youth voice as a key component of their program design. Program staff in McGregor solicit feedback through focus groups and surveys, and they also use a youth advisory board to provide input on program design and offerings. Based on the information collected, the program has revised its marketing strategies, increased program offerings, and created group clubs based on youth-identified interests.

Participating students have seen academic and social gains. One of the most successful offerings has been small-group mentoring, an activity that targets youth who have low academic achievement, poor attendance, high incidence of behavioral violations, and other indicators of risky behaviors or vulnerability. The groups meet weekly to check school progress and participate in recreational activities, enrichment, and service projects. Eighty percent of participants in small-group mentoring made gains in achievement, decreased behavioral violations, and increased attendance. The program has found the greatest academic gains have occurred with multiyear participation. After participating in the program for 2 to 3 years, many students have increased their grades to a "B" average, or a GPA of 3.00.

Improvements in Student Learning and Behavior

Data provided by grantees show that Minnesota's 21st Century Community Learning Centers are on the right track. In communities across the state, large numbers of high-need students have increased opportunities to participate and engage in learning outside of the classroom. Innovative approaches to programming, with an emphasis on personal and social development as well as academic improvement, are showing promising results. Annual performance reporting shows that regular participation in 21st Century Community Learning Centers has had a positive impact on student behaviors. In 2009–10, school-day teachers reported that 68% of 21st Century Community Learning Centers regular attendees (participants who attended programming 30 days or more) improved their academic performance. Teachers also reported the following improvements in student behavior of regular attendees:

> In communities across the state, large numbers of high-need students have increased opportunities to participate and engage in learning outside of the classroom.

- *Completing homework satisfactorily (65%)*

- *Participating in class (65%)*

- *Turning homework in on time (61%)*

- *Being attentive in class (59%)*

- *Coming to school motivated to learn (58%)*

- *Getting along well with others (55%)*

- *Behaving well in class (53%)*

- *Attending class regularly (45%)*

- *Volunteering for extra credit or responsibility (44%)*

Conclusion

The design of the 21st Century Community Learning Centers initiative invites local school-community partners to create learning and support opportunities to meet their students' needs. To share and encourage "what works," the Minnesota Department of Education and a coalition of strategic partners, including the University of Minnesota's Extension Center for Youth Development and the state's afterschool network, provide resources, training, and coaching to grantees as they assess their programs with an emphasis on quality improvement and innovation.

This statewide infrastructure of support and collaboration for continuous improvement, combined with innovative, local school-community programming and partnerships and a focus on results, constitutes a winning combination for quality afterschool opportunities and for the children and youth in 21st Century Community Learning Centers.

ABOUT THE AUTHORS

Allison Anfinson is the former results measurement director for the 21st Century Community Learning Centers grant program at the Minnesota Department of Education. Anfinson came to the Department in 2006 with experience in research, evaluation, and community development.

Sheila Oehrlein leads the Safe and Healthy Learners at the Minnesota Department of Education. She has staffed the 21st Century Community Learning Centers grant program for the department for 6 years. Oehrlein has nearly 20 years of experience working with or on behalf of youth, having worked in a variety of settings including schools, and child care centers.

REFERENCES

American Indian Math Project. (2011). *21st Century Community Learning Centers end-of-year progress report, 2011.* Unpublished report submitted to the Minnesota Department of Education, Roseville, MN.

Deschenes, S. N., Arbreton, A., Little, P. M., Herrera, C., Grossman, J. B., & Weiss, H. B. (with Lee, D.). (2010). *Engaging older youth: Program and city-level strategies to support sustained participation in out-of-school time.* Retrieved from Harvard Family Research Project website: http://www.hfrp.org/out-of-school-time/publications-resources/engaging-older-youth-program-and-city-level-strategies-to-support-sustained-participation-in-out-of-school-time

Durlak, J. A., & Weissberg, R. P. (2007). *The impact of after-school programs that promotepersonal and social skills.* Chicago, IL: Collaborative for Academic, Social, and Emotional Learning.

ENCORE. (2011). *21st Century Community Learning Centers end-of-year progress report, 2011.* Unpublished report submitted to the Minnesota Department of Education, Roseville, MN.

Little, P. M. D., Wimer, C., & Weiss, H. B. (2007). *After school programs in the 21st century: Their potential and what it takes to achieve it* (Research Brief No. 10). Retrieved from Harvard Family Research Project website: http://www.hfrp.org/publications-resources/browse-our-publications/after-school-programs-in-the-21st-century-their-potential-and-what-it-takes-to-achieve-it

Minneapolis Beacons Network. (2011). *21st Century Community Learning Centers end-of-year progress report, 2011.* Unpublished report submitted to the Minnesota Department of Education, Roseville, MN.

Christina MacDonald
Program Specialist, 21st Century
Community Learning Centers Program,
New Hampshire Department of Education

Suzanne Birdsall
Education Consultant, 21st Century
Community Learning Centers Program,
New Hampshire Department of Education

Providing Rich Academic and Learning Supports Through New Hampshire's 21st Century Community Learning Centers Initiative

Let's put our minds together and see what life we can make for our children.
- **Sitting Bull**

The New Hampshire 21st Century Community Learning Centers program currently serves 24 communities and more than 10,000 youth across the state. Evaluation data show that individual programs serve significant populations of at-risk students who can benefit from the rich academic and social supports provided by these programs. In particular, 55% of enrolled students are eligible for free or reduced price lunch, 16% are eligible for special education services, 8% are Limited English Proficient (LEP), and 32% and 40% perform below proficient on the state reading and mathematics assessment, respectively. These percentages all exceed statewide averages.

In evaluation surveys (Russell & Woods, 2012), principals overwhelmingly report that the 21st Century Community Learning Centers contributed to

- *improved social skills for students (97%);*

- *improved literacy skills (90%); and*

- *improved math skills (86%).*

Evaluation findings (Russell and Woods, 2012) also revealed that students reported

- *high levels of satisfaction with the program,*

- *high levels of satisfaction with engagement in learning,*

- *high levels of satisfaction with the positive interactions with staff and their peers in programs, and*

- *high levels of satisfaction with an emphasis on skill-and mastery-focused activities.*

The strength of New Hampshire's 21st Century Community Learning Centers program lies in the quality and dedication of its local program sites and its ability to function cohesively towards common goals and shared outcomes.

Through a close-knit and well-networked set of program grantees, New Hampshire has created a foundation and support structure to meet the needs of children and their families across the state, as well as to maximize resources and opportunities for educational innovation through expanding learning time after school and during the summers. Two specific ways that New Hampshire is accomplishing this include building a collaborative community and constructing statewide data collection systems for program improvement.

Building a Community

The strength of New Hampshire's 21st Century Community Learning Centers program lies in the quality and dedication of its local program sites and its ability to function cohesively towards common goals and shared outcomes. Recognized by its peers nationwide as consisting of a remarkably well-networked and cohesive group of local grantees, the 21st Century Community Learning Centers program in New Hampshire is founded on a community of shared interest and aspirations and is grounded in a strong belief that the potential for greatness is far greater when implementation begins from a place of shared strength. This core principle resonates at each level—among staff at each site and among sites across the state—thus creating opportunities for shared learning, collaborative problem solving, and a team-based approach to creating high quality afterschool opportunities for youth, families, and communities. Building this community of shared interest and strength has been accomplished intentionally over the past 10 years through the implementation of deliberate strategies and actions.

At the state level, local program directors meet bimonthly with 21st Century Community Learning Centers state coordinators to launch initiatives, receive information, network, and share challenges and opportunities regarding their individual and statewide programs. Meetings often begin with a protocol facilitated by an experienced program director to encourage sharing and building personal and professional connections among the participants. Directors are often invited formally or informally to discuss the various processes, approaches, and resolutions they have developed in response to cross-cutting challenges or issues. As a result, they come to know each other's strengths and are comfortable looking to each other for support. This opens the door for a variety of grassroots support strategies including mentorships, peer site visits, and regional collaboration for professional development and advocacy events, such as Lights On Afterschool—a nationwide effort led by the Afterschool Alliance to build understanding and support for quality afterschool programs.

A formalized network of site coordinators has been established to create a platform for those managing day-to-day operations to connect. This group, facilitated by one of the current 21st Century Community Learning Centers program directors, meets regularly, up to five times per year. The agenda includes professional development training, as well as opportunities to share and distribute program resources, strategies for resolving day-to-day program challenges, and curriculum ideas. Both the format and the topics are generated internally, based on the self-identified needs of the participants. Additionally, the site coordinator network hosts an annual showcase highlighting successful clubs and program strategies. Though optional, each of these meetings attracts over half of the site coordinators who state that these are a highly valued resource.

We like roundtables at conferences because we learn so much from each other.

- 21st Century Community Learning Centers Coordinator

This kind of networking and capacity-building also occurs at a multistate/regional level. New Hampshire's state coordinators are members of the New England regional network that meets quarterly to share successes and resources, strategize around shared challenges, and identify opportunities to collaborate on common goals and initiatives. These meetings have established strong relationships of support in which the coordinators serve as resources for each other, both in and outside of these formal meetings to address their needs and challenges. The regional structure also provides a venue to share policies, strategies, and initiatives, including, for example, evaluation strategies, competition processes, and opportunities for innovation. It also generates opportunities to collaborate on professional development, funding opportunities, and regional partnerships with external stakeholders.

Collaborative Leadership

New Hampshire's success in building a community of best practice among its 21st Century Community Learning Centers sites is not solely a product of collegial relationships and partnering. Rather, it also involves a process of collaborative leadership in which the members share a vision and responsibility for improving the work.

New Hampshire's Record of Successes

....

Anytime-Anywhere Learning: High level partnerships lead to education reform

Anytime-Anywhere Learning is a keystone for education reform in New Hampshire. In 2005 the State Board of Education established mastery of course competencies as the standard for earning high school credit, rather than mere seat time. The board also included the flexible use of time and place in the state's School Approval Standards, which allowed for extended learning opportunities to become an alternate pathway for credit toward graduation for high school students. Subsequently, in 2006, New Hampshire was awarded a Supporting Student Success grant through the National Governor's Association and Council of Chief State School Officers with C.S. Mott Foundation funding. This grant supported the formation of high-level partnerships to implement extended learning opportunities. Building on this collaboration among the Governor's Office, the New Hampshire Department of Education, and PlusTime New Hampshire (the state's afterschool network), Supporting Students Success Through Extended Learning Opportunities was launched as a 3-year pilot program at four high schools in 2007 with funding from the Nellie Mae Education Foundation. These sites, in turn, shared their knowledge and expertise with newly designated 21st Century Community Learning Centers high school sites, as well as other high schools throughout the state. The 21st Century Community Learning Center program application for new funding now includes extended learning opportunities as an option at funded high school sites.

> ... the State Board of Education is proposing that it be a requirement, not an option, for all high schools to offer extended learning opportunities to their students.

Building on the successes of this pilot, the State Board of Education is proposing that it be a requirement, not an option, for all high schools to offer extended learning opportunities to their students. Students throughout New Hampshire would be able to earn credit towards graduation via individual or group competency-based learning opportunities designed in collaboration with community partners and highly qualified teachers. These activities could include designing and implementing a research study with the local hospital, developing a marketing plan for the neighborhood farm stand, or teaching a dance class for the local preschoolers.

....

New Hampshire's summer conference

It is through this collaborative style that the state's 21st Century Community Learning Centers annual summer conference is planned. Each year a group of 6–8 program directors volunteer to work with the state coordinators to identify the content and structure the conference. From identifying topic areas and recruiting presenters to coordinating the schedule and conference format, the directors are heavily involved in ensuring that the conference meets the needs of their school and community administrators, their peers, and their direct staff.

Local program directors as a statewide asset

Local program directors have become an asset statewide in helping address larger education reform issues. Directors actively participate on state-level advisory committees pertaining to the 21st Century Community Learning Centers program and the other education-related issues, including evaluation and data systems, the Child and Adult Care Food Program Advisory Council, New Hampshire Children's Alliance, and Extended Day. These professionals serve not only as representatives, giving voice to the interests and potential impacts on their programs, but also serve as key problem solvers and strategists. Their creative thinking, out-of-the box ideas, and on-the-ground experience provide insight and motivation for a new level of innovation. Through this process they are developing increased professional capacity and are honing their leadership skills.

Program improvement

One of the most important resources in program improvement and growth is the ability to use data to inform the strategies, policies, and practices. This capacity is being developed in a three-pronged approach:

1. **Evaluation design.** A new statewide evaluation with an external evaluator was launched in the spring of 2012. The new evaluation system was designed to streamline data collection and increase consistency across programs. Survey data previously captured at the local level has been integrated into the statewide evaluation, allowing programs to compare their progress with state-level aggregates while minimizing duplication of effort. Additionally, capitalizing on existing state-level online data collection systems has significantly expanded local capacity by eliminating time consuming data entry and providing immediate access to results.

    Maintaining a collaborative approach, the state coordinators and program directors have come together in an effort to identify what data is currently being collected, where, and how; how existing data systems interact; and what information can be extrapolated. The goal has been to identify the resources and opportunities currently available for programs to assess their impact and to think critically about how to use this data to map out a path of continued progress and increased youth outcomes.

2. **Constructing statewide data collection systems.** Efforts to integrate 21st Century Community Learning Centers program information into existing data systems have increased significantly. In addition to developing a process to upload 21st Century Community Learning Centers participation data into the state Department of Education's data warehouse, programs have increased use of the national PPICs[1] and New Hampshire's own Performance Pathways. The aim has been to extract meaningful data and reports that can be used both internally, to support program development and quality, and also to be able to share program successes with stakeholders in a way that clearly demonstrates the impact and value added to the community.

3. **Program improvement.** This new system also links to existing educational data sources, allowing for deeper and more meaningful analysis of the social and academic impacts of the 21st Century Community Learning Centers at both the state and local levels and across a variety of programmatic and demographic characteristics. As a result, this evaluation not only enhances the ability of the state and local programs to assess program successes and identify opportunities for improvement but also establishes a unified system that streamlines data collection, minimizes data burden, and capitalizes on existing systems to maximize the availability of data at the state and local level.

Conclusion

The 21st Century Community Learning Centers program in New Hampshire has all the essential elements of successful expanded learning programs—providing enriching programming to youth during high-risk hours, a focus on increased academic success, and targeted professional development for afterschool professionals. Yet, what makes New Hampshire's efforts distinctive are strong networking, collaborative leadership, capacity-building, and an evaluation design linked to the development of state-level data collection systems that can be mined to inform improved program development.

> A man is called selfish not for pursuing his own good, but for neglecting his neighbor's.
> - *Richard Whately*

Because of these successes, more young people are receiving more quality learning opportunities, and the 21st Century Community Learning Centers initiative is also regarded as an important state asset by serving as a learning lab and resource for other efforts to improve educational outcomes for many more children and youth across New Hampshire.

ABOUT THE AUTHORS

Christina MacDonald is a state coordinator for the 21st Century Community Learning Centers Program in New Hampshire. A former teacher, she is dedicated to supporting local programs in their quest for high quality, sustainable learning opportunities that meet youth needs and cultivate a passion for life-long learning.

Suzanne Birdsall has worked at the New Hampshire Department of Education administering the 21st Century Community Learning Centers program since 2002. Prior to this she was an elementary school teacher and founded a nonprofit afterschool enrichment program. Her vision for afterschool includes engaging cohesive groups of afterschool professionals to create fun, relevant, and invigorating opportunities to New Hampshire's youth.

REFERENCES

Russell, C., & Woods, Y. (2012). *Evaluation of the New Hampshire 21st Century Community Learning Centers: Findings from the 2011–12 school year*. Washington, DC: Policy Studies Associates.

1. According to the PPICS website (http://ppics.learningpt.org), "The purpose of this system is to collect basic information about 21st CCLC programs across the United States. PPICS was created in 2003 at the commission of the U.S. Department of Education (ED). The system was built to help ED track 21st CCLC programming following the transition from federal to state administration, which took place in 2001. Each year, PPICS is used to collect program data from some 3,000 21st CCLC grants covering close to 9,000 centers serving 1.5 million student attendees."

Susan Inman
Director of Learning Opportunities, Options and Supports, Oregon Department of Education, and Administrative Licensure Coordinator, Willamette University

Pete Ready
Education Specialist, 21st Century Community Learning Centers, Oregon Department of Education

Jenni Deaton
Administrative Specialist for the Learning Opportunities, Options and Supports Team, Oregon Department of Education

Oregon's 21st Century Community Learning Centers: A Key Component of Student Success in College, Work, and Citizenship

In 2011, Oregon's legislature affirmed a clear and ambitious education goal for the state, known as the "40-40-20" goal. This goal states that by 2025, 40% of adult Oregonians will hold a bachelor's or advanced degree, 40% will have an associate's degree or a meaningful postsecondary certificate, and *all* adult Oregonians will hold a high school diploma or equivalent—including the remaining 20% who will likely choose not to pursue postsecondary education beyond a high school diploma. Leaders across the state have been working to advance Oregon's educational attainment rates, but the passage of the goal into law through Oregon Senate Bill 253 has prompted a new drive for action and change.

Against that backdrop, Oregon's 21st Century Community Learning Centers have been working to increase academic achievement to enable students to close the achievement gap. Every year more than 25,000 students attend 128 centers located in areas of high poverty across the state of Oregon. According to a 2011–12 report by Learning Point Associates, teachers report that

The passage of Senate Bill 253 has now intensified the necessity of offering even stronger academically based programs, along with enrichment activities that expand students' intellectual and developmental horizons.

- *72% of the attendees in the 21st Century Community Learning Centers afterschool programs improved in their academic performance, and*

- *2/3 increased their rates of homework completion (Learning Point Associates, 2012).*

The passage of Senate Bill 253 has now intensified the necessity of offering even stronger academically based programs, along with enrichment activities that expand students' intellectual and developmental horizons. So it is more important than ever that Oregon's afterschool programs learn from and use current research to make improvements.

Expanded Learning Opportunities and Time

Building systems of support and sustainability, while ensuring quality programming, is the overriding mission of Oregon's 21st Century Community Learning Centers office at the Oregon Department of Education (ODE). Oregon's expanded learning activities and enrichment services, implemented by local programs and community partners, provide students with rich learning experiences that prepare them for success in college, in the workplace, and as citizens.

Outcomes of expanded learning time depend on many factors, including how effectively the extra time and opportunities are used and to whom they are directed. As Silva (2007) points out,

> *Research shows that extending the right kind of time to the students who need it most can improve student learning and effectively close the achievement gap between poor and minority students and their more affluent peers. . . . But the preponderance of evidence on extending time in schools suggests that the benefits of adding to the school day or year are by no means certain or universal (p. 9).*

Programs that focus on specific, predetermined academic and social outcomes tend to have a greater impact than those that focus too narrowly on academic outcomes or, alternately, those that lack focus or specified outcome goals. Programs are most successful when they offer a variety of structured, age-appropriate choices, when the environment is supportive, and when the experience is not perceived as punitive. According to a 2005 RAND Corporation report, nine common characteristics are associated with high quality, effective out-of-school-time programs:

- *a clear mission*
- *high expectations and positive social norms*
- *a safe and healthy environment*
- *a supportive emotional climate*
- *a small total enrollment*
- *stable, trained personnel*
- *appropriate content and pedagogy, relative to the children's needs and the program's mission, with opportunities to engage*
- *integrated family and community partners*
- *frequent assessments (Bodilly & Beckett, 2005, p. xv)*

Given the emerging research on afterschool program quality and its relationship to outcomes, it is clear that . . . quality afterschool programs also share the following features: appropriate supervision and structure, an environment that fosters positive youth-adult relationships, intentional programming with opportunities for autonomy and choice, and good relationships among the various settings in which program participants spend their day (Little, 2007, p. 8).

In the Oregon Department of Education, efforts are being made to increase sustained participation in well-designed afterschool programs because studies have shown that all children, particularly disadvantaged children, may gain a host of benefits that lead to better overall educational outcomes. Many of these are also building blocks specifically to improve student achievement. (See Durlak and Weissberg's article elsewhere in this volume, which finds that broad-based, quality programs have a positive effect on achievement and test scores.)

Oregon's Leading Indicators for Program Quality

Based on the growing research and evaluation studies that show afterschool and summer programs can and do make a positive difference, the Oregon 21st Century Community Learning Centers Program, in collaboration with the Oregon Leading Indicators Advisory Group; long-time partner Oregon Afterschool for Kids Network (Oregon ASK); and staff at the American Institutes for Research, developed leading indicators for program quality and continuous improvement.

The following are Oregon's defined leading indicators by category:

••

Collaboration and Partnership

- *Partners associated with the center are actively involved in planning, decision making, evaluating, and supporting the operations of the afterschool program.*

- *Staff from partner organizations are meaningfully involved in the provision of activities at the center.*

- *Staff at the center will be engaged in intentional efforts to collaborate and communicate frequently about ways to improve program quality.*

- *Steps are taken by the center to establish linkages to the school day and use data on student academic achievement to inform programming.*

••

Staff

- *Staff at the center are provided with training and/or professional development.*

- *Staff at the center complete one or more self-assessments during the programming period.*

- *Staff at the center are periodically evaluated/assessed during the program period.*

Intentionality in Student Program Offerings

- *There is evidence of alignment between (a) program objectives relative to supporting youth development, (b) student needs, and (c) program philosophy/ model and the frequency/extent to which key opportunities and supports are provided to youth.*

- *There is evidence of alignment between (a) program objectives relative to the academic development of students, (b) student needs, and (c) program philosophy/model and activities being provided at the center.*

- *There is evidence of intentionality in activity and session design among staff responsible for the delivery of activities intended to support student growth and development in mathematics and reading/language arts.*

Intentionality in Family Program Offerings

- *Steps are taken by the center to reach out and communicate with parents and adult family members of participating students.*

- *There is evidence of alignment between (a) program objectives relative to supporting family literacy and related development, (b) family needs, and (c) program philosophy/model and activities being provided at the center.*

These indicators demonstrate clear connections that school day and data analysis are key elements on the path to strengthening the capacity and quality of afterschool programs statewide.

Initiatives for Student Success in Strategic Areas

With a strong foundation in the basics of systems building, 21st Century Community Learning Centers program grantees are required to integrate statewide programs in the areas of reading and math, with additional options for federally funded science, technology, engineering, and math (STEM) and English language acquisition initiatives that match their program and community partners' vision of desired program outcomes. Describing measures of growth for anticipated student academic and social outcomes has become a critical part of program quality and improvement. The strategic alignment of extended learning opportunities with school-day academic programs increases program effectiveness and the quality of each child's experience in afterschool programs.

> The strategic alignment of extended learning opportunities with school-day academic programs increases program effectiveness and the quality of each child's experience in afterschool programs.

The primary academic initiative for 2011–12 was provided with support from Oregon's STEM leadership team. A two-phase program, emphasizing regional partnerships and professional development for paid and volunteer staff resulted in 25 of the 31 grantees receiving approved STEM implementation grants. Five of the implementing programs also qualified for professional development STEM grants. The outcomes included increased student access to technology, science, math, and engineering during the extended learning time offered afterschool and during the summer, as well as increased teacher training for improved program quality. What follows are two examples of program successes in Oregon with the STEM initiative: Salem-Keizer Education Foundation and Springfield Public School Afterschool Programs.

There is growing enthusiasm for Salem-Keizer Education Foundation's (SKEF) successful school gardens program, which is one component of their 21st Century Community Learning Centers' STEM offerings. In partnership with the Oregon Department of Agriculture, Marion-Polk Food Share, Life Source, and countless volunteers, students are tending to their school gardens on a daily basis and are enjoying the harvest for lunch. The program will open a new aquaponic greenhouse during the winter of 2012–13. SKEF is also the first program in Oregon to implement Mouse Squad, a nationally acclaimed program that creates technology-based opportunities for student success in today's information society.

For the past 5 years, Springfield Public School Afterschool Programs have provided students in grades 1–12 with a variety of hands-on STEM programs. Building bridges between school-day and out-of-school-time instruction, the Hamlin Middle School STEM Summer Program offered three 1-week robotics sessions in July 2012. At Springfield High School, afterschool students in the Music Recording Studio learn songwriting, basic music theory, digital audio engineering, beat production and studio management. They write their own lyrics and sing and record their own songs. Springfield's afterschool classes are designed to support quality academic and career-related experiences while sparking students' imagination and creativity.

New Emphasis on Program Sustainability

Since the system of 21st Century Community Learning Centers programs across Oregon anticipates a decline in funding rates in the coming years, program sustainability has become a focus of program quality planning. Importantly, to build broader ownership for sustainability, the Oregon Department of Education recently provided funding for the statewide afterschool alliance affiliate OregonASK to present a statewide webinar for all 21st Century Community Learning Centers grantees on program sustainability. The Finance Project, based in Washington, DC, facilitated the webinar.

Currently 11 Oregon 21st Century Community Learning Centers grantees are working through an intensive program of sustainability planning exercises facilitated by OregonASK Americorps/VISTA volunteers. Building a local sustainability team is the launching point for the great work of Oregon's programs to continue into 2012–13, resulting in a strategy for the inevitable reduced levels of state funding as the programs mature.

Conclusion

Oregon's statewide infrastructure of support and collaboration to provide academic enrichment opportunities for students, coupled with the innovation of local district programs and partners, create a powerful combination of quality afterschool services and supports for Oregon youth in 21st Century Community Learning Center programs. These programs will contribute significantly to the achievement of Oregon's 40-40-20 goal, and they are a tremendous learning resource for many struggling students across the state.

ABOUT THE AUTHORS

Susan Inman is the director of learning opportunities, options and supports at the Oregon Department of Education, as well as the administrative licensure coordinator at Willamette University. Inman has served in various positions in education during the past 25 years. She has taught in grades kindergarten through postsecondary and served as a school principal for 10 years. Susan has supervised English language learning programs, migrant education, 21st Century Community Learning Centers, and charter schools for the Oregon Department of Education since 2011.

Pete Ready has been an education specialist for Title IV-B, 21st Century Community Learning Centers at the Oregon Department of Education since 2006. Ready's background includes teaching middle school and high school English language arts and middle school special education, and serving as coordinator of community-based alternative schools, and Head Start program director.

Jenni Deaton is an administrative specialist for learning opportunities, options and supports at the Oregon Department of Education. Deaton has been with the department since 2009, and was part of the communications staff in the superintendent's office prior to joining the Learning Opportunities team in 2011.

REFERENCES

Bodily, S. J., & Beckett, M. K. (2005). *Making out-of-school-time matter: Evidence for an Action Agenda*. Santa Monica, CA: RAND Corporation. Retrieved from http://www.rand.org/pubs/monographs/MG242

Little, P. (2007). *The quality of school-age child care in after-school settings*. (Research-To-Policy Connections No. 7). New York, NY: Child Care & Early Education Research Connections.

Learning Point Associates. (2012). *Changes in student behavior among regular attendees (Federal Teacher Survey Results): All states–2012*. Retrieved from Profile and Performance Information Collection System website: http://ppics.learningpt.org/ppics/reports/aprBehaviorChangesFed.asp

Silva, E. (2007). *On the clock: Rethinking the way schools use time*. Retrieved from http://www.educationsector.org/sites/default/files/publications/OntheClock.pdf

Ayeola Fortune
Director of Education Initiatives,
United Way Worldwide

Strengthening Out-of-School-Time Initiatives to Support Student Success: The Role of United Way in Afterschool, Weekends, and Summer Learning

Any effort to improve education must factor in the reality that students spend only 20% of their time in school (Davis & Farbman, 2002). Boosting youths' opportunity for success—in school, work, and life—must therefore include a robust strategy for using out-of-school time to expand learning opportunities.

> Working with our partners at the national, state, and local level, we want to cut the number of high school dropouts—currently 1.3 million students every year—in half.

This strategy must include a shared vision, collaboration, aligned activities, and collective action among all sectors to reach our youth with high quality, well-designed, and well-implemented afterschool, summer, and weekend programs.

This is an issue that matters to United Way. Education is a priority for our network of 1,200 state and local United Ways. Working with our partners at the national, state, and local level, we want to cut the number of high school dropouts—currently 1.3 million students every year (Alliance for Excellent Education, 2010)—in half. Quality afterschool and summer programs can address the very factors (such as poor attendance, failing grades, misbehavior, very low test scores, and disengagement from schools) that have been linked to dropping out (Hammond, Linton, Smink, & Drew, 2007).

That means ensuring that meaningful supports and opportunities exist for all children—especially children from disadvantaged families—from birth through young adulthood.

It also means seizing every opportunity. United Way network surveys have found that some 95% of local United Ways fund out-of-classroom learning, but far fewer actually collaborate strategically with program providers and other key stakeholders to develop a system of well-placed, quality afterschool, weekend and summer learning programs that strategically capture the energy of many different providers and build strong school-community-family partnerships.

As program funders, United Ways have a unique opportunity to help advance

- *academic enrichment and supports that expand learning in engaging ways after the school day ends and during the summer and that do not merely provide youth with "more of the same" from the typical school day;*

- *opportunities for youth to build personal skills, cultivate new interests, and develop meaningful relationships with peers and supportive adults; and*

- *opportunities for youth to engage in constructive extracurricular activities that support learning and development.*

Yet, communities also need systemic approaches to address ongoing challenges around access, quality, participation, alignment, coordination, and sustainability.

United Ways are respected as community conveners, communicators, connectors, and funders. Increasingly, they are using their considerable capacity to fill these roles in their communities to help individuals and institutions better understand and fully realize the potential of afterschool, summer, and weekend programs to improve student success. They are mobilizing the community around expanding quality afterschool and summer learning programs, while working to deepen and strengthen existing efforts to ensure that community and school-based programs are high quality, relevant, engaging, age appropriate, accessible, and effectively targeted to serve those most in need.

That is happening across the country. In Boston, the United Way of Massachusetts Bay and Merrimack County brought together key stakeholders to examine the challenge, to plan, and then to act in alignment. The group fielded a survey on existing youth assets, developed summer literacy and employment programs, and organized a donated playground in a housing development.

The aim was to maintain or increase student reading skills, build the capacity of afterschool and summer staff, and increase school partnerships and family engagement. The coalition (involving three United Ways) integrated literacy into expanded learning time programs in underperforming school districts, targeting more than 1,800 youth in seven communities. Some 68 hours of training for 100 staff helped integrate language and literacy into out-of-school-time learning, bring school and program staff together to learn from each other, and improve school-program-family partnerships.

Results for the Boston Summer Literacy Initiative showed that 85% of the participating youth tested better than expected—with 68% showing academic gains, according to a study commissioned by the MA Department of Early Education and Care (Love, 2011). Youth read more, improved their vocabulary and reading comprehension, and improved their attitudes toward reading.

In Austin, Texas, the United Way for Greater Austin made community engagement a focus of its expanded learning time work, including youth focus groups that informed an action agenda. Afterschool, school community partnerships, and family involvement were incorporated as a cornerstone of the United Way's new Middle School Matters initiative, a partnership with 16 agencies, including expanded learning time providers, to provide tutoring, parent education, mentoring, and afterschool programs in the three lowest-performing schools.

Leveraging both organizational and individual partnerships is the "sweet spot" for many United Ways. These organizations are uniquely positioned in communities to support afterschool and summer learning coalitions by tapping

> . . . the United Way for Greater Austin made community engagement a focus of its expanded learning time work, including youth focus groups that informed an action agenda.

- *their ability to reach across sectors (e.g., local government, schools, cultural and philanthropic institutions, faith and community-based organizations, non-profit agencies);*
- *their annual workplace campaigns that engage individual donors;*
- *and their strong business relationships.*

For example, as part of United Way's national call to action to recruit one million education volunteers, United Ways are recruiting employees of local businesses as mentors and tutors for youth who may not have adult role models. By identifying and developing these mentors, volunteers, and tutors from the business community—and by regarding them appropriately as "second-shift caring adults" or "community teachers"—United Ways can give added significance and attention to this vitally important community learning resource.

In Grand Rapids, the Heart of West Michigan United Way is bringing the community together around 900 struggling students in its most disadvantaged neighborhoods. Some 1,200 community volunteers work one-on-one in the Schools of Hope initiative, with more than 60 companies giving their employees paid time off to mentor or tutor after school. The strategy is paying off, as kids are gaining academic and other skills.

Driving systemic improvements in afterschool, summer, and weekend programs requires understanding what works and replicating success. Since 2008, with the support of JCPenney, United Way Worldwide invested in out-of-school-time initiatives in 10 communities. These pilots have dug deep to strengthen existing, or build new, expanded learning time coalitions; map the availability and quality of programs in their communities; address the gaps in data, services, and opportunities; and engage key constituencies (for example, youth, parents, teachers) to get a better sense of needed supports.

Collectively, these learnings suggest that United Ways can significantly strengthen these efforts in their communities by taking these steps:

● **Map the expanded learning time landscape.** *Without knowing where quality afterschool, weekend, and summer learning assets are located and needed, good and informed decisions are impossible. Many communities begin without a clear understanding of where the programs are, who they serve, and what kinds of outcomes they are producing. Gaining this understanding can be transformative, identifying unmet needs and galvanizing support.*

● **Measure program quality.** *Many programs do not have a way to assess their own impact and quality. Programs often use different approaches to show impact, so comparisons cannot be made. United Ways can help develop a common language and understanding of quality across programs. As funders, United Ways can invest in quality improvement approaches that tie professional development to specific areas that need support. There is a growing body of research that is finding factors that are linked to better program results.*

● **Leverage passion to develop professionals.** *People working in youth development are very passionate, but they often operate in isolation. Participating in professional convenings can therefore be an important way to generate an enhanced sense of professionalism. Also, connecting youth development professionals and community volunteers with educators and schools can produce more engaging, interesting, and quality afterschool, weekend, and summer programs. This takes thoughtful and focused collaborative planning among schools and community teachers or second-shift caring professionals. United Ways can insist on, fund, and help lead such collaboration.*

● **Create and coordinate an aligned network.** *"Connecting the dots" within a community matters. It is crucial to coordinate services to close gaps, avoid duplication, and demonstrate contributions of many community stakeholders. United Ways have relationships with stakeholders—providers, schools, community and faith-based organizations, arts and cultural groups, colleges, businesses, etc.—that can be leveraged to create stronger alignment, coordination, and communication.*

Achieving all of this requires a systemic, big-picture approach that is not piecemeal or focused on individual programs.

That means we must ensure a shared community vision and coordinated action—along with mutual accountability, sustained effort, and measured results—across a diverse coalition. It means working collaboratively on communitywide and community-based strategies that can drive real change. Finally, it means bringing people from all walks of life together to work in meaningful ways—not just giving but also advocating and volunteering—to advance these community strategies.

"Driving with data" is critical. In Jacksonville, Florida, the United Way of Northeastern Florida and its partners used local data, experts, and community conversations to create Achievers for Life, an effort to target struggling middle schoolers who showed attendance, behavior, and self-esteem problems (based on school data). Key strategies included improving the quality and availability of out-of-school-time supports and employing Family Advocates to work with families. After one year, participants showed a 31% boost in GPA (United Way of Northeast Florida, 2008).

These are the kinds of creative partnerships and *results* that United Ways want to achieve in every community. The following are some suggestions for community organizations seeking to work with United Ways:

- *Attend United Way events and introduce yourself and your work. United Ways staff members meet many people this way that they would not otherwise know.*

- *Invite local United Way staff to your events and to see your program. United Ways spend a lot of time doing this to understand emerging best practices/ programs that might be off their radar.*

- *Ask about ways to get involved and who else you should get to know. United Ways have a good vantage point in the community and can help facilitate introductions to others.*

- *Share program outcomes and the demographics of the populations you serve. This way, United Ways can better align resources to meet needs.*

- *Be a liaison to the communities you serve. This will help United Ways understand how best to help bring resources to that neighborhood or community.*

- *Advocate and educate the public on important community, state, and national issues concerning education, income, and health.*

Conclusion

Evidence continues to mount that quality afterschool, weekend, and summer programming can turn out-of-school time into a positive learning opportunity, helping constructively fill the 80% of waking hours that young people are not in school. These expanded learning opportunities can also help address some of the key factors contributing to young people dropping out of school, including absenteeism, behavioral problems, and poor course performance. To leverage this time in a cost-effective manner requires bold, and often new, community-school collaborations, taking advantage of the many youth-serving organizations and volunteers who are interested in working with children and youth, as well as applying school resources in some new ways in the expanded learning time and space.

We know that "more of the same" is expensive and unlikely to make much difference. New partnerships, new ways of working, and new levels of collaboration are needed. Because of the United Ways' broad reach in the community—active in 1,200 communities and in relationship with 50,000 employers—they can be a vitally important, positive force to support and drive the expansion of engaging learning opportunities after school hours and during summers and weekends by working closely with schools, community organizations, and volunteers. It is imperative that community and youth-serving organizations, schools, and voluntary organizations work together with their United Ways to capitalize systemically on the power of expanded learning after school, during the summers, and over weekends. Working in new ways to generate new, more engaged learning and positive youth development opportunities can help dramatically improve the odds for success for many of America's youth.

For More Information

Please contact your local United Way's community impact staff. Contact information is usually on its website, or track down your United Way at http://www.liveunited.org.

ABOUT THE AUTHOR

Ayeola Fortune is the director of education initiatives at United Way Worldwide, leading the organization's work to improve middle grade success and boost high school graduation. She helped lead the development of United Way's education roadmaps, which outline core community strategies, high-impact implementation approaches, and roles United Ways can play to reach United Way's goal to cut high school dropout numbers in half by 2018. Previously, she served as the director of Extended Learning Opportunities and Development Project at the Council of Chief State School Officers. Fortune has also been a middle and high school teacher and has taught and developed curricula at the University of Pittsburgh.

REFERENCES

Alliance for Excellent Education. (2010). *High school dropouts in America*. Retrieved from http://www.all4ed.org/files/HighSchoolDropouts.pdf

Davis, J., & Farbman, D. A. (2002). Schools alone are not enough: After-school programs and education reform in Boston. *New Directions for Youth Development*, (94), 65–87. Retrieved from http://www.stanford.edu/dept/SUSE/projects/ireport/articles/afterschool/schools%20are%20not%20enough.pdf

Hammond, C., Linton, D., Smink, J., & Drew, S. (2007). *Dropout risk factors and exemplary programs: A technical report*. Retrieved from http://www.dropoutprevention.org/sites/default/files/uploads/major_reports/DropoutRiskFactorsandExemplaryProgramsCoverPages5-16-07.pdf

Love, M. L. (2011). *Evaluation of summer 2010 out-of-school time literacy and learning promotion grant*. Retrieved from http://www.eec.state.ma.us/docs1/Final_OST_Evaluation_2_4_11.pdf

United Way of Northeast Florida. (2008). *Achievers for life: Addressing the dropout crisis*. Retrieved from http://www.uwnefl.org/documents/UWAchieversForLife_OneYearProgress.pdf

Priscilla Little
Research and Strategy Consultant

School-Community Learning Partnerships: Essential to Expanded Learning Success

For the past decade the 21st Century Community Learning Centers initiative has asked schools to work in partnership with community- and faith-based organizations to support children's learning during the hours after school and during the summertime. Consequently, there has been tremendous growth across the nation in intentional efforts to forge meaningful partnerships between schools and afterschool and summer programs.

Increasingly, the field is recognizing that these partnerships are essential to efforts to expand *when, where, how,* and *what* students learn (Little, 2011). This article begins with an overview of the benefits of school-community partnerships to students, schools, and community organizations. It then examines the role of partnerships in the 21st Century Community Learning Centers initiative, reviewing national data on the numbers and kinds of partners that 21st Century Community Learning Centers nationwide are engaging with to support student success. The article concludes with a discussion of four features of effective learning partnerships.

The Benefits of School-Community Partnerships

When schools and community organizations work together to support learning, everyone benefits. Partnerships can serve to strengthen, support, and even transform individual partners, resulting in improved program quality, more efficient use of resources, and better alignment of goals and curricula (Harvard Family Research Project, 2010).

First and foremost, learning partnerships can support student outcomes (see, for example, Little, Wimer, & Weiss, 2008). For example, the *Massachusetts Afterschool Research Study* found that afterschool programs with stronger relationships with school teachers and principals were more successful at improving students' homework completion, homework effort, positive behavior, and initiative. This may be because positive relationships with schools can foster high quality, engaging, and challenging activities, along with promoting staff engagement (Miller, 2005).

In addition to supporting student learning directly, partnerships can have additional benefits to students and their families. They can

- *provide continuity of services across the day and year, easing school transitions and promoting improved attendance in after school programs;*

- *facilitate access to a range of learning opportunities and developmental supports, providing opportunities for students and teachers alike to experiment with new approaches to teaching and learning;*

- *facilitate information sharing about specific students to best support individual learning; and*

- *provide family members with alternative entry points into the school day to support their student's learning.*

Using Partners to Complement Program Offerings

Being a Lifelong Achiever Starts Today (BLAST) is a 21st Century Community Learning Centers initiative program in Atlanta, Georgia. It has an effective collaboration with Atlanta Memorial Hospital and New Attitudes Health and Fitness Center. Students are taught and mentored to help improve their lifestyle by making dietary changes and exercising properly and regularly. Students have access to a full array of health professionals and services at the center and can participate in a 10-week wellness program. At the end of the 10-week course, known as "The Body Shop," the student who has made the greatest transformation receives a New Attitudes membership. This membership provides access to the entire wellness and fitness center for one year. Many students also learn how to swim and overcome their fear of the water. Since there is no community pool or community gym available, this partnership has made resources available to students that would otherwise not be available to them (Manhattan Strategy Group, 2011).

Learning partnerships can also greatly benefit schools. They can

- *complement the academic curriculum with a wider range of services and activities, particularly enrichment and arts activities that may not available during the school day;*

- *support transitions across the school years, particularly the critical middle to high school transition, which research indicates is a key predictor of high school graduation (Neild, Balfanz, & Herzog, 2007);*

- *reinforce concepts taught in school without replicating the school day, often exposing classroom teachers working in the after school program to new pedagogies;*

- *improve school culture and community image through exhibitions and performances that help "shine the light" on students whose talents may not be apparent in the classroom; and*

- *gain access to mentors, afterschool staff, and other resources to support in school learning and improve the teaching and learning in the classroom itself.*

Finally, learning partnerships with schools can strengthen and support community partners. They can

- *help gain access to and recruit groups of students most in need of support services;*

- *improve program quality and staff engagement, particularly when there is crossover between school and community organization staff;*

- *foster better alignment of programming to support a shared vision for learning, one which aligns curriculum to support state and local standards; and*

- *maximize resource use such as facilities, staff, data, and curriculum.*

Community Partners Can Support School Partners

Roger Williams, a Title I School in Providence, Rhode Island, is one of three anchor schools for a wide range of afterschool programs in the South Side/West End AfterZone supported and coordinated by the Providence After School Alliance (PASA). While Roger Williams struggles to make AYP, its partnership with PASA, city agencies, and community-based organizations to expand afterschool services has contributed to improved school performance. The partnership with PASA has played a critical role in improving the scale and quality of afterschool services at Roger Williams, currently reaching more than 360 youth in 45 different programs. Funding and staffing support from PASA has provided resources to expand academic and enrichment program options and double the number of participants. PASA also improves program quality by supporting partnerships with high quality providers that include community- based organizations, individual instructors, the school district, and the local police department (Providence After School Alliance, internal communication, 2011).

The Role of Partnerships in 21st Century Community Learning Centers

Partnerships are a critical component of 21st Century Community Learning Centers, and each year since 2006 the number of partners has continued to grow. By 2010, the 3,450 funded grantees engaged over 30,000 partners, with an average of almost 9 partners per grantee. Community-based organizations were the most common partners in 2010, almost three times higher than any other type of partner. For-profit corporations and school districts were the second and third most utilized partners, with colleges and universities also playing a main partnership role.

Partners perform a number of important roles: They offer programming, provide in-kind services, and provide paid and volunteer staffing (see Table 1). Further, Table 1 illustrates that more partners have steadily made more contributions to 21st Century Community Learning Centers over the past 5 years.

Table 1. Number of grants with a partner providing a given contribution type across 5 years of annual performance reporting.

Partner Contribution	2006	2007	2008	2009	2010
Programming	2,464	2,582	2,695	2,881	3,139
Paid Staffing	1,782	1,814	1,906	1,965	2,046
Volunteer Staffing	1,833	1,924	1,933	2,042	2,185
In-Kind Goods	2,113	2,246	2,351	2,477	2,698
Funding	813	872	968	915	929
Evaluation Services	1,043	1,076	1,049	1,078	1,160

School-Day Staff Can Support Student and Staff Recruitment Efforts

The City Day Extended Academy Mentoring Program is a 21st Century Community Learning Centers initiative program in Salt Lake City, Utah. To create cohesion between the school-day and afterschool programs, school-day teachers are highly involved in the planning and implementation of programs, and all afterschool staff must follow the same policies and procedures regardless of site. Staff are recruited for specific roles within the programs. The Project Director creates a list of required qualifications for particular programs that principals must heed when hiring afterschool staff. Along with the Project Director's recommendations, consulting teachers in the district complete staff observations and provide a list of individuals who have demonstrated skills and characteristics that may be well suited to the afterschool program. Principals make a concerted effort to hire program staff who have been with the district for 3 or more years and who have appropriate professional licenses; new teachers, or those changing grade levels, are not actively recruited in order to allow them sufficient time to get acclimated before gaining additional responsibility within the district (Manhattan Strategy Group, 2011).

Analysis of the financial support that partners contribute by providing the services listed above reveals that in 2010 alone, partners contributed over $230 million to the 3,450 initiative grantees. Over the past 5 years partners have contributed over $1 billion to support 21st Century Community Learning Centers programming.

Together, these data suggest that partners are an essential component of the 21st Century Community Learning Centers initiative and they have been growing significantly in all dimensions over the past 5 years. Partners provide vital in-kind services and supports, as well as real dollars, which add significant value to the work of 21st Century Community Learning Centers. As centers consider bringing on more partners it is important that project and site directors understand how to develop and cultivate effective partnerships. The next part of this article discusses the features of effective partnerships.

> Over the past 5 years partners have contributed over $1 billion to support 21st Century Community Learning Centers programming.

Features of Effective School-Community Partnerships

There is emerging consensus on an inter-related set of features that help promote and sustain healthy school-community partnerships (Harvard Family Research Project, 2010):

- **A shared vision for learning and developmental outcomes for students.** *This vision acknowledges the critical, complementary roles of schools, community partners, and families. A shared vision also helps partners avoid working against each other and instead pursue a common vision of student success. When school leaders embrace a vision for student success that considers students' physical, emotional, and social well-being in addition to academic outcomes, the partnership is more likely to be successful than when competing agendas operate during the expanded learning day.*

- **A diverse set of partners with effective communications mechanisms and relationships among multiple staff at multiple levels.** *Strong and sustainable partnerships need relationships that are built at multiple levels (for example, at the district, school, and classroom levels) and among multiple school staff, including district and nonteaching staff. Working with partners at different levels helps the afterschool and summer programs become integral to the daily life and culture of the school at all levels, from the principal to the custodian. In addition, relationships at various levels can help mitigate the effects of staff turnover at other levels; for example, strong relationships with teachers can help sustain the partnership in the event of a change in principals.*

- **Intentionally blended staffing with role clarity to promote understanding of how the work is relevant to all.** *For afterschool and summer programs, this means hiring staff who have legitimacy in the school building and who are skilled at building relationships with school staff. Some programs do this by hiring licensed teachers, people who "speak the same language" as school-day teachers, can substitute and consult in classrooms, and can participate in professional development activities. Hiring licensed teachers who also teach at a host school facilitates information sharing and forges connections with other teachers who might not otherwise make time for "outside" programs or services. Blended staffing may also mean a liaison who serves an important bridging function between the school and the afterschool or summer program.*

- **Clear data-sharing processes and agreements.** *One feature of a strong collaboration is the ability of partners to access information and data from each other, including, if possible, student-level academic data (e.g., test scores and grades). Afterschool and summer programs can use these data both to track and strengthen student performance and to demonstrate the impact of their services. In addition to getting data from schools, some programs provide their own data to schools to promote reciprocal data sharing.*

As efforts to expand learning opportunities and time continue to grow under a variety of approaches and models—whether afterschool, summer learning, expanded or extended learning day or year, or out-of-school time—it is important that all these efforts build on the strong base of effective partnerships already present among schools and afterschool and summer programs, capitalizing in particular on the rich history of partnerships advanced by 21st Century Community Learning Centers.

For More Information

School-Community Partnership Resources

- **Afterschool: The Bridge Connecting Schools and Communities**
  www.statewideafterschoolnetworks.net/afterschool-bridge-connecting-schools-and-communities. This brief highlights how afterschool programs can serve as bridges that connect schools and communities, positively benefiting youth and families, schools, community-based organizations, and the community as a whole.

- **A Guide for School Principals**
  www.statewideafterschoolnetworks.net/guide-school-principals. This guide was produced by The After-School Corporation (TASC) to help support principals in their efforts to build and sustain partnerships with TASC-funded afterschool programs.

- **Meaningful Linkages between Summer Programs, Schools, and Community Partners: Conditions and Strategies for Success**
  www.nmefdn.org/uploads/Meaningful%20Linkages%20full%20report%20rev%2010.09.pdf. This report documents and describes how to create and sustain meaningful partnerships between high-quality summer learning programs and schools.

- **Afterschool: The Bridge Connecting Schools and Communities**
  http://www.afterschoolalliance.org/issue_30_bridge.cfm. This issue brief describes the benefits of family, school, and community partnerships.

- **Strengthening Connections Between Schools and Afterschool Programs**
  www.learningpt.org/afterschool/strength.pdf. This guide examines comprehensive program planning to better integrate afterschool programming with the school day.

ABOUT THE AUTHOR

Priscilla Little is an independent research and strategy consultant who has been working on issues related to effective afterschool and summer learning programs for over a decade. Her clients include national education research firms, state education agencies, not-for-profit agencies, and private foundations. She is currently working for The Wallace Foundation to support its afterschool system-building work, and with the U.S. Department of Education on a research study to investigate good and innovative practices in 21st Century Community Learning Centers programs. The views represented in this article are solely her own and do not represent those of her clients.

REFERENCES

Harvard Family Research Project. (2010). *Partnerships for learning: Promising practices in integrating school and out-of-school time program supports*. Retrieved from http://www.hfrp.org/publications-resources/browse-our-publications/partnerships-for-learning-promising-practices-in-integrating-school-and-out-of-school-time-program-supports

Little, P. (2011). *Expanded learning opportunities in Washington state: Pathways to student success*. Retrieved from http://www.schoolsoutwashington.org/UserFiles/File/ELO%20Policy%20Brief%20Single%20Pages.pdf

Little, P., Wimer, C., & Weiss, H. (2008). *Afterschool programs in the 21st century: Their potential and what it takes to achieve it* (Issues and Opportunities in Out-of-School Time Evaluation No. 10). Retrieved from http://www.hfrp.org/content/download/2916/84011/file/OSTissuebrief10.pdf

Manhattan Strategy Group. (2011). *High school promising practices project for the 21st Century Community Learning Centers program, Addendum 1*. Washington, DC: U.S. Department of Education.

Miller, B. M. (2005). *Pathways to success for youth: What counts in after-school*. Retrieved from United Way of Massachusetts Bay and Merrimack Valley website: http://supportunitedway.org/

Neild, R. C., Balfanz, R., & Herzog, L. (2007). An early warning system. *Educational Leadership*, 65(2), 28–33.

Conclusion

Richard W. Riley
U.S. Secretary of Education, 1993–2001

Terry K. Peterson
Senior Director and Fellow, Afterschool Network,
College of Charleston

Conclusion:
Leveraging the Power of Quality Afterschool and Summer Learning: An Important Strategy for Student Success Across America

As a result of rigorous academic standards recently adopted by almost all of our states, teaching and learning are improving all across America. Yet too many of our students are still struggling to master basic skills and learn well the core subjects.

In the 21st century, it is more imperative than ever that all of our students master the skills and behaviors that lead to high school graduation—the critical first rung on the ladder to economic success and a productive future, both for our students and our great country. To achieve this goal, though, our schools are being called upon to do much more but with many fewer resources.

In today's multimedia, 24/7 environment, our young people are taking in information and ideas 100% of the time. Yet schools—full of learning resources—are often closed and locked 75 to 80% of the time.

At the same time, many parents have to work all day, leaving them to worry about those hours after school ends, when their children and adolescents may be at home alone or otherwise unsupervised.

We know from successful experience that hundreds of thousands of arts, cultural, sports, and other youth organizations, as well as civic and faith-based groups, want to partner with educators and schools to expand, broaden, and reinforce learning. Far too often, however, potential community partners are disconnected from schools and the students who could benefit from their support.

Well-designed expanded learning opportunities provided during the afterschool hours and summers through school-community partnerships are outstanding and cost-effective ways to address gaps in learning and to foster positive development. These enriching learning opportunities can be designed and developed by the partners to maximize use of all available school and community resources. They can be delivered during the "worrisome 3:00–6:00 p.m." hours, during the summer and, where needed, before school and on weekends.

The need to leverage the power of expanded learning opportunities in afterschool and summers has never been greater. To prepare our students adequately for their life in the 21st century, we must strengthen basic skills, provide next-generation learning opportunities, foster community-school partnerships, and promote family engagement.

As our world has become increasingly complex, we have come to recognize that schools alone cannot support all of the learning needs of children and youth to be prepared for careers, college, and life. Today's reality is that young people will require a new set of knowledge, skills, and dispositions to succeed in our rapidly changing, knowledge-based, global economy. This requires that learners have opportunities to explore, test, venture, and create so they can develop the assets they will need to benefit from and contribute to an increasingly information-filled world. Innovative expanded learning afterschool and during summers with school-community partnerships are well suited to provide these opportunities.

We are pleased that educators, youth-serving organizations, and community- and faith-based organizations now have access in one place to the knowledge and expertise contained in the nearly 70 articles and studies in *Expanding Minds and Opportunities*. This extensive compendium comprises a significant body of literature about the powerful benefits of expanded learning programs for America's future. These articles demonstrate clearly that high quality, engaging afterschool and summer experiences complement school instruction, provide affordable and sustainable means to accelerate achievement and attainment, and build partnerships that lead to student, family, and community success. They describe a variety of effective strategies and partnerships that extend and build on learning from the school day into the nonschool hours.

One of the most significant catalysts for expanded learning opportunities afterschool and during summers has been the 21st Century Community Learning Centers initiative. With the addition of the 21st Century Community Learning Centers program to the Elementary and Secondary Education Act with bipartisan support in Congress, this federal funding stream has united school and community partners to provide active, engaged learning opportunities that expand the minds of children and youth to leverage learning whenever and wherever it happens.

During the second term of the Clinton administration, the positive impact of the program grew dramatically as the president and first lady both made it a strong education priority to scale up 21st Century Community Learning Centers in thousands of schools and communities across America. Their leadership, supported by several congressional champions, brought annual funding increases for 21st Century Community Learning Centers from $1 million to $1 billion. In the years since, members of Congress from both sides of the aisle have continued to approve the program's funding level.

This compendium offers evidence and stories from high quality, local 21st Century Community Learning Centers programs across the country, as well as findings from other initiatives, that illustrate the positive impact of quality afterschool and summer programs on children, families, and communities.

The authors of the studies, articles, and commentaries in this volume represent a diverse array of educators, community leaders, and youth-serving participants in the expanded learning and afterschool field, including researchers, practitioners, funders, policy makers, and thought leaders. A central theme pervades and connects all the articles in the compendium: *Expanded learning programs can assist and support many more children and youth with opportunities to learn and grow so they can succeed educationally and lead productive lives.*

The learning and developmental results and impact that high quality expanded learning, afterschool, and summer programs can yield are potent.

Fundamentally, expanded learning programs help students stay on track with academic basics as well as foster school success through better attendance, study habits, and attitudes. Expanded learning opportunities also hold compelling promise to push the leading edge of learning by engaging young people in activities that involve

- *digital and blended learning;*
- *exploratory science, technology, engineering, and mathematics (STEM) experiences;*
- *opportunities for creativity and innovation through the arts;*
- *development of cultural competence; and*
- *building international and entrepreneurial awareness.*

The learning and developmental results and impact that high quality expanded learning, afterschool, and summer programs can yield are potent. Afterschool and summer programs promote essential social and emotional capacities that advance cognitive and academic development. Equally powerful are the benefits to families and communities. Quality afterschool programs promote parent/family engagement in their children's learning, as well as essential partnerships between schools and a wide array of community entities—universities, businesses, museums, libraries, cultural and arts organizations, and civic and faith-based institutions.

During the past 15 years, such relationships have cultivated infrastructures designed to build program quality and capacity through various local, regional, state, and national networks. These coalitions of public and private stakeholders have focused intentionally on continuous improvement through training and professional development, interagency collaboration, evaluation and accountability systems, and leveraging funding streams to ensure affordability and sustainability.

> . . . it is clear that a very important tool for contemporary education improvement and reform is expanding learning opportunities during afterschool and summers.

With these infrastructures in place, the potential is high for scaling up to more schools and communities that want and need quality afterschool and summer learning programs.

For example, after a little more than 15 years, the 21st Century Community Learning Centers initiative is now funding nearly 11,000 school- and community-based centers throughout all 50 states. Moreover, the program now annually serves more than 1.5 million students, involves nearly 300,000 parents and other adult family members, and engages the support of tens of thousands of community partners across the country. This means that over the past 10 years alone, almost 15 million students and 2.5 million adult family members have participated in learning opportunities provided and leveraged by the 21st Century Community Learning Centers initiative. Notably, these numbers reflect the involvement of—and impact on—some of the most economically needy families in the country.

We encourage you to use this compendium as a resource in your work to support the learning and development of children, youth, families, and communities. Good progress has been made, but much more needs to be done. There are almost 50,000 public schools with more than 40% of their children from low-income backgrounds. In almost all 100,000 of our nation's public schools, there are struggling students from all income levels who could benefit from participating in high quality expanded learning experiences.

Recommendations

Given the growing body of evidence of effectiveness and the many different examples of best practices and positive school-community partnerships, it is clear that a very important tool for contemporary education improvement and reform is expanding learning opportunities during afterschool and summers.

Many entities—school districts, municipalities, county governments, United Ways and foundations, as well as state governments—can take steps that will incentivize and leverage these powerful learning experiences. We recommend the following actions.

1. Provide resources to deploy a full-time coordinator for school-community partnerships and afterschool/summer learning for each school or neighborhood that needs and wants significant expansion of learning opportunities and learning supports. A full-time coordinator helps link and pool appropriate local/community and school resources.

2. Provide funding and regulatory support so students can be transported easily from school to/from community, cultural, college, youth-serving, and workplace opportunities that are a formal component of the afterschool and summer learning partnership with schools.

3. Change policies and practices so that middle and high school students can earn additional credits for high school graduation and career and college readiness through afterschool, weekend, and summer learning programs in school partnerships with employers and/or other educational institutions—museums, libraries, 2- and 4-year colleges, cultural and science centers, etc.

4. Support the development and strengthening of local and state afterschool and summer learning networks to rally an array of elementary and secondary education resources; community and youth-serving organizations (4-H, YM/WCA, Boys and Girls Clubs, Communities in Schools, etc.); higher education; faith-based groups; health, fitness, arts, and cultural resources; and interested employers to expand learning any time and in credible places.

5. Connect and support strongly the professional development, technical assistance, and coaching services available to expand learning in afterschool and summers. This will help improve program quality, effectiveness, and resource alignment that, in turn, will contribute positively to factors that lead to greater student success, achievement, and attainment. At the same time, students will be provided engaging, motivating, broadening, and hands-on learning and development opportunities.

6. Include indicators in evaluation and accountability systems for expanded learning afterschool and summer programs that are linked to student success in moving from grade to grade and graduating on time and to boosting overall post-secondary technical and college enrollment rates. These include, for example, such indicators as student attendance, grades in core subjects, homework completion, engagement and interest in learning, participation in career and college awareness and preparation programs, and standardized achievement scores. Many of these indicators can be collected and used to inform quality advancement efforts during the actual time during the year that afterschool and summer learning programs are operating. These indicators also can and should be collaboratively used with school personnel for joint improvement endeavors.

Finally, action at the federal level is warranted. Although the 21st Century Community Learning Centers initiative currently funds about 11,000 school-community partnerships annually, there remain almost 30,000 to 40,000 schools with significant numbers of struggling children and youth. It makes fiscal sense for Congress to increase significantly the funding for 21st Century Community Learning Centers to address this gap.

As the expansive evidence in *Expanding Minds and Opportunities* documents, we know that expanded learning opportunities are essential to help our struggling students catch up, keep up, and get ahead. They also benefit all students by broadening their knowledge and skills. By building school-community partnerships, we can keep more young people of all ages on track for success in school, in the community, and in life… and we can do it cost effectively.

Expanding and improving afterschool and summer learning partnerships is a positive way to advance the American dream. We urge you to join us in taking action to ensure these powerful learning opportunities are accessible to young people in every school and community in America who want and need them.

ABOUT THE AUTHORS

Richard W. Riley, former secretary of education and former governor of South Carolina, is a leader and advocate for improving education. *Time* magazine named him as one of the top 10 Cabinet members in the 20th Century. Riley currently serves in leadership capacities in the National Commission on Teaching and America's Future, the Carnegie Corporation of New York, the KnowledgeWorks Foundation, the Riley Institute at Furman University, and the ACT Board. He is a senior partner at Nelson Mullins Riley & Scarborough LLP, where he counsels clients on business, governance, and financial matters. He started his involvement in education improvement as a PTA co-president and state legislator.

Terry K. Peterson, a longtime associate of Dick Riley, is also a leader and advocate for educational reform and improvement. In addition to serving as one of Secretary and Governor Riley's principal go-to persons in designing and implementing a number of successful state and national education reforms, he has a long history of also working at the grassroots level and even internationally for educational change and advancement. Peterson has been a classroom teacher and parent-involvement specialist, taught statistics and research design courses, testified in a dozen states on school reform issues, and has provided advice to education reformers in Brazil, Argentina, South Korea, Mongolia, and Denmark.